The Reformation

THE REFORMATION
OF THE CHURCH

*

*A Collection of Reformed and Puritan
Documents on Church Issues*

*

Selected with Introductory Notes by
IAIN H. MURRAY

THE BANNER OF TRUTH TRUST

THE BANNER OF TRUTH TRUST
3 Murrayfield Road, Edinburgh EH12 6EL
PO Box 621, Carlisle, Pennsylvania 17013, USA

*

First published 1965
Reprinted 1987
ISBN 0 85151 118 X

*

Printed and bound at
Billing & Sons Ltd., Worcester

Contents

INTRODUCTION   7

SECTION I

THE NATURE OF THE CHURCH   15

SECTION II

THE RULE FOR REFORMATION — THE WORD OF GOD

1. Liberation from Human Authority   30
   Martin Luther
2. The Reformers and the Regulative Principle   38
   William Cunningham
3. The Regulative Principle and Things Indifferent   55
   John Hooper
4. The Abolition of Vestments   63
   John à Lasco
5. Scripture and the Ordering of Worship   75

SECTION III

THE NEED OF REFORMATION

1. The Necessity for Reformation: The Admonition to
   Parliament 1572   85
   Thomas Wilcox
2. Concerning a National Church   99
   William Ames
3. The Relation of Church and State   107
   Charles Hodge
4. Episcopacy: The Petition for the Prelates Examined   127
5. The Grounds of Nonconformity   151
   Edmund Calamy

[5]

SECTION IV

NEW TESTAMENT CHURCH GOVERNMENT

1. The Book of Discipline 1587   178
2. A True Description of the Visible Church 1589   196
   Henry Barrow
3. The Form of Presbyterial Church Government 1645   207
   Westminster Divines
4. The Cambridge Platform 1648   234
5. The Savoy Platform 1658   276
6. The Difference between Independency and Presbytery   285
   Jeremiah Burroughs
7. A Presbyterian View of the Difference with Independency   294
8. The Heads of Agreement 1691   301

SECTION V

THE UNITY OF THE CHURCH

1. The Way to Peace   314
   Walter Cradock
2. What We Are to Bear with in Others   326
   Jeremiah Burroughs
3. Union among Protestants   345
   John Owen
4. The Scandal of Division among the Godly   358
   James Durham

APPENDICES

1. The Church Membership of Children   383
   Thomas Shepard
2. Episcopalian Writers on Church Government   410

Introduction

I T M A Y be regretted that at a time when the Christian Faith is commanding so little influence in the nation, the Church herself should be engaged with questions which affect her own life rather than the life of the masses of the people. Issues such as the Church-State relationship, the place of Episcopacy and the order and unity of the visible Church are dominating themes in the contemporary ecclesiastical debate and they may appear to be subjects far removed from the urgent problem of the spiritual apathy of the average man and woman.

But the ecumenical leaders who have been responsible for the prominence given to these issues would be quick to assert the shallowness of such an assessment. It is *because* of the prevailing religious apathy, they would say, that the Church must set her own house in order. If paganism is not to engulf us then the Churches must settle their divisions and find a new solidarity before they can effectively address their message to the world. The ecumenical discussion which is now going on in almost all denominations has therefore a practical end in view and it is general agreement about that end which is giving church leaders the enthusiasm to find solutions to the difficulties arising out of long-standing denominational differences. Indeed such is the momentum which this enthusiasm has now gained in the Churches, that traditional denominational loyalties are already in the melting-pot. Dr Eric Baker, Secretary of the Methodist Conference, was only one of the many spokesmen of the new spirit when he declared in March 1964, 'Denominationalism is doomed. It is time to burst its bands.'

We may ask, however, how it is that, as so many of the issues which are once more in prominence are subjects which have already been dealt with extensively in the literature of former centuries (particularly in the Reformation and Puritan era), there is no attempt to examine this literature. Questions about Church Unity, Schism, Episcopacy, Church and State, etc., bulk large in seventeenth-century works. Between 1640 and 1662 it is estimated that 30,000 books and pamphlets were written on matters relating to the Church:[1] this was the material which Thomas Carlyle

---

[1] This estimate is that of Thomas M'Crie, the younger. H. M. Dexter records how his research into sixteenth-century Puritanism led him to draw up a bibliography of works on church government and related themes which contained some eighteen hundred titles for that century alone! *The Congregationalism of the Last Three Hundred years*, 1879, vi.

found in the archives of the British Museum in the mid-nineteenth century, 'printed, written, to the extent of tons and square miles'. Yet, in 1912, H. Hensley Henson could speak of this 'vast literature' as something 'which is wholly dead save for an occasional excursion of the curious'.[2] Today the way in which Reformers and Puritans treated Church issues is almost entirely forgotten and the works which would give the information which is needed are largely unobtainable.

The cause of this neglect can be traced ultimately, no doubt, to the fact that the whole Reformed-Puritan approach to the doctrine of the Church is suspect. To some the suspicion is probably nothing more than the prejudice that these authors were the men responsible for the troubles of the sixteenth and seventeenth centuries, and for the rise of divisions within Protestantism at that period; but traced more accurately – for the above charge is no more accurate than the charge that Elijah troubled Israel in the days of King Ahab – the neglect of this literature can be attributed to the definite rejection on the part of modern Protestantism of the principle that Scripture is a sufficient and perfect rule for the ordering of the Church of Christ. It was upon this principle that all Puritan endeavours for Church reformation were based and it is precisely for this reason that their works are judged to be no help in our ecumenical age. Bishop Hensley Henson put his finger on this when he wrote: 'The attitude of unquestioning and literal acceptance which determined the Puritan's handling of the Bible, and made it for him a sufficient directory of conduct in all situations, has passed for ever.'[3] *The Anglican-Methodist Conversations* of 1963 categorically affirm that Scripture 'does not contain all things expedient or even needful for the proper conduct of life and the ordering of the Church'.[4] The Archbishop of Canterbury, Dr Ramsey, is so far from regarding Scripture as a norm for Church issues that he writes, 'to burrow in the New Testament for forms of ministry and imitate them is archaeological religion'.[5] These statements reveal the real character of the ecumenical movement. While it professes to seek Church unity and a resolution of differences in order to address the non-churchgoing masses with greater authority, the message which such a 'united Church' would give to the people would not be one requiring unqualified obedience to the Word of God. How could it be when the need for such obedience has already been set aside? If the whole approach to present Church discussions

---

[2] *Puritanism in England*, H. Hensley Henson, p. 76.
[3] Op. cit., p. 78.
[4] *Conversations between the Church of England and the Methodist Church*, p. 16.
[5] *The Gospel and the Catholic Church*, A. M. Ramsey, p. 69.

is one which refuses to take Scripture as a sure and final guide, it is only too obvious that the end product of a 'Church' formed on such a basis is not going to be the preaching of a message which calls sinners to listen to Scripture as the voice of the living God. The crisis today is therefore much more than a disagreement about the outward life of the Churches. It has come to the point when the question has to be asked whether the Churches which treat Scripture in this manner are Christian Churches at all. 'They only be the church,' wrote the Reformation martyr John Hooper, 'that embrace this holy book, the Bible, heareth it, learneth it, and followeth the judgment of it. He is a Christian man, that leaveth the word of man, and keepeth the Word of God. . . . It is not sufficient for a Christian man to believe one part of the Scripture; but faith is a right persuasion and willing consent unto the whole Word of God.'[6] Where would the denominations stand today if they were tried by this test?

The documents provided in this book, which are mainly selected from the period 1550–1662, will be of help only to those who are prepared to bring everything to the judgment of Scripture. The authors of this material did not belong to one group, they were not always exegetically accurate, they did not claim a perfect understanding of the Scriptures, nor to have succeeded in putting into practice all that God's Word requires. They could say with Robert Rollock: 'Whilst I live I never expect to see a perfect Reformation in the Church.' Their vision for the Church was one which stretched beyond the boundaries of time and earth; by faith they saw her in her future beauty as the faultless bride of Jesus Christ. Yet this view, far from making them complacent about existing conditions, rather gave them the passion and determination to see that God's people upon earth acted as consistently as it was possible for redeemed sinners to act in relationship to the claims of the Saviour who had purchased the Church by His Blood. To them, love to Christ meant keeping His written commandments – commandments relating not only to their individual welfare but to the corporate welfare of the people who are His Body. Consequently Puritanism was never just an 'ecclesiastical' movement in the sense that it was conducted by ministers apart from the common people. Its essential appeal of faithfulness to Christ reached the hearts of Christians in all walks of life, and in the great historic struggle for further reformation in the Church there was exhibited a sense of the worth of the Church as a Divine institution upon earth such as has never since been exceeded in British Church history. When we read of ordinary women like Margaret Lauchlison and Margaret Wilson enduring the sentence of drowning in the waters of the

[6] *Early Writings of John Hooper*, Parker Society, p. 139.

Solway rather than submitting to an earthly ruler governing Christ's Church, or when we hear the exhortations of a Lancashire mother, Elizabeth Heywood, to her family when she was dying, we see the place which the Church held in the affections of Christians three hundred years ago. Addressing her husband and children, Mrs Heywood exclaimed, 'O Sirs, let the church of God lie near your hearts, it lies near God's heart: "They shall prosper that love Zion": prefer Jerusalem before and above your chief joy!'

It is the manner in which the Reformers and Puritans viewed the Church which explains why they endured so much mental labour and often physical suffering in contending against religious abuses and setting forth scriptural principles; and it also explains how they succeeded in arousing the attention of the people to regard these issues as matters which were bound up with their spiritual privileges and Christian freedom. A re-examination of such documents as are here reprinted should assist in re-awakening the same attitude in evangelicals today. All too often in recent years it has been customary for us to act as though the Gospel could prosper on earth independently of the condition of the visible Church; and evangelicals have been content to meet in organizations and societies as though the denominational differences which divide them are incapable of any scriptural solution. There are encouraging signs that this evangelical outlook on Church issues is now breaking up. There is a growing recognition of the fact that as long as the major denominations represent in the eyes of the nation the voice of Christianity, there is a formidable hindrance to the reception of the *true* Christian Faith – just as there was before the Reformation when a corrupt Papacy was the spokesman for the 'Gospel'. There are also indications of an awareness that it is corruption in the Churches which has contributed so much to the unbelief of the masses, and, further, that the presence of this corruption is an evidence of Divine judgment in that God has allowed Satan to have sway over a nominal Christianity which has deserted the commission Christ gave to His Church (Matt. 28: 20). For the principle is still true: 'Because thou servedst not the Lord thy God with joyfulness, and with gladness of heart, for the abundance of all things; therefore shalt thou serve thine enemies which the Lord shall send against thee' (Deut. 28: 47, 48).

Yet this is not all: the solution to the present situation does not lie merely in a denunciation of denominational apostasy. The ultimate fact to be considered is that in the present situation true Christians in all the churches are being chastened and humbled by God into a recognition of their profound need of His Presence. We ourselves are under judgment and any attempt to seek remedies which ignore this is bound to fail (Hosea 5: 13, 15).

It is through this humbling process that hope arises. It creates a new desire to please God and keep His Word (Psa. 119:67), it delivers us from a desire to defend traditional positions for which there may be no scriptural warrant, and it therefore enables us to approach church issues upon which evangelicals have been long divided in a new way and with a new concern to be united with all those who love the truth. A common attachment to the Scriptures and a determination to seek grace to resolve difficulties in that light is the only sure basis of Church unity.

If we look at Church questions in this way we are, whether consciously or not, following the same approach as was adopted by the authors of the various documents here reprinted. These writers had as their objective the conformity of Christians to the New Testament Church pattern and this led them to consider the same kind of obstacles as are still with us today. From such material enormous benefit can be gained: on some issues we believe they succeeded in proving the Biblical position over against their opponents; on other points their writings went far to eliminate differences between orthodox Christians and yet left a residue of difficulties which were unresolved. That the denominational positions have remained so little changed in these past 300 years is not because at that time all possible discussion was exhausted, it is rather because no subsequent generation of Christians has given the same degree of attention to the subjects which were then handled. There is certainly more light to break forth from the Word, but what light has previously been given by Christ through pastors and teachers who drew deep from Scripture is already our heritage and to possess it in our minds will provide us with a great advantage at this present time.

For this new compilation and arrangement of documents I am responsible, but I am also indebted to my friends Mr John J. Murray and Mr Michael Boland for considerable help in the preparation of the material for the press and for assistance in the provision of the additional editorial notes which precede each document or extract. We hope that the book will be of service to the number of evanglical ministers at the present time who are re-examining the subjects here dealt with in fraternals and in other gatherings.

IAIN MURRAY.

December 1964

SECTION I

The Nature of the Church

[1]

WILLIAM TYNDALE

MARTYRED AT VILVORDE OCTOBER 1536

From An Answer to Sir Thomas More's Dialogue[1]

THERE is another question, whether the church may err, which if ye understand of the pope and his generation, it is verily as hard a question as to ask whether he which had both his eyes out be blind or no; or whether it be possible for him that hath one leg shorter than another to halt. But I said that Christ's elect church is the whole multitude of all repenting sinners that believe in Christ, and put all their trust and confidence in the mercy of God; feeling in their hearts that God for Christ's sake loveth them, and will be, or rather is, merciful unto them, and forgiveth them their sins of which they repent; and that he forgiveth them also all the motions unto sin, of which they fear lest they should thereby be drawn into sin again. And this faith they have without all respect of their own deservings, yea, and for none other cause than that the merciful truth of God the Father, which cannot lie, hath so promised and so sworn.

And this faith and knowledge is everlasting life; and by this we be born anew, and made the sons of God, and obtain forgiveness of sins, and are translated from death to life, and from the wrath of God unto his love and favour. And this faith is the mother of all truth, and bringeth with her the Spirit of all truth; which Spirit purgeth us, as from all sin, even so from all lies and error, noisome and hurtful. And this faith is the foundation laid of the apostles and prophets; whereon Paul saith (Eph. 2) that we are built, and thereby of the household of God. And this faith is the rock, whereon Christ built his congregation. Christ asked the apostles (Matt. 16) whom they took him for. And Peter answered for them all, saying, 'I say that thou art Christ, the Son of the living God, that art come into this world.' That is, We believe that thou art he that was promised unto Abraham, that should come, bless us, and deliver us. Howbeit, Peter yet wist not, by what means. But now it is opened throughout all the world, that, through the offering of his body and blood, that offering is a satisfaction for the sin of all that repent, and a purchasing of whatsoever they can ask, to keep them in favour; and that they sin no more. And Christ answered, 'Upon this rock I will build my congregation:' that is, upon this faith. And against the rock of this faith can no sin, no hell, no devil, no lies nor error prevail.

[1] Tyndale: *Answer to More*, Parker Society, 30–31.

[15]

For whatsoever any man hath committed, if he repent and come to this rock, he is safe. And that this faith is the only way by which the church of Christ goeth unto God, and unto the inheritance of all his riches, testify all the apostles and prophets, and all the Scripture, with signs and miracles, and all the blood of martyrs. And whosoever goeth unto God, and unto forgiveness of sins, or salvation, by any other way than this, the same is an heretic out of the right way, and not of Christ's church.

For this knowledge maketh a man of the church. And the church is Christ's body (Col. 1) and every person of the church is a member of Christ (Eph. 5). Now it is no member of Christ that hath not Christ's Spirit in it (Rom. 8); as it is no part of me, or member of my body, wherein my soul is not present and quickeneth it. And then, if a man be none of Christ's, he is not of his church.

[11]

From his Prologue to
An Exposition upon Chapters V, VI, and VII of Matthew[1]

And as all they that have their hearts washed with this inward baptism of the Spirit are of the church, and have the keys of the Scripture, yea, and of binding and loosing, and do not err; even so they that sin of purpose, and will not hear when their faults be told them, but seek liberties and privileges to sin unpunished, and gloss out the law of God, and maintain ceremonies, traditions and customs, to destroy the faith of Christ, the same be members of Satan, and all their doctrine is poison, error and darkness; yea, though they be popes, bishops, abbots, curates, and doctors of divinity, and though they can rehearse all the Scripture without book, and though they be seen in Greek, Hebrew, and Latin: yea, and though they so preach Christ and the passion of Christ, that they make the poor women weep and howl again. For when they come to the point, that they should minister Christ's passion unto the salvation of our souls, there they poison altogether and gloss out the law, that should make us feel our salvation in Christ, and drive us in that point from Christ, and teach us to put our trust in our own works for the remission and satisfaction of our sins, and in the apish play of hypocrites, which sell their merits instead of Christ's blood and passion.

[1] Tyndale: *Expositions*, Parker Society, 12.

[III]

JOHN BRADFORD

MARTYRED AT SMITHFIELD 1ST JULY 1555

From The Hurt of Hearing Mass[1]

If we behold the face of the popish church in respect of Christ's true church whose beauty indeed is all inward, being replenished with the Spirit of Christ and the fruits of the same, outwardly being but simple, for she will add nothing to Christ's commandments in God's service and religion, otherwise than for order's sake – if, I say, we behold the face of the popish church, Lord, how it glistereth, and gorgeous it is in comparison of Christ's true church! which is discerned in these days but by the word of God truly preached, the sacraments purely ministered, and some discipline nothing so much as hath been, might be, and should be. Whereas the popish church wants nothing to set herself forth to the show – as he that considereth the persons (pope, cardinals, legates, archbishops, bishops, suffragans, abbots, priors, deans, prebendaries, archdeacons, canons, monks, friars, parsons, vicars, subdeacons, etc., and a thousand more), the power, riches, honours, promotions, lands, houses, fair services (as singing, saying, ringing, playing, censing, etc.), implements (crosses, chalices, relics, jewels, basins, copes, cruets, vestments, books, bells, candles, etc.) – he, I say, that considereth these things, he cannot but with Samuel, thinking Eliab had been he whom God had chosen, think this to be the catholic church and spouse of Christ.

But this sentence (Ps.45) saith, the beauty of God's paramour is 'within': and therefore this may be suspected to be the rose-coloured whore St John speaketh of in the Apocalypse, for whom her ministers watch night and day, how to maintain their mistress and whore-madam, with endowing her with the riches, power, and pleasures of the earth. Whereas the ministers of Christ's true church watch and labour how to enrich and beautify God's people with heavenly riches, even with the knowledge of God and his Christ; and therefore they use daily preaching and public praying, and using the sacrament so as may edify; they urge men to hoard up their treasures in heaven, etc. And this gear the world liketh not, but murmureth at the ministers, contemneth them, pilleth them, that for poverty and living's sake they might speak to please, as experience hath taught here in England.

[1] Bradford: *Writings*, Parker Society, 345-7.

[IV]

JOHN HOOPER

MARTYRED AT GLOUCESTER 9TH FEBRUARY 1555

From his Godly Confession and Protestation of the Christian Faith[1]

Now I will declare my faith concerning the external and visible church of Christ, and of the ministers thereof. I call this visible church a visible congregation of men and women, that hear the gospel of Christ, and use his sacraments as he hath instituted them: in the which congregation the Spirit of God worketh the salvation of all believers, as St Paul saith, 'The gospel is the power of God to the salvation of the believer.' As though he had said, by the Gospel of Christ, where it is heard and believed, the mind is changed by the virtue of the Holy Ghost from the love of sin unto the love of virtue: the will is wrought to consent; and the consent so assisted by the Holy Ghost, that faith obtaineth the remission of sin, and the beginning of everlasting life. And these two marks, the true preaching of God's word and right use of the sacraments, declare what and where the true church is.

Unto the which church I would all Christian men should associate themselves, although there may happen to be some things desired in manners and discipline. For no church, as touching this part, can be absolutely perfect. But where as the doctrine is sound, and no idolatry defended, that church is of God, as far as mortal man can judge. And where as this doctrine and right use of sacraments be not, there is no church of Christ, though it seem never so holy. For in the blessed Virgin's time the Pharisees and bishops were accounted to be the true church; yet by reason their doctrine was corrupt, the true church rested not in them, but in Simeon, Zachary, Elisabeth, the shepherds, and other. The same doth St Paul teach us, that whosoever he be that preacheth other doctrine than the word of God, is not to be credited, though he were an angel of heaven. Neither will such as know God hearken unto them, but will hear Christ, the prophets, and apostles, and no other.

---

[1] Hooper: *Later Writings*, Parker Society, 87–8.

[v]

NICHOLAS RIDLEY

MARTYRED AT OXFORD 16TH OCTOBER 1555

*From a document by Ridley and Latimer, setting forth their views in
the form of a conference between themselves and one of their
persecutors[1]:*

Ridley – The holy catholic or universal church, which is the communion
of saints, the house of God, the city of God, the spouse of Christ, the body
of Christ, the pillar and stay of the truth; this church I believe, according
to the Creed; this church I do reverence, and honour in the Lord. But
the rule of this church is the word of God, according to which rule we
go forward unto life. And as many as walk according to this rule, I say
with St Paul, 'Peace be upon them, and upon Israel which pertaineth unto
God.' The guide of this church is the Holy Ghost. The marks whereby this
church is known unto men in this dark world, and in the midst of this
crooked and froward generation, are these: the sincere preaching of God's
holy word, the due administration of the sacraments, charity, and faithful
observing of ecclesiastical discipline, according to the word of God. And
that the church or congregation which is garnished with these marks, is
in very deed that heavenly Jerusalem, which consisteth of those that be
born from above. This is the mother of us all, and by God's grace I will
live and die the child of this church.

Persecutor – That church which you have described unto me is invisible,
but Christ's church is visible and known. For else why would Christ have
said, 'Dic ecclesiae', i.e. 'Tell it unto the church'. For he had commanded
in vain to go unto the church, if a man cannot tell which it is.

Ridley – The church which I have described is visible, it hath members
which may be seen; and also I have afore declared, by what marks and
tokens it may be known. But if either our eyes are so dazzled, that we cannot
see it, or that Satan hath brought such darkness into the world, that it is
hard to discern the true church; that is not the fault of the church, but
either of our blindness, or of Satan's darkness. But yet, in this most deep
darkness, there is one most clear candle, which of itself alone is able to
put away all darkness: 'Thy word is a candle unto my feet, and a light
unto my steps.'

[1] Foxe: *Acts and Monuments*, VII, 412–13.

[19]

[VI]

HUGH LATIMER

MARTYRED AT OXFORD 16TH OCTOBER 1555

The exhortation to return to the unity of the church was frequently made to the Reformers by their persecutors. The following exchange between the Bishop of Lincoln and Latimer indicates the incompatibility of their respective conceptions of the church[1]:

Lincoln – We, upon due repentance of your part, shall receive you, reconcile you, acknowledge you no longer a strayed sheep, but adjoin you again to the unity of Christ's church, from the which you in the time of schism fell. So that it is no new place to the which I exhort you; I desire you but to return thither from whence you went. Consider, master Latimer, that without the unity of the church is no salvation, and in the church can be no error.

Latimer – Your lordship often doth inculcate the catholic church, as though I should deny the same. No, my lord, I confess there is a catholic church, to the determination of which I will stand; but not the church which you call catholic, which sooner might be termed diabolic. And whereas you join together the Romish and catholic church, stay there, I pray you. For it is one thing to say Romish church, and another thing to say catholic church.

[VII]

GEORGE MARSH

MARTYRED AT CHESTER 24TH APRIL 1555

During his examination by the Bishop of Chester and his subordinates, Marsh, urged to submit to the church of Rome, replied in the following terms[1]:

To whom the said George Marsh answered that he did acknowledge and believe (though much evil be withal annexed) one holy catholic and apostolic church, without which there is no salvation, and that this church

---

[1] *Acts and Monuments,* VII, 529, 540–1.   [1] *Acts and Monuments,* VII, 48–9.

is but one; because it ever hath, doth, and shall, confess and believe one only God, and him only worship; and one only Messiah, and in him only trust for salvation: which church also is ruled and led by one Spirit, one word, and one faith; and that this church is universal and catholic, because it ever hath been since the world's beginning, is, and shall endure to the world's end, and comprehending within it all nations, kindreds, languages, degrees, states, and conditions of men; and that this church is builded only upon the foundation of the prophets and apostles, Jesus Christ himself being the head corner-stone; and not upon the Romish laws and decrees, the bishop of Rome being the supreme head.

And whereas they said, the church did stand in ordinary succession of bishops, being ruled by general councils, holy fathers, and the laws of holy church, and so had continued by the space of fifteen hundred years and more; he made answer that the holy church, which is the body of Christ, and therefore most worthy to be called holy, was before any succession of bishops, general councils, or Romish decrees neither yet was bound to any time or place, ordinary succession, general councils, or traditions of fathers, neither had any supremacy over empires and kingdoms; but that it was a little poor silly flock, dispersed and scattered abroad, as sheep without a shepherd in the midst of wolves, or as a flock of orphans and fatherless children; and that this church was led and ruled by the only laws, counsels, and word of Christ, he being the Supreme Head of this church, and assisting, succouring, and defending her from all assaults, errors, troubles, and persecutions, wherewith she is ever compassed about.

[VIII]

THOMAS CAUSTON AND THOMAS HIGBED
MARTYRED IN ESSEX 26TH MARCH 1555

Part of their Confession of Faith[1] *delivered to the Bishop of London, for which they were burnt:*

We believe, that there is a catholic church, even the communion of saints, 'built upon the foundation of the prophets and apostles,' as St Paul saith, 'Christ being the head corner-stone.' For the which church Christ gave

[1] *Acts and Monuments*, VI, 734.

himself, to make it to himself a glorious congregation, without fault in his sight.

We believe, that this church of herself, and by her own merits, is sinful, and must needs say, 'Father! forgive us our sins': but, through Christ and his merits, she is freely forgiven; 'for he in his own person', saith St Paul, 'hath purged her sins, and made her faultless in his sight': 'Besides whom, there is no Saviour', saith the prophet: 'Neither is there salvation', saith St Peter, 'in any other name.'

We believe, as he is our only Saviour, so he is our only Mediator. For the apostle St Paul saith, 'There is one God, one Mediator between God and man, even the man Jesus Christ.' Wherefore, seeing none hath this name, God and man, but Jesus Christ, therefore there is no Mediator but Jesus Christ.

We believe, that this church of Christ is and hath been persecuted, by the words of Christ, saying 'As they have persecuted me, so shall they persecute you: for the disciple is not above his master.' 'For it is not only given unto you to believe in Christ', saith St Paul, 'but also to suffer for his sake. For all that will live godly in Christ Jesus, must suffer persecution.'

We believe that the church of Christ teacheth the word of God truly and sincerely, putting nothing to, nor taking any thing from: and also doth minister the sacraments according to the primitive church.

We believe, that this church of Christ suffereth all men to read the Scriptures, according to Christ's commandment, saying, 'Search the Scriptures; for they testify of me.' We read also out of the Acts, that when St Paul preached, the audience daily searched the Scriptures, whether he preached truly or no. Also the prophet David teacheth all men to pray with understanding: 'For how shall the unlearned', saith St Paul 'say amen, at the giving of thanks, when they understand not what is said?' And what is more allowed than true faith, which, St Paul saith, 'cometh by hearing of the word of God?'

We believe, that the church of Christ teacheth, that God ought to be worshipped according to his Word, and not after the doctrine of men: 'For in vain', saith Christ, 'ye worship me, teaching nothing but the doctrine of men.'

Also we are commanded of God by his prophet, saying, 'Walk not in the traditions and precepts of your elders: but walk', saith he, 'in my precepts: do that I command you: put nothing thereunto, neither take any thing from it.' Likewise saith Christ, 'You shall forsake father and mother, and follow me.' Whereby we learn, that if our elders teach otherwise than God commanded, in that point we must forsake them.

[22]

[ix]
JOHN CALVIN
[1509–1564]

From a letter to the King of France, October 1557[1]:

We believe that the order of the church which Jesus Christ has established on his authority, ought to be held sacred and inviolable; and yet that church cannot be held together unless there be pastors who have the office of teaching, and these pastors we are bound to honour and listen to with respect, when they are duly called and faithfully discharge their duty, in which belief we detest those missionaries who would annihilate, as far as in them lies, the preaching of the word of God.

We believe that we ought to observe and keep up the unity of the church, and that all those who separate themselves from it are perverse persons whom we ought to shun as deadly pests. Nevertheless we are of opinion that we ought prudently to discern which is the true church, because several falsely abuse this title. We declare then, that it is the society of the faithful who agree to follow the word of God and that pure religion which depends on it, and who profit therein throughout the whole course of their lives, increasing and confirming themselves in the fear of God, according as they have need to make progress, and tending always to that which is beyond. Moreover, that, whatever efforts they make, it behoves them incessantly to have recourse to Christ for the remission of their sins.

We believe that the sacraments are conjoined with the word for ampler confirmation, to be the pledges and earnests of the grace of God, and by this means to comfort and aid our faith, because of the infirmity and hardheartedness which is in us. We hold also that the substance thereof is Jesus Christ, for being separated from him they lose all efficacy.

[1] Calvin: *Letters*, edited by Jules Bonnet, III, 375.

SECTION II

The Rule for Reformation —
The Word of God

Liberation
from Human Authority

Martin Luther

[1483-1546]

THE FOLLOWING EXTRACT IS FROM A SERMON PREACHED BY LUTHER IN *1538 in a series of expositions on the Gospel of John. The Reformer's expositions on this Gospel have recently been published in English for the first time by Concordia Publishing House as part of a 56-volume edition of Luther's Works. This particular passage, reprinted by permission of the publishers, will be found in vol. 22, pp. 254–261. The context of the extract is a treatment of John 2: 23, 24 in which Luther (unlike many later commentators) interprets the many who 'believed' in Christ's name because of His miracles on the occasion of His first public visit to Jerusalem, as genuine but weak believers who could not yet be trusted by Christ. Whether linked legitimately to his text or not, Luther's pungent digression on the place which is to be given to Scripture is characteristic of the spirit which kindled the Reformation movement and liberated thousands from a false reverence of human authority.*

In connection with Luther's view of Scripture, M. Reu, Luther and the Scriptures (Wartburg Press, Ohio, 1944), is a helpful statement of his belief in its perfect Divine authority – a fact which has sometimes been contested.

The immense strength which Luther came to draw from his knowledge that Scripture is the voice of God, and the practical implications which this had upon his heroic conflict can be seen in his Letters, vol. 1 (covering the years 1507–1522 and published as vol. 48 of the Concordia edition of Luther). Returning from the historic meeting at Worms in 1521, Luther writes to the Emperor Charles V from Friedberg on April 28: 'Since (the Word of God) is above everything it has to be held absolutely free and unbound in all things, as Paul teaches. (The Word of God) is never subject to any man's whim to lower its importance or challenge it, no matter how great, how numerous, how learned, and how holy the men are. This is true to such an extent that St Paul in Galatians 1 (v. 8) dares to exclaim and reiterate, "If we or an angel from heaven should preach to you a gospel (contrary to that which we preached to you) let him be accursed".'

Liberation from Human Authority

ALTHOUGH we must always expect the best from man, especially from the believers, we remember that they may err and go astray. If this truth had been observed in Christendom, we would have had neither the pope nor all the filth and stench of his anti-Christian doctrine with which the Christian Church was later seduced. In the papacy one concluded: 'Oh, he is a holy man and, consequently, all that he says must be true!'

Take, by way of illustration, Saints Ambrose, Gregory, Augustine, and Jerome, and all the others, down to Bernard, Benedict, Dominic and Francis. In the end all the sayings and doctrines of anyone with a reputation for holiness were collected.

I need to be warned against such a practice. I must say: 'I shall gladly believe that the men I have mentioned – such as Gregory, Ambrose and Augustine – were holy men; but I do not trust myself to them. For their holiness does not make them infallible, and it does not imply that one must rely and depend on all the dicta of the fathers or approve and believe all their teachings. Rather take the touchstone of God's Word into your hands. Let this be your criterion for testing, trying and judging all that the fathers have preached, written and said, as well as all the precepts and human ordinances that have been promulgated. Otherwise one will be easily misled and deceived. And since this polishing stone was not applied to the pope in times past, he ran rampant and covered the church with errors.

Therefore I say: I want to see whether any doctrine concurs with Christ. I dare not forget the clear rule which St Paul gives us Christians: to pay attention to what conforms to the doctrine of Christ and to the faith. In Rom. 12: 7 he says: 'Let it be in conformity with the faith'; that is, it must be in harmony and conformity with Christ. And St Peter declares: 'Whoever speaks, let him speak as the word of God' (1 Peter 4: 11). You must not go only to St Bernard and St Ambrose, but it is imperative that you take them with you to Christ and see whether they agree with His teaching. If they do not, but have added something to that which Christ has taught, or have evolved something from their own piety and taught this, I shall let them answer for that. But I must not convert it into an article of faith; nor am I to believe it, since they do not entirely agree with Christ. For I am to adhere to Christ alone; He has taught neither too much nor too little. He has taught me to know God the Father, has revealed Himself to me, and has also acquainted me with the Holy Spirit. He has also instructed me how to live and how to die and has told me what to hope for. What more do I want? And if anyone wishes to teach me anything now, let him beware of any innovations. If he tries to present anything new, I must say to him: 'I will not believe it, dear pastor, dear preacher, dear St Ambrose, dear St Augustine. For anything that goes beyond and above the man who is called Christ is not genuine. It is still flesh and blood, and Christ warned us against relying on that. He Himself did not trust Himself to man.'

But because in the past we disobeyed this instruction of Christ, everything that was spoken by St Gregory, Thomas Aquinas, and others was approved. And this produced all the monks and nuns. In fact, all the pilgrimages and the invocation of the saints sprang from this source.

No one will believe how great an ordeal it is and how severe a shock when a person first realizes that he must believe and teach contrary to the fathers, especially when he sees that so many excellent, intelligent, and learned men, yes, the best of them taught thus, and that the majority of the people in the world shared their views; among these were so many holy men, like Saints Ambrose, Jerome, and Augustine. I, too, have often experienced this shock. But in spite of all this, that one man, my Lord and Saviour Jesus Christ, must have greater weight with me than all the holiest people on earth put together. Yea, He must also outweigh all the angels in heaven (Gal. 1: 8) if they teach anything at variance with the Gospel, or if they add to or detract from the doctrine of the divine Word. And then when I read the books of St Augustine and discover that he, too, did this and that, it thoroughly appals me. And when, over and above this, the hue and the cry is raised: 'The church! The church!', this dismays one most of all. It is truly difficult to subdue one's own heart in these matters, to deviate from people who are so highly respected and who bear such a holy name – indeed, from the church herself – and no longer to have any confidence and faith in the church's teaching. I mean, of course, that church of which they say: 'Lo, the church has decreed that the precepts of Saints Francis and Dominic and the orders of monks and nuns are proper, Christian, and good.' This truly bewilders and dismays a person. But after all is said and done, I must say that I dare not accept whatever any man might say; for he may be a pious and God-fearing man and yet be mistaken and err. Therefore I shall not trust myself to them all, as the Lord, according to this text, did not trust Himself to man either. And in another passage, found in the Gospel of Matthew, Christ earnestly warns us to beware of false prophets who will appear and not merely declare that they are Christians, but will also 'show great signs and wonders, so as to lead astray, if possible, even the elect' (Matt. 24: 24).

Therefore we should place no reliance in any of the fathers or in their writings, but we should crawl under the wings of our Brood Hen, the Lord Jesus, and depend solely on Him. For of Him God the heavenly Father Himself said: 'This is My beloved Son, with whom I am well pleased; listen to him' (Matt. 17: 5). God insists that we give ear to Christ alone, for He said neither too little nor too much.

Moses, who shines with the greatest lustre in Scripture, is authorized to say: 'You shall not add to the word which I command you, nor take from it, but leave it unaltered as I taught it to you' (Deut. 4: 2). And if Moses, the servant, lays claim to such honour and authority, how much more is Christ the Lord entitled to it, of whom God the Father bore witness from heaven that we should listen to Him and to no other! For Christ has taught us how to know the Father and Himself, how to live in our several estates, and also how to pass through the sore trials and the agonies of the hour of death, for all of which He gave us His Word and Sacraments. And we dare not add to or subtract from these.

But the pope acts arbitrarily, and he has the audacity to add to and to subtract from them. Thus he deprives the laity of the one kind in Holy Communion, contrary to the words of God, which say: 'Listen to Him!' Who authorized him to do this? And if it was forbidden to take away from Moses, the servant's words, why, then, should one want to curtail or mutilate the words of the Lord Christ? Therefore, pope or no pope, I may believe that you are pious, but I will not trust you. For you detract from the divine Word, and your message and doctrine are not in conformity with the faith, as St Paul demands (Rom. 12: 7). The pope also adds to the divine Word, as is manifest in his indulgences, his pilgrimages, also in his claim that it is a sin to eat butter and meat on certain days. Who authorized him to add this? My Lord Christ says that I am to be untrammelled, free to eat what God grants me and what is put before me by man, if only I know the Father and believe in Him.

But in the papacy they counter with the cry: 'The fathers! The fathers!' You must reply: 'I am ready to believe and to concede that they were pious people during their lifetime; however, whenever they talk and teach contrary to Christ, I do not believe them. How are you going to harmonize the pope's decree, "Whoever eats meat on Friday is of the devil, accursed and damned," with Christ's teaching to the contrary? St Paul says that all food should be received and used with thanksgiving to God (1 Tim. 4: 4). Does the pope's prohibition agree with the doctrine of Christ? I do not question that Ambrose and Augustine taught abstinence from meat on certain days; but since this contradicts Holy Scripture, I shall not comply with it or obey you.'

If I say: 'St Benedict was a holy man, St Gregory was pious and one of the elect!' it does not follow by any means that then everything they said and did was holy and good and must be accepted and taught. Do not draw such a conclusion. For they, too, were human. This text tells us that many believed in Christ, but that nevertheless He did not trust Himself to them. Why, then, do you insist on trusting yourself to these men and following them? There is more in man than just his faith. There is the old Adam; flesh and blood still cling to us. Furthermore, the devil desires to sift man as wheat is sifted, as Christ says to St Peter (Luke 22: 31). Therefore man can indeed err and fall.

Now how will you proceed? Will you condemn these men? No, I do not intend to condemn Benedict and others. But I do propose to take their books and carry them to Christ and to His Word as a criterion for comparison, to submit St Francis' rule to Christ's Gospel for a judgment. If their doctrine agrees with the Gospel, I shall accept it; if not, I shall say: 'You may be a holy man, but you will never subject me to your rule; for it is a human bauble. Therefore let the devil adopt it! I do not want it!'

That should have been our policy long ago. But everybody is hesitant about doing this and will not do it even today, since no one is willing to concede that the church is fallible. But take hold of Christ, as John the Baptist also sends his disciples to Him. Subject the saints, too, to the scrutiny of Christ. Rules cannot be formulated on the basis of the actions of prophets and holy men. You must judge everything solely in the light of the words of Christ the Lord; for it is written: 'Listen to Him (Matt. 17: 5). And if you give ear only to him, then I want you to know that everything you say and do in faith in the Son will also have My approval. If not, then all your actions and words will be displeasing to Me.' We know from experience what will happen if the opinions of men become all-important. When St Augustine, Jerome, or Ambrose spoke or taught anything we closed our eyes, accepted and believed it without questioning and argument, on the assumption that the church and the saints must be respected. But man's disposition to sin and to err was left out of consideration.

It is dangerous to say, as the pope has, that, since St Benedict was a holy man who abstained from meat on Fridays and Saturdays, it is salutary to copy him in this respect. What if St Benedict had been motivated by

[33]

thirst for honour and carnal zeal? Or should you say: 'Behold, I want to ape St Francis because the pope declares that he was a holy man, that he disdained money, wore a grey cowl and wooden shoes'? No, Christ did not command the wearing of a grey cowl, though St Francis thought it was a good idea. But what if the Holy Spirit did not inspire him to do this, but the old Adam, who always tries to be so clever in spiritual matters? Human devotion and reason prompted St Francis to do this. Christ the Lord, however, is content to see you dressed in any garment you may choose. Just remain with Christ, and let nothing lead you away from Him. Crawl under His wings, just as little chicks crawl under the brood hen and follow her wherever she may lead them; otherwise a hawk may tear them to pieces and devour them.

The Reformers and
the Regulative Principle

William Cunningham

[1805-1861]

THE EARLY NINETEENTH CENTURY SCOTTISH THEOLOGIAN JOHN DICK
wrote concerning the Church in his Lectures on Theology (*vol. 4, p. 324, 1838*):
'*Some have supposed that the government of the Church is ambulatory; by which they mean, that no precise form has been prescribed, and that it is left to the wisdom of men to vary the form according to circumstances; to adapt it to the genius, and habits, and civil constitution of different nations. This is a summary mode of terminating all disputes about the subject.*' *Although this latitudinarian way of dealing with Church issues had found many supporters in England since the decline of Puritanism, it was not until the second half of the nineteenth century that a widespread attempt was made in Scotland to abandon the historic position that Scripture alone is the rule of the Church.*

One of the leading popularizers of this new view was Dr John Tulloch, who in his Leaders of the Reformation, *published in 1859, made the following statement:* '*The Christian Scriptures are a revelation of divine truth and not a revelation of church polity. They not only do not lay down the outline of such a polity, but they do not even give the adequate and conclusive hints of one; and for the best of all reasons, that it would have been entirely contrary to the spirit of Christianity to have done so; and because, in point of fact, the conditions of human progress do not admit of the imposition of any unvarying system of government, ecclesiastical or civil.*' *This earned from William Cunningham, Principal of New College, Edinburgh, a trenchant reply in* The British and Foreign Evangelical Review *and the article was reprinted in a posthumous volume of his writings,* The Reformers and the Theology of the Reformation, *1862. It is from this reply to Tulloch that the following statement of the regulative principle of Scripture is taken.*

Bibliography

Historical Theology, 2 vols., William Cunningham, 1862, reprinted 1960, cf. vol. 1, pp. 64–73, where he expounds the conviction that: 'It is unwarrantable and unlawful to introduce into the government and worship of the Christian Church any arrangements and ordinances which have not been positively sanctioned by Christ or His apostles'.
The Necessity of Reforming the Church; The True Method of Giving Peace to Christendom and Reforming the Church, John Calvin. These two tracts, which contain some of the clearest of Calvin's statements on the regulative principle, will be found in his Tracts and Treatises, 3 vols., 1844–1851, reprinted 1958.

The Reformers and the Regulative Principle

O<small>F</small> the views generally held by the Reformers on the subject of the organization of the Church, there are two which have been always very offensive to men of a loose and latitudinarian tendency – viz. the alleged unlawfulness of introducing into the worship and government of the Church anything which is not positively warranted by Scripture, and the permanent binding obligation of a particular form of Church government. The second of these principles may be regarded, in one aspect of it, as comprehended in the first. But it may be proper to make a few observations upon them separately, in the order in which they have now been stated.

The Lutheran and Anglican sections of the Reformers held a somewhat looser view upon these subjects than was approved of by Calvin. They generally held that the Church might warrantably introduce innovations into its government and worship, which might seem fitted to be useful, provided it could not be shown that there was anything in Scripture which expressly prohibited or discountenanced them, thus laying the *onus probandi*, in so far as Scripture is concerned, upon those who opposed the introduction of innovations. The Calvinistic section of the Reformers, following their great master, adopted a stricter rule, and were of opinion that there are sufficiently plain indications in Scripture itself, that it was Christ's mind and will that nothing should be introduced into the government and worship of the Church, unless a positive warrant for it could be found in Scripture. This principle was adopted and acted upon by the English Puritans and the Scottish Presbyterians; and we are persuaded that it is the only true and safe principle applicable to this matter.

The principle is in a sense a very wide and sweeping one. But it is purely prohibitory or exclusive; and the practical effect of it, if it were fully carried out, would just be to leave the Church in the condition in which it was left by the apostles, in so far as we have any means of information – a result, surely, which need not be very alarming, except to those who think that they themselves have very superior powers for improving and adorning the Church by their inventions. The principle ought to be understood in a common-sense way, and we ought to be satisfied with reasonable evidence of its truth. Those who dislike this principle, from whatever cause, usually try to run us into difficulties by putting a very stringent construction upon it, and thereby giving it an appearance of absurdity, or by demanding an unreasonable amount of evidence to establish it. The principle must be interpreted and explained in the exercise of common sense. One obvious modification of it is suggested in the first chapter of the *Westminster Confession of Faith* where it is acknowledged 'that there are some circumstances, concerning the worship of God and government of the Church, common to human actions and societies, which are to be ordered by the light of nature and Christian prudence, according to the general rules of the Word, which are always to be observed'. But even this distinction between things and circumstances cannot always be applied very certainly; that is, cases have occurred in which there might be room for a difference of opinion, whether a proposed regulation or arrangement was *a distinct thing* in the way of innovation, or merely a *circumstance* attaching to an authorized thing and requiring to be regulated. Difficulties and differences of opinions may arise about details, even when sound judgment and good sense are brought to bear upon the interpretation and application of the principle; but this affords no ground for denying or doubting the truth or soundness of the principle itself.

In regard to questions of this sort there are two opposite extremes, into which one-sided minds are apt to fall, and both of which ought to be guarded against. The one is to stick rigidly and doggedly to a general principle, refusing to admit that any limitations or qualifications ought to be permitted in applying it; and the other is to reject the principle altogether, as if it had no truth or soundness about it, merely because it manifestly cannot be carried out without some exceptions and modifications, and because difficulties may be raised about some of the details of its application which cannot always be very easily solved. Both these extremes have been often exhibited in connection with this principle. Both of them are natural, but both are unreasonable, and both indicate a want of sound judgment. The right course is to ascertain, if possible, whether or not the principle be true; and if there seem to be sufficient evidence of its truth, then to seek to make a reasonable and judicious application of it.

With regard to the Scripture evidence of the truth of the principle, we do not allege that it is very direct, explicit, and overwhelming. It is not of a kind likely to satisfy the coarse, material literalists, who can see nothing in the Bible but what is asserted in express terms. But it is, we think, amply sufficient to convince those who, without any prejudice against it, are ready to submit their minds to the fair impression of what Scripture seems to have been intended to teach. The general principle of the unlawfulness of introducing into the government and worship of the Church anything which cannot be shown to have positive Scriptural sanction, can, we think, be deduced from the Word of God by good and necessary consequence. We do not mean at present to adduce the proof, but merely to indicate where it is to be found. The truth of this principle, as a general rule for the guidance of the Church, is plainly enough involved in what Scripture teaches concerning its own sufficiency and perfection as a rule of faith and practice, concerning God's exclusive right to determine in what way He ought to be worshipped, concerning Christ's exclusive right to settle the constitution, laws, and arrangements of His kingdom, concerning the unlawfulness of will-worship, and concerning the utter unfitness of men for the function which they have so often and so boldly usurped in this matter. The fair application of these various Scriptural views taken in combination, along with the utter want of any evidence on the other side, seems to us quite sufficient to shut out the lawfulness of introducing the inventions of men into the government and worship of the Christian Church.

There is no force in the presumption, that, because so little in regard to the externals of the Church is fixed by Scriptural authority, therefore much was left to be regulated by human wisdom, as experience might suggest or as the varying condition of the Church might seem to require. For, on the contrary, every view suggested by Scripture of Christianity and the Church, indicates that Christ intended His Church to remain permanently in the condition of simplicity as to outward arrangements, in which His apostles were guided to leave it. And never certainly has there been a case in which it has been more fully established by experience, that the foolishness of God, as the apostle says, is wiser than men; that what seems to many men very plausible and very wise, is utter folly, and tends to frustrate the very objects which it was designed to serve. Of the innumerable inventions of men introduced into the government and worship of the Church, without any warrant from Scripture, but professedly as being indicated by the wisdom of experience, or by the Christian consciousness of a particular age or country, to be fitted to promote the great ends of the Church, not one can with any plausibility be shown to have had a tendency to contribute, or to have in fact contributed, to the end contemplated; while, taken in the mass – and of course no limitation can be put to them unless the principle we maintain be adopted – they have inflicted fearful injury upon the best interests of the Church. There is a remarkable statement of Dr Owen's on this subject, which has been often quoted, but not more frequently than it deserves; it is this – 'The principle that the church hath

[40]

power to institute any thing or ceremony belonging to the worship of God, either as to matter or manner, beyond the observance of such circumstances as necessarily attend such ordinances as Christ Himself hath instituted, lies at the bottom of all the horrible superstition and idolatry, of all the confusion, blood, persecution, and wars, that have for so long a season spread themselves over the face of the Christian world.' It is no doubt very gratifying to the pride of men to think that they, in the exercise of their wisdom, brought to bear upon the experience of the past history of the Church, or (to accommodate our statement to the prevalent views and phraseology of the present day) in the exercise of their own Christian consciousness, their own spiritual tact and discernment, can introduce improvements upon the nakedness and simplicity of the Church as it was left by the apostles. Perhaps the best mode of dealing with such persons, is to call upon them to exemplify their own general principle, by producing specific instances from among the innumerable innovations that have been introduced into the Church in past ages, by which they are prepared to maintain that the interests of religion have been benefited; or, if they decline this, to call upon them for a specimen of the innovations, possessed of course of this beneficial character and tendency, which they themselves have devised and would wish to have introduced; and then to undertake to show, what would be no very difficult task, that these innovations, whether selected or invented, have produced, or would produce if tried, effects the very reverse of what they would ascribe to them.

There is a strange fallacy which seems to mislead men in forming an estimate of the soundness and importance of this principle. Because this principle has been often brought out in connection with the discussion of matters which, viewed in themselves, are very unimportant – such as rites and ceremonies, vestments and organs, crossings, kneelings, bowings, and other such *ineptiae* – some men seem to think that it partakes of the intrinsic littleness of these things, and that the men who defend and try to enforce it, find their most congenial occupation in fighting about these small matters, and exhibit great bigotry and narrow-mindedness in bringing the authority of God and the testimony of Scripture to bear upon such a number of paltry points. Many have been led to entertain such views as these of the English Puritans and of the Scottish Presbyterians, and very much upon the ground of their maintenance of this principle. Now, it should be quite sufficient to prevent or neutralize this impression, to show, as we think can be done, 1st, That the principle is taught with sufficient plainness in Scripture, and that, therefore, it ought to be professed and applied to the regulation of ecclesiastical affairs. 2nd, That, viewed in

[41]

itself, it is large, liberal, and comprehensive, such as seems in no way unbecoming its divine Author, and in no way unsuitable to the dignity of the Church as a divine institution, giving to God His rightful place of supremacy, and to the Church, as the body of Christ, its rightful position of elevated simplicity and purity. 3rd, That, when contemplated in connection with the ends of the Church, it is in full accordance with everything suggested by an enlightened and searching survey of the tendencies of human nature, and the testimony of all past experience. And with respect to the connection above referred to, on which the impression we are combating is chiefly based, it is surely plain that, in so far as it exists *de facto*, this is owing, not to anything in the tendencies of the principle itself or of its supporters, but to the conduct of the men who, in defiance of this principle, would obtrude human inventions into the government and worship of the Church, or who insist upon retaining them permanently after they have once got admittance. The principle suggests no rites or ceremonies, no schemes or arrangements; it is purely negative and prohibitory. Its supporters never devise innovations and press them upon the Church. The principle itself precludes this. It is the deniers of this principle, and they alone, who invent and obtrude innovations; and they are responsible for all the mischiefs that ensue from the discussions and contentions to which these things have given rise.

Men, under the pretence of curing the defects and shortcomings, the nakedness and bareness, attaching to ecclesiastical arrangements as set before us in the New Testament, have been constantly proposing innovations and improvements in government and worship. The question is, How ought these proposals to have been received? Our answer is, There is a great general Scriptural principle which shuts them all out. We refuse even to enter into the consideration of what is alleged in support of them. It is enough for us that they have no positive sanction from Scripture. On this ground we refuse to admit them, and, where they have crept in, we insist upon their being turned out, although, upon this latter point, Calvin, with his usual magnanimity, was always willing to have a reasonable regard to times and circumstances, and to the weaknesses and infirmities of the parties concerned. This is really all that we have to do with the mass of trumpery that has been brought under discussion in connection with these subjects. We find plainly enough indicated in Scripture a great comprehensive principle, suited to the dignity and importance of the great subject to which it relates, the right administration of the Church of Christ – a principle 'majestic in its own simplicity'. We apply this principle to the mass of paltry stuff that has been devised for the purpose of improving and adorning the Church, and thereby we sweep it all away. This is all that we have to do with these small matters. We have no desire to know or to do anything about them; and when they are obtruded upon us by our opponents, we take our stand upon a higher platform, and refuse to look at them. This is plainly the true state of the case; and yet attempts are constantly made, and not wholly without success, to represent these small matters, and the discussions to which they have given rise, as distinctively characteristic of English Puritans and Scottish Presbyterians; whereas, in all their intrinsic littleness and paltriness, they are really characteristic only of those who contend for introducing or retaining them.

It was a great service, then, that Calvin rendered to the Church when he brought out and established this principle, in correction of the looser views held by the Lutheran and Anglican Reformers. If all the Protestant churches had cordially adopted and faithfully followed this simple but comprehensive and commanding principle, this would certainly have prevented a fearful amount of mischief, and would, in all probability, have effected a vast amount of good. There is good ground to believe, that, in that case, the Protestant churches would have been all along far more cordially united together, and more active and successful in opposing their great common enemies, Popery and infidelity, and in advancing the cause of their common Lord and Master.

There is another principle that was generally held by the Reformers, though not peculiar to them, which is very offensive to Dr Tulloch and other latitudinarians, – viz. the Scriptural authority or *jus divinum* of one particular form of Church government. This general principle has been held by most men who have felt any real honest interest in religious matters, whether they had adopted Popish, Prelatic, Presbyterian, or Congregational views of what the government of the Church should be. The first persons who gave prominence to a negation of this principle, were the original defenders of the Church of England in Queen Elizabeth's reign, Archbishop Whitgift and his associates, who scarcely ventured to claim a Scriptural sanction for the constitution of their Church. They have not been generally followed in this by the more modern defenders of the Church of England, who have commonly claimed a divine right for their government, and not a few of whom have gone the length of unchurching Presbyterians and Congregationalists. But they have been followed by some men in every age who seemed anxious to escape from the controlling authority of Scripture, that they might be more at liberty to gratify their own fancies, or to prosecute their own selfish interest.

From the time of Whitgift and Hooker down to the present day, it has

[43]

been a common misrepresentation of the views of *jure divino* anti-prelatists to allege that they claimed a divine right – a positive Scripture sanction – for the *details* of their system of government. Dr Tulloch seems to have thought it impossible to dispense with this misrepresentation; and accordingly he tells us that Presbyterianism 'not merely asserted itself to be wise and conformable to Scripture, and therefore divine, but it claimed the direct impress of a divine right for all its details and applications'. This statement is untrue. There may be differences of opinion among Presbyterians as to the extent to which a divine right should be claimed for the subordinate features of the system, and some, no doubt, have gone to an extreme in the extent of their claims. But no Presbyterians of eminence have ever claimed 'the direct impress of a divine right for *all* the details and applications' of their system. They have claimed a divine right, or scriptural sanction, only for its fundamental principles, its leading features. It is these only which they allege are indicated in Scripture in such a way as to be binding upon the Church in all ages. And it is just the same ground that is taken by all the more intelligent and judicious among *jure divino* Prelatists and Congregationalists.

Dr Tulloch, in the last of the quotations we have given from his book, endeavours to prove that no form of Church government was or could have been laid down in Scripture, so as to be permanently binding upon the Church. His leading positions are embodied in this statement:

'The Christian Scriptures are a revelation of divine truth, and not a revelation of church polity. They not only do not lay down the outline of such a polity, but they do not even give the adequate and conclusive hints of one. And for the best of all reasons, that it would have been entirely contrary to the spirit of Christianity to have done so; and because, in point of fact, the conditions of human progress do not admit of the imposition of any unvarying system of government, ecclesiastical or civil.'

Dr Tulloch admits that the Scriptures are 'a revelation of divine truth'; and since the truth revealed in them is not the theology of the Reformation, we hope that some time or other he will enlighten the world as to what the 'divine truth' is which they do reveal. As to the position that 'the Scriptures are not a revelation of church polity', we venture to think, that it is possible that something may be taught in Scripture on the subject of Church polity for the permanent guidance of the Church; and if there be anything of that nature taught there, then it must be a portion of the 'divine truth' which the Scriptures reveal. Whether anything be taught in Scripture on the subject of Church polity, must be determined, not by such an oracular deliverance as Dr Tulloch has given, but by an examina-

[44]

tion of Scripture itself, by an investigation into the validity of the Scriptural grounds which have been brought forward in support of the different theories of Church government. Dr Tulloch will scarcely allege, that there is nothing whatever taught in Scripture as to what should be the polity of the Church; and if there be anything taught there upon the subject, it must be received as a portion of divine truth. He is quite sure, however, that the sacred Scriptures 'not only do not lay down the outline of such a polity, but they do not even give the adequate and conclusive hints of one'. Here we are directly at issue with him. We contend that not merely 'hints', but what may be fairly called an 'outline' of a particular Church polity, are set forth in Scripture in such a way as to be binding upon the Church in all ages.

We admit, indeed, that when this position is discussed in the abstract as a general thesis, a good deal of the argument often adduced in support of it is unsatisfactory and insufficient, as well as what is adduced against it. When the position we maintain is put in the shape of an abstract proposition, in which the advocates of all the different forms of Church government – Papists, Prelatists, Presbyterians, and Congregationalists – may concur; in other words, when the general position is laid down, that a particular form of Church government, *without specifying what,* is sanctioned by Scripture, we admit that the materials which may be brought to bear in support of this position are somewhat vague and indefinite, and do not tell very directly and conclusively upon the point to be proved. The strength of the case is brought fully out only when it is alleged that some one particular form of Church government specified, as Prelacy or Presbyterianism, is sanctioned and imposed by Scripture. The best and most satisfactory way of establishing the general position, that the Scripture sanctions and imposes a particular form of Church government, is to bring out the particular principles, rules, and arrangements in regard to the government of the Church which are sanctioned by Scripture, and to show that these, when taken together, or viewed in combination, constitute what may be fairly and reasonably called a form of Church government. By this process not only is the general proposition most clearly and directly established, but, what is of much more importance, the particular form of Church government which Scripture sanctions, and which, therefore, the Church is under a permanent obligation to have, is brought out and demonstrated.

Attempts, indeed, have been made to prove and to disprove the general thesis in the abstract by *a priori* reasonings, but most of these reasonings appear to us to possess but little force or relevancy. It is contended on *a*

[45]

priori grounds, on the one hand, that there *must* have been a particular form of Church government laid down in Scripture; and it is contended on similar grounds, on the other hand, that this *could not* be done, or that it was impossible consistently with the general nature of the Christian Church, and the circumstances in which it was, and was to be, placed. But the truth is, that nothing which can be fairly regarded as very clear or cogent can be adduced in support of either of these abstract positions, unless the idea of a form of Church government be taken, in the first of them, in a very wide and lax, and in the second, in a very minute and restricted sense. On the one hand, while there is a large measure of *a priori* probability, that Christ, intending to found a Church as an organized, visible, permanent society, very different in character from the previously subsisting Church of God, especially in regard to all matters of external organization and arrangement, should give some general directions or indications of His mind and will as to its constitution and government, we have no certain materials for making any assertion as to the extent to which He was called upon to carry the rules He might prescribe as of permanent obligation, or for holding that He might be confidently expected to give rules so complete and minute as to constitute what might with any propriety be called a form of Church government. And, on the other hand, while it is evident that the Christian Church was intended to be wholly different in external organization from the Jewish one, and to have no such minute and detailed system of regulations, as being intended for all ages and countries; and while on these grounds, but little, as compared with the Jewish system, was to be subjected to precise and detailed regulations, and something might thus be left to the Church to be determined by the light of nature and providential circumstances – there is no antecedent improbability whatever, arising from any source or any consideration, in the idea that Christ might give such general directions on this subject as, when combined together, might justly have the designation of a form of Church government applied to them. On these grounds we do not attach much weight to those general *a priori* considerations, by which many have undertaken to prove, on the one hand, that Christ *must* have established a particular form of government for His Church, or, on the other hand, that He *could not have* done so; and we regard the case upon this whole subject as left in a very defective and imperfect state, until the advocates of the principle of a scripturally sanctioned or *jure divino* form of Church government, have shown what the particular form of Church government is which the Scripture sanctions, and have produced the evidence that Scripture does sanction *that* form, and, of course, *a* form – which will be a sufficient answer to the allegation that He *could not have done so*.

We think we can prove from Scripture statement and apostolic practice, the binding obligation of certain laws or rules, and arrangements, which furnish not only 'hints', but even an 'outline of church polity', and which, when combined together, may be fairly said to constitute *a form of church government*. In this way, we think we can show that there is a particular form of church government which, in its fundamental principles and leading features, is sanctioned and imposed by Scripture, viz. the Presbyterian one.

If the general *a priori* considerations which have been frequently brought into the discussion of this subject are insufficient to establish the true position, that Scripture does sanction one particular form of church government, much less are they adequate to establish the false position that it does not. Dr Tulloch, as we have seen, asserts that we have 'the best of all reasons' to show that the Scriptures do not lay down even an 'outline' of a Church polity. But his 'best of all reasons' are not likely to satisfy any but those who are determined beforehand to be convinced. His reasons are two: 1st, 'It would have been entirely contrary to the spirit of Christianity to have done so'; 2nd, 'The conditions of human progress do not admit of the imposition of any unvarying system of government, ecclesiastical or civil.' This is the whole proof which he adduces; and these he calls 'the best of all reasons'. This, forsooth, is to prove that it is impossible that even the 'outline' of a Church polity could have been set forth in Scripture as permanently binding. Even Divine Wisdom, it would seem, could not have devised an outline of a Church polity which would have been accordant with 'the spirit of Christianity and the conditions of human progress'. Our readers, we presume, will not expect us to say anything more for the purpose of refuting and exposing this. 'The spirit of Christianity and the conditions of human progress' might have had some bearing upon the question in hand, if there had been on the other side the maintenance of the position, that the Scriptures imposed upon the Church a full system of minute and detailed prescription of external arrangements, similar in character and general features to the Jewish economy. But when it is considered how entirely different from everything of this sort is all that is contended for by intelligent defenders of the divine right of a particular form of Church government, most men, we think, will see that Dr Tulloch's appeal, for conclusive evidence against its possibility, to the spirit of Christianity and the conditions of human progress, is truly ridiculous.

The disproof of the position, which has been received so generally among professing Christians, that Scripture does sanction and prescribe the outline of a Church polity, cannot be effected by means of vague and

[47]

ambiguous generalities, or by high-sounding declamation. It can be effected, if at all, only by the method of exhaustion; that is, by the detailed refutation of all the different attempts which have been made to establish from Scripture the divine right of a particular form of Church government. And this species of work is much more difficult, requires much more talent and learning, than declaiming about 'the spirit of Christianity and the conditions of human progress'.

At the same time, we must admit that it has become somewhat common and popular in modern times, to scout and ridicule the advancing of a claim to a divine right on behalf of any particular form of Church government. This has arisen partly, no doubt, from the ignorant and injudicious zeal with which the claim has been sometimes advocated, even by those whose views upon the subject of Church government were, in the main, sound and Scriptural; but principally, we are persuaded, from certain erroneous notions of the practical consequences that are supposed to follow necessarily from the establishment of this claim.

All Papists and many Prelatists, in putting forth a claim to a divine right on behalf of their respective systems of Church government, have openly, and without hesitation, deduced from their fancied success in establishing this claim, the conclusion that professedly Christian societies which had not *their* form of government were, for this reason, to be refused the designation and the ordinary rights of Christian Churches, or even to be placed beyond the pale within which salvation is ordinarily possible. This mode of procedure, in applying the claim to a divine right, universal among Papists, and by no means uncommon among a certain class of Prelatists, must appear to men who know anything of the general genius and spirit of the Christian system, and who are possessed of any measure of common sense and Christian charity, to be absurd and monstrous; and by many the disgust which has been reasonably excited by this conduct, has been transferred to the general principle of claiming a *jus divinum* on behalf of a particular form of Church government, from which it was supposed necessarily to flow. All this, however, is unwarranted and erroneous. Presbyterians and Congregationalists have as generally set up a claim to a divine right on behalf of their systems of Church government as Papists and Prelatists have done; but we do not remember that there has ever been a Presbyterian or a Congregationalist of any note who unchurched all other denominations except his own, or who refused to regard and treat them as Christian Churches merely on the ground that they had adopted a form of government different from that which he believed to have, exclusively, the sanction of the Word of God.

[48]

But many seem to suppose that Presbyterians and Congregationalists, in not unchurching other denominations on the ground of rejecting what they believe respectively to be the only Scripturally sanctioned form of Church government, are guilty of an amiable weakness, and fall into inconsistency, by declining to follow out their assertion of a *jus divinum* in judging of others, to its natural and legitimate consequences. This notion is erroneous and unjust, as will appear by attending to the true state of the case. All that is implied in claiming a divine right for Presbyterianism, for instance, is that the person who does so believes, and thinks he can prove, that Christ has plainly enough indicated in His Word His mind and will, that the fundamental principles of Presbyterianism should always and everywhere regulate the government of His Church. Prelatists and Congregationalists, professing equally to follow the guidance of the sacred Scriptures and to submit to the authority of Christ, have formed a different and opposite judgment as to the true bearing and import of the materials which Scripture furnishes upon this subject, and have in consequence set up a different form of government in their Churches. This being the true state of the case, the sum and substance of what any candid and intelligent Presbyterian, even though holding the *jus divinum* of presbytery, has to charge against them is just this, – that they have mistaken the mind and will of Christ upon this point, that they have formed an erroneous judgment about the import of the indications He has given in His Word, as to how He would have the government of His Church to be regulated. And this, which is really the whole charge, does not, upon principles generally acknowledged, afford of itself any sufficient ground for unchurching them, or for refusing to recognize and treat them as Christian Churches. It is a serious matter to adopt and to act upon erroneous views in regard to any portion of divine truth, anything which God has made known to us in His Word, and we have no wish to palliate this in any instance. But let the case be fairly stated, and let the principles ordinarily and justly applied to *other errors* be applied to this one. There can be no possible ground for holding, that the adoption and maintenance of an error on the subject of the government of the Church, by words or deeds, involves more guilt, or should be more severely condemned, than the adoption and maintenance of an error upon a matter of doctrine in the more limited sense of that word; and on the contrary, there is a great deal in the nature of the subject, viewed in connection with the general character, spirit, tendency, and objects of the Christian economy, and in the kind and amount of the materials of evidence which Scripture affords us for forming a judgment upon such questions, which indicates that errors in regard to government should be treated with less severity of condemnation, and should less materially affect the intercourse of churches with each other, than errors (within certain limits) with regard to doctrine, which are not usually considered to warrant the unchurching of other denominations, or to form an insuperable obstacle to the maintenance of friendly relations with them.

These grounds, on which we establish the unwarrantableness and unfairness of the common allegation, that claiming a divine right for one particular form of Church government, implies the unchurching of other denominations who may have come to a different conclusion as to the bearing of the Scripture testimony upon this subject, apply equally to the wider and more comprehensive principle, formerly explained, of the unlawfulness of introducing anything into the government and worship of the Church which is not positively sanctioned by Scripture. Lutherans and Anglicans generally contend that this principle is not taught in Scripture, and, on this ground, refuse to be so strictly tied up in regard to the introduction of ceremonies and regulations. We believe that, in denying this principle, they have fallen into an error in the interpretation and application of Scripture, and that the ceremonies and regulations which, in opposition to it, they may have introduced, are unlawful, and ought to be removed. But we never imagined, that because of this error in opinion, followed to some extent by error in practice, these denominations were to be unchurched, or to be shut out from friendly intercourse, espesially as the Scriptural evidence in favour of the principle, though quite sufficient and satisfactory to our minds, is of a somewhat constructive and inferential description, and as differences sometimes arise among those who concur in holding it about some of the details of its application.

If these views, which are in manifest accordance with the dictates of common sense, and with principles generally recognized in other departments of theological discussion, were admitted, there would be much less disinclination to yield to the force of the Scripture evidence in support of the two principles which we have explained, and which form, we are persuaded, the only effectual security for the purity of Church administration, and the authority of Church arrangements.

But there are, in every age, some men who seem anxious to have the reputation of being in advance of all around them in the enlightened knowledge of theological subjects, and who, with this view, are very desirous to escape from the trammels of implicit deference to the authority of Scripture. The great source of error in religious matters is that men do not fully and honestly take the Word of God as their rule and standard.

The Regulative Principle
and Things Indifferent

John Hooper
[c. 1495-1555]

THE FOLLOWING DOCUMENT, NOW PRINTED IN ENGLISH FOR THE FIRST time, is of particular importance in revealing that disagreement among Protestants over the regulative principle of Scripture did not first emerge as an issue in the Elizabethan period, but rather that the principle was very definitely presented by a group of English Reformers in the reign of Edward VI in an attempt to secure 'a perfect and apostolical reformation'. They disagreed with the official Protestant policy, formulated by Thomas Cranmer, on the ground that it permitted 'a mixed and mingled religion' in which God's truth was associated with 'the superstitious invention of man'.

Of this group John Hooper was a leading spokesman. A Cistercian monk, Hooper had been converted some time in the last ten years of Henry VIII's reign and forced to go into exile. After studying at Zurich he returned home in the third year of Edward's reign (1549) and at once became so influential through his power-ful pulpit ministry that he was called to preach a course of Lent sermons before the King and Court in 1550. The result was his once famous expositions of Jonah, in which he reflected at various points on the imperfections of the English reformation settlement. For this he incurred the displeasure of the Church leaders, yet he was offered the See of Gloucester by the Lord Chancellor. Hooper declined a nomina-tion to this bishopric, specifying as a reason his inability to wear the vestments re-quired by the existing Ordinal. The Privy Council were at first prepared to waive his scruples, but the bishops (notably Cranmer and Nicholas Ridley), conscious that a question of principle and policy was involved in Hooper's nonconformity, de-clined to proceed with his consecration. In the deadlock which ensued Hooper wrote a defence of his position, which is printed here from an incomplete manuscript (the only copy known to have survived) to which Ridley replied in a letter to the Privy Council (cf. Writings of Bradford, Letters, Treatises, Parker Society pp. 373–395).

The crux of the case against Hooper was that vestments were an 'indifferent' thing which therefore needed no express Scripture warrant for their use. In Hooper's brief reply he lays down certain rules to distinguish what things are genuinely indifferent, in order to show that his opponents' plea was invalid. Because of the brevity of his statements in this document (which is a précis rather than a full statement of his case) his meaning is not at once clear and Ridley took advantage of this in his reply. In his first rule or 'token', Hooper's argument is apparently that although things indifferent – by virtue of very definition – do not have express scriptural warrant, they nevertheless need to be in accord with Scripture in the sense that Scripture lays down general directions governing the use of things in-different in such chapters as Romans 14, and therefore such things can only be used in faith if they are consistent with the teaching of such passages. The obscurity of Hooper's language on this point may be due in part to imperfections in the surviving manuscript, which is not the original but a copy made by another hand. Hooper's second rule is that if a necessary inference can be justly made from Scripture, then such an inference has the same force as an explicit command or prohibition, and

[53]

therefore vestments are not 'indifferent', because their use is contrary to what may be inferred from scriptural teaching. His third and fourth rules are straightforward: namely, that indifferent things must be seen to have a usefulness in the Church before they are practised, and that if their practice is made obligatory and enforced by compulsion, then they cease to be 'indifferent'. All these arguments were expanded and stated with more precision and scriptural proofs by the later Puritans.

Hooper's resistance to the official policy on this matter resulted in the extraordinary situation of his being committed to the Fleet prison, from which he was only released when he wrote a letter of submission to Cranmer on February 15, 1551. The letter (printed in G. C. Gorham's Reformation Gleanings, 1857*) shows that Hooper did not recant his principles, as the modern Catholic historian, Philip Hughes, wrongly asserts* (The Reformation in England, *II, p. 119*), *but that the strength of the opposition from other Protestants led him to doubt the wisdom of continuing his particular stand against vestments. The controversy did not resolve the main issue at stake, which was the regulative principle of Scripture: the 1550 controversy was perhaps the first clear evidence that failure in Protestant unity was inevitable where this principle was not accepted. When the Elizabethan Puritans re-stated the principle and met with even fiercer opposition than Hooper had encountered, the ultimate division of English Protestantism, as it occurred in 1662, became inevitable.*

Thanks are due to the Warden and Fellows of New College, Oxford, for permission to consult and translate this document, and to Mr Edward P. C. Greene for the translation.

Bibliography

The Early Writings of John Hooper, edited by Samuel Carr, 1843 (Parker Society).

The Later Writings of John Hooper, edited by Charles Nevinson, 1852 (Parker Society).

Ecclesiastical Memorials, John Strype, Bk. I, chapter 28.

Memorials of Thomas Cranmer, John Strype, Bk. II, chapter 17.

The Acts and Monuments of John Foxe, revised by Josiah Pratt, vol. 6, pp. 636–676.

Original Letters relative to the English Reformation, 1537–1558 (Parker Society, 1846–47).

Martin Bucer and the English Reformation, C. Hopf, 1946.

Cranmer and the Reformation under Edward VI, C. H. Smyth, 1926.

The Vestments Controversy, J. H. Primus, 1960.

The Regulative Principle and Things Indifferent

NOTHING should be used in the Church which has not either the express Word of God to support it, or otherwise is a thing indifferent in itself, which brings no profit when done or used, but no harm when not done or omitted.

The peculiar and special vestments in the ministry are not enjoined by the Word of God, nor are they things indifferent in themselves. Therefore they should not be used.

The first part of the argument is so obviously true that it needs no proof. But I prove the second part from nature and the properties of all indifferent things, which must necessarily have these four conditions or qualities, or otherwise are not indifferent:

FIRST TOKEN OR CONDITION

Indifferent things must have their origin and foundation in the Word of God. For what cannot be proved from the Word of God is not of faith, for faith depends on hearing the Word of God (Rom. 10). But what is not of faith cannot be any mediate and indifferent thing, but, as Scripture says, is really sin (Rom. 14), and that which cannot please God, is for that reason also to be rooted up, like the plant which the heavenly Father hath not planted (Matt. 15), and must be cherished by no man.

SECOND TOKEN OR CONDITION

Although a thing may have its origin in Scripture, if it is to be indifferent, it is nevertheless required that there be no positive precept by which it is ordered, nor any negative one by which it is prohibited, but that it be left to us as something free, to use or not to use, as shall seem useful or otherwise to the conscience of the person using it. Consequently, whether anyone uses it or does not use it, the thing itself will bring profit and assistance to the conscience of the person using it, not harm or impediment. For those things which are ordained by God must always of necessity be kept. But those things which are prohibited, those must always and of necessity be avoided and shunned. But not only what is ordained or prohibited by the express Word of God, but also every judgment of the Divine will, which follows by necessary inference and can be gathered from a collation and comparison of the Scriptures among themselves, has the force and the nature of divine precept, either for commanding or for prohibiting, so long as it conforms to the nature, and proportion of faith and Scripture. Just as we are commanded to baptize infants, not indeed by the express words of Scripture, but by a collation of the Scriptures, which in this matter has a power equal to the express commandment of God. Similarly also we admit women to the Communion of the Lord's table, although we have no express commandment to do so in the Word of God.

THIRD TOKEN OR CONDITION

Indifferent things must have a manifest and open usefulness, known in the Church, lest they may seem to be received for no purpose, or to be forced into the Church by treachery and deceit. The civil magistrate and minister of the Church must take the utmost care to see that this does not happen. To each of the two (as Paul says), power is given to edification and not to destruction (I Cor. 14) and so that they may act on behalf of truth and not against it (2 Cor. 13). For neither of them has the power to bring into the Church those things which do not edify.

FOURTH TOKEN OR CONDITION

Indifferent things ought to be set up in the Church by a certain apostolic and evangelical tolerance and freedom, not with a violent tyranny, to establish a necessity and compulsion, since in matters of that kind Christian liberty should be free. Whatever that is which is held to be indifferent in the ministry of the Church, if once it has degenerated and fallen into that tyranny and slavery, it ceases to be an indifferent thing.

These are the tokens or signs by which indifferent things can be distinguished, so that henceforth we may not hold nor think any of those things indifferent which does not contain in itself these four conditions. But let us come now to the position of this particular controversy of our own, which is concerned with special vestments and those allotted and assigned to ministers of the Church, and to the ministry. Our controversy does not touch on that which concerns the civil government. Consequently I would far prefer that the position of this contention of ours should not be turned aside from the ecclesiastical to the civil polity: this is what our opponents commonly do and they also do not readily allow their case to be examined and decided in their own ecclesiastical court, but they beg resources and help from the civil court and the magistrates. Also they try to persuade the magistrates of this: that if they should be deprived of the freedom and power to use this solemn parade of vestments in the Church, which they themselves idly think pertains to conserving the usefulness, decorum and order in the ministry, immediately from this will follow contempt of the magistrates and the greatest diminution of its own authority in civil administration and government. O sons of this age, wiser in your generation than the children of light (Luke 16)! You, who can so easily persuade the magistrates that enemies are friends, and friends enemies, and that the office of magistrates, who are the vice-gerents of God Himself here on earth, is rather to promote, uphold, support, honour and defend your superstitious and blind church, rather than that perfect and enlightened Church of the Apostles. But because this matter has come up for enquiry, if the magistrates decide that you should be compelled to take this case of yours back into your own hands, and examine it by the sacred volume of the Bible, which is both your Book and mine, your Judge and mine; or by the example of the apostolic Church, or any other church which in your present age is governed by the Word of God – if I shall not convince you that my case is good, but that yours is bad, I promise that I shall not refuse to undergo the same punishment as the man who wished to introduce a new law, and could not find fault with the old law by any fair reasoning: I shall deserve, with him, to be punished with death for my audacious enterprise.

CONCERNING VESTMENTS

If that first token of indifferent things is sought concerning vestments, whether they have their origin and source in the Word of God, so that a minister might use them in the Church, that certainly is quite apparent in the writings of the apostles and evangelists, which place before us most clearly the annulment of the rituals of Aaron, his ceremonies, priesthood, images, and peculiar figures, and the institution of the new and perfect priesthood of Christ. They must demonstrate to us from these books the grounds and occasion when some peculiar and special vestments should be worn in the ministry, for the adornment of the ministry itself, or for the preferring of its decorum, or for some distinctive mark, by which the minister can be distinguished from the people, as once was ordained by the Lord in the ministry of Aaron's priesthood. But the statutes, canons and decrees of the apostles and evangelists make no mention of this matter. Therefore, since they lack this first property which is required in indifferent things, we do exclude vestments from the number of indifferent things. (Afterwards he cites Polydore Vergil, Book 4, chap. 7, and Book 6, chap. 12.)

Vestments lack the second token and condition of indifferent things. What is prohibited by God can in no way be indifferent, as we have given warning above. For this is the doctrine of Paul in Gal. 2, that whatever re-establishes things that have been annulled in Christ, transgresses the will of God. And the same author clearly teaches that the priesthood of Aaron has been abolished by the priesthood of Christ (Heb. 7, 8, 10) with all its rites, vestments, shavings, anointings, consecrations, and other similar things. If then those semblances of Aaron's priesthood cannot stand with Christ's priesthood, far less can that Popish priesthood, which according to the testimony of their books is derived either from Aaron or from the heathen (Polydore *ut supra*). Neither indeed is it without its mystery that our Saviour Jesus Christ hung naked from the Cross. For Aaron's priests used vestments in their own ministry because the reality of their priesthood, Christ Himself, had not yet come. But when Christ Himself was to be sacrificed, stripped of all clothing, displaying in this way His own priesthood, which since He was Reality itself, now had no further need of veils or semblances.

So also the use of these vestments is examined by the other two tokens. . . . [1]

---

[1] The manuscript is incomplete at this point.

The Abolition of Vestments

John à Lasco

[1499-1560]

JOHN À LASCO WAS PROBABLY THE MOST TRAVELLED OF THE LEADING
*Continental Reformers and his influence was felt in many lands. Born of a family
of Polish nobility, he studied in Italy, Paris and Basle, before returning to his
native land where positions of honour in the Romish Church had been assigned to
him since childhood: 'I was once', he later wrote, 'a Pharisee of repute, adorned with
many roles and dignities, splendidly endowed with many and rich benefices from
the days of my boyhood.' In 1538, however, when à Lasco was Archdeacon of
Warsaw, he declined the King's offer of the bishopric of Cujavia and instead re-
linquished all his titles and went into exile. Thereafter he laboured in poor and
martyr churches in the Rhineland and in Belgium, before crossing to England at the
invitation of Cranmer in 1548.*

*The thoroughness of à Lasco's convictions was already known, and in his letter
of invitation Archbishop Cranmer had said, 'We are desirous of setting forth in our
churches the true doctrine of God, and have no wish to adapt it to all tastes, or
to deal in ambiguities.' Though à Lasco's stay at Lambeth appears to have strengthened Cranmer, the Polish reformer returned to his work in East Friesland in 1549,
until the following year when increasing persecution led him to fulfil the desires of
a number in England who were eager for his presence and leadership. Thus à
Lasco was back in London in the critical year of the Vestment controversy and he
was the most theologically able of those reformers, who, like Hooper, were concerned
for a more decided policy of reform based on a recognition of the regulative principle
of Scripture.*

*Besides his intellectual powers and charm of character, à Lasco was a forceful
leader, and by letters patent from King Edward he was given leave to organize the
some 5,000 strong 'Strangers' Church', made up of refugees, according to principles
which had not been put into practice in the English Church. In a statement à Lasco
made after the death of Edward, he declared that the young king was a knowing
supporter of the plan that the refugees 'should have churches of their own in which
they should freely regulate all things according to primitive methods, without any
regard to existing rites: so that the English churches might be incited to embrace
apostolic purity'. It was because Nicholas Ridley recognized the implications of
having such a large congregation in the heart of London, which claimed freedom
from the jurisdiction and ecclesiastical acts of the English Church, that he contested
the right of the refugees to worship in ways other than those laid down in English
law.*

*The document which is here reprinted after 400 years, was first printed by the
English Puritans in 1566, in a collection of tracts entitled* The Fortress of the
Fathers. *The following is a fresh English translation of à Lasco's original Latin
manuscript. The manuscript is dated September 20th, in the fifth year of Edward's
reign. It thus belongs to the period of the Vestment Controversy, in which à Lasco –
in contrast to the mediating roles adopted by Martin Bucer and Peter Martyr –
gave forthright support to the position taken by Hooper.*

Other documents of à Lasco's, throwing light on the Edwardian period of the

[61]

English Reformation, have still to be printed in English, particularly Letter 29 in Abraham Kuyper's Latin edition of à Lasco's works, in which the reformer gives his reasons to Cranmer for those differences in practice in the 'Stranger's Church' to which Ridley objected, and states what he believed to be the scriptural case to establish that: 'Nothing ought to be added to public worship concerning which God has given no command.'

After the death of Edward, à Lasco, returning to the Continent with members of his congregation, was shipwrecked on the Danish coast, and only after many hardships reached Friesland and later Frankfurt. In 1556 he returned to Poland, but the early promise of a great Reformation in that country was terminated by the reformer's death on January 8, 1560. One of his last letters was to the new Queen Elizabeth, urging her to follow the religious policy of her late brother. The letter, he declared, was: 'From a dying man. The Lord has seen fit to lay me under an illness, so that I cannot finish the letter with my own hand.'

Testimonies to the worth of this forgotten reformer can be found in the words of many of his contemporaries, including Cranmer, Latimer, Hooper and Calvin.

For the translation of this document from Latin thanks are due to Mr David Clines.

Bibliography
Johannes à Lasco Opera, 2 vols., edited with introduction by A. Kuyper, 1866.
Life of John à Lasco, H. Dalton, translated into English by M. J. Evans, 1886. (Unfortunately the second part of Dalton's life of à Lasco was never translated into English; it was printed in German at Gotha in 1881.)
History of the Presbyterians in England, A. H. Drysdale, 1889, pp. 40–51, 'John à Lasco and His Early Presbyterian Organization in London'.
History of the Reformation in Europe in the Time of Calvin, J. H. Merle d'Aubigné, Vol. VII, pp. 529–584 (English edition, 1876).

The Abolition of Vestments

I T is my belief that among all things in the Church of Christ, some ought to be preserved perpetually, some are indifferent, but others are not on any account to be tolerated. Those that ought to be permanent in the Church are the pure teaching of the prophets and apostles, which ought to be set forth diligently through God's ministers to the flock of Christ, as the food of the soul. Additional to this are the sacraments of Baptism and the Lord's Supper administered according to the apostolic rite described in three apostolic gospels; to these ecclesiastical discipline is most fittingly joined. But whatever things are done for the useful and convenient administration of the Word and sacraments are indifferent; so long as they have their source in the Scriptures let there be no prohibition, let their usefulness to the Church be clear, and let there be no tyranny which strangles men's consciences. Of this kind are questions of gathering at this or that hour of day in church, using this or that sort of speech in administration of the sacraments, and celebrating the Lord's Supper once or more often in the year.

The things which ought definitely to be kept out of the Church are twofold: certain things are so obviously impious that they can never deceive even those who are but little instructed in the Word of God, such as the worship of images, adoration of the bread and wine, profanation of the Lord's Supper by the mass, invocation of the sacraments, prayer for the dead, and innumerable similar monstrosities which Antichrist has brought into Christ's Church. There are other things, introduced by the same Antichrist, which contend strongly with Christian liberty, obscure Christ, increase hypocrisy, and bring pride into the Church. At the same time, however, they bear upon them the appearance of utility and splendour. Of this sort are appointed fast days, limitation of foods, much singing which is not understood in the Church, the playing of organs, and the use of vestments in the administration of the sacraments. There is not now the space to record how much harm has crept into the Church from these individual things, and how much more could creep in if they are not abolished; I can here only treat of the use of vestments, because they must by no means be tolerated any longer in the reformed Church of Christ by a pious teacher. Although much can be thought out in its defence by ingenious men, we regard not the reasonings of man's intellect but upon the command of the divine will.

First, by means of the argument by which Christ and the prophets together with the apostles expel from the Church human dogmas and inventions as a plague (Matt. 12, Isa. 29, Col. 2), I too am convinced that vestments are a human invention which ought to be removed from the Church. A witness of this is Polydore Vergil, Book 6, *De Inventoribus Rerum*, chap. 12. The practice has been borrowed from the Hebrews that priestly vestments should be consecrated along with the altar covers and other things necessary for temple use, and that the vestments themselves should be assigned to priests and other initiates, so that they might put them on when they were about to perform their sacred duties. Pope Stephen I was the first among us to lay down that this should be done. For in the beginnings of the new religion, the priests used not to put on anything extra when they were going to carry out divine service, since they were anxious rather to clothe themselves inwardly with spiritual virtues and put off the vices of the flesh than to put on new apparel. Now I conclude that if they did not change their clothes before performing sacred duties, then they used none for them that were admitted into the ministry of the Gospel. Laying on of hands with fasting and prayer was sufficient for Paul and Barnabas. Paul, when he carefully laid down all the duties of a bishop for Timothy and Titus, made no mention of special vestments and other ceremonies.

It is clear enough from the decree of Celestinus, the first bishop of Rome, that the use of vestments did not pervade all the Churches at once; these are his words against special vestments of this kind for bishops: We ought to be distinguished, he says, from the common people or from others by our teaching, not our dress; our behaviour, not our appearance; and our purity of mind, not our clothing, for if we begin to be anxious for novelty, we shall trample under foot the order handed down to us by our fathers, and make a place for empty superstitions. Therefore we ought not to lead the simple minds of the faithful to such things, but should teach them rather than deceive them. Nor is an imposition to be made on their eyes, but rather precepts should be poured upon their minds. Thus far Celestinus.

However we cannot deny, since our people are prone to superstition, that before his time the use of certain kinds of vestments, though quite simple, had crept into many Churches. Certainly Sylvester gave the opportunity, but Charlemagne finished the matter, as the histories witness. Thus it is clear that the use of special vestments in the Church for ecclesiastical personages is a human invention, and is for this cause to be done away with if there were no more.

[64]

Those who wish to retain the use of vestments in the Church as a divine institution refer to the priesthood of Aaron. But let them take a little care of what they are saying, for according to the Scriptures Christ is a priest according to the order not of Aaron but of Melchizedek, and the priesthood of Aaron has in Christ been abolished, together with all its parts, among which we number vestments. And thus Christ, the very wisdom of the Father, did not use in divine service any new or special kind of vestments or prescribe their use, for the foreshadowing priesthood was done away with by the true priest Christ. All those therefore who bring back Aaronic vestments into the Church defile the priesthood of Christ, as if there should be need of shadows when there is the light itself. Nor will there be room for your defence that you are not recalling the whole Aaronic priesthood, but only a part thereof, and he who receives part does not receive the whole; but it is undoubted that the whole foreshadowing priesthood of Aaron is to be rejected, because it is abrogated. And all those who restore again those things which have been destroyed and abrogated by the authority of the divine Word are without doubt transgressors of the divine law (Gal. 2). Furthermore, Paul rightly teaches (Gal. 4), 'The handmaid is to be cast out, along with her son' – signifying that all bondage of the law after the rising of the gospel's light is to be cast out; and it means that we should on no account allow ourselves to be moved from our liberty in Christ.

Now it is clear that teaching and commandment of a special kind of vestments in God's ministry is a transgression of the divine law because the Aaronic priesthood is thus recalled.

If anyone is induced by the foregoing argument to deny that vestments are part of the Aaronic priesthood, and says that by a certain expression of liberty they were introduced by the Roman bishops to adorn the order of the priesthood, even so he has not produced sufficient reason why they should be retained. We know that the Roman Pope is the very Antichrist; wherefore his priesthood also is Antichristian, by which the whole priesthood of Christ is utterly trampled upon. But forasmuch as the principal part of the papistical priesthood consists in ceremonies, anointing, shaving of hair, mitres and vestments, (for without these things they do not regard anyone as a bishop, and by the quality of these ornaments they judge the quality of the bishop) it follows that if we condemn the Pope's priesthood because it is of Antichrist, we ought also to avoid all its parts and manifestations. For the more the pious and Christian heart loves the sacrilegious marks of the papistical priesthood, the more the Christian priesthood is defiled. Wherefore he who hates the priesthood of Antichrist ought also to hate its individual manifestations. Again, he who loves the part cannot hate the whole.

Moreover, if it is agreed that the Pope's priesthood with all its marks is the priesthood of Antichrist (and every work of Antichrist is a work of Satan), we ought not to promote it but destroy it, if indeed we wish to be co-workers with Christ, who came to destroy the works of the devil, as the Scriptures testify.

Nor let us imagine that anyone may, of his own authority, institute, abolish, or keep, the use of these vestments; for all power is given for edification (as Paul says) and not for destruction. And in the same place he says, 'We can do nothing against the truth, but for the truth'. And edification is to build the faithful upon Christ, in faith, hope, and love, and in innocence of life, by always stretching out towards what is more perfect; but vestments promote none of these things; nay rather they obscure the face of Christ, they induce a certain connection with the profane priesthood of Antichrist, or a falling back to the shadows of Aaron from the body of Christ. It is the truth for which apostolic men and Christian magistrates ought to labour. It is certain that Christ is content with that order which he himself left, and that the shadows should no more be sought. Wherefore they will labour for the truth, not against it by recalling those things which Christ destroyed and abolished.

In this regard Paul simply admitted nothing into the Church unless it edified, that is, increased godliness. Special vestments in the ministry do not edify but destroy; they are therefore not to be tolerated. Nor do those things edify which provide an imaginary occasion for piety, but they must provide Christians with a compelling opportunity for piety. But vestments, on the contrary, sometimes increase pride in those who use them, sometimes hypocrisy, sometimes both. It is very easy for them to provide an opportunity for hypocrisy, indeed it is unavoidable; if there is really in oneself that virtue which you imagine to be signified by vestments, why do you receive a reward from men by declaring it? But there is not, and the hypocrite in you is shown up, who are a different man from what you appear to be. Nor will you escape if you say that no inner virtue is signified by these private garments, but that of the office is indicated. What then was it that indicated the office of the apostles? Was it vestments or the Spirit of the Lord and love of the Church and of Christ? His disciples do not forget their office when they take off these vestments. Why do they not rather meditate upon the Word of the Lord day and night and by it correct their ways, for it penetrates to the inmost recesses of the heart, while vestments can move only the outward man. What did Christ

[66]

demand of Peter the third time that his office should be indicated in feeding the sheep? Indeed, nothing but love.

Moreover, there is a danger that a reputation of merit or some such foolish thing should be occasioned by the idea that the dignity of the ministers or the sacraments or the preaching of the Word is violated unless it is supplied with this useless and pernicious clothing.

This fear alone of human merit should move us to exclude from the temple vestments, together with the other ceremonies introduced by human invention.

It is an impious thing to furnish an occasion of stumbling in this way to the weak for whom Christ died. Experience has taught how easy it is to put one's trust in these things, so much so that he who does not consider or care for these things does not seem to be able to escape the imputation of impiety. Nor is it possible that they should excuse themselves by claiming that in vestments there resides nothing either of good or bad. For in order for us to grant this, you would have to argue that this was realized by those emperors when first vestments were introduced by the bishops. We are not born for ourselves alone, but that we should serve the Church and also posterity; it cannot but be that to leave to them the religion of Christ in as pure a form as possible is a thing most pleasing to God. No dying man willingly leaves to his sons a will unless it is provided with all that is necessary to remove all cause of contention. Why do we not show the same diligence and faithfulness in reference to the testament of God?

I know that it is objected by some that sacred services are adorned by vestments. Nay, they are much obscured. For vestments assail the eyes of men and remove their minds from the contemplation of the sacred things which are taking place in the sacraments and lead them to the pleasures of the senses. Holy simplicity commends the institutions of God. Through them are given to us the example of Christ and the apostles and the early Church, which it is safer and more holy and more useful to imitate than to pervert and to condemn Christ by acting otherwise. Here I add what Paul remarked concerning the doctrines of men which 'have an appearance of wisdom and humility of mind and afflicting of the body, not through any honour to the satisfying of the flesh' (Col. 2).

Tyranny finally is brought in and vestments are imposed whether they are wanted or not. And this tyranny brings it about that if something is of itself free and indifferent, it ceases to be indifferent. Paul instructs Christians in plain words not to put themselves under tyranny or superstitions. Thus, 'If you are dead to the elements of this world', etc. And again, 'Do not become servants of men'. And indeed it is a most hard slavery to be compelled to a certain kind of vestment in the Church, which savours of paganism or the Aaronic priesthood or the heresy of Antichrist, and which is in so many ways pernicious, and useful in no way at all.

But why does it please us so much to strain ourselves with popish filth? Why do we not give the same honour to the priesthood of Jesus Christ as the popish priests give to the priesthood of Antichrist? There is not the slightest thing prescribed by him (no matter how far he differs from Christ) which they do not most religiously observe; why do we for our part not obey Christ in everything, content with his simple truth?

Finally, since Paul commands us to beware of every kind of evil, and we have shown that to prescribe vestments in the administration of holy things is truly an evil, who will not judge that they should be avoided, for they are indeed a human invention, parts of the Aaronic or papistical priesthood, edifying nothing, but begetting pride, hypocrisy, and the reputation of merit.

Certain objections are made by the advocates of these vestments to which it will be sufficient to subjoin brief answers, for they will hardly refute our previous arguments.

Obj. In indifferent matters the weakness of our brethren is to be considered, according to the example of the apostles.

Ans. You would surely deny that those things are indifferent which obscure the priesthood of Christ, and produce from themselves nothing except hypocrisy, sects, and pride in the church, have no source in the scriptures, and are commanded with tyranny unworthy of Christians. The apostles are never said to have done such things; let us not falsely pervert the pious concern of the apostles for the founding of the church of Christ. Again, since our opponents claim that the understanding of the weak is to be taken account of, why do they not allow a free use to the strong? And when will the weak better learn that these things are stupid, foolish, and pernicious, than when they see them abrogated? How can the simple and ignorant think otherwise than that some godliness consists in those things that yet remain, when they see so many other things which were used in times past done away? Thus infirmity is not helped, but rather harmed, if vestments or similar ceremonies are retained. For they are retained for the sake of the reputation of merit, and we measure the dignity of the sacraments by external things.

Further, they bring forward the decree of the magistrate concerning the retention of vestments. Indeed the piety, prudence, and goodwill of our magistrate is well-known to me, so that when he perceives carefully the danger of these ceremonies, he would rejoice that there are some who wish to run in the law of the Lord, and make the path plain for others, so that he might restore everything to the integrity of the apostolic order. They know that to them is given power in the church for edification, not for destruction, that they should stand for the truth, not against the truth. And since the ready piety of our magistrate is well-known, I doubt that blame can be withheld if anyone under his patronage wishes to defend tyrannically human traditions, or to force them upon others against their will, contrary to the commandment of God. But those things which we have ourselves chosen are apt to please us more than those which God's laws prescribe. Nor need there be any fear of uproar if human dogmas and those superstitions by which we provoke the anger of God are removed from the church; nay rather we ought to hope for greater peace and tranquillity in the kingdom the nearer we come to the institutions of Christ and the further we retreat from Antichrist. The prudence of human reason is deceptive, which seeks for itself and promises to itself peace by illegitimate means. Saul, by seeking the favour of God with the forbidden sacrifices of the Amalekites, foolishly destroyed himself. There is one way of safety if we altogether turn to repentance: believe the gospel of Christ, walk in innocence of life, and retain nothing in the church which does not either have the express word of God, or else take its infallible origin from that source. Then let true pastors, zealous for teaching, be set over the churches, and let dumb and wicked pastors be shut out; thus king will flourish with people, according to the promises of God often repeated by His prophets.

Scripture and the
Ordering of Worship

From the Preface to the Geneva Service Book of 1556

THAT THE VESTMENT CONTROVERSY OF 1550 HAD DONE NOTHING TO *terminate differences among the English Protestant leaders was made apparent by renewed disagreement over the second Book of Common Prayer, which was completed in 1552. One of King Edward's chaplains, John Knox, now became the chief spokesman of those who could not agree to the official claim that the latest revision (the first Edwardian Prayer Book had appeared in 1549) had made the book 'fully perfect'. Knox's influence secured a few alterations before the Prayer Book was enforced by law, but only eight months were to pass before this settlement was overthrown by the death of Edward on July 6, 1553.*

In the persecution which ensued after the accession of Mary, the Protestant leaders who remained in England bore witness to their common faith in the Gospel by their martyrdoms, while others who escaped to the Continent formed congregations of English refugees. One of the first of these congregations was gathered in Frankfort in 1554, and as its prevailing outlook was in sympathy with that of Knox – whom they called to be one of their ministers – the full use of the 1552 Prayer Book was discontinued and in place of the English liturgy a new order of service was drawn up by Knox, Whittingham, Gilby, Foxe and Cole. This was not, however, brought into immediate use due to the lack of full agreement in the congregation, and when a new party of refugees arrived in March 1555, who were representatives of the 'official' reformation policy of Cranmer and Ridley, harmony became impossible and it was necessary for Knox and those who shared in a concern for further reformation to withdraw to Geneva where a new English congregation was formed in November 1555. This became the strongest and most influential English congregation in the exile period and it has often been spoken of as the cradle of English Puritanism.

The order of service drawn up in Frankfort was now brought into use and it was published early in 1556 under the title: 'The Form of Prayers and Ministration of the Sacraments, etc., used in the English congregation at Geneva'. The Preface to this 'Book of Geneva', as it became known, gives the first statement by an English Church that the regulative principle of Scripture is foundational to the Church's government and worship. It was probably written by William Whittingham, who was to become one of the leaders of Elizabethan Puritanism, and a man who was more than once in trouble with the ecclesiastical authorities before his death at Durham in 1579. The Geneva Book became the Service Book of the Church of Scotland, was secretly used by English Puritans, and was being reprinted as late as 1644. The Contents page of the Geneva Book was as follows:

1. *The confession of the Christian faith*
2. *The order of electing Ministers, Elders, and Deacons*
3. *The assembly of the Ministry every Thursday*
4. *An order for the interpretation of the Scriptures, and answering of doubters, observed every Monday*
5. *A confession of our sins used before the sermon and framed to our state and time*
6. *Another confession for all states and times*

7. *A general prayer after the sermon, for the whole estate of Christ's Church*
8. *The ministration of Baptism, and the Lord's Supper*
9. *The form of Marriage, the visitation of the sick and the manner of burial*
10. *An order of ecclesiastical discipline*
11. *One and fifty Psalms of David in metre*
12. *The Catechism of M. Calvin etc.*

The extract which follows is taken from the Preface.

Bibliography

The Works of John Knox, edited by David Laing, 6 vols., 1846–64, The Geneva Book is printed in vol. 4.
Life of John Knox, Thomas M'Crie, new edition 1873. Reprinted 1960, though unfortunately without the valuable notes of the earlier editions.
John Knox, P. Hume Brown, 2 vols., 1895.
A Brief Discourse of the Troubles Begun at Frankfurt In The Year 1554, About The Book of Common Prayer and Ceremonies. This important historical document, first printed anonymously by an English Puritan (possibly William Whittingham) in 1575, was last reprinted in 1908 with notes by Edward Arber.
John Knox and the Church of England, Peter Lorimer, 1875. In an appendix Lorimer reprints a short life of Whittingham.
The Marian Exiles: A Study in the Origins of Elizabethan Puritanism, C. H. Garrett, 1938. This book by a strongly anti-evangelical author is unfortunately the only work so far written on the subject.
John Knox's Geneva Service Book, W. D. Maxwell, 1931.
Plain Mr Knox, Elizabeth Whitley, 1960.

Scripture and the Ordering of Worship

BECAUSE there is no way more ready or sure to come to him, than by framing ourselves altogether to his blessed will, revealed unto us in his Word; we, to whom though God hath given more liberty, yet no less lamenting your bondage than rejoicing in our own deliverance from that Babylonian slavery and antichristian yoke, have earnestly endeavoured, amongst other things which might bring us to the worthy consideration of God's Word, to frame our lives, and reform our state of religion in such sort, that neither doubt of the certainty thereof should make us fear, nor yet man's judgment discourage us, and cause us to shrink from this enterprise most acceptable to God, comfortable to his Church, and necessarily appertaining to every Christian man's duty.

We, therefore, not as the greatest clerks of all, but as the least able of many, do present unto you which desire the increase of God's glory, and the pure simplicity of his Word, a form and order of a reformed Church, limited within the compass of God's Word, which our Saviour hath left unto us as only sufficient to govern all our actions by; so that whatsoever is added to this Word by man's device, seem it never so good, holy, or beautiful, yet before our God, which is jealous and cannot admit any companion or counsellor, it is evil, wicked, and abominable. For he that is the wisdom of the Father, the brightness of his glory, the true light, the word of life, yea truth and life itself, can he give unto his Church (for the which he paid the ransom of his bood) that which should not be a sufficient assurance for the same? Can the word of truth deceive us? The way of life misguide us? The word of salvation damn us? God keep us from such blasphemies, and so direct our hearts with his Holy Spirit, that we may not only content ourselves with his wisdom, but so rejoice in the same, that we may abhor all things which are contrary.

The which considerations, dear brethren, when we weighed with reverent fear and humbleness; and also knowing, that negligence in reforming that religion which was begun in England, was not the least cause of God's rods laid upon us, having now obtained by the merciful providence of our heavenly Father a free Church for all our nation in this most worthy city of Geneva, we presented to the judgment of the famous man John Calvin, and others learned in these parts, the order which we minded

[75]

to use in our Church: who approving it, as sufficient for a Christian congregation, we put the same in execution, nothing doubting but all godly
men shall be much edified thereby. And as for the Papists, or malicious
men and ungodly, we have not laboured to satisfy them, because we knew
no sovereign medicine for their cankered sore, except it may please God,
by our prayers, to be merciful to them, and call them home, if they be not
already forsaken.

But yet, for as much as there are some, which through continuance in
their evil, rather delighting in custom than knowledge, cannot suffer that
men should once open their mouths against certain old and received
ceremonies, we thought good in this place somewhat to touch that scru-
pulosity. For as ceremonies grounded upon God's Word, and approved in
the New Testament, are commendable (as the circumstance thereof doth
support), so those that man hath invented, though he had never so good
occasion thereunto, if they be once abused, import a necessity, hinder
God's Word, or be drawn into a superstition, without respect ought to be
abolished.

For if Hezekiah was commended by the Holy Ghost for breaking in
pieces the brazen serpent, which Moses had erected by God's commandment, and now had continued above 800 years, which thing of itself was
not evil, but rather put men in remembrance of God's benefit; yet because
it began to minister occasion to the people to commit idolatry, was not
to be borne withal: how much more ought we to take heed, that through
our occasion men commit not idolatry with their own imaginations and
fantasies? It was not without great cause, commanded by Almighty God,
that the places, and other appurtenances, which had served to idolatry
should be utterly consumed, lest babes and children, through occasion
remembering the same, should fall into like inconvenience. And think you
that we ought to be wiser? and not rather take heed, that those things
which the Papists and other idolaters have invented, or else observe as
invented by man, may not enter into Christ's church, as well to the end
that the weak may not be confirmed in their error, as that we may altogether separate ourselves from that idolatrous Babylon and temple of
Belial, wherewith Christ hath no concord nor agreement?

There was no one ceremony more ancient, nor yet of better authority,
than the washing of the disciples' feet, which was observed a long time in
the Church, and instituted by Christ himself; yet when some were persuaded that it was a portion of the Lord's Supper, and others thought it
served instead of Baptism, the godly churches in St Augustine's time
thought it better to leave that which was ordained for a good use, than

by retaining the same, confirm an error or superstition. The Corinthians, for the relief of the poor, and to increase brotherly amity together, did institute a feast, immediately after the Lord's Supper. But how sharply St Paul did reprehend the same, condemning in comparison, that men should add anything to the Lord's institution, it appeareth by that he saith, 'I have received of the Lord that which I gave you.'

We read also, that Hezekiah and his nephew Josiah restored the use of the Passover, which had been a very long time discontinued; but in the ministration thereof, they observed no other ceremonies than God had left to Moses from the beginning. Circumcision, likewise a sacrament, was evermore after one sort ministered, even as the Lord commanded it. But such is the nature of flesh, it will be wise, and have a stroke in God's doings; yea, and how wilfully it causeth man to maintain his own fantasies, it is manifest to them which have perused the ancient records of the Church. For beginning at Jerusalem, and so coming to the rest of the churches, as Constantinople, Antioch, Alexandria, and Rome, he shall see plainly that their greatest disturbance and overthrow chanced through ceremonies. What conflict was at all times betwixt the Latin and Greek Churches for the same, no Christian can consider without tears. And was there anything more objected against St Paul, both of the Galatians and also of others, than that he would not observe the ceremonies as the chief Apostles did? and yet he kept them whilst any hope was to gain the weak brethren, and therefore circumcised Timothy; but when he perceived that men would retain them as necessary things in the Church, he called that which before he made indifferent, wicked and impious, saying, that whosoever was circumcised, Christ could nothing profit them. Fearing also, lest he had taken pains among them in vain, which joined Christ with beggarly ceremonies. Therefore, dear brethren, being hereby persuaded, and with many more reasons confirmed (which opportunity permitteth not here to write), we have contented ourselves with that wisdom which we have learned in God's Book, where we be taught to preach the Word of God purely, minister the Sacraments sincerely, and use prayers and other orders thereby approved, to the increase of God's glory, and edification of His holy people.

[77]

SECTION III

The Need of Reformation

The Necessity of Reformation:
An Admonition to the Parliament 1572

Thomas Wilcox

[1549-1608]

APART FROM ITS VALUE TO THOSE WHO ARE CONCERNED ABOUT CHURCH
*reformation in our own day, the Admonition to Parliament is a historical document of
great significance. Although ostensibly intended for the House of Commons, it was
printed and widely circulated and is the first clear written statement of the Puritan
objections to the Church of England settlement established by Elizabeth I. It marks
a definite step towards the organization of the Puritan movement.*

*The Admonition was anonymous, but even so, on July 7, 1572, two young
London ministers, John Field and Thomas Wilcox, were arrested, and admitted to
being its authors. Field (1545–1588) was curate of St Giles', Cripplegate and had
contributed to the pamphlet* A View of Popish Abuses, *which formed the second
part of the Admonition and which is not here reprinted. Wilcox (1549–1608) was
curate of All Hallows and wrote the Admonition proper. For their offence, the two
men were sentenced in October 1572 to one year's imprisonment. After their release,
Field and Wilcox were not allowed to continue their regular ministry in the
Church of England, but they were both active until their deaths, preaching, and
advocating reform, despite several times being brought before the authorities. Field
was secretary of a conference of London ministers and a gifted organizer. Wilcox,
who outlived him by twenty years, gained a reputation as an adviser to those
troubled in conscience. Though not scholars of the order of Thomas Cartwright or
Walter Travers, Field and Wilcox were influential figures in the early formative
stages of the Puritan movement.*

*Not content with punishing its authors the authorities were unwilling that the
pamphlet should be unanswered and John Whitgift, Master of Trinity College,
Cambridge, and later Archbishop of Canterbury, was deputed to answer it. Whitgift's* Answer to the Admonition *appeared in February 1573. By May of the same
year a* Reply to the Answer, *by Thomas Cartwright, had also issued from the
press. The controversy was prolonged, Whitgift producing a* Defence of the
Answer, *and Cartwright a* Second Reply. *Another work evoked by this controversy was Richard Hooker's famous and monumental* Laws of Ecclesiastical Polity, *a classic defence of the religious principles embodied in the Elizabethan settlement.*

*The Admonition was an explosive document because it attacked the whole
hierarchical and liturgical framework of the Elizabethan settlement. The Admoni-
tioners claimed that:* 'We in England are so far off from having a church rightly
reformed according to the prescript of God's Word that as yet we are not come to
the outward face of the same.'

*In the study of this document most attention has been given to the rejection of
episcopacy and the demand for the equality of all ministers and the introduction of
lay elders (or seniors). But the Admonition is much more than an attack on bishops.
It is an attempt to indicate how the Reformed principle of the authority of Scripture
may be applied more consistently to the worship, discipline and order of the English
Church.*

Bibliography

Sources: *Puritan Manifestoes* ed. by W. H. Frere and C. E. Douglas, 1907; *Works*, John Whitgift (Parker Society), which includes all Whitgift's writings on the Admonition controversy as well as some of Cartwright's; *Zurich Letters* (Parker Society); Lives of Parker, Grindal and Whitgift, by John Strype.

Historical background: *Thomas Cartwright and Elizabethan Puritanism (1535–1603)*, A. F. Scott Pearson, 1925; *Tudor Puritanism*, M. M. Knappen, 1939; *Matthew Parker*, V. J. K. Brook, 1962; *The Admonition Controversy*, D. J. McGinn (recent but unsatisfactory); 'John Field and Elizabethan Puritanism', P. Collinson, in *Elizabethan Government and Society*, Essays presented to Sir John Neale, 1961 (informative if unsympathetic); *Reformation and Reaction in Tudor Cambridge*, H. C. Porter, 1958.

For sympathetic accounts of the history of those who adhered to what became known as the Puritan or Presbyterian position cf. *History of The Presbyterians in England*, A. H. Drysdale, 1889; *Annals of English Presbytery*, T. M. M'Crie, 1872; 'Early English Presbyterian History', an article by Peter Lorimer in *The Catholic Presbyterian*, May 1880.

The Necessity of Reformation

S EEING that nothing in this mortal life is more diligently to be sought for, and carefully to be looked unto,[1] than the restitution of true religion and reformation of God's Church: it shall be your parts (dearly beloved) in this present Parliament assembled, as much as in you lieth to promote the same, and to employ your whole labour and study; not only in abandoning all popish remnants both in ceremonies and regiment, but also in bringing in and placing in God's Church those things only, which the Lord Himself[2] in His Word commandeth. Because it is not enough to take pains in taking away evil,[3] but also to be occupied in placing good in the stead thereof. Now because many men see not all things, and the world[4] in this respect is marvellously blinded, it hath been thought good to proffer to your godly considerations, a true platform of a Church reformed, to the end that it being laid before your eyes, to behold the great unlikeness betwixt it and this our English Church: you may learn either with perfect[5] hatred to detest the one, and with singular love to embrace, and careful endeavour to plant the other: or else to be without excuse before[6] the majesty of our God, who (for the discharge of our conscience, and manifestation of His truth) hath by us revealed unto you at this present the sincerity and simplicity of His Gospel. Not that you should either[7] wilfully withstand, or ungraciously tread[8] the same under your feet, for God doth not disclose His will to any such end, but that you should yet now at the length with all your main and might, endeavour that Christ (whose[9] easy yoke and light burden we have of long time cast off from us) might rule and reign in His Church by the sceptre of His Word only.

May it therefore please Your Wisdoms to understand, we in England are so far off from having a Church rightly reformed, according to the prescript of God's Word, that as yet we are not come to the outward face of the same. For to speak of that wherein all consent, and whereupon all writers accord: The outward marks whereby a true Christian Church is

---

[1] 2 Kings 23; 2 Chron. 17; 29: 29, 30, 31; Ps. 132: 2, 3, 4; Matt. 21: 12; John 2: 15.
[2] Deut. 4: 2; 12: 32.   [3] Ps. 37: 27; Rom. 12: 9.   [4] 1 Cor. 2: 14.
[5] Ps. 31: 6; 139: 22.   [6] John. 15. 22.   [7] 1 Tim. 3: 8.
[8] Matt. 7: 6.   [9] Matt. 11: 31.

[85]

known, are preaching of the Word purely, ministering of the sacraments sincerely, and ecclesiastical discipline which consisteth in admonition and correction of faults severely. Touching the first, namely the ministry of the Word, although it must be confessed that the substance of doctrine by many delivered is sound and good, yet herein it faileth, that neither the ministers thereof are according to God's Word proved, elected, called, or ordained: nor the function in such sort so narrowly looked unto, as of right it ought, and is of necessity required. For whereas in the old church a trial was had[10] both of their ability to instruct, and of their godly conversation also: now, by the letters commendatory of some one man, noble or other, tag and rag, learned and unlearned, of the basest[11] sort of the people (to the slander of the Gospel in the[12] mouths of the adversaries) are freely received. In those days[13] no idolatrous sacrificers or heathenish priests were appointed to be preachers of the Gospel: but we allow, and like well of popish mass-mongers, men for all seasons, King Henry's priests, King Edward's priests, Queen Mary's priests, who of a truth (if God's Word were precisely followed) should from the same be utterly removed. Then[14] they taught others, now they must be instructed themselves, and therefore like young children they[15] must learn catechisms. Then election was made by the common[16] consent of the whole Church: now every one picketh out for himself some notable good benefice, he obtaineth the next advowson, by money or by favour, and so thinketh himself to be sufficiently chosen. Then the congregation[17] had authority to call ministers: instead thereof now, they run, they ride, and by unlawful suit and buying, prevent other suitors also. Then no[18] minister placed in any congregation, but by the consent of the people, now, that authority is given into the hands of the bishop alone, who by his sole authority thrusteth upon them such, as they many times as well for unhonest life, as also for lack of learning, may, and do justly dislike. Then, none admitted to the ministry, but[19] a place was void beforehand, to which he should be called: but now, bishops (to whom the right of ordering ministers doth at no hand appertain) do make 60, 80, or a 100 at a clap, and send them abroad into the country like masterless men. Then, after just trial and vocation they were admitted to their function, by laying on of the hands of the company of the[20] eldership only: now there is (neither of these being

[10] Acts 1: 12; 6: 3; 1 Tim. 3: 2, 7, 8; Tit. 1. 6.   [11] 1 Kings 12: 31.
[12] Rom. 2: 24.   [13] Heb. 5: 4; Ezek. 44: 10, 12, 13; Jer. 23.   [14] 1 Tim. 4: 11.
[15] Ministers of London enjoined to learn Nowell's Catechism.
[16] Acts 1: 26.   [17] Acts 6: 2, 3.
[18] Acts 14: 23; 2 Cor. 8: 19.   [19] Acts 1: 25.   [20] 1 Tim. 4: 14.

looked unto) required an alb, a surplice, a vestment, a pastoral staff, beside that ridiculous, and (as they use it to their new creatures) blasphemous saying, Receive the Holy Ghost. Then every pastor[21] had his flock, and every flock his shepherd, or else[22] shepherds: Now they do not only run frisking from place to place (a miserable disorder in God's Church) but[23] covetously join living to living, making shipwreck[24] of their own consciences, and being but one shepherd (nay, would to God they were shepherds and not wolves) have many flocks. Then the ministers were[25] preachers: now bare readers. And if any be so well disposed to preach in their own charges, they may not, without my Lord's licence. In those days known[26] by voice, learning and doctrine: now they must be discerned from others by popish and Antichristian apparel, as cap, gown, tippet, etc. Then, as God gave utterance[27] they preached the Word only: now they read homilies, articles, injunctions, etc. Then[28] it was painful: now gainful.[29] Then poor and ignominious: now rich and glorious. And therefore titles, livings, and offices by Antichrist devised are given to them, as Metropolitan, Archbishop, Lord's Grace, Lord Bishop, Suffragan, Dean, Archdeacon, Prelate of the garter, Earl, County Palatine, Honour, High Commissioners, Justices of peace and Quorum, etc. All which, together with their offices, as they are strange and unheard of in Christ's church, nay plainly[30] in God's Word forbidden: So are they utterly with speed out of the same to be removed. Then ministers were not tied to any form of prayers invented by man, but as the spirit[31] moved them, so they poured forth hearty supplications to the Lord. Now they are bound of necessity to a[32] prescript order of service, and book of common prayer in which a great number of things contrary to God's Word are contained, as baptism[33] by women, private[34] Communions, Jewish[35] purifyings, observing[36] of holy days, etc., patched (if not all together, yet the greatest piece) out of the Pope's portuis. Then[37] feeding the flock diligently: now teaching quarterly. Then preaching[38] in season and out of season: now once in a month is thought sufficient, if twice, it is judged a work of supererogation. Then nothing taught but God's Word, Now

[21] Acts 20: 28; Eph. 4: 11; Tit. 1: 5; 1 Pet. 5: 2.   [22] Acts 14: 23.
[23] Is. 5: 8.   [24] 1 Tim. 1: 14.   [25] Phil. 2: 20, 25; Col. 1: 7; Luke 9: 2.
[26] 1 Sam. 9: 18; Matt. 26: 48; 26: 73.   [27] John. 6: 38; 12: 49; 1 Cor. 11: 23.
[28] 1 Tim. 3: 1.   [29] Phil. 4: 11; 2 Cor. 6: 4; 8: 10.
[30] Matt. 23: 11, 12; Luke 22: 25; 1 Cor. 4: 1; 1 Pet. 5: 2, 3.
[31] Rom. 8: 26; 1 Tim. 1: 2.
[32] Damasus the first inventor of this stuff. Well furthered by Gregory VII.
[33] Matt. 28: 19; 1 Cor. 14: 35. The first appointer hereof was Victor I, anno 198.
[34] 1 Cor. 11: 18.   [35] Acts 15: 10.   [36] Ex. 20: 9.
[37] 1 Pet. 5: 2.   [38] 1 Tim. 4: 2.

Princes' pleasures, men's devices, popish ceremonies, and Antichristian rites in public pulpits defended. Then they[39] sought them, now they seek theirs.

These, and a great many other abuses are in the ministry remaining, which unless they be removed and the truth brought in, not only God's justice shall be poured forth, but also God's Church in this realm shall never be builded. For if they which seem to be workmen, are no workmen in deed, but in name, or else work not so diligently and in such order as the workmaster commandeth, it is not only unlikely that the building shall go forward, but altogether impossible that ever it shall be perfected. The way therefore to avoid these inconveniences, and to reform these deformities is this: Your Wisdoms have to remove Advowsons, Patronages, Impropriations, and bishops' authority, claiming to themselves thereby right to ordain ministers, and to bring in that old and true election, which was accustomed to be[40] made by the congregation. You must displace those ignorant and unable ministers already placed, and in their rooms appoint such as both can, and will by God's assistance[41] feed the flock. You must pluck down and utterly overthrow without hope of restitution, the court of Faculties, from whence not only licences to enjoy many benefices, are obtained, as Pluralities, Trialities, Totquots, etc., but all things for the most part, as in the court of Rome, are set on sale, licences to marry, to eat flesh in times prohibited, to lie from benefices and charges, and a great number beside, of such like abominations. Appoint to every congregation a learned and diligent preacher. Remove homilies, articles, injunctions, a prescript order of service made out of the mass book. Take away the Lordship, the loitering, the pomp, the idleness, and livings of Bishops, but yet employ them to such ends as they were in the old church appointed for. Let a lawful and a godly Seignory look that they preach, not quarterly or monthly, but continually: not for filthy lucre' sake, but of a ready mind. So God shall be glorified, your consciences discharged, and the flock of Christ (purchased[42] with His own blood) edified.

Now to the second point, which concerneth ministration of Sacraments. In the old time, the Word was[43] preached, before they were ministered: now it is supposed to be sufficient, if it be read. Then, they were ministered in public[44] assemblies, now in private houses. Then[45] by ministers only, now by midwives, and deacons, equally. But because in treating of both the sacraments together, we should deal confusedly: we will therefore

[39] Phil. 2: 20, 21.   [40] Acts 1: 26; 6: 2, 3; 14: 13.   [41] 1 Pet. 5: 2.
[42] Acts 20: 28.   [43] Matt. 3: 1.   [44] Mark 1: 5; 1 Cor. 11: 18.
[45] Matt. 28: 19; 1 Cor. 4: 1.

[88]

speak of them severally. And first for the Lord's supper, or holy communion.

They had no introit, for Celestinus a pope brought it in, about the year 430. But we have borrowed a piece of one out of the mass book. They read no fragments of the Epistle and Gospel: we use both. The Nicene creed was not read in their Communion: we have it in ours. There was then, accustomed to be an examination of the communicants, which now is neglected. Then they ministered the Sacrament with common[46] and usual bread: now with wafer cakes, brought in by Pope Alexander, being in form, fashion and substance, like their god of the altar. They received it[47] sitting: we kneeling, according to Honorius' Decree. Then it was delivered generally, and indefinitely, Take ye[48] and eat ye: we particularly, and singularly, Take thou, and eat thou. They used no other words but such as Christ left: We borrow from papists, The body of our Lord Jesus Christ which was given for thee, etc. They had no *Gloria in excelsis* in the ministry of the Sacrament then for it was put[49] to afterward. We have now. They took it with conscience. We with custom. They shut men by reason of their[50] sins, from the Lord's Supper. We thrust them in their sin to the Lord's Supper. They ministered the Sacrament plainly. We pompously, with singing, piping, surplice and cope wearing. They simply as they[51] received it from the Lord. We, sinfully, mixed with man's inventions and devices. And as for Baptism, it was enough with them, if they[52] had water, and the party to be baptized faith, and the minister to preach the Word and minister the sacraments.

Now, we must have surplices devised by Pope Adrian, interrogatories ministered to the infant, godfathers and godmothers, brought in by Higinus, holy fonts invented by Pope Pius, crossing and such like pieces of popery, which the church of God in the Apostles' times never knew (and therefore not to be used), nay (which we are sure of) were and are man's devices, brought in long after the purity of the primitive church. To redress these, Your Wisdoms have to remove (as before) ignorant ministers, to take away private communions and baptisms, to enjoin deacons and midwives not to meddle in ministers' matters, if they do, to see them sharply punished. To join assistance of elders, and other officers, that seeing men will not examine themselves, they may be examined, and brought to[53] render a reason of their hope. That the statute against wafer cakes may more prevail than an Injunction. That people be appointed to receive the Sacrament, rather sitting, for avoiding of superstition, than kneeling, having in

[46] Acts 2: 46; 20: 7.   [47] Matt. 26: 20; Mark 14: 18; Luke 22: 14; John. 13: 28.
[48] Matt. 26: 26; Mark 14: 12; 1 Cor. 11: 24.
[49] Telesphorus, in anno 130.   [50] 1 Cor. 5: 11.   [51] 1 Cor. 11: 23.
[52] Acts 8: 35, 36, 37; 10: 47.   [53] 1 Cor. 11: 28; 1 Pet. 3: 15.

[89]

it the outward show of evil, from[54] which we must abstain. That Excommunication be restored to his old former force. That papists nor others, neither constrainedly nor customably, communicate in the mysteries of salvation. That both the Sacrament of the Lord's Supper and Baptism also, may be ministered according to the ancient purity and simplicity. That the parties to be baptized, if they be of the years[55] of discretion, by themselves and in their own persons, or if they be infants, by their parents (in whose room if upon necessary occasions and businesses they be absent, some of the congregation knowing the good behaviour and sound faith of the parents) may both make rehearsal of their faith, and also if their faith be sound, and agreeable to Holy Scriptures, desire to be in the same baptized. And finally, that nothing be done in this or any other thing, but that which you have the express warrant of God's Word for.

Let us come now to the third part, which concerneth ecclesiastical discipline. The officers that have to deal in this charge, are chiefly three, ministers, preachers or pastors of whom before; Seniors or Elders; and Deacons. Concerning Seniors, not only their office but their name also is out of this English Church utterly removed. Their office was to[56] govern the Church with the rest of the ministers, to consult, to admonish, to correct, and to order all things appertaining to the state of the congregation. Instead of these Seniors in[57] every church, the Pope hath brought in and we yet maintain the Lordship of one man over many churches, yea over sundry Shires. These Seniors then, because their charge was not overmuch, did execute their offices in their own persons without substitutes. Our Lords bishops have their under-officers, as Suffragans, Chancellors, Archdeacons, Officials, Commissaries, and such like. Touching Deacons, though their names be remaining, yet is the office foully perverted and turned upside down, for their duty in the primitive church was to[58] gather the alms diligently, and to distribute it faithfully, also for the sick and impotent persons to provide painfully, having ever a diligent care, that the charity of godly men were not wasted upon loiterers[59] and idle vagabonds. Now it is the first step to the ministry, nay, rather a mere order of priesthood. For[60] they may baptize in the presence of a bishop or priest, or in their absence (if necessity so require) minister the other Sacrament, likewise read the holy Scriptures and homilies in the congregation, instruct the youth in the Catechism, and also preach, if he be commanded by the bishop. Again, in the old church every[61] congregation had their Deacons. Now they are

[54] 1 Thess. 5: 22.   [55] Matt. 3: 6.   [56] Acts 15: 4; 1 Cor. 12: 28.   [57] Rom. 12: 8.
[58] Rom. 12: 8.   [59] 2 Thess. 3: 10.   [60] Pontifi. tit. The ordering of deacons.
[61] Phil. 1: 1; John. 13: 27; Acts 6: 5; 1 Tim. 3: 8.

tied to Cathedral churches only, and what do they there? gather the alms and distribute to the poor? nay, that is the least piece or rather no part of their function. What then? to sing a gospel when the bishop ministereth the Communion. If this be not a perverting of this office and charge, let every one judge. And yet lest the reformers of our time should seem utterly to take out of God's Church this necessary function, they appoint somewhat to it concerning the poor, and that is, to search for the sick, needy and, impotent people of the parish, and to intimate their estates, names, and places where they dwell to the Curate, that by his exhortation they may be relieved by the parish, or other convenient alms. And this as you see, is the highest part of his office, and yet you must understand it to be in such places where there is a Curate and a Deacon: every parish cannot be at that cost to have both, nay, no parish so far as can be gathered, at this present hath. Now then, if you will restore the church to his ancient officers, this you must do. Instead of an Archbishop or Lord bishop, you must make[62] equality of ministers. Instead of Chancellors, Archdeacons, Officials, Commissaries, Proctors, Doctors, Summoners, Churchwardens, and such like: you have to plant in every congregation a lawful and godly seignory. The Deaconship[63] must not be confounded with the ministry, nor the Collectors for the poor, may not usurp the Deacon's office: But he that hath an[64] office, must look to his office, and every man must keep himself within the bounds and limits of his own vocation. And to these three jointly, that is, the Ministers, Seniors, and deacons, is the whole regiment of the church to be committed. This regiment consisteth especially in ecclesiastical discipline, which is an order left by God unto his Church, whereby men learn to frame their wills and doings according to the law of God, by[65] instructing and admonishing one another, yea and by correcting and punishing all wilful persons, and contemners of the same. Of this discipline there are two kinds, one private, wherewith we will not deal because it is impertinent to our purpose, another public, which although it hath been long banished, yet if it might now at the length be restored, would be very necessary and profitable for the building up of God's house. The final end of this discipline, is the reforming of the disordered, and to bring them to repentance, and to bridle such as would offend. The chiefest part and last punishment of this discipline is excommunication, by the consent of the Church determined, if the offender be obstinate, which how miserably it hath been by the Pope's proctors, and is by our new Canonists

___

[62] 2 Cor. 10: 7; Col. 1: 1.—[Phil. 1: 1; 1 Thess. 1: 1].
[63] 1 Tim. 3: 8.   [64] Rom. 12: 7; 1 Cor. 7: 20.
[65] James 5: 16; Matt. 18: 15, 16, 17.

abused, who seeth not? In the primitive church it was in[66] many men's hands: now one alone excommunicateth. In those days it was the last censure of the Church, and never went forth but for[67] notorious crimes: Now it is pronounced for every light trifle. Then excommunication was greatly regarded and feared. Now because it is a money matter, no whit at all esteemed. Then for[68] great sins, severe punishment, and for small offences, little censures. Now great sins either not at all punished, as[69] blasphemy,[70] usury, etc., or else slightly passed over with pricking in a blanket, or pinning in a sheet, as[71] adultery, whoredom, drunkenness, etc. Again, such as are no sins (as if a man conform not himself to popish orders and ceremonies, if he come not at the whistle of him, who hath by God's Word no authority to call, we mean Chancellors, Officials, Doctors, and all that rabble) are grievously punished, not only by excommunication, suspension, deprivation and other (as they term it) spiritual coercion, but also by banishing, imprisoning, reviling, taunting, and what not? Then the sentence was tempered according[72] to the notoriousness of the fact. Now on the one side either hatred against some persons, carrieth men headlong into rash and cruel judgment: or else favour, affection, or money, mitigateth the rigour of the same, and all this cometh to pass, because the regiment left of Christ[73] to His Church, is committed into one man's hands, whom alone it shall be more easy for the wicked by bribing to pervert, than to overthrow the faith and pity of a zealous and godly company, for such manner of men indeed[74] should the Seigniors be. Then it was said, Tell[75] the church: now it is spoken, Complain to my Lord's grace, primate and Metropolitan of all England, or to his inferior, my Lord Bishop of the diocese; if not to him, show the Chancellor or Official, or Commissary or Doctor. Again, whereas the excommunicate were never received till they had[76] publicly confessed their offence, now for paying the fees of the court, they shall by master Official, or Chancellor, easily be absolved in some private place. Then the congregation, by the wickedness of the offender grieved, was by his public penance satisfied. Now absolution shall be pronounced, though that be not accomplished. Then the party offending should in his own person, hear the sentence of Absolution pronounced. Now, Bishops, Archdeacons, Chancellors, Officials, Commissaries and such like, absolve one man for another. And this is that order of

[66] 1 Cor. 5: 4.   [67] 1 Cor. 5: 11; 2 Thess. 3: 14.   [68] 1 Tim. 1: 20; 1 Cor. 5.
[69] Lev. 24: 14, 16; Num. 15: 34, etc.   [70] Deut. 23: 19, 20.
[71] Lev. 20: 10; Deut. 22: 22.   [72] 1 Tim. 1: 20.
[73] Matt. 18: 17; 1 Cor. 12: 28; Rom. 12: 8; 1 Tim. 5: 17; Acts 15: 2, 4; 6: 22, 23.
[74] Ex. 18: 21; Deut. 1: 13.   [75] Matt. 18: 17.   [76] 2 Cor. 2: 7.

ecclesiastical discipline which all godly wish to be restored, to the end that every one by the same, may be kept within the limits of his[77] vocation, and a great number be brought to live in godly conversation. Not that we mean to take away the authority of the civil[78] Magistrate and chief governors, to whom we wish all blessedness, and for the increase of whose godliness we daily[79] pray: but that Christ being restored into His kingdom, to rule in the same by the sceptre of His Word, and severe discipline: the Prince may be better obeyed, the realm more flourish in godliness, and the Lord Himself more sincerely and purely according to His revealed will served than heretofore He hath been, or yet at this present is. Amend therefore these horrible abuses, and reform God's Church, and the[80] Lord is on your right hand, you shall not be removed for ever. For he will deliver and defend you from all your enemies either at home or abroad, as he did faithful Jacob[81] and good[82] Jehoshaphat. Let these things alone, and God is a righteous judge, he will one day call you to your reckoning. Is a reformation good for France? and can it be evil for England? Is discipline meet for Scotland? and is it unprofitable for this Realm? Surely God hath set these examples before your eyes to encourage you to go forward to a thorough and a speedy reformation. You may not do as heretofore you have done, patch and piece, nay rather go backward, and never labour or[83] contend to perfection. But altogether remove whole Antichrist, both head, body and branch, and perfectly plant that purity of the Word, that simplicity of the sacraments, and severity of discipline, which Christ hath commanded, and commended to His Church. And here to end, we desire all to suppose that we have not attempted this enterprise for vain glory, gain, preferment, or any other worldly respect: neither yet judging ourselves, so exactly to have set out the state of a church reformed, as that nothing more could be added, or a more perfect form and order drawn: for that were great presumption, to arrogate so much unto ourselves, seeing that as we are but weak and simple souls, so God hath raised up men of profound judgment and notable learning. But thereby to declare our good wills toward the setting forth of God's glory, and the building up of His Church, accounting this as it were, but an entrance into further matter, hoping that our God, who hath in us begun this good work,[84] will not only in time hereafter make us strong and able to go forward therein: but also move other, upon whom he hath bestowed greater measure of his gifts and graces, to labour more thoroughly and fully in the same.

[77] 1 Cor. 7: 20.   [78] Rom. 13.   [79] 1 Tim. 2: 2.
[80] Ps. 16: 8.   [81] Gen. 35: 5.   [82] 2 Chron. 17: 10.
[83] Heb. 6: 1.   [84] Phil. 1: 6.

The God of all glory so open your eyes to see his truth, that you may not only be inflamed with a love thereof, but with a continual care seek to promote, plant, and place the same amongst us, that we the English people, and our posterity, enjoying the sincerity of God's gospel for ever, may say always: The Lord be praised. To whom with Christ Jesus His Son our only Saviour, and the Holy Ghost our alone Comforter, be honour, praise, and glory, for ever and ever.   Amen.

Concerning a
National Church

William Ames
[1576-1633]

WHEN WILLIAM PERKINS, THE PURITAN LEADER IN CAMBRIDGE, DIED IN *1602 there were two men outstandingly fitted to carry on the work – Paul Baynes, who succeeded Perkins as lecturer at St Andrew's Church, and William Ames, Fellow of Christ's and likely to be one day Master of the College. But the year following Perkins' death saw the succession of James I, who soon uttered his famous threat to the Puritans that he would make them conform, or 'harry them out of the land'. Under Archbishop Bancroft, opposition to Puritanism stiffened and the Cambridge leaders were among many ministers who were confronted with the choice of conformity or suppression. Refusing the former alternative, Baynes was suspended from his ministry and silenced, and Ames was forced, about 1610, to leave the University and find refuge on the Continent.*

Even on the Continent, Ames was closely watched by the English ecclesiastical authorities, who prevented his appointment to a professorship at Leyden and sought to block all Puritan influence by the suppression of such agencies as the Pilgrim Press at Leyden – a press run by John Robinson and Thomas Brewster, with which Ames was suspected of having connections (see the fine life of Robinson by W. H. Burgess, 1920). Nevertheless, in 1622, Ames was invited to the Chair of Divinity at the University of Franeker, in Friesland. Here he remained for twelve years and to his classes students flocked from as far as Hungary and Poland.

In 1633, due to his ill-health in Friesland and a desire to minister to his own countrymen, Ames accepted a call to the English Church at Rotterdam, where he became the colleague of Hugh Peters. From here Ames had intended to take part in the emigration movement to New England, but his family had later to sail alone, as he died of asthma at the age of 57 in the year of his arrival at Rotterdam. Many years later Ames's memory was still revered in New England, both for his strength and accuracy as a theologian and for his warm heart: 'He seldom preached without tears,' says Cotton Mather, 'and when upon his death bed, had most wonderful foretastes of glory.'

In the twenty years preceding the overthrow of the English hierarchy in 1641 Ames was responsible for two books which were among the most damaging to the cause of the hierarchy. For the first he had only an indirect responsibility; this was The Diocesan's Trial, *by his old friend Paul Baynes who had died in 1617, which Ames published with a lengthy preface in 1621. The second book was Ames's own best-known work,* A Fresh Suit Against Human Ceremonies. *Behind the book lay a protracted controversy. In 1610 Bishop Morton had published a* Defence of Three Nocent Ceremonies, *viz. the surplice, the sign of the cross in baptism, and kneeling to receive the Sacrament. In 1622 an* Anonymous Reply *appeared, possibly from the pen of Ames himself, and in 1631 a* Rejoinder *to this was written by Dr John Burgess, Prebend of Lichfield Cathedral. Ames's* Fresh Suit, *from which the following extract is taken, is principally a reply to Burgess's* Rejoinder *(hence the abbreviation in the text, 'the Rej. teacheth'); it is also a full Puritan statement of those issues which were opposed by the defenders of the status quo in England. The work was influential in determining the Nonconformity of such a man as Richard Baxter, and it was referred to by the ejected Puritans of 1662 as an unanswered case against conformity.*

The following passage shows how deeply divided was English Protestantism over the practical definition of 'the Church'. To the bishops a congregation was 'a church' if it belonged to the national unit of 'The Church of England' – the mother of all parish churches and the grandmother of all believers. To the Puritans a congregation was only a church if it possessed the scriptural marks of a true church, and if it lacked those marks no connection with any other unit could give it such a status. The episcopal view of 'The Church of England' as the mother of parish churches, they rejected as an utterly unscriptural concept. What makes particular churches partake in the unity of the whole Church is not national and political laws, nor subjection to the human institution of an episcopate, but the possession of a common faith and subjection to one Redeemer. Congregations so united in a profession of the truth may by the accidental facts of nationality be particularly associated within a nation (such was the vision of the Puritans of both Presbyterian and Independent convictions) and in a spiritual sense they are the Church of Jesus Christ in a nation; this is entirely different from asserting that the government of a nation may institute a visible 'Church' and test the church standing of all particular congregations by whether or not they conform to this national 'Church'. As David Calderwood writes, nowhere in the New Testament is 'a visible Church endowed with power of ecclesiastical government taken for a whole shire or county . . . City churches and town churches the Scripture knoweth, but not country churches. For when the Scripture speaketh of a Province or Country, it speaketh in the plural number churches, *not* church, *in the singular'* (The Altar of Damascus, *1621, pp. 82, 83).*

The issue in the following pages thus reverts to the whole foundation principle of the Puritan movement. As Ames states in the Preface to his Fresh Suit: *'We stand upon the sufficiency of Christ's institution for every thing pertaining to divine worship, and that the Word of God, and nothing else, is the only standard in matters of religion.'*

Concerning a National Church

O F the faithful congregations, wherein we were born, baptized, and nourished up in faith, there is no question made, but they are our loving and beloved mothers: Yet much question ariseth concerning that which the Rejoinder teacheth, viz. *That all these churches together have one mother, and so we have a grandmother, that is the Church of England, considered as one church: and that by way of representation, as the convocation house, (2) by way of association and combination into one profession, worship and discipline, which includeth the orders and officers, that is, the Hierarchy, pertaining thereunto, but not by any other collective consideration.*

1. I never read either in Scripture, or in any orthodox writer, of a visible particular Church, either grandmother of Christians, or mother of other Churches; if the Rej. hath, he should do well to inform us where we may find this doctrine explained. 2. I would willingly know, whether Christians and Christian churches also were not in England before this great grandmother? I think the Rej. will not deny it, nor yet fly for succour to his physicians, who have found out an herb, which is called of them, *Son before the Father*, to justify his intention of *Daughter before the Mother:* He must confess that this Grandmother is only a mother in law, and that law also to be man's, not God's. 3. All the churches of England may as well be considered as one in unity of profession, without any new motherhood, as all the Latin Schools of England one, in the unity of the same Grammar, or all Galenical, or Platonical Schools, one in their kind. 4. A Representative mother is the image of a mother, and an image, with commanding authority in religion, without God's command, is an Idol: It was well, therefore, to this purpose said by Zwinglius (Explan. arti. 8): *That you be a representative church, we willingly believe, for you are not the true church: But show, I beseech you, whence you had this name, who styled you with this title? who gave you power of meeting, and combining together? who granted you authority of coining decrees and Canons, differing from the word of God? who suffered you to impose these upon men? who persuaded you thus to burden Consciences? who enjoined you to call evil good, and good evil? You are therefore an hypocritical church, which hath nothing sound in it, and substantial, but all things feigned and painted. But you are not that true church, that bride beseeming our Saviour, who stays herself upon the truth alone and the Spirit of God. He*

speaketh these things of those, which under the name of Representative churches, imposed their inventions upon true churches, without Scripture, which is a true representation of our representative convocation. 5. The Rej. confesseth, that this Hierarchical convocation is human and not divine, and he will not deny but Christians and Christian congregations are Divine. Now what a monstrous and preposterous generation then doth he make (as it were in a chimerical dream) of Divine Children, proceeding from human mothers and grandmothers: Our Saviour was of another mind, when he made these two opposite, from earth, and from heaven: The Rej. hath found out so great consent between these two, that earth may be the mother and grandmother of heaven: Besides the human mother of Divine children is not of their Heavenly Father's choice, nor by him appointed, to bear the person of their true mother: But she was first put into this office by the presumption of men, and afterward authorized, by the Archmother of Rome, continuing her profession, by sleight and might, to represent those, from whom she can show no other letters of credence, for the power she usurpeth, than she maketh herself, or hath gotten by stealth from civil power.

6. This representative mother is very seldom extant, viz. when there is a Parliament, which now we have not had these divers years: And when she appeareth, she can give no milk to her children, further than she hath commission from man: None of her children can have access unto her, only she appointed many years since, certain servants of hers, with restraint of their father's allowance, to diet them, with dry ceremonies, and scourge them, with silencing, deprivation, excommunication, if they find fault with that provision, which is very pap, with a hatchet; Is not such a mother worthy of grand titles and honour?

7. The examples of such motherhood, which the Rej. fetcheth from the assemblies of Israel, Scotland, and our Parliament, have no agreement. For (1) we read of no assemblies of Elders (by office in Israel) from whence all other were excluded, styled either Mothers of Israel or all Israel: Neither was there in any such assemblies this motherly authority exercised, of appointing human sacred ceremonies unto Israel. (2) The assembly of Scotland, before Perth, had no such state, as our convocation, nor power of commanding, but only advised of, and directed those things which God had appointed, and the churches were known to desire, yet might their judgment be well called, *the judgment of the Church of Scotland*, because they pronounced nothing but that which all the churches of Scotland did publicly profess, even in their solemn confession. (3) Our Parliament is not styled, the *Mother commonwealth of England*, yet in civil affairs, more

liberty is left for style and power, unto public assemblies, than in religious: But if the lower house of Parliament were not more freely chosen, and of greater power, than the poor lower house of Convocation, a query might be made, whether the state or commonwealth of England were there or no.

Now for the second way of one church, by association, and combination of all particular churches into one profession, worship, and discipline: This is good, thus far, and the very same with that collective consideration, which the Repl. mentioned, and the Rej. termed *a new misty inexplicable nothing,* except combination doth mistily cover under it, the swallowing up of particular congregations, by national, provincial, diocesan churches. But as for that clause, that this must needs include such orders and offices as our Hierarchy: this is either a begging or a stealing of the main question: For (1) this Hierarchy consisteth of officers and orders (by the Rej.'s own confession) human, not divine: now association of profession, worship and discipline may certainly be had by officers and orders divine. (2) The reformed churches of France have their association and combination without any Hierarchy. (3) The Hierarchy doth not associate churches under it, but subdue all to itself, so that, as the Pope is sometime esteemed the Church of Rome, and sometime, he with his assistants, so is our Hierarchy in England. Beza in his notes of the church not far from the end giveth warning of this: *I most willingly leave the whole frame of Episcopal authority to the papists, of which (I openly profess) the Holy Spirit of God was never the author, but human policy, which if we do not observe to be accursed by God, we certainly as yet see nothing at all: and nourish we do a viper in our bosoms which will kill the mother.* This prophecy is too true of the Hierarchy as in other respects, so in this, that it seemeth to devour our mother church's title, liberty, right and power, and in a great part hath prevailed.

9. It was added by the Replier, that the Hierarchy is a creature of *man's making,* and may more lawfully be removed, when it pleaseth man, than ever she was by him erected. To this the Rej. answereth, confessing, that *sundry offices and orders in our church are human, and not divine: adding, that accidental forms of discipline are not determined in the Word of God, but left in the church's liberty, to devise, as all but Anabaptists and such as edge too near upon them consent.*

Which words are worthy of a note or two: For he (1) acknowledgeth our Hierarchy of Archbishops, Bishops, Deans, Archdeacons, etc., to be creatures of man's making, not divine: Now of these principally consist our convocated mother church, as it is well known, a few ministers being added to her, for fashion's sake, so that this church is a church of man, not of God, by his own confession, and this church is said to be devised by the church. Now it soundeth strangely, *A church of the church's devising:* Nor know I well what the devising church of England can be. The Rej. telleth us, that there be but two ways of considering the Church of England as one, either in the convocation house, or in that combination, which must needs (saith he) include the orders and officers pertaining thereunto: Now in both of these ways Hierarchical orders and officers are supposed and included, so that the Church of England neither of these ways could possibly devise these orders and officers. (3) The distinction used betwixt the *essentials of discipline,* and *the accidental forms* thereof, is obscure: And if these terms may be interpreted by that sense which is given by the *Rej. of Doctrinal and Ritual, substantial, circumstantial worship, that must be essential which is commanded in the word, that is accidental which is not commanded, but permitted.* Then the Rej. in affirming essentials to be determined, and accidentals not, saith nothing else, but that which is determined is determined, and that which is not determined is not determined. (4) If he mean by accidental forms, circumstances of time, number, place and occasional course of proceeding, then he accuseth unjustly, not only us, but the Anabaptists themselves, of opposing so manifest a truth, by all men confessed. (5) It would be worth a little pain of his to declare, how, and in what sense our Hierarchy is accidental to the church and discipline of England? The Bishops are efficient causes, even in a high rank, of our Discipline, they are principal members of our Diocesan churches, they have an Ecclesiastical rule and command over the particular congregations within their Dominion, by them and in their name, the essentials of ordination, institution, introduction, suspension, deprivation, excommunication, etc., are dispensed and disposed of: who will say, that these things can agree to accidental forms? (6) Concerning edging upon Anabaptists, in this point it may with better reason be objected to those that maintain Diocesan Bishops, than to those that oppose them, for it is well known that the Anabaptists, in Holland, Zeeland, and Friesland, have their Bishops, which have care of many congregations, within a certain circuit, and in all of them (though there be others that teach) they only, at their visitations, perform some main things belonging to the pastoral office. (7) The position (that our Bishops are human creatures of man's making) is not only to us, but to many of themselves, sufficient to condemn their office, some of them having publicly protested that, if it were so, they would not keep their places one day.

The Relation
of Church and State

Charles Hodge

[1797-1878]

WHEN HENRY VIII ASSUMED WHAT HAD FORMERLY BEEN THE PRERO-
*gatives of the Pope in relation to the Church in England, the Church-State con-
nection became a dominating issue in the course of English Protestantism. Cranmer
built his policy on the supreme place of the civil magistrate in the visible Church,
and by this means was able to carry through in the reign of Edward VI, without
the consent of the English Church (which was still predominantly Papist in its
faith), the distinctive legislation of the English Reformation. The precedent which
was thus established was, however, soon put to a different use in the reign of
Mary, when the State again became 'the hangman for the Church', and at the
opening of Elizabeth's reign in 1558 there was a growing body of Protestants who
questioned the position which had been assigned to the monarch in the Church. The
change of Elizabeth's title from 'Supreme Head' to 'Supreme Governor' did not allay
their fears and the Queen soon made known the force of her religious authority –
even to the extent of suspending the Puritan sympathizer, Edmund Grindal, from
his office as Archbishop of Canterbury in 1577. Only the royal intervention prevented further reformation of the Church in the Elizabethan era, and from that
time till the Civil Wars the authority of the Crown, while upholding nominal
Protestantism, was used by a submissive episcopate to suppress Puritan influence and
preaching.*

*Though Archbishop Whitgift, the strongest upholder of Elizabeth's religious
settlement, accused the Puritans of making 'the church and state distinct bodies',
the Puritans sought to hold to what they believed to be a Biblical balance by attri-
buting to the civil magistrate an important degree of authority in matters concerning
the Church while at the same time asserting that the Church must never be subjected to the State. Hence the frequent Puritan attempts, beginning in 1572, to
implement their policy for reform through Parliament, and their views on what
degree of authority the Scripture allows to the civil magistrate were finally embodied in the Westminster Confession (Section 23). The first strong spiritual
challenge to this Puritan view came from the Separatists in the 1590s, who reasoned
that the Puritan policy for reform rested on a wrong dependence on the Church-
State connection, and, while they did not hold that the civil powers could be
legitimately neutral towards the Gospel, they emphasized that if the State should
disobey Scripture, Christians had no warrant to delay reformation until 'God shall
incline the prince's heart'.*

*The view that the earlier Puritans and the Westminster Confession gave too
much to the magistrate was developed by the English Independents (in the Commonwealth period) and the differences between them and the Presbyterians are to
be seen in the way the Savoy Declaration varies from the Westminster Confession in the section 'Of the Civil Magistrate'. The American Presbyterian Church
likewise amended the Wertminster Confession on this point in 1788 (cf. A. A.
Hodge, The Confession of Faith 1958, pp. 22, 23), and Charles Hodge represents this later outlook in the following historical survey of the various ways in
which the subject has been treated. The article was first printed in Princeton*

Review, *1863, and reprinted in the author's* The Church and Its Polity, *1879. In another important article,* A Nation's Right to Worship God *(printed in Britain in* The British and Foreign Evangelical Review, *1860), Hodge argues that while a union of Church and State 'either gives the state some sort of control over the church, as in England, or gives the church some control over the state, according to the Papist theory', nevertheless, the separation of Church and State does not imply that 'the state, as such, has no duties to God, and no religious character'. It was this latter truth which the defenders of the Established Church of Scotland were principally concerned to safeguard in Scotland in the famous Voluntary Controversy of the 1830s (when opposite sides were taken by William Cunningham and John Brown of Broughton Place), and the issue was again prominent in Scotland in the 1860s when it was one factor which prevented the union of the Free Church with the United Presbyterian Church (cf.* The Church of Christ, *James Bannerman, vol. 2, pp. 345–403, 1960).*

The whole controversy is again being revived in England today by the pressure of the dominant party in the Church of England – the successors of the Tractarians – to release the Church from Parliamentary control and from existing Protestant legislation. There is consequently an urgent need for a scriptural re-assessment of the question, lest we simply adopt a course which existing circumstances appear to indicate is most likely to be favourable to us, and thus, resolving our difficulties by expediency instead of Scripture, repeat the mistake which has often been made in the past when, as Hodge says, 'the actual relation between the Church and State is determined historically, i.e. by the course of events, and then a theory invented to explain and justify it'.

Bibliography

Truth and Innocence Vindicated, John Owen, 1669 (the authority of the civil magistrate over the conscience of subjects in matters of religion).

Discussions on Church Principles, William Cunningham, 1863.

Statement of the Difference, Thomas M'Crie, with Preface by George Smeaton, 1871.

National Christianity and Scriptural Union, George Smeaton, 1871.

Church and State, A. F. Scott Pearson, 1928 (a study especially of the ideas of Thomas Cartwright).

The Law of Christ respecting Civil Obedience, John Brown, 1839 (3rd edition).

The Relation of Church and State

THIS is an exceedingly complicated and difficult subject. There are three aspects under which it may be viewed.

I. The actual relation which at different times and in different countries has subsisted between the two institutions.

II. The theory devised to justify or determine the limits of such existing relation.

III. The normal relation, such as should exist according to the revealed will of God, and the nature of the state and of the Church.

Before the conversion of Constantine, the Church was of course so far independent of the state, that she determined her own faith, regulated her worship, chose her officers, and exercised her discipline without any interference of the civil authorities. Her members were regarded as citizens of the state, whose religious opinions and practices were, except in times of persecution, regarded as matters of indifference. It is probable that much the same liberty was accorded to the early Christians as was granted by the Romans to the Jews, who were not only allowed, in ordinary cases, to conduct their synagogue services as they pleased, but to decide matters of dispute among themselves, according to their own laws. It is also stated that Churches were allowed to hold real estate before the profession of Christianity by the Emperor.

When Constantine declared himself a Christian, he expressed the relation which was henceforth to subsist between the Church and state, by saying to certain bishops, 'God has made you the bishops of the internal affairs of the Church, and me the bishop of its external affairs.' This saying has ever since been, throughout a large portion of Christendom, the standing formula for expressing the relation of the civil magistrate to the kingdom of Christ.

According to this statement, it belongs to the Church, through her own organs, to choose her officers, to regulate all matters relating to doctrine, to administer the Word and sacraments, to order public worship, and to exercise discipline. And to the state to provide for the support of the clergy, to determine the sources and amount of their incomes, to fix the limits of parishes and dioceses, to provide places of public worship, to call together the clergy, to preside in their meetings, to give the force of laws to their decisions, and to see that external obedience at least was rendered to the decrees and acts of discipline.

And this, in general terms, was the actual relation between the two institutions under the Roman emperors, and in many of the states which rose after the dissolution of the Roman empire. But it is easy to see that the distinction between the internal affairs which belonged to the bishops, and the external which belonged to the civil ruler, is too indefinite to keep two mighty bodies from coming into collision. If the magistrate provided the support of the bishops and sustained them in their places of influence, he felt entitled to have a voice in saying who should receive his funds, and use that influence. If he was to enforce the decisions of councils as to matters of faith and discipline, he must have some agency in determining what those decisions should be. If he was to banish from his kingdom those whom the clergy excluded from the Church, he must judge whether such exclusion was in itself just. And on the other hand, if the Church was recognized as a divine institution, with divinely constituted government and powers, she would constantly struggle to preserve her prerogatives from the encroachments of the state, and to draw to herself all the power requisite to enforce her decisions in the sphere of the state into which she was adopted, which she of right possessed in her own sphere as a spiritual, and, in one sense voluntary, society.

Simple and plausible, therefore, as the relation between the Church and state, as determined by Constantine, may at first sight appear, the whole history of the Church shows that it cannot be maintained. Either the Church will encroach on the peculiar province of the state, or the state upon that of the Church. It would require an outline of ecclesiastical history, from Constantine to the present day, to exhibit the conflicts and vacillations of these two principles. The struggle though protracted and varied in its prospects, was decided in favour of the Church, which under the papacy gained a complete ascendancy over the state.

The papal world constituted one body, of which the Pope, as vicar of Christ, was the head. This spiritual body claimed a divine right to make its own laws, appoint its own officers, and have its own tribunals, to which alone its officers were amenable, and before whom all persons in the state, from the highest to the lowest, could be cited to appear. All ecclesiastical persons were thus withdrawn from the jurisdiction of the state; while all civil persons were subject to the jurisdiction of the Church. The Church being the infallible judge of all questions relating to faith and practice, and it being the obvious duty of all men to receive the decisions and obey the injunctions of an infallible authority, the state was bound to receive all those decisions and enforce all those commands. The civil magistrate had no judgment or discretion in the case; he was but the secular arm of the Church, with whose judgments, no matter how injurious he might regard them to his own prerogative, or to the interests of his people, he had no right to interfere. The Church, however, claimed the right to interfere in all the decisions of the civil power; because she only could judge whether those decisions were or were not inimical to the true faith, or consistent with the rule of duty. Hence arose what is called the indirect power of the Church in the temporal affairs of the state. Even without going to the extreme of claiming for the Pope, by divine right, a direct sovereignty over the Christian world, moderate Romanists of the Italian school claimed for the Pope this indirect power in the civil affairs of kingdoms; that is, power of deciding whether any law or measure was or was not hurtful to the Church, and either to sanction or to annul it. And in case any Sovereign should persist in a course pronounced by an infallible authority hurtful to the Church, the obligation of obedience on the part of his subjects was declared to be at an end, and the Sovereign deposed.

In most cases, the actual relation between the Church and state is determined historically, i.e., by the course of events, and then a theory invented to explain and justify it; but in the case of the papacy, it is probable the theory preceded and produced the actual relation. On the assumption of the external unity of the whole Church under a visible head, and of the infallibility of that visible body when speaking through its appropriate organ, the relation of the Church to the state, which Gregory strove to realize, and which did for ages subsist, is the normal relation; and it is therefore, at the present day, the very theory which is held by the great body of Romanists.

In practice, however, it was found intolerable, and therefore, especially in France, and later in Austria, the kings have resisted this domination, and asserted that as the state no less than the Church is of divine origin, the former has the right to judge whether the acts and decisions of the Church are consistent with the rights and interests of the state. The kings of France, therefore, claimed indirect power in the affairs of the Church, and exercised the right of giving a *placet*, as it was called, to acts of the Church; that is, they required that such acts should be submitted to them, and receive their sanction before taking effect in their dominions.

As the Reformation involved the rejection of the doctrine of the visible unity of the Church under one infallible head, it of necessity introduced a change in the relation between the state and the Church. This relation, however, was very different in different countries, and that difference was evidently not the result of any preconceived theory, but of the course of events. It was, therefore, one thing in England, another in Scotland, and another in Germany.

The Church of England. With regard to England, it may be said, in general terms, that the Reformation was effected by the civil power. The authority by which all changes were decreed, was that of the king and parliament. The Church passively submitted, subscribing articles presented for acceptance, and adopting forms of worship and general regulations prescribed for her use. This fact is so inconsistent with the high-church theory, that every effort is made by advocates of that theory, to evade its force, and to show that the change was the work of the Church itself. It is admitted, however, by episcopal writers themselves, that in the time of Henry and Edward, the great majority both of the clergy and the people, i.e. the Church, was opposed to the reformation.

Henry rejected the authority of the Pope, though he adhered to the doctrines of Romanism. He declared himself by Act of Parliament the head of the Church, and required all the bishops to give up their sees, suspending them from office, and then made each take out a commission from the crown, in which it was declared that all ecclesiastical power flowed from the Sovereign, and that the bishops acted in his name, and by virtue of power derived from him.

The six articles were framed by his authority, in opposition to Cranmer and the real Reformers, and enacted by Parliament, and made obligatory under severe penalties, upon all the clergy. These articles affirm all the distinguishing doctrines of Romanism.

The clearest proof that they rested on the authority of the king is, that as soon as he died they were discarded, and a doctrinal formulary of an opposite character adopted.

Under Edward VI, the actual practice was for the crown to appoint a certain number of the clergy to prepare the requisite formularies or measures, and then these, if approved by the king, were published in his name, and enforced by act of Parliament. The convocation and the clergy then gave their assent. It was thus the Prayer Book was prepared and introduced. Thus, too, the Articles of Religion were, under Edward, the act of the civil power alone. They were drawn up under Cranmer's direction, and with the assistance of other divines, but they were not the work of the Convocation, as their preamble would seem to imply; nor were they set forth by any authority but that of the crown. Under Elizabeth they were revised by the Convocation.

The actual relation of the Church to the state in England is sufficiently indicated by these facts. The king was declared to be the supreme head of the Church, i.e., the source of authority in its government, and the supreme judge of all persons and causes ecclesiastical, of whatever kind. The clergy were brought with great difficulty to make this acknowledgment, and therefore it cannot be said to be the spontaneous act of the Church. It was rather a usurpation. It is said that the acknowledgment was made with the saving clause, *quantum per Christi legem licet*, with regard to which, there is a dispute, whether it was in the first acknowledgment. The preponderance of evidence, so far as we know, is against it; and certain it is, it is not now in the oath. And it can make little difference, because the very end of the oath was to declare that Christ did allow the king the power which he claimed and exercised.

The king then, as head of the Church, changed the form of worship, introduced new articles of faith, suspended and appointed bishops, visited all parts of the Church to reform abuses, issued edicts regulating matters of discipline, granted commissions to the bishops to act in his name, and by act of Parliament declared that all jurisdiction, spiritual and temporal, emanates from him, and that all proceedings in the episcopal courts should be in his name.

These principles have ever been acted on in the Church of England; though with less flagrancy of course in the settled state of the Church than at the Reformation. All the proceedings, however, of Elizabeth; all the acts of James I against the Puritans; of Charles I in Scotland, in the introduction of episcopacy into that country; of Charles II at his restoration, and even of William III at the Revolution, when the non-juring bishops were excluded, were founded on the assumption of the absolute power of the state over the Church. And everything still rests on that foundation. The king still appoints all the bishops, and has the legal right to suspend them; all the binding authority of the Articles and Prayer Book rests on acts of Parliament. No man can be refused admission to the Church, no matter what his opinions or character, against the will of the state; and no man can be excommunicated but by civil process; and the ultimate decision, even in the trial of a bishop for heresy, is rendered by the king in council.

Different theories have been devised to justify this entire subordination of the Church to the state. The early Reformers, Cranmer especially, were thoroughly Erastian; and held that the king was entrusted with the whole care of his subjects, as well concerning the administration of the Word, as in things civil and political; and as he had under him civil officers to act in his name, so he had Church officers, the one class being assigned, appointed, and selected by the authority of the king, as much as the other. Cranmer did not even hold to the necessity of any ordination by Church officers, considering the king's commission all-sufficient. This whole theory rests on an exorbitant notion of the regal power.

A second theory supposes that there is no difference between a Christian state and a Church. A Church is a people professing Christianity, and they may adopt what form of government they please. This supposes not only that the details of Church government are not prescribed in Scripture, but that there is no government in the hands of Church officers at all ordained by Christ; but in whatever way the will of the sovereign power, i.e. of the people, is expressed and exercised, is, as to its form, legitimate; and hence the best and most healthful form of Church government is that which most fully identifies the Church with the state. This is the doctrine of Dr Arnold. Though this theory, if sound, might justify the existing state of things in England, it cannot justify the Reformation; for that was not carried on by the people; i.e. the Church in its state capacity, but by civil authority, in despite both of the clergy and the people.

High churchmen take different grounds. Some admit the irregularity in the mode of proceeding under Henry and Elizabeth, but justify it on the ground of necessity, or of extraordinary emergency, calling for the exercise of extraordinary powers. Others, as Mr Palmer, deny that the Church is responsible for those acts, or that she is to be judged by the preamble of acts of Parliament, or by the claims or acts of the crown, but exclusively by her own declarations and acts. And he endeavours to show that all the leading facts of the Reformation were determined by the Church. To do this, however, he is obliged to maintain that what the king did on the advice of a few divines, was done by the Church, which is as unreasonable as to refer the sanitary or legal regulations of a kingdom to the authority of the physicians or lawyers who may be consulted in drawing them up.

Mr Palmer falls back on the theory suggested by Constantine, which assigns the internal government of the Church to bishops, and the external to the king. He accordingly denies that the king can, either by himself or by officers deriving their authority from him, pronounce definitions of faith, administer the Word or sacraments, or absolve or excommunicate. He may, however, convene Synods, and preside in them; sanction their decisions, and give them the force of laws; he may refuse to sanction them, if contrary to the doctrines of the Catholic Church, or injurious to the state; he may receive appeals from Church courts; preserve subordination and unity in the Church; prevent, by civil pains and penalties, all secession from her communion, and found and endow new bishoprics.

This doctrine rests on the assumption, 1. That it is the design of the state, and the duty of its officers, to promote and sustain religion by civil pains and penalties; 2. That the Church is a divine institution, with a prescribed faith and discipline; and 3. That the marks of the true Church are so plain that no honest man can mistake them.

The only point in which this system differs from the papal doctrine on this subject is, that it allows the civil magistrate discretion whether he will enforce the decisions of the Church or not. This difference arises from the fact that tractarians do not pretend that provincial synods are infallible; and with such only has the king anything to do; whereas Romanists maintain that the Pope, speaking *ex cathedra*, is infallible. There is room, therefore, for discretion in reference to the decisions of the former, but none in reference to those of the latter.

Mr Palmer, however, is far from maintaining that the actual state of things corresponds with his theory, and most tractarians are loud in their complaints of the bondage under which the Church in England is now groaning.

Lutherans. In Germany the course of the Reformation was very different from what it was in England, and consequently the relation between the Church and state received a different form. The movement took its rise, and was guided in all its progress, in the former country, by Luther and his associates, and was sanctioned cordially by the people. He did not wait to be called up by the Elector to denounce the errors of popery, or to reform its abuses. He did both, and the people joined him. They besought the civil authorities to sanction these changes, and to protect and aid them in carrying them out. And the Electors slowly and cautiously granted their sanction. The Reformation here, therefore, did not proceed from the state, but really and truly from the Church, i.e. the clergy and people, and the state sanctioned and joined it. Had the bishops generally co-operated in the work, it is probable, from the frequent declarations of Luther and Melanchthon, they would in Germany, as in Sweden, have been allowed, not as a matter of right, but of expediency, to retain the executive power in their hands. But as they had not only greatly neglected all discipline in the Church, and finally sided with Rome, the Reformers called on the electors to appoint *consistories*, to be composed, as they expressed it, 'of honest and learned men', to supply the deficiency. These bodies were at first designed simply to administer discipline. They were to be Church courts, for the trial and punishment of spiritual offences. As, however, the bishops withdrew, the powers of the consistories were enlarged, and they became on the one hand the organ of the Church. As the members of these consistories are appointed by the state, and as they are the organs of administering both the internal and external affairs of the state, the prince is, in Lutheran countries, the real possessor of Church power, i.e. it is regarded as inhering in him. The whole administration of its affairs is in his hands, and whatever changes are introduced, are made by his authority. Accordingly, the union of the Lutheran and Reformed Churches and the introduction of a new liturgy was the act of the late king of Prussia. At first it was only advisory on his part, but he subsequently began to coerce compliance with his will. This extreme exercise of authority, however, met with great opposition, and was, by a large part of the Church, considered as transcending the legitimate power of the state. The present king disclaims such power, and says he wishes to know the mind of the Church, and stands ready to carry out her wishes, if consistent with his conscience.

The actual power of the state in Lutheran countries was the result of the Reformation, and not of a theory of what ought to be the relation of the Church and state. Different theories have been suggested, in order to give form and intelligibility to this relation. The most common is, that the prince is there, and, by the will of the Church, heir to the power of the bishops. His power is therefore called an episcopate. This theory includes the following points. 1. Civil and ecclesiastical government are distinct. 2. The object of Church government is mainly the preservation of the truth. 3. Church power belongs by the ordinance of God to the Church itself, and to the prince as the highest member of the Church, and since the religious peace, by the legal devolution on him of the power of the bishops. 4. This authority is, however, only external, a *potestas externa*, in the exercise of which he is bound to act according to the judgment of the clergy, and the people have the right to assent or dissent. This is the doctrine of the three orders, as it is called, that is, that Church power belongs to the Church as composed of prince, clergy, and people.

5. Hence the Prince possesses civil and ecclesiastical power in different ways and on different subjects. This is considered the orthodox, established doctrine of the Lutheran Church on the relation of the Church and state. It is the doctrine of all the older, eminent theologians of that Church. The other theories are the Territorial, i.e. Erastian; the collegiate (voluntary union) and the Hegelian – that the state is God's kingdom; the Church but a form of the state. The prince is the point of unity; having the full power of both. He appoints (not merely confirms) bishops, prescribes liturgies,

and gives the contents as well as the binding form to all Church decisions.

Reformed Church. According to the Reformed Church of Geneva, Germany, France, Holland, and Scotland, the relation of the state and Church is taught in the following propositions as given and sustained by Turretin, Lec. 28, Ques. 34.

1. Various rights belong to the Christian magistrate in reference to the Church.

This authority is confined within certain limits, and is essentially different from that of pastors. These limits are thus determined: (*a*) The magistrate cannot introduce new articles of faith, or new rites or modes of worship. (*b*) He cannot adminster the Word and sacraments. (*c*) He does not possess the power of the keys. (*d*) He cannot prescribe to pastors the form of preaching or administration of the sacraments. (*e*) He cannot decide on ecclesiastical affairs, or on controversies of faith, without consulting the pastors.

On the other hand: (*a*) He ought to establish the true religion, and when established, faithfully uphold it, and if corrupted, restore and reform it. (*b*) He should, to the utmost, protect the Church by restraining heretics and disturbers of its peace, by propagating and defending the true religion, and hindering the confession of false religions. (*c*) Provide proper ministers, and sustain them in the administration of the Word and sacraments, according to the Word of God, and found schools as well for the Church as the state. (*d*) See that ministers do their duty faithfully according to the canons of the Church and the laws of the land. (*e*) Cause that confessions of faith and ecclesiastical constitutions, agreeable to the Scriptures, be sanctioned, and when sanctioned adhered to. (*f*) To call ordinary and extraordinary synods, to moderate in them, and to sanction their decisions with his authority.

The question, 'whether the state can rightfully force its subject to profess the faith', is answered in the negative. The question, 'whether heretics should be capitally punished', is answered in the affirmative, provided their heresy is gross and dangerous to the Church and state, and provided they are contumacious and malignant in the defence and propagation of it.

The Westminster Confession, as adopted by the Church of Scotland, taught the same general doctrine. The 23rd chapter of that Confession contains the following clause: 'The civil magistrate may not assume to himself the administration of the Word and sacraments, or the power of the keys of the kingdom of heaven, yet he hath authority, and it is his duty, to take order that unity and peace be preserved in the Church, that the faith of

[115]

God be kept pure and entire, that all blasphemies and heresies be suppressed, all corruptions and abuses in worship and discipline be prevented or reformed, and all the ordinances of God duly settled, administered, and observed; for the better effecting whereof he hath power to call synods, to be present at them, and to provide that whatsoever is transacted in them be according to the mind of God'.

When this Confession was adopted by our Church in 1729, this clause was excepted, or adopted only in a qualified manner; and when our present constitution was adopted in 1789, it and the corresponding passages in the Larger Catechism were omitted. It has, however, always been part of the Confession of the Church of Scotland (and was, it is believed, retained in the Cambridge and Saybrooke Platforms as adopted in New England).

In words, this clause seems to cover all the ground taken by Mr Palmer. History shows, however, that the Church in Scotland has ever been, in a great measure, independent of the state, and for generations in conflict with it. The practical interpretation, therefore, of the doctrine here taught, has been to deny to the civil magistrate any real control in ecclesiastical affairs.

The late Dr Cunningham, in one of his tracts, occasioned by the recent controversies, thus expounds the doctrine of this passage.

1. He says, by the civil magistrate is to be understood the supreme civil power; and that the Confession merely teaches what the civil ruler will find to be his duty when he comes to the study of the Word of God.

2. That the rule of all his judgments is the Word of God.

3. That the Confession denies to the civil magistrate all right to the ministration of the Word and sacraments, or to the power of the keys, that is, to the management of the ordinary affairs of the Church of Christ; and states, that as it is the duty of every private person to judge for himself whether the doctrines, discipline, and decisions of a Church, are according to the Word of God, and if so, then to receive, obey, and promote them; so also it is the duty of the civil magistrate, in his sphere, and in the exercise of his legitimate authority and influence, to do the same.

In that branch of the Reformed Church which was transported to this country by the Puritans, and established in New England, this same doctrine as to the duty of the magistrate, and relation to the Church and state, was taught, though under a somewhat modified form. The New England theory was more of a theocracy. All civil power was confined to the members of the Church, no person being either eligible to office, or entitled to the right of suffrage, who was not in full communion of some Church. The laws of the Church became thus the laws of the land, and the two institutions were in a measure merged together. The duty of the magistrate to make and enforce laws for the support of religion, for the suppression of heresy and punishment of heretics, was clearly taught. John Cotton even wrote a book to prove that persecution was a Christian duty.

The theory on which this doctrine of the Reformed Church is founded, is, 1. That the State is a divine institution, designed for promoting the general welfare of society, and as religion is necessary to that welfare, religion falls legitimately within the sphere of the state. 2. That the magistrate, as representing the state, is, by divine appointment, the guardian of the law, to take vengeance on those who transgress, and for the praise of those who obey; and as the law consists of two tables, one relating to our duties to God, and the other to our duties to men, the magistrate is, *ex officio*, the guardian of both tables, and bound to punish the infractions of the one, as well as of the other. 3. That the Word of God determines the limits of the magistrate's office in reference to both classes of his duties; and as, under the Old Testament, there was a form of religion, with its rites and officers prescribed, which the magistrate could not change, so there is under the New. But under the Old, we find with this Church government the kings were required to do, and in fact did do much, for the support and reformation of religion, and the punishment of idolaters; so they are now bound to act on the same principles, making the pious kings of the Old Testament their model.

The American Church. The doctrine current among us on this subject is of very recent origin. It was unknown to the ancients before the advent. In no country was religion disconnected with the state. It was unknown to the Jews. The early Christians were not in circumstances to determine the duty of Christian magistrates to the Christian Church. Since the time of Constantine, in no part of Christendom, and by no denomination, has the ground been assumed, until a recent period, that the state and Church should be separate and independent bodies. Yet to this doctrine the public mind in this country has already been brought, and to the same conclusion the convictions of God's people in all parts of the world seem rapidly tending. On what grounds, then, does this novel, yet sound, doctrine rest? This question can only be answered in a very general and superficial manner on the present occasion.

1. In the first place it assumes that the state, the family, and the Church, are all divine institutions, having the same general end in view, but designed to accomplish that end by different means. That as we cannot infer from the fact the family and the state are both designed to promote the welfare of men, that the magistrate has the right to interfere in the domestic economy of the family; so neither can we infer from the Church

and state having the same general end, that the one can rightfully interfere with the affairs of the other. If there were no other institution than the family, we might infer that all the means now used by the Church and state, for the good of men, might properly be used by the family; and if there were no Church, as a separate institution of God, then we might infer that the family and the state were designed to accomplish all that could be effected. But as God has instituted the family for domestic training and government; the state, that we may lead quite and peaceable lives, and the Church for the promotion and extension of true religion, the three are to be kept distinctive within their respective spheres.

2. That the relative duties of these several institutions cannot be learned by reasoning *a priori* from their design, but must be determined from the Word of God. And when reasoning from the Word of God, we are not authorized to argue from the Old Testament economy, because that was avowedly temporary, and has been abolished; but must derive our conclusions from the New Testament. We find it there taught,

(1) That Christ did institute a Church separate from the state, giving it separate laws and officers.

(2) That he laid down the qualifications of those officers, and enjoined on the Church, not on the state, to judge of their possession by candidates.

(3) That he prescribed the terms of admission to, and the grounds of exclusion from, the Church, and left with the Church its officers to administer these rules.

These acts are utterly inconsistent with Erastianism, and with the relation established in England between the Church and state.

3. That the New Testament, when speaking of the immediate design of the state, and the official duties of the magistrate, never intimates that he has those functions which the common doctrine of the Lutheran and Reformed Church assign him. This silence, together with the fact that those functions are assigned to the Church and Church officers, is proof that it is not the will of God that they should be assumed by the state.

4. That the only means which the state can employ to accomplish many of the objects said to belong to it, viz. pains and penalties, are inconsistent with the example and commands of Christ; with the rights of private Christians, guaranteed in the Word of God (i.e., to serve God according to the dictates of his conscience) are ineffectual to the true end of religion, which is voluntary obedience to the truth, and productive of incalculable evil. The New Testament, therefore, does not teach that the magistrate is entitled to take care that true religion is established and maintained; that right men are appointed to Church offices; that those officers do their

duty; that proper persons be admitted, and improper persons be rejected from the Church; or that heretics be punished. And on the other hand, by enjoining all these duties upon the Church, as an institution distinct from the state, it teaches positively that they do not belong to the magistrate, but to the Church. If to this it be added that experience teaches that the magistrate is the most unfit person to discharge these duties; that his attempting it has always been injurious to religion, and inimical to the rights of conscience, we have reason to rejoice in the recently discovered truth, that the Church is independent of the state, and that the state best promotes her interests by letting her alone.

Episcopacy:
The Petition for the Prelates Examined

Jeremiah Burroughs (?)
[1599–1646]

THOUGH, ACCORDING TO THE ELIZABETHAN DIVINE, JOHN RAINOLDS, *'all who have laboured in reforming the church for five hundred years, have taught that all pastors, whether they are entitled bishops or priests, have equal authority and power by God's Word'*, vocal opposition to the Episcopacy of the Church of England is generally traced back to Thomas Cartwright's Cambridge lectures and the 1572 Admonition to Parliament (see pp. 81 ff.). In the 1570s the only effective obstacle to reform was the civil power. Elizabeth I regarded her own interests as indissolubly connected with those of the bishops, and the phrase: *'No bishop, no king'*, supposedly coined by her successor, James I, is in fact a true description of the Queen's own outlook.

In the next century, with the ritualistic innovations of Laud, opposition to the bishops increased, and their unpopularity was aggravated by their association with the period of personal rule by Charles I which was to lead to the Civil Wars. Writers who reflected on episcopacy were savagely punished: Alexander Leighton was whipped, branded in the face, had his ears cut off and his nose slit, and was then imprisoned in revolting conditions for publishing his Sion's Plea against the Prelacy in 1628. Ironically, it was the King's attempt to impose bishops on presbyterian Scotland that brought about his and their downfall in England. To raise money for his army he was forced to summon Parliament in 1640, after an interval of ten years, and the pent-up opposition burst forth. When the Long Parliament met in November 1640, petitions for church reform poured in, especially directed against Episcopacy. The 'Root and branch' petition from London, which bore 15,000 signatures, stated that: 'Whereas the government of Archbishops and Lord Bishops, etc., hath proved very prejudicial and dangerous both to the church and Commonwealth . . . we therefore most humbly pray and beseech this honourable Assembly, the premises considered, that the said Government, with all its dependencies, roots and branches, may be abolished . . . and the government according to God's Word may be rightly placed among us.' To counter this document, which was the basis of a Root and Branch Bill introduced into the Commons in May 1641, the Petition for the Prelates was drawn up and presented, pleading for the maintenance of the established government of the Church of England. This counter-petition from the episcopal side is here reprinted, along with a point-by-point examination of it which was printed anonymously in a pamphlet, The Petition for the Prelates Examined, *the authorship of which has been attributed to Jeremiah Burroughs (see p. 353).*

These two documents cover basically the same ground as the mass of pamphlet literature that was published on both sides during this period. Notable on the episcopal side were the two treatises by Joseph Hall, Bishop of Exeter: Episcopacy by Divine Right Asserted, *1640, and* An Humble Remonstrance to the High Court of Parliament, *1641. The famous tract* Smectymnuus, *the title of which was made up of the initials of its five authors: Stephen Marshall, Edmund Calamy, Thomas Young, Matthew Newcomen and William Spurstowe, was a reply to Hall's* Remonstrance. *The great poet John Milton also took up cudgels in sup-*

port of the Smectymnuans and against Hall, though not principally on scriptural grounds.

While the reformation of Episcopacy was viewed as a necessity by the Long Parliament there was no unanimity over the extent to which reform should be carried. Some regarded the removal of all political power from the bishops as sufficient (a step which was accomplished in 1642 when episcopal seats in the House of Lords were abolished). Others desired the reduction of diocesan episcopacy to a more primitive form in which a bishop would be only a 'first among equals' in a local presbytery. This latter view had the support of Edward Reynolds and James Ussher, Archbishop of Armagh. The main Puritan stream, however, which had growing support in the Commons, regarded as unscriptural the claim that a bishop was anything more than a preaching elder in a local congregation: the Scriptures teach that these various names belong to one office and that there is no other permanent order of ministers besides presbyters. This conviction virtually triumphed in 1643 when Parliament abolished Episcopacy and joined with Scotland in drawing up the famous Solemn League and Covenant, in which the two nations pledged to extirpate church government by Archbishops, Bishops, etc., and to seek 'the reformation of religion in the kingdoms of England and Ireland, in doctrine, worship, discipline, and government, according to the Word of God and the example of the best Reformed Churches'.

Despite all the discussion concerning Episcopacy in the 1640s no reconciliation of views was found to be possible. When after 1660 the Bishops were restored, the old differences remained, and Smectymnuus was again reprinted from the Puritan side in 1669. There were also successors of James Ussher who were seeking a via media by a compromise form of 'primitive episcopacy', for example, Richard Baxter and Robert Leighton. But with the increasingly latitudinarian attitude towards Scripture which developed in the latter part of the seventeenth century, the view which came to command increasing influence was that which was defended by Edward Stillingfleet, Bishop of Worcester, namely that Scripture does not determine the question of the form of church government and therefore the preservation of Episcopacy may be argued from considerations which lie outside the scope of Scripture. On this comparatively pacific note the whole controversy fell largely into abeyance until the Tractarian Movement of the 1830s revived it with all the old intensity. According to the Tractarian position there can be no true Church without Diocesan Bishops in lineal succession from the Apostles. Such a belief rests on an essentially Roman Catholic definition of the Church; so it is not surprising to find that those who hold it today regard Episcopacy as necessary not only for the Church of England but for all churches as a prerequisite for the reunion of Christendom. Because those who defend this outlook do not accept Scripture as the sole means of knowing God's will for the Church, they find no inconsistency in asserting that Episcopacy is to be revered because of its 'Divine origin' even though the episcopal system is not appointed in the Word of God. While this modern view is akin to the defence of Episcopacy by opponents of the Puritans, there are *still those who would take lower ground to defend a modified Episcopacy while adopting the same view of Scripture as Stillingfleet and not claiming for the system Divine (i.e. scriptural) authority.*

The present century has witnessed a widespread abandonment of any attempt to reject Episcopacy on scriptural grounds – largely because apostasy in the churches has made many indifferent to Biblical authority – nevertheless it may yet be seen that the only sure grounds upon which to controvert a system hallowed with age and buttressed by many errors is to bring it to the sure test of the Word of God.

Bibliography

At a very early stage in the English Reformation William Tyndale denied the legitimacy of episcopal church government in his *Practice of Prelates,* 1530 (reprinted in Tyndale's *Works,* Parker Society, 1849). In the later sixteenth century, Episcopacy was opposed in the English Church by the main stream of Puritans and by those Christians who withdrew from the Establishment, cf. Henry Barrow, *A Brief Discoverie of the False Church,* 1590, reprinted 1962 in *The Writings of Henry Barrow,* edit. L. H. Carlsen. In the seventeenth century a multitude of books and pamphlets appeared against Episcopacy, including David Calderwood, *The Altar of Damascus,* 1621; Paul Baynes, *The Diocesan's Tryall,* 1621; M. Poole and Seabrook, *The Divine Right of the Gospel Ministry,* 1654; David Clarkson, *No Evidence for Diocesan Churches* (as well as other works on episcopacy by the same author); shorter treatment of Episcopacy was given by others such as Lord Brooke, Vavasour Powell, Zachary Crofton and John Gailhard.

The case for a modified form of Episcopacy may be found in Archbishop Ussher's *Works;* R. Baxter, *A Treatise of Episcopacy,* 1681; and a recent historical survey of this viewpoint will be found in an article by J. C. Spalding and M. F. Brass entitled 'The Reduction of Episcopacy as a Means of Unity in England, 1640–1662', *Church History,* December 1961.

A comprehensive bibliography of orthodox Puritan, Scottish and continental works against Episcopacy will be found in *The Church of Christ,* James Bannerman, 1869, reprinted 1960, vol. 2, pp. 440–450.

References to the leading works in defence of the Anglican form of Episcopacy are given in *Old Priest and New Presbyter,* 'Episcopacy and Presbyterianism since the Reformation with especial relation to the Churches of England and Scotland', Norman Sykes, 1956. An answer to Sykes, who only seeks to preserve the *status quo* of Episcopacy on historical grounds, was written from the Anglo-Catholic (i.e. Tractarian) position by A. L. Peck, *Anglicanism and Episcopacy,* 1958. On the bearing of Episcopacy on Church Unity, various works have appeared from the Anglican position, e.g. *Episcopacy and Unity,* H. A. Wilson, 1912, and *Episcopacy and Reunion,* E. R. Fairweather and R. F. Hettlinger, 1953. The recent series of *Star Books on Reunion,* 1962, under the general editorship of the Bishop of

Bristol, shows the extent to which writers of almost all denominational backgrounds assume that Episcopacy of some kind must be the form of Church government accepted in a reunited Church. In contrast to the almost entire contemporary absence of scriptural literature against Episcopacy, a considerable quantity of Anglo-Catholic books are available, one of the most important of which is *The Gospel and the Catholic Church*, A. M. Ramsey. The latter work is important not so much as an outstanding statement of the Anglo-Catholic case, but because the errors therein defended by a man who is the Archbishop of Canterbury and a foremost ecumenical leader reveal how far true Christianity will be eclipsed if such views of Episcopacy are allowed to prevail.

Episcopacy:
The Petition for the Prelates Examined

It will seem nothing strange, that amidst so many petitions against Prelacy, from all the parts of the Kingdom, someone should set forth, and appear for it; if we consider how many Papists and Popishly affected have for many years found peace and ease under the shadow thereof; how many members of the Prelatical Hierarchy do feel their foundations shaken, and their hopes blasted; how many worldly men do fear the yoke of Christ, and shun to be brought under the obedience of the Gospel; and how many there be that are mistaken with the concept of the external pomp and glory of the Church, of the governing of the Church by the rules of human policy, and of the dangers which may ensue upon alterations. We know that even Baal had the men of the city who pleaded for him: that cursed Jericho found favour with Hiel the Bethelite, that many cried out, Great is Diana; and that the ruin of Babylon, although a matter of Hallelujah to the godly, who find in her the blood of prophets, and of saints, is bewailed and lamented by the merchants of the earth, and such as have lived deliciously with her. The Prelacy was of late grown to such greatness in this kingdom, that it were a wonder, if it should not find some to uphold it; and yet to such insolence, that it were a wonder, if at this opportunity, it should not fall. We do for our parts find ourselves bound, both to warn, and call upon all men to be wise, and to observe the wonderful work of God, lest haply they be found fighting against God; and also to remove stumbling blocks out of the way, that the weak be not hindered or discouraged in praying and petitioning for Reformation, which is all that is aimed at, in these following pages.

THE PRELATICAL PETITION
To The
Knights, Citizens, etc.
The Humble Petition of, etc.
Humbly showeth

That whereas there has of late a petition subscribed by many (who pretend to be inhabitants of this city) been delivered, received, and read in this Honourable House, against the ancient, present, and by Law established Government of the Church, and that not so much for the Reformation of Bishops, as for the utter subversion and extirpation of episcopacy itself. We whose names are underwritten to show there be many, and those of the better sort of the inhabitants of this city, otherwise and better minded, do humbly represent unto this Honourable House these following considerations:

1. That Episcopacy is as ancient as Christianity itself in this Kingdom.

2. That Bishops were the chief instruments in the Reformation of the Church against Popery, and afterwards the most eminent Martyrs for the Protestant religion, and since, the best and able champions for the defence of it.

3. That since the Reformation, the times have been very peaceable, happy, and glorious, notwithstanding Episcopal government of the Church, and therefore that this government can be no cause of our unhappiness.

4. We conceive that not only many learned, but diverse other godly persons would be much scandalized and troubled in conscience, if the government of Episcopacy, conceived by them to be an Apostolical institution, were altered, and since there is so much care taken, that no man should be offended in the least ceremony, we hope there will be some, that such men's consciences may not be pressed upon, in a matter of an higher nature and consequence, especially considering that this government by Episcopacy is not only lawful and convenient for edification, but likewise suitable and agreeable to the Civil policy and Government of this State.

5. That this Government is lawful, it appears by the immediate, universal and constant practice of all the Christian world grounded upon Scripture, from the Apostles' time to this last Age; for above 1,500 years together. It being utterly incredible, if not impossible, that the whole Church for so long a time, should not discover by God's Word this government to be unlawful, if it had been so: To which may be added, that the most learned Protestants, even in those very Churches which now are not governed by Bishops, do not only hold the government by Episcopacy to be lawful, but wish that they themselves might enjoy it.

Again, that the Government by Episcopacy is not only lawful, but convenient for edification, or as much, or more conducive to piety and devotion than any other, it appears because no modest man denies that the primitive times were most famous for piety, constancy, and perseverance in the faith, notwithstanding more frequent and more cruel persecutions, than ever have been since, and yet it is confessed, that the Church in those times was governed by Bishops.

Lastly: That the Government of the Church by Episcopacy is most suitable to the frame and form of the Civil government here in this Kingdom, it appears by the happy and flourishing union of them both, for so long a time together, whereas no man can give us an assurance how any Church government besides this (whereof we have had so long experience) will suit and agree with the Civil policy of this State: And we conceive it may be of dangerous consequence for men of settled fortunes to hazard their estates, by making so great an alteration, and venturing upon a new form of Government, whereof neither we, nor our ancestors have had any trial, or experience; especially considering that those, who would have Episcopacy to be abolished, have not yet agreed, nor (as we are verily persuaded) ever will or can agree upon any other common form of government to succeed in the room of it, as appears by the many different and contrary drafts, and platforms they have made and published, according to the several humours and sects of those that made them, whereas, seeing every great alteration in a Church or State must needs be dangerous, it is just and reasonable that whosoever would introduce a new form instead of an old one, should be obliged to demonstrate and make it evidently appear aforehand: that the Government he would introduce is proportionably so much better, than that he would abolish, as may recompense the loss we may sustain, and may be worthy of the hazard we must run, in abolishing the one, and in introducing and settling of the other. But this we are confident can never be done, in regard of this particular.

And therefore our humble and earnest request to the Honourable House is, that as well in this consideration, as all the other aforesaid, we may still enjoy that Government, which most probably holds its institution from the Apostles and most certainly its plantation with our Christian faith itself in this Kingdom, where it has ever since flourished and continued for many ages without interruption or alteration, whereby it plainly appears, that as it is the most excellent government in itself: so it is the most suitable, most agreeable, and every way most proportionable to the Civil constitutions and temper of this State: and therefore we pray and hope will always be continued, and preserved in it and by it, notwithstanding the abuses and corruptions which in so long tract of time through the errors or negligence of men have crept into it, which abuses and corruptions being all of them (what and how many soever they may be) but merely accidental to Episcopacy. We conceive and hope, there may be a Reformation of the one, without destruction of the other, which is the humble Suit of, etc.

THE PETITION FOR THE PRELATES BRIEFLY EXAMINED

We whose names are underwritten, to show there be many and those of the better sort of the inhabitants of this city, otherwise and better minded, do humbly represent unto this Honourable House, these considerations.

How much better these Petitioners are than the former, let not their own judgments, but their work determine. We will not examine their minds, what they think, but their considerations, what they publish, which are:

1. *That Episcopacy is as ancient as Christianity itself in this Kingdom.*

This is a consideration to gain time by; how far about must we go to search all antiquity, before the strength of this consideration can come to

[129]

an issue. The most speedy and best way of determining, is to go to that which is most ancient, the certain infallible rule.

History tells us, that Christianity came into England by Simon Zelotes, and Joseph of Arimathaea[1], who lived in the times of penning that Scripture which must be the rule of our Church government; put us not off therefore with the rust of your antiquity, but give us the gold of divine truth.

If wheresoever mention is made of Bishops in the History of Antiquity, you bring it to prove the lawfulness of your Bishops in controversy, you abuse the reader; for we say that Bishops indeed are ancient, but such Bishops as the Scriptures speak of, namely, Presbyters in several congregations. St Patrick in his time had founded in Ireland three hundred and sixty five churches, and ordained so many Bishops. Eusebius tells us of one Soticus, Bishop of the Village of Comanbind; Theodoret of Mares, Bishop of a small town called Solicha; Jerome of Asclepias, Bishop of a small town in Africa. What antiquity relates concerning the government of churches within themselves, and how smaller churches in villages came to be under the power of Pastors of greater churches in cities, is very observable. Thus we find it written. The policy of the churches was like that of members in one body, where all suffer together, and are helpful each to other : hence we have so many epistles to Churches and Teachers written to others, which came neither from subjection or authority, but from love and desire of edifying; but because the light of the Gospel, set up in the same one city, by little and little did enlighten the lesser towns adjacent, therefore those churches did acknowledge and reverence that city, from whence the light of the Gospel sprung to them, as their Mother; and did consult with the Officers thereof in controversies and things pertaining to the Church; and if any thing were not well done, they did admonish and freely rebuke one another, and friendly subject each to other. Those that excelled in gifts lorded it not over others, but ministered unto them; but those churches where the Apostles and other eminent men taught, were of great esteem and honoured accordingly. But this custom afterwards grew to a law, as appears by the Nicene Council, where some churches, with their Bishops, are made subject by law, and compelled to obey some other one church and her Bishop. And in this age, namely, the second century, the story saith, it cannot be showed by the testimony of any approved author, that of so many churches as were planted by the

---

[1] This was a generally accepted belief of the period, being held by such Elizabethan Protestant historians as Matthew Parker. There is no historical evidence, however, for the tradition although Christianity may have been introduced into England as early as the apostolic age.—Ed.

Apostles, any one did arrogate superiority over others, by divine or Apostolical authority, neither did other churches acknowledge, or honour any one of them as superior, whose Bishop should have power to appoint Ceremonies or make Decrees, to which all should be bound.

The Constitution of Diocesan Bishops in England was first in imitation of the Heathens, who had their Arch-Flamins, and Flamins, instead whereof that the Christians might gain them to their Religion, the seat of the Arch-Flamins of London, York, and Chester were changed into the sees of three Archbishops, and of the Flamins into the sees of Bishops; and one Devotus, Bishop of Winchester, had all the possessions of the pagan Flamins, even twelve miles compass round about the city conferred upon him and his Clergy, in which were contained thirty-two villages.

The Christian world knew no Diocese made up of many Parishes, till the year 267, as Polydore Vergil testifies, therefore Diocesan Bishops cannot be so ancient as Christianity in England.

Suppose Bishops were so ancient, as you pretend, yet they may be Antichristian, because the Scripture tells us, that Antichrist began to work in the Apostles' time.

2. *That Bishops were the chief instruments in the reformation of the Church against Popery.*

That some good men should not see the evil of Episcopacy in the darkness of Popery, it is no marvel.

If their places were therefore good, because the men were instruments of reformation, then now their places are naught, because they are inlets and instruments of so much corrupting innovation.

Most of the Bishops then were the chief hinderers of the reformation, witness Martin Bucer in a speech of his to King Edward, Your Majesty (saith he) doth see, that this restoring again the kingdom of Christ, which we require, yea, which the salvation of us all requireth, may in no wise be expected to come of the Bishops, seeing there be so few among them which do understand the power and proper offices of this kingdom, and very many of them by all means (which possibly they can and dare) either oppose themselves against it, or defer and hinder it.

Had not King Edward, though young, set his heart for reformation more than the best of the Bishops, it had never proceeded so far as it did. When Cranmer and Ridley pressed him to permit his sister the Lady Mary to have Mass in her house, the King having heard what they could say, replied out of the Scriptures so fully, that they were enforced to give place to his replication, and grant the same to be true. Then they after long debating with his Majesty in this manner, laboured politically in another sort, and alleged what dangers the denying thereof might bring to his Grace, what breach of amity on the Emperor's part, what troubles, what unkindnesses, and what occasions sundry ways it would enforce, unto whom the King answered, willing them to content themselves, for he would, he said, spend his life, and all he had, rather than to agree and grant to that he knew to be against the truth. The which when the Bishops heard, notwithstanding they urged him still to grant, and would by no means have his nay. Then the good King seeing their importunate suit, in the end his tender heart bursting out into bitter weeping and sobbing, he desired them to be content; whereat the Bishops wept as fast as he, and acknowledged the good King had more divinity in his little finger, than they had in all their bodies.

3. Bishops were most eminent Martyrs.

Of many Bishops there were some few Martyrs, but what Bishops were they? Latimer, upon the coming forth of the six Articles in King Henry VIII's time, did freely and of his own accord, resign his Bishopric, and when he put off his Rochet, suddenly he skipped for joy, feeling his shoulders so light, being discharged (as he said) of so heavy a burden, and gloried in the title of a *Quondam*.[1] Hooper was another and he made supplication to the King, desiring his Highness either to discharge him of the Bishopric, or else to dispense with him of such ceremonial orders as were required of him. Also concerning Ceremonies, he saith thus; Behold how fearful a thing it is, though the intent be never so good, even to adorn and beautify the Institutions, Decrees, and Ordinances of God, with any device of man, without the appointment of God in his Word; yea, it is no less abominable in the sight of God, than if a man should accuse him of ignorance and foolishness. Speaking of the Supper of the Lord, he saith, The outward preparation the more simple it is, the better it is, and the nearer the Institution of Christ and his Apostles. If you have bread, wine, a table, and a fair tablecloth, be not solicitous and careful for the rest, seeing they are things brought in, not by Christ, but by Popes. He also speaketh expressly against kneeling at the Lord's Supper, the Surplice, with all the monuments, tokens, and leavings of Papistry, and that excommunication should not be done by the Bishop alone, but by the Bishop and all the Parish.

[1] One of whom a certain description had formerly been true, in Latimer's case that of a bishop.—Ed.

[132]

Ridley also, when they put on his Episcopal robes for his degradation, he vehemently inveighed against that apparel, calling it foolish and abominable, yea too fond for a vice in a play.

Bishop Ferrar was another Martyr, and he was so strongly set against their superstitious ceremonies, that they made an Article against him for refusing to wear a square cap.

What Bishops have you more that were Martyrs, except Cranmer? and you see what manner of men these were, and by that little taste of their non-conformity, you may judge they would have been as forward to the work of reformation as any other, had they lived in these times.

If some Bishops, being Martyrs, argues the goodness of their place, then other Bishops being persecutors of the Martyrs, as Bonner and Gardiner, argues the evil of their places.

If you account so highly of the testimony of Martyrs, hear what that famous Martyr the Lord Cobham in Henry V's time says, that the Pope is the great head of Antichrist, the Priests and Prelates and Monks the body, and Friars the tail.

4. *And since were the best champions for the defence of it.*

The most famous champions we have had in England for the truth, have been such as have either been fully against Bishops, or that have held Presbyters and Bishops to be all one.

Doctor Barnes was condemned for saying thus, I will never believe, nor can ever believe, that one may by the law of God be Bishop of two or three cities, yea of a whole country, for that is contrary to the doctrine of St Paul, who writing unto Titus, commandeth that he should ordain a Bishop in every town.

Master Tyndale in his book of *The Obedience of a Christian Man*, page 114, says, As thou canst heal no disease, except thou begin at the root, so canst thou preach against no mischief, except thou begin at the Bishops.[1] Moreover, in his defence of the English translation, he saith: These overseers, which now we call Bishops, after the Greek word, were always abiding in one place, to govern the congregation there.

Doctor Reynolds, as great a champion for the truth as any of the Prelates, in his letter to Sir Francis Knollys, requiring his resolution, whether the authority Bishops have amongst us be God's own ordinance, answereth negatively, and proveth at large by writers old and new, that the now Archbishop Doctor Bancroft was in an error for preaching otherwise.

---

[1] Tyndale, *Doctrinal Treatises* (Parker Society, 1848), p. 186—Ed.

Doctor Fulke against the Rhemists upon Titus 1: 5 affirmeth, that albeit for order and seemly government, there was always one principal, to whom by long use of the Church the name Bishop was applied, yet in the Scripture a Bishop and an Elder is of one order and authority.

Doctor Whitaker, in his Answer to Campion's ten reasons, says, that *jure divino*, a Presbyter and Bishop are both one, and if Arius were an heretic for saying so, Jerome certainly was akin to the same heretic.

We might produce many others, as Doctor Humphry Holland, Deacon, Bale, Fox, Bradford, and others, which of necessity we forbear, to prevent tediousness. Only one who himself was a Bishop, and one of the chief champions against Papists, yet acknowledged Episcopacy not to be by divine right; for citing a place out of Austin, affirming that the office of a Bishop is above the office of a Priest, after the names of honour which the custom of the Church hath now attained, he adds himself, but not by authority of the Scripture; where also he consents to that of Jerome, Let Bishops understand that they are above Priests, rather of custom, than of any truth or right of Christ's Institution; and this he doth in opposition to Harding, pleading superiority of Bishops.[1]

5. *Since the Reformation the times have been very peaceable, happy, and glorious, notwithstanding Episcopal Government.*

To whom have the times been so? Indeed Bishops and their Creatures have lived in pomp, but how many hundreds of faithful laborious Ministers have been cast out from all their means of livelihood, themselves and their families put to lamentable extremities? How many have been imprisoned and brought to untimely ends there? How many have been driven out of their dear country? What reproaches and contempt hath been cast upon those that remain? no reformed Church in all the world can show such lamentable miseries, that their Ministers and people have been put unto for their consciences, and that in things of as low a nature, as in England can be showed.

For that prosperity we have had, no thanks to Bishops; for the lower Bishops were, as in Queen Elizabeth's time, the greater was our prosperity: But since the Bishops grew to that height (they were lately in) our prosperity hath been as much lessened, witness the lamentable complaints and outcries of the whole Kingdom against the miseries caused by them. If the lower they were, the more prosperous we were, then if they were not at all, we may very well expect more prosperity than ever.

This argument of prosperity is the same that Heathens brought against Christians. One Symmachus against whom Prudentius wrote in an Epistle

[1] The author referred to is John Jewel, Bishop of Salisbury.

to Theodosius the Emperor, used this argument to persuade continuance in the old religion of the Romans, because their Commonwealth had been most fully flourishing all the time they worshipped Jupiter, Apollo, and their other Gods. So likewise the Heathen persecutors of Christians used to say, when any evil befell them: Now are we not so fortunate as we were wont to be, because we suffer the Christians, and because we worship not our Gods with that zeal as formerly.

6. *We conceive that many learned and godly persons would be much scandalized and troubled in conscience, if the government by Episcopacy were altered.*

We confess in things indifferent, that governors in commanding and all men in practising ought to be very careful in giving offence, the Scripture lays down rules for ordering us in things indifferent, which bind governors as well as others. The Apostles had as much authority in the Church as ever any since, and yet they durst not enjoin a thing indifferent, which was offensive, but counted it necessary to abstain from that which was offensive, though in its own nature indifferent as in the matter of eating blood, Acts 15. But in such things wherein we are not at all left to our liberty, the rules of offence take no place; if any will be offended for doing our duty, we must not therefore forbear.

The keeping in of Bishops in these times wherein God so clearly opposes them will be the greatest offence that ever was given to the people of England and other reformed Churches, and a special hardening of our adversaries, even the Papists themselves, who do extremely contend for Episcopacy to be *jure divino,* witness that book of Franciscus a Sancta Clara, called *Apologia pro Episcopis;* and that Canon of the Council of Trent: If any man shall say, that Bishops are not above Presbyters, let him be Anathema. And that you may see what a dangerous offence it is, consider what mischievous inferences they make from thence; as that the Ministers of all reformed churches (where Episcopacy is not) are no true Ministers, and their ministry to be altogether invalid, and their churches to be no true churches; witness that of Jansenius, cited by Voetius: The Bishop only may call and ordain Elders, and whosoever in case of necessity shall be ordained by the Church and Presbyters, he is no Presbyter, and his whole ministry is invalid. Also that of the Papists, cited by Gerardus, who saith thus: The Papist laying this foundation, that Bishops are above Presbyters *jure divino,* do infer, that Luther had no power of ordaining ministers, because he was no Bishop, but only a Presbyter, and by consequence, that there are no true ministers in our churches. And no marvel, if Papists say so abroad, when our late Archprelate in open Court at home called Reverend Master Calvin rascal, and said of those Protestant churches, that they were no churches, because they had no Bishops; now what a scandal this is, let the world judge.

7. *That Episcopacy is not only lawful, but convenient for edification.*

What edification have we by Bishops, unless edification of Altars, Images, and Popery? but for edification of souls by the Word, who are greater enemies thereunto than Bishops? Preaching twice a day is sufficient to put a conformable minister into their black book, yea, to suspend him from his ministry. In catechizing they forbid any further exposition than the giving the bare grammatical sense of their form. And for prayer, wherein the Apostle makes it a chief work of the ministers of the Gospel, to give themselves to prayer as well as the ministry of the Word, they will suffer no other than reading in a book and saying over the fifty-fifth Canon.

In other reformed churches, where are no Bishops, in every congregation there is a preaching minister, but for England, where is now a settled maintenance for the ministry, and as many able men as in any other place; yet there are divers thousands of congregations without a preaching ministry, and for one sermon they preach themselves, they hinder many hundreds. It is little good that Prelates do in this kind. More of God and his Kingdom hath appeared in some one congregation, where a minister hath been whom they have silenced or deprived, than in all the Bishops' families in England; could any godly minister endure such a Parish as Lambeth is, if he had such power to reform as the Archprelate had?

When the Parliament hath examined what men the Prelates have put into places, it will appear what edification people have had by their means; what places have been more miserably provided for in all the Kingdom, than those that Prelates and Cathedrals have had the disposing of? Neither hath this been through some particular personal corruptions, but the whole Kingdom can witness how generally this hath been ever since the reformation; and if this be your edification, we beseech the Lord in mercy to deliver us from it.

8. *Episcopacy is suitable and agreeable to the civil policy and government of this State.*

What is by divine institution is agreeable to all States, and what is against it cannot be agreeable to any Christian government.

We see by our neighbours how agreeable it hath been to civil government; hath it not endangered to bring all things into confusion amongst them?

We ourselves have had full experience how the Prelates and that faction have stopped the course of Law, and lifted up themselves above it. Priests in parishes above the Magistrates there, and Bishops above the Nobles. The government of our Kingdom is by Parliamentary and Common Law, but they seek to rule against either, as appears by their Commission, which they have got for the High Commission. In the copy whereof these are their words: That you our said Commissioners, and every of you, shall diligently and faithfully execute this our Commission, and every part and branch thereof in manner and form aforesaid, and according to the true meaning thereof, notwithstanding any appellation, provocation, privilege or exemption in that behalf to be had, made, pretended or alleged by any person or persons, resident or dwelling in any place or places, exempt or not exempt within these our Realms of England, and Ireland, and the Dominion of Wales, any our Laws, Statutes, Proclamations, or other Grants, Privilege, or Ordinances which be or may seem contrary to the premisses notwithstanding.

King Philip the husband of Queen Mary thought it so inconsistent with Civil government by the Nobility, that upon his death-bed, calling his son unto him, he gave him this counsel: If you intend to rule by your Nobles, keep your Bishops low, and if you would rule by your Bishops, keep your Nobles low. What disturbance in Civil States this power of Prelates with Kings hath made, our English records do sufficiently testify, which no true English spirit can read or relate without a saddened spirit. Matthew Paris in his History tells us of the great power that Peter, Bishop of Winchester, and Peter Rivall, the Bishop's cousin, with other adherents, had with King Henry III. Great complaints were made, that by their counsel the King's heart was turned from the love of his subjects, and the hearts of them from him, and discord was sown amongst them; and that by the said counsel of the foresaid Bishop and his fellows, King John, the King's father, lost first the hearts of his Barons, after that lost Normandy, and after that other lands also, and in the end wasted all his treasure, and the Kingdom for a long time after had no quiet. By the said counsel also, England that was the Prince of Provinces, became a tributary. Moreover, through their wicked counsel, saith the story, at this present, great perturbation seemed to hang over the Realm; for if it had not been for their counsel, and if that true justice and judgment might have been administered unto the King's subjects, these tumults had never been stirred, and the King might have had his land unwasted, and his treasure unconsumed. The said Bishop impiously tells the Nobles, that the King right well might call unto him what foreigners and strangers he listed by whom he might be able to bridle his proud and rebellious subjects, and so to keep them in awe and good order: Whereupon the Nobles in great perturbation departed, promising amongst themselves in this case (which touched the state of the whole Realm) they would constantly join together, even unto death.

The great divisions in the Commonwealth presently after Constantine's times, were made by the Bishops; which the historians of those times do plentifully testify.

This is not our judgment alone; hear what Master Tyndale saith in his book of Christian obedience: Woe unto the Realms where Bishops are of the King's Counsel: as profitable are they verily unto the Realms with their counsels, as wolves unto the sheep, or the foxes unto the geese.

In France the Reformed churches not under Bishops are as good and faithful subjects unto their Prince, and so acknowledged by himself, though of another religion, as any he hath. Hence it appears, that that government which is not Prelatical, may stand with the peace and civil order of a State as well as it.

9. *That this government is lawful, appears by the immediate and constant practice of all the Christian world, grounded upon Scripture from the Apostles' time to this last age, for above fifteen hundred years together.*

To that which they say, it is grounded upon Scripture, we shall speak afterwards, but to say that this was the practice of all the Christian world for fifteen hundred years, is a bold assertion. We find in history that the Church of Scotland was not governed by Bishops till between four or five hundred years after Christ, although it had flourished in the Christian religion two or three hundred years before.

We answer as before, it is true indeed, that in all times for fifteen hundred years there were Bishops, but in this time of the Apostles and presently after, Bishops were much different from that they are now; as

1. Then they were Parochial not Diocesan.
2. Even in those times when Episcopacy began to grow to some height, yet the election of Bishops was by the whole Church, but it is not so now.
3. There was not that superiority of them over other ministers as there is now.
4. They challenged not the power of ordination and Church censures to themselves, as now they do.

These four we undertake now to show you briefly, because ere long you shall have them discussed more largely upon another occasion.

For the first—Bishops were Parochial not Diocesan; for these were

[138]

Bishops of villages and small towns, as Sozomen in his seventh book testifies; and according to Eusebius, churches wherein were Bishops, were called Parishes.

Ignatius saith, Every church should have her Communion Table, and every church her Bishop.

And Cyprian saith, The bounds of a church were not greater than a Bishop might call together the whole multitude about the affairs of it.

For the second—These Bishops were chosen by the whole church. Ambrose saith, That is truly and certainly a divine election of a Bishop which is made by the whole church.

Platina tells us, that Ludovicus the Second commanded by his letters, that the Romans should choose their own Bishop, not looking for strangers to meddle in it, for it belonged to the Citizens.

Ambrose complains to Nepotianus of the great disorder in the clergy, that they run to Bishops Suffragans, certain times of the year, and bringing some sum of money, they are ordained being chosen of none; And the Bishop without any lawful election is chosen in private of the Canons or Prebendaries only, without the knowledge of the people.

For the third—They had not superiority over other ministers, as they have now.

The Helvetian Confession, 5. 12, hath these words, Equal power is given to all ministers of the Church: from the beginning no one preferred himself before another, saving only for order, someone did call them together, propounded the matters that were to be consulted of, and gathered the voices.

The honour of a Bishop being taken from the rest of the ministers, and given to one, was the first step to Papacy.

Power of ordination belonged likewise to Presbyters, for besides the evidence of Scripture, the third Canon of the Council of Carthage says: The Bishop giving the blessing, let all the Elders there present lay on their hands.

That they had not the power of Church censures to themselves Cyprian saith, that the Presbyters and other Church Officers have as well power to absolve, as the Bishop. And in another place, For as much as absolution belongs unto all, I alone dare not do it.

And Augustine, It helpeth much to make the party more ashamed, that he be excommunicated by the whole church.

Jerome, The Elders have interest in other censures of the church, and the church itself in excommunication.

Now if there be such difference between our Bishops and the former, why do you again bring their antiquity? Your repetition leads us in our answer to come again to the same thing; may not all see how egregiously you seek to deceive the reader with great words, in pretending that Diocesan Bishops were of so long standing, because Bishops were. We see by this deceit, how dangerous it is to take words that are common to many things, and appropriate them to a particular; if it once gain the appropriation of a name or title, it will soon challenge the thing itself, and the keeping up the name after it hath been afore no marvel though men contend so much for keeping the name of Bishops. We find in the notes of the Rhemists upon that place, 1 Tim. 6. v. 20, that they contend much for the keeping their old terms, Let us keep our forefathers' words (say they) and we shall easily keep our old faith; let them say amendment, let us say penance, let them say the Lord's Supper, let us say the Mass, let them say the Communion Table, let us say the Altar, let them say Elders, Ministers, let us say Priest, let them say Superintendent, let us say Bishop, etc. They and we all have experience what power words and names have; the spirit of these Rhemists hath been lately in many of our men, they began to alter the former language, but told you at first they meant no hurt by the words and names they put upon things, and now in this controversy about Episcopacy, their chief prevailing argument is the very word Bishop, which we acknowledge to be a Scripture word, but applied so as they do, to a certain kind of superior officer in the ministry of their own devising, when God gives it to all ministers of the Gospel; this we say hath much evil in it, and the retaining of it, in this sense, is very dangerous.

10. *The most learned Protestants in those Churches which now are not governed by Bishops, do not only hold the government to be lawful, but wish that they themselves may enjoy it.*

This is boldly said, but we know quite the contrary to be true, both by their writings and by those that have lived amongst them. Gerard, in whom we may see the mind of the reformed churches as much as in any, saith: We do not acknowledge any inequality of jurisdiction that Bishops have over Presbyters *jure divino*, seeing the contrary may be gathered out of Scripture, as from Acts 20. 17, 18, and divers other places by him cited. He also brings the testimony of Jerome, Ambrose, Austin, Sedulius, Primasius, Chrysostom, Theodoret, Oecumenius, and Theophylact, and answers the contrary arguments of Bellarmine. Chamierus also, who fully knew the mind of the reformed churches, saith thus: That in the first beginning of the churches, there were no such Bishops as were afterwards instituted, to wit, such as *suo jure* were over the clergy, such saith he, were not instituted by Christ and his Apostles, and because that is best which is first, it were better for the churches, if they were all esteemed to be of equal right and degree; and when that distinct order of the Bishops from the Presbyters was first brought in, the Bishops were not the Monarchs of the Church, nor had power over the clergy, but only some of the chief were chosen to go before others in deliberation and composing of matters. And lest you should think the judgment of the Divines of the Reformed Churches to be altered, take what Voetius, Professor of Utrecht, hath formerly written, and of late said. What he hath written, you may read in his learned Tractate *De desperata causa Papatus*; where amongst much against Episcopacy, he hath these passages: We have more than abundantly proved, that pretended Episcopacy is not *jure divino*. Again, either we are not heretics in this point, or the Fathers and Doctors are heretics with us. And that you might flatter yourselves in conceiting that the reformed churches wish for your government, he saith, We who have not that order of Bishops, stand not in need of them from the English. And for his speech, when Bishop Hall's book in defence of Episcopacy came forth, he said, What will this poor fellow do? He hath of late read many lectures against the superiority and jurisdiction of the Bishops.

11. *Again, the government of Episcopacy, etc.*

Here you repeat the argument of Antiquity again, and cry up your great Diana, but concerning the Episcopacy of the Primitive times, we have said enough before. The bringing this over again, with so fair a gloss, is but to deceive the world.

12. *That the government of the Church by Episcopacy is most suitable to the frame of the Civil government in this Kingdom, appears by the happy and flourishing union of them both for so long a time together.*

Considering what persecutions and distractions there have been in both Kingdoms, by means of them, neither we nor the other Kingdom have cause to boast much of flourishing happiness.

What good hath been by the union of the Kingdoms, cannot be attributed to the Prelates; but what evil hath come by the disunion, hath been apparently by them.

13. *No man can give us assurance, how any Church government besides this will suit well the civil policy of this State.*

Whatsoever we desire in this kind, is no other than according to the Word, and we and you may assure ourselves, that so long as we walk according to that rule, peace shall be upon us, and upon the Israel of God.

This is an argument Pagans have used against the Christians: We have worshipped our Gods all this while, and if we bring in any new way of worship, we know not what the issue will be.

We are already sure that Episcopal government hath been a woeful trouble and disturbance to ours and other States, as hath been showed before.

14. *We conceive it may be of dangerous consequence, for men of settled fortunes to hazard their estates, etc.*

This seems to be a threatening clause, as if some mischievous thing were intended by the Episcopal party, suitable to the expression of one who labouring to promote the petition, urged it with this argument, that there would be no living for men in England, unless they would subscribe to it.

15. *Those who would have Episcopacy abolished, have not yet agreed, nor as we are persuaded ever can or will agree upon any other common form of government.*

If Episcopacy were gone, the agreement would be easy, as we see in Scotland; while Episcopacy was amongst them, there was no small disagreement, but since the removal thereof, they are of one heart and mind.

There is no government in any Reformed Church, from which there are so many rents, under which there are so many divisions, as the government of Episcopacy which we have in England.

Many men are afraid to discover themselves freely, for fear if Episcopacy hold, it will be hereafter revenged upon them, having had so much experience of the cruelty of men in that place, whereas if it were down, they would be more free to show their opinions, and to close with their brethren in the truth.

Reformed Churches in all places do agree, and why should not we think there would be agreement amongst us, if Episcopacy were removed?

They who seem most to differ, yet they differ not one from another so much, as they all differ from Episcopacy. They profess one to another, that they can walk as brethren together in enjoying communion one with another in peace and love.

You seem to rejoice in the supposal of dissensions between others, thinking thereby to gain time, but that you may see there is not so vast a difference amongst us as you think, in these things we are all agreed.

Church discipline is to be learned from the plain and perfect Word of

God, and in such particulars as are common to the Church with other Societies, is to be directed by the light of nature, the Church observing always the general rules of the Word.

A particular Church consisteth of such as in the use of the ordinances of Christ do join together in one body and society, to walk in all the ways of Christ neither are there any other members of a particular Church, but such as in profession are believers and saints.

The Church may have no office nor office-bearers, but such as are by divine appointment, which are Elders or Deacons, or more particularly, Pastors, Teachers, Elders, and Deacons, by which Christ hath provided for all the necessities of the Church.

Although the civil and ecclesiastical government be different kinds of governments, yet it is a principal part of the civil Magistrate, who is keeper of both Tables, to have a care of the Church, and to exercise his authority for the preserving of religion, and for the peace and safety of the Church, and where the Magistrate does his duty, it is a special blessing of God, and he is to be obeyed in all things lawful.

Each particular Church hath her own power and authority, and the use and benefit of all the Ordinances of Christ, neither is there anything to be done without the express or tacit consent of the congregation, in matters which are proper and peculiar to a particular Church, whether in election or ordination of ministers, or in admitting or excommunicating of members.

It is in many respects expedient both for the members of each church, whether ministers or people, and for the right governing and well-being of the particular churches in a nation professing the Christian religion, that besides their particular assemblies and Elderships, they convene by their Commissioners, Ministers, and Elders in greater Assemblies, that matters that concern all the churches within their bounds respective, may with common advice and consent be agreed upon for their good and edification.

16. *It is just and reasonable, that whosoever would introduce a new form, should be obliged to demonstrate aforehand, that the government he would introduce be better than the other, and able to recompense the loss thereof.*

There can be no loss of an evil, and therefore you need not call for a recompense either before or after, seeing Prelacy is an evil, as we have proved and shall prove, it is neither to be recompensed, nor moderated, nor reserved, but presently and wholly to be taken away, whatever the consequence may be. The presence of an error hinders men from seeing the truth; if the government be for the present hurtful, and the exercise

[143]

mischievous to others, we need not, we ought not to spare it till we know what shall come in the room.

And further we all see a platform before us amongst our brethren in the reformed churches, which we conceive would give satisfaction in the main, being according to the former six Propositions, and what alteration is to be made in such things wherein one reformed church differs from another, the same may be effected with more peace than the Episcopacy can be continued.

17. *We may still enjoy that government which most probably holds its institution from the Apostles.*

We are glad you suspect your cause so far, having no other than a sandy foundation of probability; what an evil is it that so many thousands have suffered such sore things, in souls and bodies, in estates, liberties, and names, for mere probabilities! We bless God we have more to say for our cause against Episcopacy than probables, and our reasons from Scripture are these.

The whole charge of all the affairs of the Church of Ephesus was left to the Elders, Acts 20, where Saint Paul tells them, that the Holy Ghost had made them overseers over that flock which they were ποιμàινειν and the word signifies in the judgment of all, both to feed and to rule.

Whatsoever you make to belong to Episcopacy, as Episcopacy, is either matter of jurisdiction, or ordination. Jurisdiction doth not belong to the Bishop; for our Saviour Christ saith, Go tell the Church, which to interpret of one man, is against that place, because he saith, Whatsoever ye bind, against the course of Scripture, because one man is never called a Church, and against common sense, because the word Church, there signifies an assembly. And for Ordination, the Apostle saith unto Timothy, The gift that is in thee, which was given thee by prophecy, with the laying on of the hands of the Presbytery, 1 Tim. 4: 14, therefore Ordination also belongs unto the Elders.

We find no rules, nor instructions in Scripture for the ordering of Bishops, as distinguished from Elders, Pastors, and Teachers, and therefore we cannot believe that there is any such distinct office: *Judicent nobis loca*, as Voetius speaks, let them show us those places of Scripture, where is that peculiar ministry, and where are those special instructions which belong to the Bishops alone, and not unto other Pastors?

We find in the judgment of the Holy Ghost, that a Bishop and an Elder are all one, as appears in Acts 20, by comparing the seventeenth verse with the twenty-eighth; those that are called Elders in the seventeenth, are called Bishops in the twenty-eighth; which the English translates 'overseers', and only here. So Titus 1: 5 compared with verse 7 where those who are said to be Elders in the fifth verse, are each of them called a Bishop in the seventh; otherwise there should be no force in the particle, 'for'. This is the arguing of the Apostle, Ordain Elders, verse 5, if any be blameless, verse 6, for a Bishop must be blameless, verse 7.

One Bishop now has jurisdiction over diverse counties and hundreds of churches, but in the Apostle's times, there were diverse Bishops in every city, Titus 1: 5: Elders in every city; who (as we have proved before) are the same with Bishops, Phil. 1: 1, Bishops and Deacons at Philippi; it is certain in these places they were not all Christians, it is most likely, very few of them, and yet those few had divers Bishops set over them; other kind of Bishops than these the Scripture knows not. Yet in these times the Elders had extraordinary gifts, as appears James 5, where the Apostle sets down a rule for all churches in those times, that when any was sick, the Elders should anoint him with oil, and so he should recover; if the Elders had then miraculous gifts, and yet there were divers appointed for every city, then it cannot be conceived, that now when Elders have no such extraordinary gifts, yet that one should be set over many counties, it may be thousands of congregations.

The Scripture acknowledgeth no superiority or inferiority between officers of the same kind. One Apostle was not over another, nor one Evangelist over another, nor one Prophet over another (indeed the Scripture saith, the spirits of the Prophets are subject to the Prophets, but the subjection was mutual, one not having more power over another, than that other had over him), neither is one Deacon over another; and what colour of reason can be given, that one Pastor or Teacher should have power over another.

There is no mention in Scripture of any under an Apostle or Evangelist, that did perform any work of office in any place but in his own particular church; the Apostles and Evangelists which are made distinct officers in the 4th of Ephesians, had their Commission general for all places without any limitation; but in this latitude of the Commission, they have no successors. There was no place where Apostles or Evangelists came, but they had the same power, which we suppose none of our Bishops dare arrogate to themselves. If therefore they succeed not Apostles and Evangelists in the largeness of their Commission, then their succession must be of those Pastors and Teachers, whom we find the Holy Ghost hath set over particular Congregations.

If Church Officers be not limited to several congregations, then there

[145]

is no limitation by any divine Institution, and if so, then a Pastor may have many, yea, all churches in the world under him, and so the Popedom must be granted at most inconvenient, and not against any divine Institution. If it should be said, that though one can oversee divers, yet it follows not that he can oversee all, we answer, that no man can oversee divers, but by substitutes, and by substitutes he may oversee all, and so the difference will be only in the inconvenience, and not in the unlawfulness, which is in the nature of the thing. You have here our Arguments, and if they be weighed without prejudice, surely you yourselves will judge them to be more than probabilities. We have not answered to every passage of this Petition; for we find many tautologies. Only one passage there is more, which we cannot pass by, to which we answer briefly, and then we have done.

18. *You say, that this government by Bishops hath continued many ages without any alteration.*

If an alteration be made unto the better, what cause hath any to complain, *nullus pudor est ad melior a transire*, Ambrose. Epist. 31 ad Valent. It is no shame to change for the better.

If this government hath been without any alteration, then it is the same every way it was before the Reformation, and if so, then it is the very same Antichrist had retained many hundreds of years. Now we will leave it to the consideration of any indifferent man, whether he can think in his conscience, that it is any way probable, that Antichrist should retain the government of Christ so long in the simplicity and purity of it. Is it not the great design of Antichrist, to lift up himself above Christ and his people? and by what means could he more readily effect this, than by corrupting the government? Had he not power to do it, seeing for many years he did what he listed in the Church? All doctrines that stood in his way, he hath corrupted, and can it be thought, that he should leave government entire, according to institution, which was most opposite to his design? Pride and arrogancy cause men above all things to seek to bring government under their own wills; and whoever since the beginning of the world swelled with more pride and arrogancy than Antichrist hath done? which appears by his interdicting of Kingdoms, and bringing Princes under his feet. But now we hope God will stir up the spirits of the Princes of the earth, to cast off with indignation that base bondage and Babylonish tyranny they have so long been under; for which, both we and all the churches of God, both do, and shall cry to heaven to hasten.

The Grounds of the Nonconformity of the Ministers who were Ejected

Edmund Calamy

[1671-1732]

THE RESTORATION OF CHARLES II IN 1660 BROUGHT BACK INTO POWER all those spiritual influences against which the Puritans had stood prior to the Civil Wars. Episcopacy, compulsory liturgy and uniformity in ceremonies were again to be the state religion. A meeting at the Savoy in 1661 between Episcopalians and Presbyterians indicated the futility of any hope of accommodation, and rather than comply with the terms of the Act of Uniformity, which was imposed in the following year, some 2,000 Puritans gave up their churches and livings. This Great Ejection of 1662 was one of the most decisive events in the history of English Protestantism, hardening the division between Conformity and Nonconformity for three centuries to come.

In view of the significance of the event it may be surprising that comparatively little contemporary literature appeared on the Puritan side explaining their non-compliance with the Uniformity Act. It was not until 1696 that a mass of autobiographical and other material from Richard Baxter's papers entitled Reliquiae Baxterianae gave some account of the ejected ministers, and a new century had come before Edmund Calamy, the grandson of the Westminster divine, published his Abridgement of Mr Baxter's History of His Life and Times in 1702. Calamy's work, however, was more than an abridgment of Baxter's Reliquiae: it contained an important new chapter on the reasons for the ejected ministers' Nonconformity, drawn partly from Baxter's Nonconformity Stated and Vindicated (1689) as well as from other sources. It is this chapter which is reproduced with certain omissions in the following pages.

There are reasons for the seemingly small volume of writers for Nonconformity after 1662. In the quarter century of persecution which followed the Ejection – a period when it seemed that the very foundations of true Christianity in England might be destroyed – many of the Puritan leaders were engaged in other literary work of a more fundamental nature. But a principal reason for the little emphasis their writings gave to their Nonconformity lies in the fact that their reasons had already been fully and amply stated in such writers as Calderwood and Ames: all that Calamy needed to do was to sum up the arguments which had been urged against the half-reformed character of the national Church ever since the reign of Edward VI. The Uniformity Act of 1662 was not an ignorant blunder, it was a deliberate refusal of Biblical truth. The Puritans had long contended that elements alien to the Gospel were in the Establishment, and 1662 was a final proof just how strong these elements were.

Bibliography

Reliquiae Baxterianae, 1696.
An Abridgement of Mr Baxter's History of His Life and Times, Edmund Calamy, 1702.
The Nonconformists' Memorial, Samuel Palmer, 1774.
Calamy Revised, A. G. Matthews, 1933.

A Collection of Farewell Sermons, Preached by the late London Ministers, 1662.

England's Remembrancer, being a collection of Farewell Sermons preached by divers Nonconformists in the country, 1663.

Sermons of the Great Ejection, 1962 – a selection from the above two volumes, republished to commemorate the tercentenary of the Great Ejection.

The Two Thousand Confessors of 1662, 2nd edit., Thomas Coleman, 1861.

St. Bartholomew Bi-centenary Papers, being Lectures by Thomas M'Crie and others, 1862.

English Puritanism, Documents relating to the Settlement of the Church of England by the Act of Uniformity of 1662, Peter Bayne, 1862.

'The Demise of English Presbyterianism, 1660–1760', an article by J. C. Spalding in *Church History,* March 1959.

The Grounds of the Nonconformity of the Ministers who were Ejected

IT is not to supposed that two thousand men, pick them where you will, should be all of a mind. Among the excluded ministers there was a diversity of sentiments. Some could have gone much farther than others in compliance with authority. But as the terms of conformity were settled, they durst not yield, some upon one account, others upon another, and several upon many reasons at once, fearing they should thereby have offended God. Many eyes were upon them; their refusal was public; the gap made by their ejection wide and great; and the consequences very considerable. The censures which were afterwards passed upon them were harsh and severe; and at length it became modish to run them all down, as a pack of unreasonable and humoursome complainants. Posterity must and will judge in the case, when plaintiffs and defendants are all in their graves. For their help and assistance, I have here drawn up the plea of those who were the sufferers, which compared with the arguments and replies of the aggressors, may help in passing an impartial judgment. I desire only it may be observed that the following abstract contains the reasons of those who were the most moderate, and least fond of separation.

The things imposed upon them, if they would keep their livings or lectureships, or any post of service in the established Church were these five. They must be re-ordained, if not Episcopally ordained before. They must declare their unfeigned assent and consent to all and everything contained and prescribed in and by the Book of Common Prayer, and administration of the Sacraments, and other rites and ceremonies of the Church of England; together with the psalter, and the form or manner of making, ordaining and consecrating of bishops, priests, and deacons, etc. to which was superadded an equivalent subscription. They must take the Oath of Canonical Obedience, and swear subjection to their Ordinary according to the Canons of the Church. They must abjure the Solemn League and Covenant.[1] And they must also abjure the taking arms upon any pretence whatsoever against the King, or any commissioned by him.[2] These things were all straitly enjoined without anything to qualify or soften them, or room for a dispensation. So that if any man scrupled but

---

[1] This point is omitted in the present selection.—Ed.
[2] This point is also omitted.—Ed.

one point, and could have complied in all the rest, he was as certainly ejected as if he had scrupled all. And all of them were indeed scrupled by many, who weighing them maturely could not regard them (as circumstances stood) as things indifferent, or barely inconvenient, but refused them as flatly sinful, according to the best light they could gain by their utmost enquiries. I will view them distinctly, in the order in which I have mentioned them.

I. They must be re-ordained, if not Episcopally ordained before. This was plain in the Act of Uniformity, by which it was enacted that from and after the feast of St Bartholomew 1662, no incumbent, in possession of any parsonage, vicarage, or benefice, that was not in holy orders by Episcopal ordination, should enjoy the same, but be *ipso facto* deprived; his ecclesiastical promotions being void as if he were naturally dead, etc. Room indeed was left for receiving Episcopal orders (if till then wanting) between the time in which the act passed, and Bartholomew Day, August the 24th. But though there could have been a compliance in all other respects, if Episcopal ordination were then found wanting, they were by the Act, *ipso facto* ejected. This affected the far greatest part of those who came into the ministry after that Diocesans were put down in England by the power of the Parliament. For they were ordained by an assembly of senior pastors, who were then in possession of that power. And though after due examination as to their qualifications, they were solemnly set apart to the sacred ministry by fasting, and prayer, and imposition of hands, and had the blessing of heaven for many years attending their sacred ministrations, they must yet now be doomed to silence, unless re-ordained by Diocesans.

This was what they could not submit to, because it would in their apprehension be a nullifying their past ordination. This seemed not to them a light matter, but very momentous, inasmuch as the peace of their own consciences, the credit of the Reformed Churches abroad, and the good and welfare of the people among whom they had laboured, were all very nearly concerned in it. Their consciences would not allow them to play with holy things; in pretending to be moved by the Holy Ghost, to take upon them the office of a deacon, when they knew themselves already fixed sufficiently in the higher office of Presbyters. It appeared to them a taking God's name in vain, solemnly to pray to him for what they were assured they had already; and to seem to be first invested with a sacred authority, which they had received long before. Neither durst they pour such contempt upon the Reformed Churches abroad, as their submission in this particular would in their esteem have carried in it, by disowning them and their ministers, who had no other ordination, such as that which they had before received.

II. They were required to declare their unfeigned assent and consent to all, and everything contained and prescribed in and by the book, entitled, 'The Book of Common Prayer, and administration of the Sacraments, and other rites and ceremonies of the Church, together with the Psalter or Psalms of David; and the Form or Manner of making, ordaining, and consecrating of Bishops, Priests and Deacons.' And they must also (and that *ex animo*) subscribe these words: 'That the Book of Common Prayer, and of ordaining Bishops, Priests and Deacons, containeth in it nothing contrary to the Word of God; and that it may lawfully be used: And that they themselves would use the form in the said books prescribed in public prayer, and administration of the Sacraments, and no other.'

The Act of Uniformity required that this declaration should be publicly made by word of mouth by all that would keep their places, on some Lord's Day before August the 24th, 1662. And by all that afterwards were presented to any ecclesiastical benefice, within two months after they were in actual possession of it. And the subscription was as peremptorily required as the declaration. But they could not herein concur for two grand reasons.

1. Because very few of them could see the Book to all things in which they were to declare their assent and consent, before the time limited by the Act was expired. For the Common Prayer Book with the alterations and amendments (for so they are called, how deservedly I enquire not) made by the Convocation, did not come out of the press till a few days before the 24th of August. So that of the 7,000 ministers in England who kept their livings, few except those who were in or near London, could possibly have a sight of the Book with its alterations, till after they had declared their assent and consent to it.

2. When they had opportunity to peruse the book, they met with several things there, which after the strictest search they could make, appeared to them not agreeable to the Word of God. For them under this apprehension (which it was not in their power to alter) to have gone to declare their satisfaction that there was nothing contrary to the Word of God, and nothing but what they could both assent to (as true) and consent to (as good and to be used) and to have subscribed this with their hands, had been doing violence to their consciences, and attempting at once to impose upon God and man.

They could not but observe the comprehensiveness of the required declaration. There must be not only consent but assent too; and that not only to all in general, but to everything in particular contained in and

[153]

prescribed by the Book of Common Prayer. Words could scarce be devised by the wit of man, more full, and more significant, whereby they might testify their highest justification and commendation of every point and syllable, every rite and ceremony, every matter and thing contained in the whole Book, and in every page and line of it. A man might almost be tempted to imagine that the framers of this imposed declaration and subscription, had had this Book of Common Prayer dropping down among them immediately from heaven, and that they looked upon it as nothing else but a continued oracle from first to last.

Such a declaration as was required of them concerning it, was in their apprehension as much as could be desired or done concerning the Book of God, the Bible itself. Yea they questioned whether many a sober man might not have scrupled to declare so much concerning any copy of the Bible now extant in the world, there being hardly any one to be found, but what may have such faults and slips, as may make an unfeigned assent and consent to every tittle, a matter of rational scruple. But as for the Book of Common Prayer, etc. they found such marks of human infirmity, in the frame and contexture and the particular offices of it, that they durst not make the subscription and declaration required, till they could receive satisfaction, with reference to sundry exceptions they had to bring in, which appeared to them of great weight and consequence.

1. The subscription and declaration required, they found, would take in the doctrine of real Baptismal Regeneration, and certain salvation, consequent thereupon. And that whether the persons baptized were qualified subjects of baptism or not. It would be an approbation of the rubric at the end of the public office for baptism, where it is said, 'it is certain by God's Word that children which are baptized, dying before they commit actual sin, are undoubtedly saved'. It would have been well if they had quoted the place, for the dissenting ministers freely confessed their ignorance, that they knew of no such word in Scripture. It would also be an agreement to use constantly after baptism that thanksgiving: 'We yield thee hearty thanks, most merciful Father, that it hath pleased thee to regenerate this infant with thy Holy Spirit.'' Now when they should be obliged to baptize all comers, without a liberty of refusing the children of infidels, or the most scandalous sinners (provided they had but Sponsors), to bless God presently as soon as the office was over, for regenerating them by his Spirit; and lay it down as undoubtedly certain that they were saved if they died, this was what their light would not suffice for; and therefore till then it was their undoubted duty to avoid concurrence. For who can so much as question whether or no it would

have been a sin in them, to bless God with confidence for what they did not believe was real; and to lay that down as undoubtedly certain from Scripture, of which they saw not there the least foundation. They found children of the wickedest parents (of whores and adulterers living openly in all notorious sin, and wholly without God in the world) baptized without scruple; and many of them died soon after baptism. Now how could they pretend to be sure by the Word of God, and past all doubt that all such went to heaven, when God so positively declared in the Second Commandment that he would punish the iniquities of the fathers upon the children, unto the third and fourth generation? This at least might make the matter dubious to them. Suppose a Christian king should conquer a country of Pagans, or Mahometans, or Jews, and compel all their infants forthwith to be baptized, and some of them immediately expire, at least before the commission of actual sin, is the salvation of all such sure, and past all doubt, and this to be made out, and cleared by the Word of God? Is it in the power of man to make infants sure and certain of salvation? It is in the power of man to kill a poor infant, and to choose his time for doing it. Many whores murder their babes before baptism, and they might as well do it immediately after, and so assuredly (upon this hypothesis) send them to heaven, whither they shall never come themselves, without bitter and sorrowful repentance. And so might the aforesaid king and conqueror (after he by baptism had given them their sure and unquestionable passport for paradise), even in charity and kindness immediately cut the poor infants off, and so without any farther hazard, give them possession of eternal bliss. But our ministers could not tell how to apprehend that any mortals had such power over souls, as this would amount to.

It hath been pleaded by some in this case to mollify the objection that the asserting of a Baptismal Regeneration was what was mainly intended, that herein they had the concurrence of many of the most celebrated Reformed divines, and of many even of our own most admired writers; to which they had this obvious reply: that the thanksgiving after baptism mentions regenerating with the Holy Spirit; which carries the matter farther than the sign, and seems to denote the thing signified as actually given to each baptized person. Besides, the sense of the Church in this point is sufficiently cleared by the office for Confirmation, in which the bishop who officiates, in his first address to God, expresses himself thus: 'Almighty and everliving God; who hast vouchsafed to regenerate these thy servants by water and the Holy Ghost, and hast given unto them forgiveness of all their sins,' etc. This said with reference to all comers,

[155]

gives ground to all concerned to think themselves sufficiently regenerated already, and to apprehend that the Church doth not think their aiming at any farther regeneration needful, when once they are baptized and confirmed. This was a thing that appeared to our ministers of such dangerous consequence that they durst not concur in it or any way approve it, for fear of contributing to the hardening of a multitude of vain, loose, careless, secure creatures in a fatal mistake about the safety of their state; neither could they see how they could answer for it to God another day.

2. This assent, consent, and subscription, was among other things to the use of godfathers and godmothers in baptism, to the exclusion of parents.

This they esteemed sinful, not only because it jostled out the parents' right to devote their children to God in baptism, which is the thing upon which the administration of that ordinance to infants was primarily founded, but also because it opened a wide door to the profaning of one of the most awful solemnities of our holy religion. Inasmuch as godfathers and godmothers are neither required to be chosen with due care and caution (and in the case of many persons, it is really impossible to procure any serious undertakers); nor are they tied to bring the children of Christians only, nor only such as they take for their own, but without any difference may bring the children of any atheists or seducers, Jews or infidels, at pleasure, without taking any further thought or care about them. Withal these godfathers and godmothers personate the child, as believing in Christ, and renouncing sin; and that without any authority for it, either from any natural right, or positive law. And the ordinance of baptism will seem to be put upon that insufficient bottom, by any one who sedately compares the office for that purpose, with the Church Catechism. For the promise of the godfathers and godmothers, in the child's name, is in both represented as the foundation of baptismal dedication, and the ground of the claim of the benefits and blessings thence arising. Now our ministers sensibly found that this would not bear scanning. In the Church way this ordinance is so managed, as if the godfathers' faith were beneficial to the child, and not the parents': when as God requires no faith or repentance of infants, but only that they be the seed of penitent believers, and devoted to him as such; this also was an offence to many. And then they found that godfathers and godmothers were generally brought to the font to avouch a great untruth, and make themselves obnoxious to lying and perjury in the face of God and the Church. For experience showeth that what appearance soever there is of solemnity at the engaging in such a promise, yet they never (or very rarely) perform it.

3. This assent, consent, and subscription, would have obliged the

ministers to have denied the ordinance of Baptism to such as had not sponsors, although they had a real right to that ordinance, and to be thereby solemnly recognized as born members of the visible Church. Some have herein questioned the reality of the obligation; but as far as appears, upon very weak grounds. For the Canon subscribed, obliges in express words to use the form prescribed, and no other: And the Rubric declares there shall be for every male child to be baptized, two godfathers and one godmother; and for every female, one godfather and two godmothers. Consequently all that would officiate in the established Church, must by verbal declaration and subscription bind themselves to deny baptism to all children of godly parents that have not godfathers and godmothers, even though the parent be ready to do his own part, professing his faith, dedicating his child to God, and promising a religious education.

4. This assent, consent, and subscription, would oblige to sign the infants in the administration of baptism with the transient sign of the cross, and to deny baptism to the children of such as refuse it.

As for the using the sign of the cross in Baptism, some were much more against it than others: But the generality of the silenced ministers regarded it as a sacrament superadded to that which our blessed Lord had instituted.

5. This assent, consent, and subscription, would oblige them to reject all such from the Communion, as would not receive it kneeling.

That it would have herein obliged them is plain, in that the Canon forbids ministers upon pain of suspension to give the sacrament to any that do not kneel, which Canon explains the meaning of the rubric in the Liturgy, and intimates that, Give it to them kneeling, is equivalent to, Give it only to such. It was indeed asserted by the disputants on the Church side at the Savoy, that the Liturgy only required it should be given kneeling, but did not forbid the giving it to others. But it was generally contradicted by the other Commissioners, and particularly those who were upon the secret. And indeed this would be to set the Liturgy, and the Canons at variance; whereas they are really all of a piece.

Thus to exclude all that should refuse kneeling at the Communion, was what they could not consent to because it was a making new terms of Church communion; a contradicting Christ's appointed terms, which require all Christians to receive each other in love and concord, and not to doubtful disputations; a depriving Christ's members of their right; an usurpation upon men's consciences; and a tearing the Church by dividing engines.

Even those of them who could not charge kneeling as sinful, and who could themselves have complied with it, were yet afraid of excluding others upon such an account as that, by reason it was far from being a necessary matter. And withal, persons might have very good reason to be backward to yield to the altering of that posture that was used by our Saviour in the administration; and to be shy of seeming to symbolize with idolaters, in using that posture which is well known to be used by the Papists with an intention of adoration, as to the elements; which though disclaimed by the Church of England, is yet apt to be misinterpreted. Suppose a man should upon searching Church history, find that the posture of kneeling at the Communion was never required in the Church, till the Doctrine of Transubstantiation was established; this alone (though he should have nothing farther to allege) might be a valid reason for his being shy of that posture; but for ministers to enter into any such combination as to be obliged to tell such a man when offering himself to Communion: Truly sir, while you are under this scruple, though I may pity you for your weakness, yet I can't own you for a Christian, this they thought hard: and the more so, in that equal care was not taken to keep off from the Communion persons evidently unqualified, and unworthy, either through ignorance, or immorality; unless by such a method as was likely to do more hurt than good.

6. This assent, consent, and subscription, would be an allowance and approbation of that assertion, that Bishops, Priests, and Deacons are three distinct orders in the Church by divine appointment. For in the Book of Ordination, which was as much to be assented and consented to, as the Common Prayer Book itself: it is asserted, 'That it is evident to all men diligently reading the Holy Scriptures and ancient authors, that from the Apostles' time, there have been these *orders* in Christ's Church, Bishops, Priests, and Deacons as several *offices*.' And indeed the whole Book or Ordination is bottomed upon that supposition as its foundation.

Now many of the ejected ministers were conscious to themselves that they had diligently read the Holy Scriptures, and consulted ancient authors, and yet they could not see evidence of three *orders* and *offices*: and therefore to have yielded to that declaration and subscription which would have implied the contrary, had been gross prevarication. They also thought they had good reason to believe that Calvin, Beza, and many more of the first Reformers, and that such men as Blondel, Salmasius, Robert Parker, Martin Bucer, Calderwood, Cartwright, John Reynolds, Ames, Ainsworth, and many more such eminent Protestants, who had quite different apprehensions of this matter, had diligently read both Scriptures and the ancients, as well as their neighbours. Neither could they see any reason to be confident that such men as Selden, Stillingfleet (at that time when he wrote his *Irenicum*), Bishop Edward Reynolds, and many others who thought the Scripture instituted no particular forms of government, had been altogether unconversant either with the Scriptures or the Fathers. Nor did they think it necessary to run down such a man as Archbishop Ussher as a novice in either, though he often professed it his sense that Bishops are not a different order, but a different degree in the same order.

Nay, they found that even the Church of England was formerly of another mind, as may be seen in the Canons of Aelfric to Bishop Wulsne, which conclude that there were but seven ecclesiastical orders, and that the Bishops and Presbyters are not two, but one. And Bishop Stillingfleet proved as they thought by sufficient evidence, that Archbishop Cranmer and other Reformers of the Church of England were of that mind; and held that there was no difference in order between a Bishop and Presbyter, but only in degree. With what conscience then could they have yielded to such a subscription and declaration, as would represent it as their sense, that Bishops, Priests, and Deacons, were three distinct orders all along in the Church, while they thought they had good reason to apprehend the contrary, and good company in the apprehension.

Besides these, there were other things, which though by some possibly less regarded than the former, were yet such as they could not assent and consent to, without having reason and conscience fly in their face.

1. They could not consent to pronounce all saved that are buried, except the unbaptized, excommunicate, and self-murderers. The words in that office for the burial of the dead are these: 'For as much as it hath pleased Almighty God of his great mercy, to take unto Himself, the soul of our dear brother here departed'; and afterwards; 'We give thee hearty thanks for that it hath pleased thee to deliver this our brother out of the miseries of this sinful world.' And again, 'That we may rest in Him, as our hope is, this our brother doth.' This they could by no means approve of. For though they owned themselves bound to judge according to the utmost bounds of charity concerning all, yea even those with whom they would not change souls, nor be in their condition after death for ten thousand worlds, yet positively and peremptorily without all limitation or discrimination, to say and avouch concerning everyone whom they buried that God in great mercy has taken his soul, viz. by death out of the body, and taken it to Himself; this was beyond their faith, and they found nothing like it in the Gospel, which speaks altogether in another language to and of impenitent sinners. It is past contradiction that thousands are cut off by death in the midst of their sins, drunkenness, whoring, swearing, etc. without any sign of repentance from first to last, so living, and so dying.

Now, how can it be said that God took away such persons out of this world by death in mercy, in great mercy, inasmuch as at the same instant, they were taken away from all possibility of future repentance and amendment of life? They thought in such cases it might rather be feared that God took them away in wrath; provoked by the long abuse of his patience, and their own impenitency. Yet nevertheless the priest must not only say that God took away all such persons in mercy, in great mercy, but also positively affirm that God took them to himself, i.e. into heaven. Whereas the Scripture saith expressly that neither adulterers, nor fornicators, nor drunkards shall ever go to heaven, Yet hereby must they have obliged themselves, in perfect opposition, when they buried any known adulterer, fornicator, or drunkard; to declare and avouch that his soul was assuredly gone thither. They could not see how charity would excuse dangerous errors and falsehood. By this means they saw they should be necessitated to pronounce many saved at the grave, whom in their pulpits and writings they thought themselves obliged to condemn. They should hereby be in danger of speaking for God, misrepresenting his Word, and hardening the ungodly and profane in their hope of coming off safe at last, although they persisted in their dissolute and licentious course. Now they durst not damn a known adulterer, fornicator, and drunkard, while he was living, and yet save him when he was dead. Nor yet again could they commit his body to the ground, in a sure and certain hope of a happy resurrection unto eternal life. Which words must necessarily be spoken with reference to the person then interred, inasmuch as they are the continuation of the foregoing declaration: viz. God's taking his soul to himself. Besides it follows (which puts it out of doubt) in the last collect or prayer, 'That when he shall depart this life, we may rest in him (viz. Christ), as our hope is this our brother doth.' Now they thought it were easy to foresee sundry cases, in which they would be so far from having eternal life and salvation, that there would rather be a sure and certain fear of a doleful resurrection unto eternal death and damnation. And withal, it seemed to them to be but a wild and fanciful sort of charity in these men, that they should have such hopes as to persons dying under such gross sins, as murder or adultery, rebellion or blasphemy without repentance, while yet many of their consciences were too tender to allow the office to Dissenters, because they were hopeless schismatics.

2. They could not consent to a false rule for finding out Easter day. In the Common Prayer Book there is a rule for finding out the moveable feasts and holy days. Easter Day (on which the rest depend) is always the first Sunday after the first full moon, which happens next after the one and

twentieth day of March: And if the Full Moon happens upon a Sunday, Easter Day is the Sunday after. The frequent falsity of this rule may be seen by consulting the Common Almanacs; and by comparing it with the Table that follows afterward in the Common Prayer Book, to find out Easter Day for ever. So that here was a Book to be assented and consented to, that was inconsistent with itself.

3. They must consent to read Apocryphal lessons in the public Churches, which they could not agree to, because of such fabulous legends of Tobit and his Dog, Bel and the Dragon, Judith and Baruch, etc. These they found were not only to be read wholly and entirely, morning and evening two months together, but all of them also under the title and notion of Holy Scripture. For so in the whole lump together they are styled in the order, without any note of discrimination to make a distinction between one and the other. In the meanwhile in the same order (as appears by the calendar) some books of the Sacred Canon are wholly left out, and never to be read; some of them within a very little; some of them but half to be read, and many of them mutilated and curtailed as to several chapters.

This was what they could not by any means approve of. For though they could freely own there were many valuable things in the Apocryphal Books with all their faults, yet could they not have such a degree of respect for them as to think them fit to be read in Churches in the room of the Holy Scriptures. They were herein confirmed by finding even the most celebrated bishops and doctors of the Church owning there were many relations inserted in them that were false and fictitious. And they were afraid of contributing to the misleading of a great many weak and ignorant people (of which there are but too many in the nation) to fancy them of equal authority with the Holy Scriptures; of which there is therefore the more danger because in the order of reading the lessons, the title of Holy Scripture and Old Testament is given to the Apocrypha.

4. They must consent to the mistranslation of the Psalter.

The Psalter is particularly mentioned in the verbal declaration required of every incumbent. It must be assented and consented to, as having nothing in it contrary to the Word of God. To this they could not agree, because they found several mistranslations in the old version of the Psalms; which was indeed more accommodated to the Septuagint than to the original Hebrew.

5. They must assent and consent to St Athanasius' Creed. In which creed there is this expression, 'Which faith except every one do keep whole and undefiled; without doubt he shalt perish everlastingly.' This to our fathers seemed very harsh. Though they approved of the Creed in general

as heartily as their brethren, and esteemed it an excellent explication of the doctrine of the Trinity, yet could they not look upon themselves as so far called to judge other men, as to conclude all certainly damned forever that are not so well skilled in that mystery, as not to believe every word there written.

6. They must assent and consent to this Rubric, at the end of the office for confirmation, that none shall be admitted unto the Holy Communion, until such time as he be confirmed, or be ready and desirous to be confirmed.

Now though many of the ejected ministers were very desirous to have confirmation restored, and thought it would be exceeding useful, if managed with a becoming gravity and seriousness, yet to deny persons the Communion for refusing to be confirmed in the Episcopal way, was what they knew not how to justify. They found it was a thing scrupled by many persons. And were their scruples just or unjust, while the same persons were willing to own their Baptismal Covenant understandingly and seriously before the Church, and their own pastors, and to know those that laboured among them, and were over them in the Lord, and esteem them in love for their work's sake, and to be at peace amongst themselves, they durst not for their scrupling this Diocesan ceremony cast them from the communion of the Church of Christ. And therefore they durst not declare their approbation of the order that required it, nor assent and consent to it, nor subscribe that it is not contrary to the Word of God.

These were the reasons which they alleged, and printed, and published, for their refusing that assent, consent, and subscription to the Book of Common Prayer, and all and everything therein contained, which was a second thing straitly required by the Act of Uniformity.

III. They were also required to take the Oath of Canonical Obedience, and swear subjection to their Ordinary, according to the Canons of the Church.

In the form of making, ordaining, and consecrating Bishops, Priests, and Deacons, this question is required to be put to Priests and Deacons at the time of their ordination, 'Will you reverently obey your Ordinary, and other chief ministers, to whom is committed the charge and government over you; following with a glad mind and will their godly admonitions, and submitting yourselves to their godly judgments?' The answer to be returned is, 'I will so do, the Lord being my help.' An oath also is administered to the ordained of this tenor, 'I A. B. swear that I will yield true and canonical obedience to the Bishop of N— and his successors in all lawful and honest things.'

Herein they could not comply, for the reasons following:

1. Because as all obedience hath an essential relation to the laws and mandates of those whom persons are bound to obey, so the Canons of the Church, settled in its several respective Convocations, are the stated laws of the ecclesiastical government. And therefore the Oath of Canonical Obedience, which hath a reference to these stated laws or Canons of the Church, appeared to them to carry in it a plain obligation to comply with them, and submit to them in their stated practice, where they had not a dispensation. And though the obedience, that is in this case sworn, be limited to things lawful and honest, yet is it evidently supposed and taken for granted that the Canons which are in force, do require no other than such things, without leaving persons at liberty which Canons they will obey, and which they will refuse; which was a latitude which they had not found any Bishop in the land free to allow to any of their clergy. So that though in the Oath there be a limitation in words, yet they plainly saw it was only to be extended to future commands; while an obligation to comply with the things antecedently required by the Canons as lawful and honest, was supposed and taken for granted. For certainly the Church representative in its several Convocations, could not by those who profess so great a reverence for all its dictates, be supposed to require things of any other stamp or character. Now perusing the Canons, they could not be satisfied that many of the things therein required deserved that character. Nay they were not convinced, but that many things by those Canons required to have been the matter of their constant practice, would to them have been unlawful and dishonest; and therefore they durst not come under any such ensnaring obligation.

Whether they had any reason or not for thus scrupling conformity to the Canons, according to the demand of this Oath of Canonical Obedience, let any impartial persons judge, when I have briefly set before them the Canons to which they scrupled to yield conformity, with their objections against them.

By the Fourth Canon, 'Whosoever charges the Book of Common Prayer with containing anything in it that is repugnant to the Scriptures, he is to be *ipso facto* excommunicated, and not restored but by the Bishop of the place, or Archbishop, after his repentance, and public recantation of such his wicked error.'

They could not bind themselves to conform to the Canon, because though it should be allowed to be an error to bring such a charge against the Book of Common Prayer, yet could they not see that it must therefore be an error of that magnitude and wickedness, as to deserve excommunication. If all that have worse errors than that can be supposed to be, must be presently excommunicated, the Church would remain but thin. Besides they could not but esteem it a great abuse of excommunication, to have it thundered out against any persons before they were heard to speak for themselves, or told of their sin and called to repentance. Excommunications of this kind they durst not publish when commanded, for fear of offending Christ, and injuring his servants. And therefore they durst not promise or swear that they would do it. And as for those who would throw the blame in such a case upon the command of superiors, they appeared to them to open a door to the execution of any injustice or villainy in the world, supposing authority should interpose with a command.

By the Fifth Canon, 'All those are to be *ipso facto* excommunicated, etc. who affirm any of the Thirty Nine Articles agreed upon in Convocation in 1562, to be erroneous, or such as he might not with a safe conscience subscribe to.'

They could not bind themselves to conform to this Canon, for the same reasons as they scrupled conformity to that foregoing. And withal, they found the words of several of the Articles liable to exception, and some of them of small moment and dubious; they could not see the warrant of that authority ascribed to the Church in the twentieth Article. They knew of no charter Christ had given to the Church to bind men up to more than himself hath done. Neither could they esteem everything that is true an article of the Creed, or necessary to Church Communion, so that all that dissent must be presently cast out. Besides they found Bishop Jeremy Taylor overthrowing the ninth Article about original sin; and Dr Hammond refining upon the fourteenth Article, and denying the seventeenth; in which they had many followers, who were all by this Canon to be *ipso facto* excommunicated. Which was a thing in which they durst not concur, as easily foreseeing that this would make the Articles an engine of endless strife and division.

By the Sixth Canon, 'All those are *ipso facto* to be excommunicated that should affirm that the rites and ceremonies of the Church of England are superstitious, or such as being commanded by lawful authority, men who are zealously and godly affected may not with a good conscience approve and use them, or as occasion requires subscribe unto them.'

In this Canon the Church seemed to them to assume to itself a most exorbitant power, by laying so great a stress upon every one of its ceremonies, as presently to excommunicate persons that should but represent any one of them as unwarrantable. Much more could not have been said as to the Ten Commandments, or any Articles of the Creed. But besides, the ejected ministers did esteem the things above mentioned to be un-

[164]

warrantable, and therefore could not agree to excommunicate themselves, and such as concurred in the same sentiments and apprehensions with them.

By the Seventh Canon, 'All those are *ipso facto* to be excommunicated that should affirm that the government of the Church of England, by Archbishops, Bishops, Deans, Archdeacons, and the rest that bear office in the same, is repugnant to the Word of God.'

Though some of the silenced ministers could have gone farther than others in submitting to Diocesan Episcopacy, yet take that form of government in the compass of it, according to this Canon, and they found it full of corruption. The pastoral power, which was lodged by Christ in the ministers of their respective congregations, was overthrown; and the Power of the Keys put into improper hands. And that Bishops should govern the Church by others, in a secular manner, even by laymen, who do that in their name which they know nothing of; could not in their judgment be reconciled with the Word of God. And therefore they durst not bind themselves to excommunicate all such as should pass but such censures upon the frame of the ecclesiastical government as it really deserved.

By the Eighth Canon, 'All those are *ipso facto* to be excommunicated, who should affirm that the form and manner of making and consecrating Bishops, Priests, or Deacons, containeth anything in it repugnant to the Word of God.'

Though it should be supposed there were nothing amiss in this Book of Ordination, yet the belief of its innocency could not in the esteem of the silenced ministers be justly deemed a matter of that moment, as to be necessary to salvation; or that persons should be cast out of the Church for the want of it. They could not therefore take an oath, whereby they should enter into a combination of that nature, as should make them liable to be charged with the unhappy consequences.

By the Ninth, Tenth, and Eleventh Canons, 'Such as separate themselves from the Communion of the Church of England, and such as own those separate Societies to be true Churches, are all to be excommunicated, and only restored by the Archbishop.'

Canons of this kind they durst not swear subjection to, because they thought them very uncharitable. If a weak mistaken Christian may be a true Christian, though faulty; they could not see why a mistaken congregation of pious persons might not be a true Church, though faulty. Supposing it granted, that they who separated from the Church of England, and such as adhered to them, really were in an error, yet could they not see how their errors could be looked upon as comparable to those of the

Papists, who yet are so far favoured by many of the prelatical party that the Roman Church they belong to, is owned to be a true Church. Neither can it with any ground be affirmed that the ignorance, error or corruption of such Separatists is half so great as is discernible in the Muscovites, Greeks, Abassines, Coptics, Jacobites, Nestorians, and Armenians; who yet are commonly confessed to be true Churches. The greatness of the errors of those that separate from the Church of England cannot make them cease to be true Churches, when Churches much more erroneous are owned to be true. Neither can their being gathered and maintained without the consent of the ruler, presently incapacitate them from being true Churches. For he that would condemn them upon that account merely, must with the same breath disown all the Churches of Christ, which were in the world for some hundreds of years; who were all in common in that condition. The silenced ministers thought it very fit to leave those to themselves, who were so confined in their charity; as thinking it their duty to embrace all those as brethren who feared God, and wrought righteousness, and to esteem all those as true parts of the Church of Christ, among whom there was the true Christian faith and worship, how different soever their particular sentiments or modes might be, or what failures soever might be amongst them, that were consistent with an honest, upright heart and life.

By the Twenty Eighth Canon, 'Ministers are required to refuse communicants coming from other parishes.'

To this they could not submit, because in some cases the receiving of communicants from other parishes might be a duty. As particularly, if the incumbent of a neighbouring parish were vicious or scandalous, or divine ordinances were so managed, as is inconsistent with the edification of the parishioners. For them in such cases to have refused to receive persons to communion with them, would in their apprehension have been grossly uncharitable.

By the Thirty Eighth Canon, 'A minister repenting of his subscription, or afterwards omitting any of the prescribed forms or ceremonies, is first to be suspended, and then excommunicated, and then deposed from the ministry.'

This they apprehended might in many cases be to consent to cast a man out of the Church for being conscientious: To which they were afraid to submit, least they should contribute to the silencing some of those who as much deserved encouragement, as any persons whatsoever.

By the Fifty Seventh Canon, 'All that go for Baptism for their children, or the communion for themselves from their own parish, because the minister is no preacher, to another parish that hath a preaching minister, are suspended, and after a month to be excommunicated.'

To this they could not submit because they apprehended there was much more need of driving the people to preaching ministers than from them. And though they did not esteem the Sacraments null, when administered by ill-qualified ministers, yet they could not but look upon it as sinful, either to harden an ignorant and scandalous person that had intruded into the office of the ministry in his profaneness, or to encourage people that need better in being contented with such a minister.

By the Fifty Eighth Canon, 'Every Minister saying the public prayers, or ministering the Sacraments, or other rites of the Church, is required to wear a decent and comely surplice with sleeves, to be provided at the charge of the parish, and that under pain of suspension.'

The surplice as a symbolical vestment, was what they found many learned and excellent ministers had in former times been against: and it was so small a matter, of so little real necessity or use, and the great things to be eyed in the exercise of a Gospel ministry depended so little upon it that even those who would rather have submitted to it, than have been deprived of the public exercise of their ministry, yet durst not concur in the suspension of others, who were more scrupulous of it than themselves, upon that account; as they must have done, if they had subjected themselves to this Canon.

By the Sixty Eighth Canon, 'Ministers are required to baptize all children without exception, who are offered to them for that purpose.'

Though some of the silenced ministers were much straiter in their notions about the qualified subjects of baptism than others, yet they were generally against submission to this Canon, because not convinced that the children of all comers (as of atheists suppose, infidels, Jews, heretics or blasphemers; who might upon occasion, be offered as well as others) were so far in the Covenant of Grace, as to have a right to a solemn investiture in the blessings of it. And till they were convinced of this by clear proof, they esteemed it too great a domination over men's faith, to command obedience in this point upon pain of suspension. And they apprehended swearing obedience herein, to be a consenting in effect, to the profaning of one of the most sacred institutions of our religion.

By the Seventy Second Canon, 'Ministers are debarred the liberty of keeping private fasts upon any occasion, or so much as being present at them, without exposing themselves to suspension the first time, excommunication the second time, and deposition the third time.'

The silenced ministers for their part could not but esteem those to be unworthy of that sacred and honourable function, who were not to be trusted to fast and pray with their people, as occasions might require, while the law was open, to punish all abuses. And taking this to be a part of their office, they could no more renounce it, than the liberty of preaching the Gospel, when and where the necessities of souls required it.

By the Hundred and Twelfth Canon, 'The minister jointly with the parish officers is required, every year within forty days after Easter, to exhibit to the bishop or his Chancellor the names and surnames of all his parishioners, which being of the age of sixteen years, did not receive the Communion at Easter before.'

With this Canon agrees the rubric which is inserted in the Common Prayer Book, at the end of the office for the Communion; which requires every parishioner to communicate at the least three times in the year, of which Easter to be one. And if they refuse after presentation, they are to be excommunicated, and are liable to be confined in jail till they die, by virtue of the writ, *de excommunicato capiendo*.

In this the silenced ministers durst not concur, for fear of the consequences. If indeed they could have had any hopes of forcing their parishioners by a jail, out of ignorance, unbelief, and ungodliness, they would have thought it a very charitable work: But while the due and necessary qualifications were wanting, they did not know but in forcing them to the Sacrament, they might force them upon sacrilege and profaneness, to their damnation and ruin. Withal, they knew this to be a course, whereby they should distract those persons with terror, who are conscious of their unfitness; or those melancholy Christians who under temptations, tremble for fear of taking their own damnation. In a word, they were convinced this would fill the Church with such as ought rather to be kept away; occasion the casting of holy things to dogs; prevent all possibility of discipline, and be a bar to that purity, which is a great design of Christianity.

Omitting the rest, the three last Canons related to the authority of Synods: And by them all were to be excommunicated, who should affirm that a Convocation summoned by the King's authority was not the true Church of England by representation: or that the absent as well as present, were not to be subject to the decrees of such an Assembly, in causes ecclesiastical, when ratified by the King's authority: or that their Canons and constitutions were despicable, etc.

These Canons they could not oblige themselves to submit to, because of the uncertainty, and dubious and disputable nature of the matters contained in them, which they (upon that account) could not apprehend to be fit grounds of so high a censure as excommunication. That a convocation was the true Church of England by representation seemed to the silenced ministers very justly questionable, not only because the laity (whom they thought a part of the Church) were altogether excluded, but also because the clergy were far from being therein fairly represented. As to the force of the Canons of such Convocations upon absent persons as well as present, they apprehended that it depended upon the Parliament, whose ratification they looked upon as necessary, in order to their having any force or significance at all. But though they should be mistaken in points of this nature, which they thought had not been so strictly enquired into, but that they would very well bear canvassing, it seemed to them strangely and needlessly severe that an excommunication must presently be thundered out against them. And as to the credit and reputation of the Canons of any such ecclesiastical Synods or Convocations, they could not help conceiving that that depended more on their agreeableness to the Word of God, than on the commendations given them by the enacters and their admirers. But that the Church to whom our Saviour had so often recommended mildness and gentleness should be but a word and a blow, and come with the highest censures where perhaps there might be only a mistake but no malignity, this the silenced ministers esteemed not only acting without a warrant, but unsuitable to a true Christian spirit, and therefore could not swear submission.

It hath been pleaded by many, that the Oath of Canonical Obedience, doth not oblige to approve of all that is in the Canons. To which they answered that in their judgment, the case of a minister was much the same as that of a Justice of Peace. Though a Justice of Peace be not bound by his Oath to approve of every law of the land, yet he is bound to execute all of them by his place, when he is called to it. So also a minister taking the Oath of Canonical Obedience, is bound to execute the Canons, and particularly those Canons where excommunication is denounced, when called upon by his Ordinary. It hath been farther pleaded that many of these Canons are disused, and so vacated; like many laws of the land that are grown out of use. To which the reply is easy: That many of the Canons before mentioned and objected against, cannot be so much as pretended to be disused; and many of them were much less disused at that time when the ministers were ejected, than they have been at some times since. But still so long as there is neither any public declaration given that might help to distinguish among those Canons, (which were all enacted by the same authority) which were yet binding, and which superannuated; nor a liberty of judging in the case left to private ministers, so long this plea appears without any force. For let any of them appear ever so much disused, if the Ordinary thinks fit to interpose with his authority for the reviving them, the Oath obliges to submission.

2. Another capital reason why they scrupled at taking the Oath of Canonical Obedience, was because they found the Episcopal government managed by Chancellors' Courts (which were kept in the Bishop's name indeed, while they in the meantime were not suffered to act in them), where laymen exercise the Church keys, by decretive excommunications and absolutions. They found the word Ordinary mentioned in the Oath, would admit of divers senses. That it not only meant the Bishops of the Diocese, but the judges in their courts. This is the sense given by Cousins in his tables, and by all civilians.[1] And as for the other chief ministers added in the Oath, to whom subjection was to be sworn, they saw not how less could be thereby meant, than all the Archdeacons, Officials, Commissaries and Surrogates, with the rest of the attendants upon those courts.

The silenced ministers durst not bind themselves by oath to a submission of this nature, for fear of concurring to overthrow the pastoral office. They could not think the administration of the Sacraments proper and peculiar to pastors, if the keys were not so too. For the most proper use of the keys is in a way of judging who is to be admitted to Sacramental Communion, and who debarred from it. If only delivering the elements, and not judging to whom, be proper to the Pastor, then is he to see with other men's eyes. Now it was their fixed apprehension, that in a matter of so great moment and consequence, it was their duty to see with their own eyes, and not act blindfold; and that our Lord Jesus Christ had invested all that were pastors, with that measure of power which was necessary, in order to the securing the direct ends of their office. Such power, it is true, might be abused, and therefore they were not (as some have charged them) against being accountable in case of such an abuse. But then they at the same time apprehended that an appeal in such a case, would be much more properly lodged with a Synod, (whose having a fixed President or Bishop would not have disgusted the generality of them, especially if he were chosen by the Synod itself) or with a meeting consisting partly of ministers, and partly of deputies from the neighbouring churches, than with a set of wrangling lawyers, whose concern in such matters they looked upon as irrational as well as unscriptural; and whose management of them was more likely to be calculated for their own profit, rather than the credit of religion, and the purity of the Church.

As for the provision made by the Rubric before the office for the Communion in the Common Prayer Book, viz. That when a minister keeps

---

[1] Those learned in civil law.

any persons from the Sacrament, he should within forty days give an account to the Ordinary, that he might proceed against them according to the Canons; they could not acquiesce in it, because dissatisfied as to the grounds upon which these Ordinaries (whether they were mere laymen, simple Presbyters, or Diocesans) appropriated the cognizance of matters of this nature to themselves, which in the judgment of common sense was more proper for those that had the opportunity of personal inspection, than for mere strangers. They were also confirmed in their dislike of this method of procedure, because of the difficulty, tediousness, vexatiousness and expensiveness of it; because of the number that must be accused if the Canons were followed; because of the great hindrance it would be to them in their ministerial work; and in a word, because of the impossibility of keeping up any real discipline, in such a way. In which they were much confirmed by observation and experience.

And as to the submitting to the determinations and injunctions of these Ordinaries, in which they had not by this Oath and Covenant so much as a judgment of discretion left them, they durst not engage, or bind themselves, for fear of approving sacrilegious profaneness. For if it be so for mere laymen uncalled and unqualified, to usurp the other parts of the pastoral office, particularly the administration of the Sacrament (as it is generally esteemed) then they conceived it must be so too, for them to usurp the power of the keys. And if the Bishops took it for usurpation in Presbyters, to take upon them to exercise power in this case, as supposing it proper and peculiar to themselves, they could not see why they should not judge it much more so in laymen.

As for excommunications and absolutions they looked upon them as very weighty matters, and durst not agree to trifle in them. If the Bishops could trust their consciences with their chancellors, and leave them to pass sentence in their names, without ever hearing or trying the causes depending; and suffer them to excommunicate persons for them, though they knew not on whom they passed that heavy censure, nor why they did it, it was to themselves; as the ministers could not understand it, so neither could they help it; and they were not responsible for it. But when they brought these matters home to their own door, and required of them that they also should trust their consciences in the same hands, they desired to be excused, till they were better satisfied in the point. They could not yield to receive and publish their excommunications blindly, lest they should be chargeable with their irregularities and abuses; and be the instruments of molesting, worrying, and ruining as religious persons perhaps as any in their parishes. Nor durst they consent to publish the absolutions of notorious debauchees, who have given (it may be) no other proof of repentance of their crimes, besides paying the fees of the Court. These things they well knew exposed the censures of the Church to scandal and contempt, and therefore they were unwilling to give an helping hand.

And to take such an Oath as this of canonical obedience, and make such a covenant, with a reserve to themselves, afterwards to demur upon the commands of the Ordinary, when agreeable to the standing rules of the ecclesiastical administration; or make light of the Canons, which were designed to be the standing rules of their obedience, before they were repealed or superseded; they could not look upon as any other than egregious dissimulation. And therefore they thought it much safer to waive this Oath altogether, and keep themselves free from any such ensnaring bond.

SECTION IV

New Testament
Church Government

The Book of Discipline 1587

ALTHOUGH NOT PUBLISHED IN ENGLISH UNTIL 1644, COPIES OF THIS *document were in circulation for over fifty years before this date. In the Elizabethan period it was known as* The Book of Discipline. *The title-page of the 1644 edition intimates that the manuscript was found in Thomas Cartwright's study after his death, yet it seems that the author (or rather the editor) was not Cartwright, but Walter Travers.*

Travers *was closely associated with Cartwright in the leadership of Elizabethan Puritanism. He was born in Nottingham in 1548, and was a student at Trinity College, Cambridge, from 1560, becoming a fellow in 1567. In 1570 Travers was forced to leave Cambridge because of his nonconformity and went to Geneva. There he formed a lasting friendship with Calvin's successor, Theodore Beza, and completed his major work,* Ecclesiasticae Disciplinae . . . Explicatio, *which was published in 1574 and translated into English by Cartwright. The* Explicatio *was recognized as the authoritative statement of the 'Presbyterian' position (so called because of the insistence that the spiritual duties of the ministry do not lie with Diocesan bishops but with presbyters of equal standing). After a brief stay in England, Travers accepted an invitation in 1578 to be pastor of a congregation of merchants at Antwerp. In 1580 he left Antwerp, refused the offer of a Professorship at St Andrews University and settled again in England as household chaplain to Elizabeth's chief minister, Burghley, and then from 1581 as reader in the Temple Church, London. As a preacher Travers had great popularity, but five years later, after he had clashed with Richard Hooker, he was silenced and removed by Whitgift. His last official preferment came in 1594, when he was appointed Provost of the recently founded Trinity College, Dublin. From the time Travers resigned this office in 1598 until his death in 1635, he lived in comparative obscurity.*

The Book of Discipline *here reprinted should not be confused with Travers's lengthier* Explicatio. *The need for such a brief manual was felt by the Puritan ministers, and at a conference held in London towards the end of 1584 a Book of Discipline was considered (who had originally compiled it is not known), and was submitted to Travers for correction. The revised Book appeared in March 1587, and though only in manuscript form had a wide and lasting influence. It was published in 1644 at the instance of the Westminster Assembly, and there are definite similarities with the section on church order in the Westminster Confession.*

Bibliography

Directory of Church Government, 1644; reprinted in facsimile with introduction by Peter Lorimer, 1872.
Walter Travers: Paragon of Elizabethan Puritanism, S. J. Knox, 1962.
Thomas Cartwright and Elizabethan Puritanism, A. F. Scott Pearson, 1925.

The Book of Discipline 1587

The Sacred Discipline of the Church, described in the Word of God

THE discipline of Christ's church that is necessary for all times is delivered by Christ, and set down in the holy Scriptures. Therefore the true and lawful discipline is to be fetched from thence, and from thence alone. And that which resteth upon any other foundation ought to be esteemed unlawful and counterfeit.

Of all particular churches there is one and the same right order and form: therefore also no one may challenge to itself any power over others; nor any right which doth not alike agree to others.

The ministers of public charges in every particular church ought to be called and appointed to their charges by a lawful ecclesiastical calling, such as hereafter is set down.

All these for the divers regard of their several kinds are of equal power amongst themselves.

No man can be lawfully called to public charge in any church, but he that is fit to discharge the same. And none is to be accounted fit, but he that is endued with the common gifts of all the godly; that is, with faith, and a blameless life: and further also, with those that are proper to that ministry wherein he is to be used, and necessary for the executing of the same; whereupon for trial of those gifts some convenient way and examination is to be used.

The party to be called must first be elected, then he is to be ordained to that charge whereunto he is chosen, by the prayers of that church whereunto he is to be admitted; the mutual duties of him and of the church, being before laid open.

The ministers of the church are, first they that are ministers of the Word. In their examination it is specially to be taken heed unto, that they be apt to teach, and tried men, not utterly unlearned, nor newly planted and converted to the faith.

Now these ministers of the word are, first pastors, which do administer the Word and Sacraments, then teachers, which are occupied in wholesome doctrine.

[178]

Besides there are also elders, which watch over the life and behaviour of every man, and deacons, which have care over the poor.

Further, in every particular church there ought to be a presbytery, which is a consistory, and as it were a senate of elders. Under the name of elders here are contained they who in the church minister doctrine, and they who are properly called elders.

By the common counsel of the eldership all things are directed that belong to the state of their church. First, such as belong to the guidance of the whole body of it in the holy and common assembly gathered together in the name of the Lord, that all things may be done in them duly, orderly, and to edification. 2. Then also such as pertain to particular persons. First, to all the members of that church, that the good may enjoy all the privileges that belong unto them, that the wicked may be corrected with ecclesiastical censures according to the quality of the fault, private and public, by admonishing or by removing either from the Lord's Supper by suspension (as it is commonly called) or out of the church by excommunication. The which belong specially to the ministers of public charge in the church to their calling either to be begun or ended, and ended either by relieving or punishing them, and that for a time by suspension or altogether by deposition.

For directing of the eldership let the pastors be set over it, or if there be more pastors than one in the same church, let the pastors do it in their turns.

But yet in all the greater affairs of the church, as in excommunicating of any, and in choosing and deposing of church ministers, nothing may be concluded without the knowledge and consent of the church.

Particular churches ought to yield mutual help one to another, for which cause they are to communicate amongst themselves.

The end of this communicating together is, that all things in them may be so directed both in regard of doctrine and also of discipline, as by the Word of God they ought to be.

Therefore the things that belong hereunto are determined by the common opinion of those who meet so to communicate together, and whatsoever is to be amended, furthered or procured in any of those several churches that belong to that assembly. Wherein, albeit no particular church hath power over another, yet every particular church of the same resort, meeting and counsel, ought to obey the opinion of more churches with whom they communicate.

For holding of these meetings and assemblies there are to be chosen by every church belonging to that assembly, principal men from among the elders, who are to have their instructions from them, and so to be sent to the assembly. There must be also a care had, that the things they shall return to have been godly agreed on by the meetings, be diligently observed by the churches.

Further in such assemblies there is also to be chosen one that may be set over the assemblies, who may moderate and direct them. His duty is to see, that the assemblies be held godly, quiet and comely. Therefore it belongeth unto him to begin and end the conference with prayer, to know every man's instructions, to propound in order the things that are to be handled, to gather their opinions, and to propound what is the opinion of the greater part. It is also the part of the rest of the assembly to speak their opinions of the things propounded godly and quietly.

The synodical discipline gathered out of the synods and use of the churches which have restored it according to the Word of God, and out of sundry books that are written of the same, and referred unto certain heads

Of the necessity of a Calling

Let no man thrust himself into the executing of any part of public charge in the administration of the Word, sacraments, discipline or care over the poor. Neither let any such sue or seek for any public charge of the church, but let every one tarry until he be lawfully called.

The Manner of Entering and Determining of a Calling and against a Ministry of no certain place; and the Desertion of a Church

Let none be called but unto some certain charge ordained of God, and to the exercising of the same in some particular congregation. And he that is so called let him be so bound to that church that he may not after be of any other, or depart from it without the consent thereof. Let none be called, but they that have first subscribed the confession of doctrine and discipline. Whereof let them be admonished to have copies with themselves.

In the examination of ministers the testimony of the place from whence they come is to be demanded, whereby it may be understood what life and conversation he hath been of, and whether he hath been addicted to any heresy, or to the reading of any heretical books, or to curious and strange questions and idle speculations; or rather whether he be accounted sound and consenting in all things to the doctrine received in the church.

Whereunto if he agree, he is also to expound some part of the holy Scriptures twice or oftener, as it shall seem meet to the examiners, and that before the conference, and that church which is interested. Let him also be demanded of the principal heads of divinity. And whether he will diligently execute and discharge his ministry, and in the execution thereof propound unto himself not his own desires and commodities, but the glory of God and edification of the church. Lastly, whether he will be studious and careful to maintain and preserve wholesome doctrine, and ecclesiastical discipline. Thus let the minister be examined not only by one eldership, but also by some greater meeting and assembly.

Of Election

Before the election of a minister and the deliberation of the conference concerning the same, let there be a day of fast kept in the Church interested.

Of the Place of Exercising this Calling

Albeit it be lawful for a minister upon just occasion to preach in another church than that whereof he is minister, yet none may exercise any ordinary ministry elsewhere, but for a certain time upon great occasion, and by the consent of his church and conference.

Of the Office of the Ministers of the Word, and first of the Order of Liturgy, or Common Prayer

Let the minister that is to preach name a psalm or a part of a psalm (beginning with the first, and so proceeding) that may be sung by the church, noting to them the end of their singing (to wit) the glory of God and their own edification. After the psalm let a short admonition to the people follow of preparing themselves to pray duly unto God. Then let there be made a prayer containing a general confession. First of the guilt of sin both original and actual, and of the punishment which is due by the Law for them both. Then also of the promise of the Gospel, and in respect of it supplication of pardon for the said guilt and punishment, and petition of grace promised, as for the duties of the whole life, so especially for the godly expounding and receiving of the Word. Let this petition be concluded with the Lord's Prayer. After the sermon, let prayer be made again, First for grace to profit by the doctrine delivered, the principal heads thereof being remembered; then for all men, but chiefly for the universal

Church and for all estates and degrees of the people; which is likewise to be ended with the Lord's Prayer and the singing of a Psalm as before. Last of all let the congregation be dismissed, with some convenient form of blessing taken out of the Scripture, such as is Numb. 6: 24; 2 Cor. 13: 13.

Of Preaching

Let him that shall preach choose some part of the Canonical Scripture to expound, and not of the *Apocrypha*. Further in his ordinary ministry, let him not take postils (as they are called) but some whole book of the holy Scripture, especially of the New Testament, to expound in order. In choice whereof regard is to be had both of the minister's ability, and of the edification of the church.

He that preacheth must perform two things, the first that his speech be uncorrupt, which is to be considered both in regard of the doctrine, that it be holy, sound, wholesome and profitable to edification, not devilish, heretical, leavened, corrupt, fabulous, curious, or contentious; and also in respect of the manner of it, that it be proper to the place which is handled, that is, which either is contained plainly in the very words; or if it be gathered by consequent, that the same be fit and clear and such as may rise upon the property of the word, grace of speech and suit of the matter, and not be allegorical, strange, wrested or far-fetched. Now let that which is such, and chiefly which is fittest for the times and occasions of the church, be delivered. Further let the explication, confirmation, enlargement and application, and the whole treatise and handling of it be in the vulgar tongue, and let the whole confirmation and proof be made by arguments, testimonies and examples taken only out of the holy Scriptures, applied fitly and according to the natural meaning of the places that are alleged.

The second thing to be performed by him that preacheth is a reverend gravity; this is considered first in the style, phrase and manner of speech, that it be spiritual, pure, proper, simple and applied to the capacity of the people, not such as human wisdom teacheth, nor favouring of new fangledness, nor either so affected as it may serve for pomp and ostentation, or so careless, and base, as becometh not ministers of the Word of God. Secondly, it is also to be regarded as well in ordering the voice, in which a care must be had that (avoiding the keeping always of one tune) it may be equal, and both rise and fall by degrees; as also in ordering the gesture, wherein (the body being upright) the guiding and ordering the whole body is to follow the voice, there being avoided in it all unseemly gestures of the head or other parts and often turning of the body to divers sides. Finally let the gesture be grave, modest and seemly, not utterly none, nor too much neither like the gestures of players or fencers.

These things are to be performed by him that preacheth, whereby when need requireth they may be examined who are trained and exercised to be made fit to preach: Let there be, if it may be, every Sabbath day two sermons, and let them that preach always endeavour to keep themselves within one hour, especially on the weekdays. The use of preaching at burials is to be left as it may be done conveniently, because there is danger that they may nourish the superstition of some, or be abused to pomp and vanity.

Of the Catechism

Let the Catechism be taught in every church. Let there be two sorts. One more large applied to the delivering of the sum of religion by a suit and order of certain places of the Scriptures, according to which some point of the holy doctrine may be expounded every week. Another of the same sort but shorter, fit for the examination of the rude and ignorant before they be admitted to the Lord's Supper.

Of the other parts of Liturgy or Divine Service

All the rest of the liturgy or divine service consisteth in the administration of the sacraments and by the custom of the church in the blessing of marriage. The most commodious form thereof is that which is used by the churches that have reformed their discipline according to the Word of God.

Of Sacraments

Let only a minister of the Word that is a preacher minister the sacraments, and that after the preaching of the Word, and not in any other place than in the public assemblies of the church.

Of Baptism

Women only may not offer unto baptism those that are to be baptized, but the father if it may be, or in his name some other. They which present unto baptism ought to be persuaded not to give those that are baptized the names of God or of Christ, or of angels or of holy offices, as of Baptist,

Evangelist, etc., nor such as savour of paganism or popery; but chiefly such whereof there are examples in the holy Scriptures in the names of those who are reported in them to have been godly and virtuous.

Of the Communion

Let the time of celebrating the Communion be made known eight days before, that the congregation may prepare themselves, and that the elders may do their duty in going to and visiting whom they ought.

Of Signifying their Names that are to Communicate

Let them which before have not been received to the Lord's Table, when they first desire to come to it, give their names to the minister seven days before the Communion that care of enquiring of them may be committed to the elders, that if there be any cause of hindrance there may be stay made betime; but if there be no such thing let them proceed (where need may be) to the examining of their faith before some of the elders and ministers every month before the Communion. Let this whole treatise of discipline be read in the consistory, and let the ministers, elders and deacons be censured one after another; yet so that the minister concerning doctrine be censured of ministers only.

Let them only be admitted to the Communion that have made confession of their faith, and submitted themselves to the discipline; unless they shall bring letters testimonial of good credit from some other place, or shall approve themselves by some other sufficient testimony.

Children are not to be admitted to the Communion before they be of the age of 14 years except the consistory shall otherwise determine.

On the Sabbath-day next before the Communion, let mention be made in the Sermon of the examination, whereunto the Apostle exhorteth, and of the peace that is by faith. On the day of the Communion, let there be speech of the doctrine of the sacraments, and especially of the Lord's Supper.

Of Fasting

Let the day of fasting be published by the pastor according to the advice of the Consistory, either for supplication, for turning away of calamities present or threatened; or for petition of some special grace. Let the sermons upon the same day before and after noon (as on the Lord's day) be such as may be fit for the present occasion.

Of Holydays

Holydays are conveniently to be abolished.

Of Marriage

Let espousing go before marriage. Let the words of espousing be of the present time, and without condition, and before sufficient witnesses on both sides. It is to be wished that the minister or an elder be present at the espousals, who having called upon God may admonish both parties of their duties. First, may have care of avoiding the degrees forbidden both by the law of God and man: and then they may demand of them, whether they be free from any bond of marriage, which if they profess and be strangers, he may also require sufficient testimony. Further also they are to be demanded, whether they have been married before, and of the death of the party with whom they were married, which if they acknowledge and be strangers he may demand convenient testimony of the death of the other party. Finally, let them be asked if they be under the government of any; whether they whom it concerneth have consented.

The espousals being done in due order, let them not be dissolved, though both parties should consent. Let the marriage be solemnized within two months after. Before the marriage let the promise be published three several Sabbath days; but first, let the parties espoused, with their parents or governors desire the publishing thereof of the minister and two elders at the least, that they may be demanded of those things that are needful, and let them require to see the instrument of the covenant of the marriage, or at least sufficient testimony of the espousals. Marriage may be solemnized and blessed upon any ordinary day of public prayer, saving upon a day of fast.

Of Schools

Let children be instructed in Schools, both in other learning, and especially in the catechism, that they may repeat it by heart, and understand it; when they are so instructed, let them be brought to the Lord's Supper, after they have been examined by the minister, and allowed by him.

Of Students of Divinity, and their Exercises

In every church where it may conveniently be done, care is to be had that some poor scholars studious of divinity being fit for theological exercises, and especially for expounding of holy Scripture, may by the liberality of the godly rich be taught and trained up to preach.

Let that exposition as often as it shall be convenient to be had be in the presence at least of one minister, by whose presence they may be kept in order, and in the same sort, (as touching the manner of preaching) that public sermons are made. Which being ended, let the other students (he being put apart that was speaker) note wherein he hath failed in any of those things that are to be performed by him that preacheth publicly, as is set down before. Of whose opinion let the minister that is present and is moderator of their exercise, judge and admonish the speaker, as he shall think meet.

Of Elders

Let the elders know every particular house and person of the church, that they may inform the minister of the condition of every one, and the deacons of the sick, and poor, that they may take care to provide for them: they are not to be perpetual, neither yet easily to be changed.

Of Consistories

In the Consistory the most voices are to be yielded unto. In it only ecclesiastical things are to be handled. Of them; first they are to be dealt with such as belong to the common direction of the public assembly, in the order of liturgy or divine service, sermon, prayers, sacraments, marriages, and burials. Then with such also as pertain to the oversight of every one, and their particular deeds. Further, they are to cause such things as shall be thought meet to be registered and written in a book. They are also to cause to be written in another book the names of them that are baptized, with the names of their parents and sureties. Likewise of the communicants. Further also are to be noted their names that are married, that die, and to whom letters testimonial are given.

Of the Censures

None is to be complained of unto the Consistory unless first, the matter being uttered with silencing the party's name, if it seem meet so to be done by the judgment of the Consistory.

In private and less faults the precept of Christ, Matt. 18: 15, is to be kept.

Greater and public offences are to be handled by the Consistory. Further public offences are to be esteemed, first, such as are done openly before all, or whomsoever, the whole church knowing of it. Secondly, such as be done in a public place, albeit few know it. Thirdly, that are made such by pertinacity and contempt. Fourthly, that for the heinousness of the offence are to be punished with some grievous civil punishment.

They that are to be excommunicated being in public charge in the church, are to be deposed also from their charges. They also are to be discharged that are unfit for the ministry by reason of their ignorance, or of some incurable disease, or by any other such cause, are disabled to perform their ministry. But in the rooms of such as are disabled by means of sickness or age, let another be placed without the reproach of him that is discharged; and further, so as the reverence of the ministry may remain unto him, and he may be provided for liberally and in good order.

When there is question concerning an heretic, complained of to the Consistory, straight let two or three neighbour ministers be called, men godly and learned, and free from that suspicion, by whose opinion he may be suspended till such time as the conference may take knowledge of his cause.

The obstinate after admonition by the Consistory, though the fault have not been so great, are to be suspended from the Communion; and if they continue in their obstinacy, this shall be the order to proceed to their excommunication. Three several Sabbath days after the sermon publicly let be declared the offence committed by the offender. The first Sabbath let not the offender's name be published. The second let it be declared, and withal a certain day of the week named, to be kept for that cause in fasting and prayer. The third let warning be given of his excommunicating to follow the next Sabbath after, except there may be shewed some sufficient cause to the contrary: so upon the fourth Sabbath day let the sentence of excommunication be pronounced against him, that his spirit may be saved in the day of the Lord.

He that hath committed great offences, opprobrious to the Church, and to be grievously punished by the magistrate's authority, albeit he profess his repentance in words, yet for the trial thereof, and to take away the offence, let him for a time be kept from the Communion. Which how often, and how long it is to be done, let the Consistory according to their discretion determine. After which, if the party repent, he is brotherly to be received again; but not until he have openly professed his repentance before the church, by consent whereof he should have been excommunicated.

If the ministers of any public charge of the church commit any such thing, they are to be deposed from their charge.

[187]

Of the Assemblies of the Church

Particular churches are to communicate one with another by common meetings and resorts. In them only ecclesiastical matters are to be handled, and of those, only such as pertain to the churches of that resort; concerning other churches, unless they be desired, they are to determine nothing further than to refer such matters to their next common and great meeting.

Let the order of proceeding in them be this: First, let the survey be taken of those that are present, and the names of those that are absent, and should be there, be noted that they may give a reason at their next meeting of their absence, or be censured by the judgment of the assembly next. Let the acts of the last assembly of that kind be read, that if any of the same remain unfinished they may be dispatched. Then let those things be dealt in that are properly belonging to the present assembly. Where first the instructions sent from the churches are to be delivered by every one in order, as they fit together, with their letters of credence. Secondly, let the state of the churches of that resort be considered, to wit, how they are instructed and guided, whether the holy doctrine and discipline be taught and exercised in them, and whether the ministers of public charges do their duty, and such like. Furthermore they shall determine of those things that do appertain to the common state of all the churches of that resort, or unto any of the same, which way may be sufficient for the oversight of the churches. Lastly, if it seem meet, the delegates present may be censured.

They that are to meet in such assemblies are to be chosen by the consent of the churches of that assembly and conference to whom it may appertain.

Let such only be chosen that exercise public function in the church of ministry or eldership, and which have subscribed to the doctrine and discipline, and have promised to behave themselves according to the Word of God. Notwithstanding it may be lawful also to be present for other elders and other ministers, and likewise (if the assembly think it meet) for deacons and for students in divinity, especially those that exercise themselves in expounding the holy Scriptures in the conferences, and be asked their opinion. Which in students is to this end, that their judgments in handling matters ecclesiastical may be both tried and sharpened. But they only are to give voice which are chosen by the churches, and have brought their instructions signed from them.

If there fall out any very weighty matter to be consulted of, let notice of it be given to the Moderator of the assembly next going before, or to the minister of that Church where the next meeting is to be. The same is to send word of it in due time to the minister of every church of that assembly, that they may communicate it afore-hand with those to whom it appertaineth, that the delegates resorting to the next meeting may understand and report their judgments.

In appointing of the place for the assembly regard must be had of the convenient distance, and other commodities, that no part may justly complain that they are burthened above others.

In every such ecclesiastical assembly it is meet there be a Moderator. He is to have charge of the assembly, to see it kept in good order. He is always, if it may be conveniently, to be changed. The choice is to be in this manner:

The Moderator of the former assembly of that kind, or in his absence the minister of the church where they meet, having first prayed fitly to that purpose, is to move the assembly to choose a Moderator. He being chosen is to provide that the things done in the assembly may be written, that the delegates of every church may write them out and communicate them with the conferences from whence they came.

The Moderator is also by the order and judgment of the assembly, to give answer either by speech or by letters, to such as desire any answer, and to execute censures if any be to be executed. Further, he is to procure all things to be done in it godly and quietly, exhorting to meekness, moderation of spirit, and forbearing one of another where need shall be, and referring it to the assembly to take order for such as are obstinate and contentious. Lastly, he is to remember them of the next meeting following, with thanks for their pains, and exhortation to proceed cheerfully in their callings, and so courteously to dismiss the assembly. Before such time none may depart without leave of the assembly.

Those assemblies, according to their kinds have great authority, if they be greater; and less, if they be less. Therefore (unless it be a plain act, and manifest unto all) if any think himself injured by the less meeting, he may appeal still unto a greater, till he come to a general council, so that he ascend orderly from the less to the next greater. But it is to be understood, that the sentence of the assemblies be holden firm until it be otherwise judged by an assembly of greater authority.

Assemblies or Meetings are either Conferences or Synods

Conferences are the meetings of the elders of a few churches, as for example, of twelve. There are to meet in a conference chosen by the eldership of every particular church, one minister, and one elder. The conferences are to be kept once in six weeks.

They are specially to look into the state of the churches of that resort and conference: examining particularly these several points. Whether all things be done in them according to the holy doctrine and discipline of the Gospel, (to wit) whether any questions be moved concerning any point of doctrine. Whether the ecclesiastical discipline be duly observed. Whether any minister be wanting in any of those churches, that a sufficient one in due time may be procured. Whether the other ministers of public charge in the church be appointed in every congregation. Whether care be had of schools, and for the poor. Finally, they are to be demanded wherein any of them needeth the advice of the conference, for the advancement of the Gospel amongst them.

Before the end of the meeting, if it shall be so thought good by them, let one of the ministers assembled in conference either chosen by voice, or taking it by turn, preach publicly. Of his speech let the rest judge among themselves (the elders being put apart) and admonish him brotherly, if there be any cause, examining all things according to those rules that are before declared in the chapter concerning the things that are to be performed by those that preach.

Of Synods

A synod is the meeting of chosen men of many conferences. In them let the whole treatise of discipline be read. In them also (other things first being finished as was said before) let all those that are present be censured (if it may be done conveniently) and let them also have a communion in, and with the church where they were called.

There are two sorts of synods; the first is particular, which comprehendeth both the provincial and national synod. A provincial synod is the meeting of the chosen men of every conference, within the province. A province containeth four and twenty conferences.

A fit way to call a provincial council may be this. The care thereof (except themselves will determine of it) may be committed to the particular eldership of some conference within the province, which by advice of the same conference may appoint the place and time for the meeting of the provincial synod.

To that church or eldership are to be sent the matters that seemed to the particular conferences more difficult for them to take order in, and such as belong to the churches of the whole province, which is to be done diligently, and in good time, that the same may in due season give notice of the place and time of the synod, and of the matters to be debated therein, that they which shall be sent may come the better prepared and judge of them according to the advice of the conferences.

Two ministers and as many elders are to be sent from every conference unto the provincial synod. The same is to be held every half year or oftener till the discipline be settled. It is to be held three months before every national synod, that they may prepare and make ready those things that pertain to the national. The acts of the provincial synod are to be sent unto the national, by the eldership of that church in which it was holden, and every minister is to be furnished with a copy of them, and with the reasons of the same. A national synod or convocation is a meeting of the chosen men of every province, within the dominion of the same nation and civil government. The way to call it (unless it shall determine otherwise) may be the same with the provincial, that is, by the eldership of some particular church, which shall appoint the time and place of the next national convocation; but not otherwise than by the advice of their provincial synod.

Out of every provincial synod there are to be chosen three ministers, and as many elders to be sent to the national. They are to handle the things pertaining to the churches of the whole nation or kingdom, as the doctrine, discipline, ceremonies, things not decided by inferior meetings, appeals and such like. By the order of the same, one is to be appointed which may gather into one book the notes of every particular church.

Thus much for particular meetings, the universal followeth, which is called a general, or oecumenical council, which is a meeting of the chosen men of every national synod. The acts of all such councils are to be registered and reported in a book.

A True Description of the Visible Church 1589

Henry Barrow
[c. 1550-1593]

HENRY BARROW, A NATIVE OF NORFOLK, GRADUATE OF CLARE HALL, *Cambridge (B.A., 1569–70) and a student of Gray's Inn, was probably converted about the year 1580. He became associated with Christians in London who had separated from the Established Church and it was while visiting one of the imprisoned leaders of this group, John Greenwood, that Barrow himself was arrested in November, 1586. Thereafter he spent the remainder of his life in prison until he was executed, with Greenwood, on April 6, 1593.*

The following tract, the first of Barrow's writings, was written in 1589, on scraps of paper and secretly printed in Holland. It was followed the next year by his much larger work, A Brief Discovery of the False Church, *in which he argues that the parochial churches then constituted by law were not true churches of Christ.*

Foundational to Barrow's position was the belief that the church as a spiritual body cannot be co-extensive with a national or political society: 'The apostles first gathered a people by preaching unto the faith, then received and joined them to the church . . . There may none be admitted into the church of Christ but such as enter by public profession of the true faith. None remain there, but such as bring forth the fruits of faith'. As no civil law can give non-Christians a valid Church standing, Barrow treated with disdain the alleged authority of the Elizabethan Act of Uniformity which had made the nation nominally Protestant: 'All this people, with all these manners, were in one day, with the blast of Queen Elizabeth's trumpet, of ignorant papists and gross idolaters, made faithful Christians, and true professors.'

The Separatists, as they became known, held that the Puritans (such as Cartwright and Travers) while professing that 'the visible Church of Christ is a congregation of faithful men' (Article 19 of the 39 Articles) did not apply this truth in practice for in their policy of further reform they had accepted, or appeared to accept, the national 'Church' structure under the headship of the crown. This led to a lengthy controversy between Puritans and Separatists, a controversy which merged into the later Presbyterian-Independency debate.

Bibliography
Henry Barrow, Separatist, F. J. Powicke, 1900.
The Early English Dissenters in the Light of Recent Research (1550–1641), C. Burridge, 2 vols, 1912.
The Writings of Robert Harrison and Robert Brown, edited by A. Peel and L. H. Carlson, 1953. This volume, which is second in the series on Elizabethan Nonconformist Texts, contains a helpful bibliography on the Separatists.
The Writings of Henry Barrow, edited by L. H. Carlson, 1963.

A True Description 1589

A TRUE DESCRIPTION OUT OF THE WORD OF GOD, OF THE VISIBLE CHURCH

As there is but one God[1] and father of all, one Lord over all, and one spirit: so is there but one truth,[2] one faith, one salvation, one church, called in one hope, joined in one profession, guided by one rule,[3] even the word of the most high.

This church as it is universally understood, containeth in it all the elect[4] of God that have been, are, or shall be. But being considered more particularly, as it is seen in this present world, it consisteth of a company and fellowship of faithful [5] and holy[6] people gathered together in the name of Christ Jesus, their only king,[7] priest,[8] and prophet,[9] worshipping[10] him aright, being peaceably [11] and quietly governed by his officers and laws, keeping[12] the unity of faith in the bond of peace and love[13] unfeigned.

Most joyful,[14] excellent, and glorious things are everywhere in the Scriptures spoken of this church. It is called the city, house,[15] temple,[16] and mountain[17] of the eternal God: the chosen[18] generation, the holy nation, the peculiar people, the vineyard,[19] the garden enclosed,[20] the spring shut up, the sealed fountain, the orchard of pomegranate with sweet fruits, the heritage,[21] the kingdom[22] of Christ; yea, his sister,[23] his love, his spouse, his queen,[24] and his body,[25] the joy of the whole earth. To this society is the covenant[26] and all the promises made of peace,[27] of love, and

---

[1] Gen. 1: 1; Ex. 20: 3.   [2] 1 Tim. 2: 4; Phil. 1: 27; Eph. 2: 18; John 8: 41.
[3] Deut. 6: 25; Rom. 10: 8; 2 Tim. 3: 15; John 8: 51; 1 John 2: 3, 4.
[4] Gen. 17; 1 Pet. 1: 2; Rev. 7: 9; 1 Cor. 10: 3; John 17: 20.
[5] Ps. 111: 1; 149: 1; Is. 62: 12; Eph. 1: 1; 1 Cor. 1: 2; Deut. 14: 2.
[6] Deut. 12: 5; John 6: 37, 3: 14, 12: 32; Luk. 17: 3.
[7] Gen. 44: 10; Ps. 45: 6; Zech. 9: 9; Heb. 1: 8.
[8] Rom. 8:34; John 17; Heb. 5: 9, 8: 1, 4: 14.
[9] Deut. 18: 15; Mat. 17: 15; Heb. 1: 1; Gen. 14: 18.
[10] Ex. 20: 7, 8; Lev. 10: 5; John 4: 23.
[11] Mat. 11: 29; 1 Cor. 11: 16; Mark 13: 34; Rev. 22: 9.
[12] Eph. 4: 3; 1 Cor. 1: 13; Mark 9: 50.
[13] John 13: 34; 1 Cor. 13: 4; 1 Pet. 1: 22; 1 John 3: 18.   [14] Ps. 87: 2.
[15] 1 Tim. 3: 15; Heb. 3: 6.   [16] 1 Cor. 3: 17.   [17] Is. 2: 2; Mic. 4: 1.
[18] Zech. 8: 3; 1 Pet. 2: 9.   [19] Is. 5: 1, 27: 2.   [20] Cant. 4: 12; Is. 51: 3.
[21] Is. 9: 25.   [22] Mic. 3: 2; John 3: 3.   [23] Cant. 5: 2.
[24] Ps. 45: 9.   [25] 1 Cor. 12: 27; Eph. 1: 23.
[26] Gal. 4: 28.   [27] Ps. 147: 14; 2 Thess. 5: 16.

[196]

of salvation,[28] of the presence[29] of God, of his graces, of his power, and of his protection.[30]

And surely if this church be considered in her parts, it shall appear most beautiful, yea most wonderful, and even ravishing[31] the senses to conceive, much more to behold, what then to enjoy so blessed a communion. For behold, her king[32] and Lord is the king of peace, and Lord himself of all glory. She enjoyeth most holy and heavenly laws,[33] most faithful and vigilant pastors,[34] most sincere and pure teachers,[35] most careful and upright governors,[36] most diligent and trusty deacons,[37] most loving and sober relievers,[38] and a most humble,[39] meek, obedient, faithful and loving people, every stone[40] living, elect and precious, every stone hath his beauty, his burden,[41] and his order.[42] All bound to edify[43] one another, exhort, reprove and comfort one another, lovingly[44] as to their own members, faithfully[45] as in the eyes of God.

No office[46] here is ambitiously affected, no law[47] wrongfully wrested or wilfully[48] neglected, no truth[49] hid or perverted, every[50] one here hath freedom and power (not disturbing the peaceable order of the church) to utter his complaints and griefs, and freely to reprove the transgressions and errors of any without exception of persons.

Here is no intrusion[51] or climbing up another way into the sheepfold, than by the holy and free election[52] of the Lord's holy and free people, and that according to the Lord's ordinance, humbling themselves by fasting and prayer before the Lord, craving the direction of his Holy Spirit, for the trial and approving of his gifts, etc.

Thus they orderly proceed to ordination by fasting and prayer, in which action[53] the apostles used laying on of hands. Thus hath every one of the people interest in the election and ordination[54] of their officers, as also in the administration of their offices upon transgression, offences, abuse, etc., having a special care unto the inviolable order of the church, as is aforesaid.

[28] Is. 60; Ez. 47; Zech. 4: 12
[29] Is. 46: 13; Zech. 14: 17.
[30] Ez. 48: 35; Matt. 28: 20; Is. 62.
[31] Cant. 6: 4, 9.
[32] Is. 62: 11; John 12: 15; Heb. 7: 8.
[33] Matt. 11: 30; 1 John 5: 3.
[34] Acts 20.
[35] Rom. 12: 7.
[36] Rom. 12: 8.
[37] Acts 6.
[38] Rom. 12: 8; John 13: 17; Deut. 13: 17.
[39] Matt. 5: 5; Deut. 18: 10; Ez. 36: 38; Is. 60: 8.
[40] 1 Kings 7: 9; Zech. 14: 21; 1 Pet. 2: 5.
[41] Gal. 6: 2.
[42] 1 Cor. 12; Rom. 12: 3.
[43] Heb. 10: 24.
[44] Lev. 19: 17; 1 Thess. 4: 9.
[45] Col. 3: 23; 1 John 3: 20.
[46] 2 Cor. 2: 17; 3 John 9.
[47] 1 Tim. 4: 2, 3; Gal. 6: 12.
[48] 1 Cor. 5.
[49] Jer. 23: 28; 1 Tim. 3: 15.
[50] 1 Cor. 6; 14: 30; Col. 4: 17.
[51] John 10: 1.
[52] Acts 1: 23, 6: 3, 14: 23.
[53] 1 Tim. 4: 14, 5: 22.
[54] Luk. 17: 3; Rom. 16: 17; Col. 4: 17.

Likewise in this church they have holy laws,[55] as limits and bounds, which it is lawful at no hand to transgress. They have laws to direct them in the choice of every officer, what kind of men the Lord will have. Their pastor must be apt to teach,[56] no young scholar, able[57] to divide the word aright, holding[58] fast that faithful word, according to doctrine, that he may be able also to exhort, rebuke, improve, with wholesome doctrine, and to convince them that say against it: he must be a man[59] that loveth goodness: he must be wise, righteous, holy, temperate: he must be of life unreproveable, as God's steward: he must be generally well reported of, and one that ruleth his own household under obedience with all honesty: he must be modest, humble, meek, gentle, and loving: he must be a man of great patience,[60] compassion, labour and diligence: he must always be careful and watchful over the flock whereof the Lord hath made him overseer, with all willingness and cheerfulness, not holding his office in respect of persons, but doing his duty to every soul, as he will answer before the chief shepherd, etc.

Their doctor or teacher must be a man apt to teach, able to divide the word of God aright, and to deliver sound and wholesome doctrine, from the same, still building upon that sound ground-work; he must be mighty in the Scriptures, able to convince the gainsayers, and carefully to deliver his doctrine pure, sound and plain, not with curiosity or affectation, but so that it may edify the most simple, approving it to every man's conscience; he must be of life unreproveable, one that can govern his own household, he must be of manners sober, temperate, modest, gentle and loving, etc.

Their elders must be of wisdom and judgment, endued with the spirit of God, able to discern between cause and cause, between plea and plea, and accordingly to prevent and redress evils, always vigilant and intending to see the statutes, ordinances and laws of God kept in the church, and that not only by the people in obedience, but to see the officers do their duties. These men must be of life likewise unreproveable, governing their own families orderly, they must be also of manners sober, gentle, modest, loving, temperate, etc.[61]

Their deacons must be men of honest report, having the mystery of the faith in a pure conscience, endued with the Holy Ghost: they must be grave, temperate, not given to excess, nor to filthy lucre.[62]

[55] Matt. 5: 17; 1 Tim. 1: 18.   [56] Lev. 21: 17; Mal. 2: 6; 1 Tim. 3: 2.
[57] 2 Tim. 2: 15.   [58] Tit. 1: 9; 2 Tim. 4: 2.
[59] Tit. 1: 7, 8.
[60] Num. 12: 3; Is. 50: 4; Jer. 3: 15; Ez. 34: 18; Zech. 7: 11; Acts 20; 1 Pet. 5: 1–4; 1 Tim. 2: 20.
[61] Num. 11: 24; 2 Chron. 19: 8; Acts 15; 1 Tim. 5.   [62] Acts 6: 2, 1 Tim. 3: 8, 9.

Their relievers or widows must be women of sixty years of age at the least, for avoiding of inconveniences: they must be well reported of for good works, such as have nourished their children, such as have been harbourers to strangers: diligent and serviceable to the saints, compassionate and helpful to them in adversity, given to every good work, continuing in supplications and prayer night and day.[63]

These officers must first be duly proved, then if they be found blameless, let them administer, etc.[64]

Now as the persons, gifts, conditions, manners, life and proof of these officers, is set down by the Holy Ghost: so are their offices limited, severed, and diverse.[65]

The pastor's office is, to feed the sheep of Christ in green and wholesome pastures of his word, and lead them to the still waters, even to the pure fountain and river of life; he must guide and keep those sheep by that heavenly sheep-hook and pastoral staff of the word, thereby drawing them to him thereby looking into their souls, even into their most secret thoughts: thereby discerning their diseases, and thereby curing them: applying to every disease a fit and convenient medicine, according to the quality and malady of the disease, and give warning to the church, that they may orderly proceed to excommunication. Further, he must by this his sheep-hook watch over and defend his flock from ravenous beasts and the wolf, and take the little foxes, etc.[66]

The doctor's office is already set down in his description: His special care must be, to build upon the only true groundwork, gold, silver, and precious stones, that his work may endure the trial of fire, and by the light of the same fire, reveal the timber, hay, and stubble of false teachers: he must take diligent heed to keep the church from errors. And, further, he must deliver his doctrine so plainly, simply, and purely, that the church may increase with the increasing of God, and grow up into him which is the head, Christ Jesus.[67]

The office of the ancients is expressed in their description: Their especial care must be, to see the ordinances of God truly taught and practised, as well by the officers in doing their duty uprightly, as to see that the people obey willingly and readily. It is their duty to see the congregation holily and quietly ordered, and no way disturbed, by the contentious and diso-bedient, froward and obstinate: not taking away the liberty of the least,

[63] I Tim. 5: 9, 10.   [64] I Tim. 3: 10.   [65] I Cor. 12: 12, 18.
[66] Lev. 10: 11; Num. 18: 1; Ez. 44: 23, chapters 33 and 34; Ps. 23; John 21: 15; Acts 20: 28; I Pet. 5: 1; Zech. 11: 7; Rev. 22: 2; Luk. 12: 42; 2 Cor. 10: 4, 5; Heb. 8: 12.
[67] Ez. 33: 1; I Cor. 11: 19; John 10: 11, 12; Ez. 44: 24; Mal. 2: 6; I Cor. 3: 11; I Cor. 1: 7; I Tim. 4: 16 and 6: 20; Eph. 2: 20; Heb. 6: 1.

but upholding the right of all, wisely judging of times and circumstances. They must be ready assistants to the pastor and teachers, helping to bear their burden, but not intruding into their office.[68]

The deacon's office is, faithfully to gather, and collect by the ordinance of the church, the goods and benevolence of the faithful, and by the same direction, diligently and trustily to distribute them according to the necessity of the saints. Further, they must enquire and consider of the proportion of the wants both of the officers and other poor, and accordingly relate unto the church that provision may be made.[69]

The reliever's and widow's office is, to minister to the sick, lame, weary, and diseased, such helpful comforts as they need, by watching, tending and helping them: further, they must show good example to the younger women, in sober, modest, and godly conversation, avoiding idleness, vain talk, and light behaviour.[70]

These officers, though they be diverse and several, yet are they not severed, lest there should be a division in the body, but they are as members of the body, having the same care one of another, jointly doing their several duties to the service of the saints, and to the edification of the body of Christ, till we all meet together in the perfect measure of the fulness of Christ, by whom all the body being in the meanwhile thus coupled and knit together by every joint for the furniture thereof, according to the effectual power which is in the measure of every part, receiveth increase of the body, unto the edifying of itself in love: neither can any of these offices be wanting, without grievous lameness, and apparent deformity of the body, yea violent injury to the head, Christ Jesus.[71]

Thus, this holy army of saints, is marshalled here in earth by these officers, under the conduct of their glorious emperor Christ, that victorious Michael. Thus it marcheth in this most heavenly order, and gracious array, against all enemies both bodily and ghostly. Peaceable in itself as Jerusalem, terrible unto them as an army with banners, triumphing over their tyranny with patience, their cruelty with meekness, and over death itself with dying. Thus through the blood of that spotless lamb, and that word of their testimony, they are more than conquerors, bruising the head of the serpent: yea, through the power of his word, they have power to cast down Satan like lightning: to tread upon serpents and scorpions: to cast down strongholds, and every thing that exalteth itself against God. The gates of

[68] Num. 11: 16; Deut. 16: 18; 2 Chron. 19: 8; Ex. 39: 42; 1 Tim. 3: 15; 2 Tim. 1: 13; 1 Cor. 11: 16 and 14: 33; Gal. 2: 4, 5; Col. 1: 16; Acts 20; 1 Pet. 5: 1; Rom. 12: 8.
[69] Acts 6; Rom. 12: 8.
[70] 1 Tim. 5: 9; Rom. 12: 8.
[71] Luk. 9: 46; John 13: 12; 1 Cor. 12: 12, 25, 28; Eph. 4: 11, 12, 13, 16.

hell and all the principalities and powers of the world, shall not prevail against it.[72]

Further, he hath given them the keys of the kingdom of heaven, that whatsoever they bind in earth by his word, shall be bound in heaven: and whatsoever they loose on earth, shall be loosed in heaven.[73].

Now this power which Christ hath given unto his church, and to every member of his church, to keep it in order, he hath not left it to their discretions and lusts to be used or neglected as they will, but in his last will and testament, he hath set down both an order of proceeding, and an end to which it is used.[74]

And if the fault be private, private, holy and loving admonition and re-reproof, with an inward desire and earnest care to win their brother: but if he will not hear thee, yet to take two or three other brethren with him, whom he knoweth most meet to that purpose, that by the mouth of two or three witnesses, every word may be confirmed: and if he refuse to hear them, then to declare the matter to the church, which ought severally and sharply to reprehend, gravely to admonish, and lovingly to persuade the party offending: showing him the heinousness of his offence, and the danger of his obstinacy, and the fearful judgments of the Lord.[75]

If this prevail not to draw him to repentance, then are they in the name and power of the Lord Jesus, with the whole congregation, reverently in prayer to proceed to excommunication, casting him out of their congregation and fellowship, that is, out of the covenant and protection of the Lord, for his disobedience and obstinacy, and committing him to Satan for the destruction of the flesh, that the spirit may be saved in the day of the Lord Jesus, if such be his good will and pleasure.[76]

Further, they are to warn the whole congregation and all other faithful, to hold him as a heathen and a publican, and to abstain themselves from his society, as not to eat or drink with him, etc., unless it be such as of necessity must needs, as his wife, his children and family: yet these (if they be members of the church) are not to join to him in any spiritual exercise.[77]

All this notwithstanding the church is not to hold him as an enemy, but to admonish him and pray for him as a brother, proving if at any time the Lord will give him repentance.[78] For this power is not given them to the destruction of any, but to the edification and preservation of all.[79]

---

[72] Rom. 11, etc.; 1 Cor. 12; Rev. 14:12; Cant. 6:3; Revelation 12:11; Luke 10: 18, 19; Matthew 16: 18; Romans 8: 38, 39.
[73] Matt. 16: 19; John 20: 23; Matt. 18: 18.   [74] John 20: 23; Matt. 16: 19, 18: 18.
[75] Lev. 19: 17, 18; Matt. 18: 15; Deut. 19: 15; Matt. 18: 16.
[76] Matt. 18: 16; 2 Thess. 3: 15.   [77] 2 Cor. 10: 8, 12: 10; 1 Tim. 5: 20; Gal. 2: 14.
[78] 2 Thess. 3: 15.   [79] 2 Thess. 3: 15; 2 Cor. 10: 8, 13: 10.

If the offence be public, the party is publicly to be reproved, and admonished: if he then repent not, to proceed to excommunication, *ut supra*.

The repentance of the party must be proportionable to the offence, viz., if the offence be public, public: if private, private: humbled, submissive, sorrowful, unfeigned, giving glory to the Lord.[80]

There must great care be had of admonitions, that they be not captious, or curious: finding fault where none is; neither yet in bitterness or reproach, for that were to destroy and not to save our brother: but they must be carefully done, with prayer going before: they must be seasoned with truth, gravity, love and peace.[81]

Moreover, in this church is an especial care had by every member thereof, of offences: the strong ought not to offend the weak, nor the weak to judge the strong: but all graces here are given to the service and edification of each other in love and long suffering.[82]

In this church is the truth purely taught, and surely kept: here is the covenant, the sacraments, and promises, the graces, the glory, the presence, the worship of God, etc.[83]

Into this temple entereth no unclean thing, neither whatsoever worketh abominations or lies, but they which are written in the Lamb's book of life.[84]

But without this church shall be dogs and enchanters, and whoremongers, and murderers, and idolaters, and whosoever loveth and maketh lies.[85]

[80] Lev. 19: 18; Pro. 10: 12; Rom. 12: 19, 13: 10, 14 :1.
[81] Gal. 6: 1, 2; 2 Tim. 2: 24; Mark 9: 50; Eph. 4: 29; Matt. 18: 15; Jas. 5: 5, 19, 20.
[82] Luk. 17: 1; Pro. 10: 12; Rom. 14: 13, 19; Gal. 6: 2.
[83] Gen. 17; Lev. 16: 11; Is. 44: 3; Gal. 4: 28, 6: 16; Is. 60: 15; Deut. 4: 12, 13; Is. 56: 7; 1 Tim. 3: 15; Is. 52: 8.
[84] Is. 52: 1; Ez. 44: 9; Is. 35: 8; Zech. 14: 21; Rev. 21: 27.
[85] Rom. 2: 9; Rev. 22: 15.

The Form of
Presbyterial Church Government 1645

Westminster Divines

THE CONFESSION OF FAITH DRAWN UP BY THE WESTMINSTER ASSEMBLY *of Divines has been the best known and most widely used Protestant confession in the English-speaking world. The Assembly's 'Form of Presbyterial Church Government' is less well known outside Presbyterian churches, yet at the time of the Assembly itself it had probably the greater immediate practical importance. The Assembly was summoned by Ordinance of Parliament at a time when the Civil War was in progress, and met on July 1, 1643. Those initially called, including thirty laymen, numbered 151, but the average attendance was about half that number. In October Parliament ordered the Assembly to direct its attention to drawing up a directory of worship and of church government. The discussion of the latter was extremely protracted, largely because of the opposition of a small group of Independents to certain features of the proposed Presbyterian system (see pp. 283 ff.). These controversies about Church order were of more than merely academic importance since the ordination and induction of ministers to the many vacant parish churches was of pressing urgency.*

The directory of ordination was finally passed in April 1645 and both it and the form of church government were ratified by the General Assembly of the Church of Scotland. In England, however, Parliament delayed, and then in August of the same year accepted it in an extensively amended form. The Assembly however held firm and the original directory was ratified. On September 18 a committee for the ordination of ministers in London was set up – it included Cornelius Burgess, Edmund Calamy and William Gouge. A committee for Lancashire was also set up.

The greatest obstacle to the work of the Assembly with regard to Church government was the ingrained Erastianism of Parliament, which intended to hold civil and ecclesiastical power in its own hands and meant the Assembly to be confined to a purely advisory function. They therefore regarded the Assembly's vision of a single organized church, of presbyterial polity, as a threat to the authority of the civil magistrate and refused to accept such a polity as warranted by divine right and institution. Increasingly, the Parliament and Assembly were at loggerheads; the difference between them was exemplified in the debates concerning the power of excommunication: was this to be accorded to the Church without any Parliamentary restraint?

Nevertheless, though decisions on such matters of principle were left unsettled, the practical establishment of a presbyterial form of church polity went forward, and in March 1646 an Ordinance gave instructions to this end. Later the same year the Commons ordered the setting up of a Presbytery in London and a year later over 100 persons were present at the first meeting of the London synod. During the negotiations between Parliament and Charles I, the defeated King agreed to accept the continuance of Presbyterian Church government. But by this time power was passing to the Army, and first Cromwell, and then the restoration of Charles II (1660) dashed the hopes of the English Presbyterians.

Thus the Westminster Form of Presbyterial Church Government was never fully endorsed south of the border. As B. B. Warfield says of the Westminster divines: 'So far as the successful issue of their labours depended on alliance with a friendly state, their work as regards England at least, had failed. But this alliance was not the strength of the Assembly, but its weakness.'

Bibliography

Of more recent exponents of Presbyterian Church polity, the most valuable authors are W. Cunningham, J. Bannerman, R. L. Dabney, Charles Hodge, and Thomas Witherow, author of *The Form of The Christian Temple,* 1889.

Memoirs of the Westminster Divines, James Reid, 2 vols., 1811 and 1815.
Letters and Journals of Robert Baillie, edited by David Laing, 1841–42.
Scottish Theology and Theologians, James Walker. 1871.
Minutes of The Sessions of the Westminster Assembly of Divines, edited by A. F. Mitchell and John Struthers, 1874.
A History of the Creeds of Christendom, Philip Schaff, 1877.
History of the Westminster Assembly of Divines, W. H. Hetherington, edited by R. Williamson, 4th edit., 1878.
The Westminster Assembly, Its History and Standards, A. F. Mitchell, 2nd edit., 1897.
History of the Presbyterians in England, A. H. Drysdale, 1889.
The Doctrine of the Church in Scottish Theology, John Macpherson, 1903.
The Westminster Assembly and its Work, B. B. Warfield, 1931.
The Everyday Work of the Westminster Assembly, S. W. Carruthers, 1943.

The Form of
Presbyterial Church Government 1645

The Preface

JESUS CHRIST, upon whose shoulders the government is, whose name is called Wonderful, Counsellor, The mighty God, The everlasting Father, The Prince of Peace;[1] of the increase of whose government and peace there shall be no end; who sits upon the throne of David, and upon his kingdom, to order it, and to establish it with judgment and justice, from henceforth, even for ever; having all power given unto him in heaven and in earth by the Father, who raised him from the dead, and set him at his own right hand, far above all principalities and power, and might, and dominion, and every name that is named, not only in this world, but also in that which is to come, and put all things under his feet, and gave him to be the head over all things to the church, which is his body, the fulness of him that filleth all in all: he being ascended up far above all heavens, that he might fill all things, received gifts for his church, and gave officers necessary for the edification of his church, and perfecting of his saints.[2]

Of the Church

There is one general church visible, held forth in the New Testament.[3]

The ministry, oracles, and ordinances of the New Testament, are given by Jesus Christ to the general church visible, for the gathering and perfecting of it in this life, until his second coming.[4]

[1] Isa. 9: 6, 7.

[2] Matt. 28: 18, 19, 20. Eph. 1: 20, 21, 22, 23. Compared with Eph. 4: 8, 11, and Ps. 68: 18.

[3] 1 Cor. 12: 12. For as the body is one, and hath many members, and all the members of that one body, being many, are one body; *so also is Christ*. Ver. 13. For by one Spirit are we all baptized into one body, whether we be Jews or Gentiles, whether we be bond or free; and have been *all made to drink into one Spirit*. Ver. 28. And God hath set some in the church, first, apostles; secondarily, prophets; thirdly, teachers; after that miracles; then gifts of healings, helps, governments, diversities of tongues. [Together with the rest of the Chapter.]

[4] 1 Cor. 12: 28. [See before.] Eph. 4: 4. There is one body, and one Spirit, even as ye are called in one hope of your calling; Ver. 5. One Lord, one faith, one baptism. Compared with Ver. 10. He that descended is the same also that ascended up far above all heavens, that he might fill all things. Ver. 11. And he gave some, apostles; and

Particular visible churches, members of the general church, are also held forth in the New Testament.[5] Particular churches in the primitive times were made up of visible saints, *viz.* of such as, being of age, professed faith in Christ, and obedience unto Christ, according to the rules of faith and life taught by Christ and his apostles; and of their children.[6]

---

some, prophets; and some, evangelists; and some, pastors and teachers; Ver. 12. *For the perfecting of the saints, for the work of the ministry, for the edifying of the body of Christ:* Ver. 18. Till we all come *in the unity of the faith,* and of the knowledge of the Son of God, unto a perfect man, unto the measure of the stature of the fulness of Christ. Ver. 15. But, speaking the truth in love, may grow up into him in all things, which is the head, even Christ: Ver. 16. From whom the whole body fitly joined together and compacted by that which every joint supplieth, according to the effectual working in the measure of every part, maketh increase of the body, unto the edifying of itself in love.

[5] Gal. 1: 21. Afterwards I came into the regions of Syria and Cilicia; Ver. 22. And was unknown by face unto *the churches of Judea* which were in Christ. Rev. 1: 4. John to *the seven churches which are in Asia:* Grace be unto you, and peace, from him which is, and which was, and which is to come; and from the seven Spirits which are before his throne. Ver. 20. The mystery of the seven stars which thou sawest in my right hand, and the seven golden candlesticks. The seven stars are the angels of the seven churches; and the seven candlesticks which thou sawest are the seven churches. Rev. 2: 1. Unto the angel of *the church of Ephesus* write; These things saith he that holdeth the seven stars in his right hand, who walketh in the midst of the seven golden candlesticks.

[6] Acts 2: 38. Then Peter said unto them, Repent, and be baptized every one of you in the name of Jesus Christ for the remission of sins, and ye shall receive the gift of the Holy Ghost. Ver. 41. Then *they that gladly received his word* were baptized: and the same day there were added unto them about three thousand souls. Ver. 47. Praising God, and having favour with all the people. And the Lord added to the church daily *such as should be saved.* Compared with Acts 5: 14. And believers were the more added to the Lord, multitudes both of men and women. 1 Cor. 1: 2. Unto the church of God which is at Corinth, to them that are sanctified in Christ Jesus, called to be saints, with all that in every place call upon the name of Jesus Christ our Lord, both theirs and ours. Compared with 2 Cor. 9: 13. Whiles by the experiment of this ministration, they glorify God for *your professed subjection unto the gospel of* Christ, and for your liberal distribution unto them, and unto all men. Acts 2: 39. For the promise is unto you, and to your *children,* and to all that are afar off, even as many as the Lord our God shall call. 1 Cor. 7: 14. For the unbelieving husband is sanctified by the wife, and the unbelieving wife is sanctified by the husband: else were your *children* unclean; but now are they *holy.* Rom. 11: 16. For if the first-fruit be holy, the lump is also holy; and if the root be holy, so are the branches. Mark 10: 14. But when Jesus saw it, he was much displeased, and said unto them, Suffer the *little children* to come unto me, and forbid them not: for of such is the kingdom of God. Compared with Matt. 19: 13. Then were there brought unto him *little children,* that he should put his hands on them, and pray: and the disciples rebuked them. Ver. 14. But Jesus said, Suffer *little children,* and forbid them not, to come unto me; for of such is the kingdom of heaven. Luke 18: 15. And they brought unto him also *infants,* that he would touch them: but when his disciples saw it, they rebuked them. Ver. 16. But Jesus called them unto him, and said, Suffer *little children* to come unto me, and forbid them not: for·of such is the kingdom of God.

Of the Officers of the Church

The officers which Christ hath appointed for the edification of his church, and the perfecting of the saints, are, some extraordinary, as apostles, evangelists, and prophets, which are ceased.

Others ordinary and perpetual, as pastors, teachers, and other church-governors, and deacons.

Pastors

The pastor is an ordinary and perpetual officer in the church,[7] prophesying of the time of the gospel.[8]

First, it belongs to his office,

To pray for and with his flock, as the mouth of the people unto God,[9] Acts 6: 2, 3, 4, and 20: 36, where preaching and prayer are joined as several parts of the same office.[10] The office of the elder (that is, the pastor) is to pray for the sick, even in private, to which a blessing is especially

[7] Jer. 3: 15. And I will give you *pastors* according to mine heart, which shall feed you with knowledge and understanding. Ver. 16. And it shall come to pass, when ye be multiplied and increased in the land, in those days, saith the Lord, they shall say no more, The ark of the covenant of the Lord; neither shall it come to mind, neither shall they remember it, neither shall they visit it, neither shall that be done any more. Ver. 17. At that time they shall call Jerusalem the throne of the Lord; and all the nations shall be gathered unto it, to the name of the Lord, to Jerusalem; neither shall they walk any more after the imagination of their evil heart.

[8] 1 Pet. 5: 2. *Feed the flock of God* which is among you, taking the oversight thereof, not by constraint, but willingly; not for filthy lucre, but of a ready mind; Ver. 3. Neither as being lords over God's heritage, but being ensamples to the flock: Ver. 4. And when the chief Shepherd shall appear, ye shall receive a crown of glory that fadeth not away. Eph. 4: 11. And he gave some, apostles; and some, prophets; and some, evangelists; and some, *pastors and teachers;* Ver. 12. For the perfecting of the saints, for the work of the ministry, for the edifying of the body of Christ: Ver. 13. Till we all come in the unity of the faith, and of the knowledge of the Son of God, unto a perfect man, unto the measure of the stature of the fulness of Christ.

[9] Acts 6: 2. Then the twelve called the multitude of the disciples unto them, and said, *It is not reason that we should leave the word of God,* and serve tables. Ver. 3. Wherefore, brethren, look ye out among you seven men of honest report, full of the Holy Ghost and wisdom, whom we may appoint over this business. Ver. 4. But we will give ourselves continually to prayer, and to *the ministry of the word.* Acts 20: 36. And when he had thus spoken, he kneeled down, and prayed with them all.

[10] James 5: 14. Is any sick among you? let him call for the elders of the church; and *let them pray over him,* anointing him with oil in the name of the Lord: Ver. 15. And the prayer of faith shall save the sick, and the Lord shall raise him up; and if he have committed sins, they shall be forgiven him.

promised; much more therefore ought he to perform this in the public execution of his office, as a part thereof.[11]

To read the Scriptures publicly; for the proof of which,

1. That the priests and Levites in the Jewish church were trusted with the public reading of the word is proved.[12]

2. That the ministers of the gospel have as ample a charge and commission to dispense the word, as well as other ordinances, as the priests and Levites had under the law, proved, Isa. 66: 21. Matt. 23: 34, where our Saviour entitleth the officers of the New Testament, whom he will send forth, by the same names of the teachers of the Old.[13]

Which propositions prove, that therefore (the duty being of a moral nature) it followeth by just consequence, that the public reading of the scriptures belongeth to the pastor's office.

To feed the flock, by preaching of the word, according to which he is to teach, convince, reprove, exhort, and comfort.[14]

To catechize, which is a plain laying down the first principles of the

---

[11] 1 Cor. 14: 15. What is it then? I will pray with the spirit, and *I will pray with the understanding also;* I will sing with the spirit, and I will sing with the understanding also. Ver. 16. Else, when thou shalt bless with the spirit, how shall he that occupieth the room of the unlearned say Amen at thy giving of thanks, seeing he understandeth not what thou sayest?

[12] Deut. 31: 9. And Moses wrote this law, and *delivered it unto the priests* the sons of Levi, which bare the ark of the covenant of the Lord, and unto all the elders of Israel. Ver. 10. And Moses commanded them, saying, At the end of every seven years, in the solemnity of the year of release, in the feast of tabernacles, Ver. 11. When all Israel is come to appear before the Lord thy God in the place which he shall choose, *thou shalt read this law before all Israel in their hearing.* Neh. 8: 1. And all the people gathered themselves together as one man into the street that was before the water-gate; and they spake unto Ezra the scribe to bring the book of the law of Moses, which the Lord had commanded to Israel. Ver. 2. And Ezra the priest brought the law before the congregation, both of men and women, and all that could hear with understanding, upon the first day of the seventh month. Ver. 3. And *he read therein* – Ver. 13. And on the second day were gathered together the chief of the fathers of all the people, the priests, and the Levites, unto Ezra the scribe, even to understand the words of the law.

[13] Isa. 66: 21. And I will also take of them for *priests,* and for Levites, saith the Lord. Matt. 23: 34. Wherefore, behold, I send unto you *prophets,* and wise men, and scribes; and some of them ye shall kill and crucify; and some of them shall ye scourge in your synagogues, and persecute them from city to city.

[14] 1 Tim. 3: 2. A bishop then must be blameless, the husband of one wife, vigilant, sober, of good behaviour, given to hospitality, *apt to teach.* 2 Tim. 3: 16. All scripture is given by inspiration of God, and is *profitable for doctrine,* for reproof, for correction, for instruction in righteousness; Ver. 17. That the man of God may be perfect, throughly furnished unto all good works. Tit. 1: 9. Holding fast the faithful word as he hath been taught, that he may be *able* by sound doctrine both *to exhort* and *to convince* the gainsayers.

oracles of God,[15] or of the doctrine of Christ, and is a part of preaching.

To dispense other divine mysteries.[16]

To administer the sacraments.[17]

To bless the people from God, Numb. 6: 23, 24, 25, 26. Compared with Rev. 14: 5, (where the same blessings, and persons from whom they come, are expressly mentioned,[18]) Isa. 66: 21, where, under the names of Priests and Levites to be continued under the gospel, are meant evangelical pastors, who therefore are by office to bless the people.[19]

To take care of the poor.[20]

[15] Heb. 5: 12. For when for the time ye ought to be teachers, *ye have need that one teach you again* which be the first principles of the oracles of God; and are become such as have need of milk, and not of strong meat.

[16] 1 Cor. 4: 1. Let a man so account of us as of the ministers of Christ, and *stewards of the mysteries of God.* Ver. 2. Moreover, it is required in stewards, that a man be found faithful.

[17] Matt 28: 19. Go ye therefore, and teach all nations, *baptizing* them in the name of the Father, and of the Son, and of the Holy Ghost; Ver. 20. Teaching them to observe all things whatsoever I have commanded you: and, lo, I am with you alway, even unto the end of the world. Amen. Mark 16: 15. And he said unto them, Go ye into all the world, and preach the gospel to every creature. Ver. 16. He that believeth, and is baptized shall be saved; but he that believeth not shall be damned. 1 Cor. 11: 23. For *I have received of the Lord that which also I delivered unto you,* That the Lord Jesus, the same night in which he was betrayed, took bread. Ver. 24. And, when he had given thanks, he brake it, and said, Take, eat; this is my body, which is broken for you: this do in remembrance of me. Ver. 25. After the same manner also he took the cup, when he had supped, saying, This cup is the new testament in my blood: this do ye, as oft as ye drink it, in remembrance of me. Compared with 1 Cor. 10: 16. The cup of blessing which *we bless,* is it not the communion of the blood of Christ? the bread which *we break,* is it not the communion of the body of Christ?

[18] Numb. 6: 23. Speak unto Aaron, and unto his sons, saying, On this wise *ye shall bless the children of Israel,* saying unto them, Ver. 24. *The Lord bless thee, and keep thee;* Ver. 25. The Lord make his face shine upon thee, – Ver. 26. The Lord lift up his countenance upon thee, and give thee peace. Compared with Rev. 1: 4. John to the seven churches which are in Asia: *Grace be unto you, and peace, from him which is, and which was, and which is to come;* and from the seven Spirits which are before his throne; Ver. 5. And from Jesus Christ, who is the faithful Witness, and the first-begotten of the dead, and the Prince of the kings of the earth. Isa. 66: 21. And I will also take of them for priests, and for Levites, saith the Lord.

[19] Deut. 10: 8. At that time the Lord separated the tribe of Levi, to bear the ark of the covenant of the Lord, to stand before the Lord to minister unto him, and to *bless in his name,* unto this day. 2 Cor. 13: 14. *The grace of the Lord Jesus Christ, and the love of God, and the communion of the Holy Ghost, be with you all.* Amen. Eph. 1: 2. *Grace be to you,* and peace, from God our Father, and from the Lord Jesus Christ.

[20] Acts 11: 30. *Which also they did,* and sent it to the elders by the hands of Barnabas and Saul. Acts 4: 34. Neither was there any among them that lacked: for as many as were possessors of lands or houses sold them, and brought the prices of the things that were sold, Ver. 35. And laid them down at the apostles' feet: and *distribution was made unto every man according as he had need.* Ver. 36. And Joses, who by the apostles was surnamed Barnabas, (which is, being interpreted, The son of consolation,) a Levite,

And he hath also a ruling power over the flock as a pastor.[21]

Teacher or Doctor

The scripture doth hold out the name and title of teacher, as well as of the pastor.[22]

Who is also a minister of the word, as well as the pastor, and hath power of administration of the sacraments.

The Lord having given different gifts, and divers exercises according to these gifts, in the ministry of the word;[23] though these different gifts

---

and of the country of Cyprus, Ver. 37. Having land, sold it, and brought the money, and laid it at the apostles' feet. Acts 6: 2. Then the twelve called the multitude of the disciples unto them, and said, It is not reason that we should leave the word of God, and serve tables. Ver. 3. Wherefore, brethren, look ye out among you seven men of honest report, full of the Holy Ghost and wisdom, whom we may appoint over this business. Ver. 4. But we will give ourselves continually to prayer, and to the ministry of the word. 1 Cor. 16: 1. Now *concerning the collection for the saints, as I have given order to the churches of Galatia*, even so do ye. Ver. 2. Upon the first day of the week let every one of you lay by him in store, as God hath prospered him, that there be no gatherings when I come. Ver. 3. And when I come, whomsoever ye shall approve by your letters, them *will I send to bring your liberality* unto Jerusalem. Ver. 4. And if it be meet that I go also, they shall go with me. Gal. 2: 9. And when James, Cephas, and John, who seemed to be pillars, perceived the grace that was given unto me, they gave to me and Barnabas the right hands of fellowship; that we should go unto the heathen, and they unto the circumcision. Ver. 10. Only they would that *we should remember the poor;* the same which I also was forward to do.

[21] 1 Tim. 5: 17. Let the elders that *rule* well be counted worthy of double honour, especially they who labour in the word and doctrine. Acts 20: 17. And from Miletus he sent to Ephesus, and called the elders of the church. Ver. 28. Take heed therefore unto yourselves, and to all *the flock, over the which the Holy Ghost hath made you overseers,* to feed the church of God, which he hath purchased with his own blood. 1 Thess. 5: 12. And we beseech you, brethren, to know them which labour among you, and *are over you* in the Lord, and admonish you. Heb. 13: 7. Remember them which have *the rule over you,* who have spoken unto you the word of God; whose faith follow, considering the end of their conversation. Ver. 17. Obey them that have *the rule over you,* and submit yourselves: for they watch for your souls, as they that must give account; that they may do it with joy, and not with grief: for that is unprofitable for you.

[22] 1 Cor. 12: 28. And God hath set some in the church, first, apostles; secondarily, prophets; thirdly, *teachers;* after that miracles; then gifts of healings, helps, governments, diversities of tongues. Eph. 4: 11. And he gave some, apostles; and some, prophets; and some, evangelists; and some, pastors and teachers.

[23] Rom. 12: 6. Having then *gifts, differing* according to the grace that is given to us, whether prophecy, let us prophesy according to the proportion of faith; Ver. 7. Or ministry, let us wait on our ministering; or he that teacheth, on teaching; Ver. 8. Or he that exhorteth, on exhortation: he that giveth, let him do it with simplicity; he that ruleth, with diligence; he that sheweth mercy, with cheerfulness. 1 Cor. 12: 1. Now concerning spiritual gifts, brethren, I would not have you ignorant. Ver. 4. Now there are *diversities of gifts,* but the same Spirit. Ver. 5. And there are *differences of administrations,* but the same Lord. Ver. 6. And there are diversities of operations, but it is the same God which worketh all in all. Ver. 7. But the manifestation of the Spirit is given to every man to profit withal.

may meet in, and accordingly be exercised by, one and the same minister;[24] yet, where be several ministers in the same congregation, they may be designed to several employments, according to the different gifts in which each of them doth most excel.[25] And he that doth more excel in exposition of scripture, in teaching sound doctrine, and in convincing gainsayers, than he doth in application, and is accordingly employed therein, may be called a teacher, or doctor, (the places alleged by the notation of the word do prove the proposition.) Nevertheless, where is but one minister in a particular congregation, he is to perform, as far as he is able, the whole work of the ministry.[26]

A teacher, or doctor, is of most excellent use in schools and universities; as of old in the schools of the prophets, and at Jerusalem, where Gamaliel and others taught as doctors.

Other Church-Governors

As there were in the Jewish church elders of the people joined with the priests and Levites in the government of the church;[27] so Christ, who hath instituted government, and governors ecclesiastical in the church, hath furnished some in his church, beside the ministers of the word, with gifts for government, and with commission to execute the same when

[24] 1 Cor. 14: 3. But he that *prophesieth* speaketh unto men, to edification, and exhortation, and comfort. 2 Tim. 4: 2. *Preach* the word; be instant in season, out of season; *reprove, rebuke, exhort*, with all long-suffering and doctrine. Tit. 1: 9. Holding fast the faithful word as he hath been taught, that he may be able by sound doctrine both to *exhort* and to *convince* the gainsayers.

[25] [See in [23] preceding.] 1 Pet. 4: 10. *As every man hath received the gift*, even so minister the same one to another, as good stewards of the manifold grace of God. Ver. 11. If any man *speak*, let him speak as the oracles of God; if any man *minister*, let him do it as of the ability which God giveth; that God in all things may be glorified through Jesus Christ: to whom be praise and dominion for ever and ever. Amen.

[26] 2 Tim. 4: 2. *Preach* the word; be instant in season, out of season; *reprove, rebuke, exhort*, with all longsuffering and doctrine. Tit. 1: 9. Holding fast the faithful word as he hath been taught, that he may be able by sound doctrine both to *exhort* and to *convince* the gainsayers. 1 Tim. 6: 2. And they that have believing masters, let them not despise them, because they are brethren; but rather do them service, because they are faithful and beloved, partakers of the benefit. These things *teach* and *exhort*.

[27] 2 Chron. 19: 8. Moreover, in Jerusalem did Jehoshaphat set *of the Levites, and of the priests, and of the chief of the fathers of Israel*, for the judgment of the Lord, and for controversies, when they returned to Jerusalem. Ver. 9. And he charged them, saying, Thus shall ye do in the fear of the Lord, faithfully, and with a perfect heart. Ver. 10. And what cause soever shall come to you of your brethren that dwell in their cities, between blood and blood, between law and commandment, statutes and judgments, ye shall even warn them that they trespass not against the Lord, and so wrath come upon you, and upon your brethren: this do, and ye shall not trespass.

[213]

called thereunto, who are to join with the minister in the government of the church.[28] Which officers reformed churches commonly call Elders.

Deacons

The scripture doth hold out deacons as distinct officers in the church.[29] Whose office is perpetual.[30] To whose office it belongs not to preach the word, or administer the sacraments, but to take special care in distributing to the necessities of the poor.[31]

Of Particular Congregations

It is lawful and expedient that there be fixed congregations, that is, a certain company of Christians to meet in one assembly ordinarily for public worship. When believers multiply to such a number, that they cannot conveniently meet in one place, it is lawful and expedient that they should be divided into distinct and fixed congregations, for the better administration of such ordinances as belong unto them, and the discharge of mutual duties.[32]

The ordinary way of dividing Christians into distinct congregations, and most expedient for edification, is by the respective bounds of their dwellings.

[28] Rom. 12: 7. Or ministry, let us wait on our ministering; or he that teacheth, on teaching; Ver. 8. Or he that exhorteth, on exhortation: he that giveth, let him do it with simplicity; *he that ruleth*, with diligence; he that sheweth mercy, with cheerfulness. 1 Cor. 12: 28. And God hath set some in the church, first apostles; secondarily, *prophets*; thirdly, *teachers*; after that miracles; then gifts of healings, *helps, governments*, diversities of tongues.

[29] Phil. 1: 1. Paul and Timotheus, the servants of Jesus Christ, to all the saints in Christ Jesus which are at Philippi, with the bishops and *deacons*. 1 Tim. 3: 8. Likewise must the *deacons* be grave, not double tongued, not given to much wine, not greedy of filthy lucre.

[30] 1 Tim. 3: 8. Likewise must the *deacons* be grave, not double tongued, not given to much wine, not greedy of filthy lucre. [See in the Bible to Ver. 15.] Acts 6: 1. And in those days, when the number of the disciples was multiplied, there arose a murmuring of the Grecians against the Hebrews, because their widows were neglected in the daily ministration. Ver. 2. Then the twelve called the multitude of the disciples unto them, and said, It is not reason that we should leave the word of God, and serve tables. Ver. 3. Wherefore, brethren, look ye out among you seven men of honest report, full of the Holy Ghost and wisdom, whom we may appoint over this business. Ver. 4. But we will give ourselves continually to prayer, and to the ministry of the word.

[31] Acts 6: 1-4. [See before in[30].]

[32] 1 Cor. 14: 26. *Let all things be done unto edifying*. Ver. 33. For God is not the author of confusion, but of peace, as in all churches of the saints. Ver. 40. *Let all things be done decently*, and in order.

First, Because they who dwell together, being bound to all kind of moral duties one to another, have the better opportunity thereby to discharge them; which moral tie is perpetual; for Christ came not to destroy the law, but to fulfil it.[33]

Secondly, The communion of saints must be so ordered, as may stand with the most convenient use of the ordinances, and discharge of moral duties, without respect of persons.[34]

Thirdly, The pastor and people must so nearly cohabit together, as that they may mutually perform their duties each to other with most conveniency.

In this company some must be set apart to bear office.

Of the Officers of a particular Congregation

For officers in a single congregation, there ought to be one at the least, both to labour in the word and doctrine, and to rule.[35]

It is also requisite that there should be others to join in government.[36]

And likewise it is requisite that there be others to take special care for the relief of the poor.[37]

[33] Deut. 15: 7. If there be among you a poor man of one of thy brethren within any of thy gates, in thy land which the Lord thy God giveth thee, *thou shalt not harden thine heart, nor shut thine hand from thy poor brother*. Ver. 11. For the poor shall never cease out of the land: therefore I command thee, saying, Thou shalt open thine hand wide unto thy brother, to thy poor, and to thy needy, in thy land. Matt. 22: 39. And the second is like unto it, *Thou shalt love thy neighbour as thyself*. Matt. 5: 17. Think not that I am come to destroy the law or the prophets: I am not come to destroy, but to fulfil.

[34] 1 Cor. 14: 26. *Let all things be done unto edifying*. Heb. 10: 24. And *let us consider one another*, to provoke unto love, and to good works: Ver. 25. Not forsaking the assembling of ourselves together, as the manner of some is; but exhorting one another, and so much the more, as ye see the day approaching. James 2: 1. My brethren, have not the faith of our Lord Jesus Christ, the Lord of glory, with respect of persons. Ver. 2. For if there come into your assembly a man with a gold ring, in goodly apparel, and there come in also a poor man in vile raiment, etc.

[35] Prov. 29: 18. Where there is no vision, the people perish: but he that keepeth the law, happy is he. 1 Tim. 5: 17. Let the elders that rule well be counted worthy of double honour, especially they who *labour in the word and doctrine*. Heb. 13: 7. Remember them which have the rule over you, *who have spoken unto you the word of God*; whose faith follow, considering the end of their conversation.

[36] 1 Cor. 12: 28. And God hath set some in the church, first, apostles; secondarily, prophets; thirdly, teachers; after that miracles; then gifts of healings, helps, *governments*, diversities of tongues.

[37] Acts 6: 2. Then the twelve called the multitude of the disciples unto them, and said, It is not reason that we should leave the word of God, and serve tables. Ver. 8. Wherefore, brethren, look ye out among you seven men of honest report, full of the Holy Ghost and wisdom, *whom we may appoint over this business*.

The number of each of which is to be proportioned according to the condition of the congregation.

These officers are to meet together at convenient and set times, for the well ordering of the affairs of that congregation, each according to his office.

It is most expedient that, in these meetings, one whose office is to labour in the word and doctrine, do moderate in their proceedings.[38]

Of the Ordinances in a particular Congregation

The ordinances in a single congregation are, prayer, thanksgiving, and singing of psalms,[39] the word read, (although there follow no immediate explication of what is read) the word expounded and applied, catechising, the sacraments administered, collection made for the poor, dismissing the people with a blessing.

Of Church-Government, and the several sorts of Assemblies for the same

Christ hath instituted a government, and governors ecclesiastical in the church: to that purpose, the apostles did immediately receive the keys from the hand of Jesus Christ, and did use and exercise them in all the churches of the world upon all occasions.

And Christ hath since continually furnished some in his church with gifts of government, and with commission to execute the same, when called thereunto.

It is lawful, and agreeable to the word of God, that the church be governed by several sorts of assemblies, which are congregational, classical, and synodical.

Of the power in common of all these Assemblies

It is lawful, and agreeable to the word of God, that the several assemblies before mentioned have power to convene, and call before them, any person within their several bounds, whom the ecclesiastical business which is before them doth concern.[40]

---

[38] 1 Tim. 5: 17. Let *the elders that rule well* be counted worthy of double honour, especially they who labour in the word and doctrine.

[39] 1 Tim. 2: 1. I exhort therefore, that, first of all, *supplications, prayers, intercessions, and giving of thanks*, be made for all men. 1 Cor. 14: 15. What is it then? I will pray with the spirit, and I will pray with the understanding also; I will *sing with the spirit*, and I will sing with the understanding also. Ver. 16. Else, when thou shalt bless with the spirit, how shall he that occupieth the room of the unlearned say Amen at thy giving of thanks, seeing he understandeth not what thou sayest?

[40] Matt. 18: 15. Moreover, if thy brother shall trespass against thee, go and tell him his fault between him and thee alone: if he shall hear thee, thou hast gained thy brother.

They have power to hear and determine such causes and differences as do orderly come before them.

It is lawful, and agreeable to the word of God, that all the said assemblies have some power to dispense church-censures.

Of Congregational Assemblies, that is, the Meeting of the ruling Officers of a particular Congregation, for the Government thereof

The ruling officers of a particular congregation have power, authoritatively, to call before them any member of the congregation, as they shall see just occasion.

To enquire into the knowledge and spiritual estate of the several members of the congregation.

To admonish and rebuke.

Which three branches are proved by Heb. 13: 17; 1 Thess. 5: 12, 13; Ezek. 34: 4.[41]

Authoritative suspension from the Lord's table, of a person not yet cast out of the church, is agreeable to the scripture:

First, Because the ordinance itself must not be profaned.

Secondly, Because we are charged to withdraw from those that walk disorderly.

Thirdly, Because of the great sin and danger, both to him that comes unworthily, and also to the whole church.[42] And there was power and

---

Ver. 16. But if he will not hear thee, then take with thee one or two more, that in the mouth of two or three witnesses every word may be established. Ver. 17. And if he shall neglect to hear them, *tell it unto the church*; but if he neglect to hear the church, let him be unto thee as an heathen man and a publican. Ver. 18. Verily I say unto you, Whatsoever ye shall bind on earth shall be bound in heaven; and whatsoever ye shall loose on earth shall be loosed in heaven. Ver. 19. Again I say unto you, That if two of you shall agree on earth as touching any thing that they shall ask, it shall be done for them of my Father which is in heaven. Ver. 20. For where two or three are gathered together in my name, there am I in the midst of them.

[41] Heb. 13: 17. *Obey them that have the rule over you,* and submit yourselves: for they watch for your souls, as they that must give account; that they may do it with joy, and not with grief: for that is unprofitable for you. 1 Thess. 5: 12. And we beseech you, brethren, to know them which labour among you, and are over you in the Lord, and admonish you; Ver. 13. And to esteem them very highly in love for their work's sake. And be at peace among yourselves. Ezek. 34: 4. The diseased have ye not strengthened, neither have ye healed that which was sick, neither have ye bound up that which was broken, neither have ye brought again that which was driven away, neither have ye sought that which was lost; but with force and with cruelty have ye ruled them.

[42] Matt 7: 6. Give not that which is holy unto the dogs, neither cast ye your pearls before swine, *lest they trample them under their feet, and turn again and rend you.* 2 Thess. 3: 6. Now we command you, brethren, in the name of our Lord Jesus Christ, that ye

authority, under the Old Testament, to keep unclean persons from holy things.[43]

The like power and authority, by way of analogy, continues under the New Testament.

The ruling officers of a particular congregation have power authoritatively to suspend from the Lord's table a person not yet cast out of the church:

First, Because those who have authority to judge of, and admit, such as are fit to receive the sacrament, have authority to keep back such as shall be found unworthy.

Secondly, Because it is an ecclesiastical business of ordinary practice belonging to that congregation.

When congregations are divided and fixed, they need all mutual help one from another, both in regard of their intrinsical weaknesses and mutual dependence, as also in regard of enemies from without.

Of Classical Assemblies

The scripture doth hold out a presbytery in a church.[44]

A presbytery consisteth of ministers of the word, and such other public officers as are agreeable to and warranted by the word of God to be church-

---

withdraw yourselves from every brother that walketh disorderly, and not after the tradition which he received of us. Ver. 14. And if any man obey not our word by this epistle, note that man, and have no company with him, that he may be ashamed. Ver. 15. Yet count him not as an enemy, but admonish him as a brother. 1 Cor. 11: 27. Wherefore, whosoever shall eat this bread, and drink this cup of the Lord, unworthily, shall be *guilty of the body and blood of the Lord*. [See on to the end of the Chapter.] Compared with Jude, Ver. 23. And others save with fear, pulling them out of the fire; hating even the garment spotted by the flesh. 1 Tim. 5: 22. Lay hands suddenly on no man, *neither be partaker of other men's sins*; keep thyself pure.

[43] Lev. 13: 5. And the priest shall look on him the seventh day: and, behold, if the plague in his sight be at a stay, and the plague spread not in the skin; *then the priest shall shut him up seven days more*. Numb. 9: 7. And those men said unto him, We are defiled by the dead body of a man: *wherefore are we kept back*, that we may not offer an offering of the Lord in his appointed season among the children of Israel? 2 Chron. 23: 19. And *he set the porters* at the gates of the house of the Lord, *that none which was unclean in any thing should enter in*.

[44] 1 Tim. 4: 14. Neglect not the gift that is in thee, which was given thee by prophecy, with the laying on of the hands of *the presbytery*. Acts 15: 2. When therefore Paul and Barnabas had no small dissension and disputation with them, they determined that Paul and Barnabas, and certain other of them, should go up to Jerusalem unto the apostles and elders about this question. Ver. 4. And when they were come to Jerusalem, they were received of the church, and of the apostles and elders, and they declared all things that God had done with them. Ver. 6. And *the apostles and elders came together for to consider of this matter*.

governors, to join with the ministers in the government of the church.[45]

The scripture doth hold forth, that many particular congregations may be under one presbyterial government.

This proposition is proved by instances:

I. *First,* Of the church of Jerusalem, which consisted of more congregations than one, and all these congregations were under one presbyterial government.

This appeareth thus:

First, The church of Jerusalem consisted of more congregations than one, as is manifest:

1*st,* By the multitude of believers mentioned, in divers [places], both before the dispersion of the believers there, by means of the persecution,[46] and also after the dispersion.[47]

2*dly,* By the many apostles and other preachers in the church of Jerusalem. And if there were but one congregation there, then each apostle preached but seldom;[48] which will not consist with Acts 6: 2.

---

[45] Rom. 12: 7. Or *ministry,* let us wait on our ministering; or he that teacheth, on teaching; Ver. 8. Or he that exhorteth, on exhortation: he that giveth, let him do it with simplicity; *he that ruleth,* with diligence; he that sheweth mercy, with cheerfulness. 1 Cor. 12: 28. And God hath set some in the church, first apostles; secondarily, prophets; thirdly, teachers; after that miracles; then gifts of healings, helps, *governments,* diversities of tongues.

[46] Acts 8: 1. And Saul was consenting unto his death. And at that time there was *a great persecution* against the church which was at Jerusalem; and they were all scattered abroad throughout the regions of Judea and Samaria, except the apostles. Acts 1: 15. And in those days Peter stood up in the midst of the disciples, and said, (the number of the names together were about *an hundred and twenty.*) Acts 2: 41. Then they that gladly received his word were baptized: and the same day there were added unto them about *three thousand souls.* Ver. 46. And they, continuing daily with one accord in the temple, and breaking bread from house to house, did eat their meat with gladness and singleness of heart, Ver. 47. Praising God, and having favour with all the people. And the Lord added to the church daily such as should be saved. Acts 4: 4. Howbeit many of them which heard the word believed; and the number of the men was about *five thousand.* Acts 5: 14. And believers were the more added to the Lord, *multitudes both of men and women.* Acts 6: 1. And in those days, when *the number of the disciples was multiplied,* there arose a murmuring of the Grecians against the Hebrews, because their widows were neglected in the daily ministration. Ver. 7. And the word of God increased: and the number of the disciples multiplied in Jerusalem greatly: and *a great company of the priests* were obedient to the faith.

[47] Acts 9: 31. Then had the *churches* rest throughout all *Judea,* and *Galilee,* and *Samaria,* and were edified; and walking in the fear of the Lord, and in the comfort of the Holy Ghost, were *multiplied.* Acts 12: 24. But the word of God *grew and multiplied.* Acts 21: 20. And when they heard it, they glorified the Lord, and said unto him, Thou seest, brother, how *many thousands* of Jews there are which believe; and they are all zealous of the law.

[48] Acts 6: 2. Then the twelve called the multitude of the disciples unto them, and said, *It is not reason that we should leave the word of God,* and serve tables.

3*dly*, The diversity of languages among the believers, mentioned both in the second and sixth chapters of the Acts, doth argue more congregations than one in that church.

Secondly, All those congregations were under one presbyterial government; because,

1*st*, They were one church.[49]

2*dly*, The elders of the church are mentioned.[50]

3*dly*, The apostles did the ordinary acts of presbyters, as presbyters in that kirk; which proveth a presbyterial church before the dispersion, Acts 6.

4*thly*, The several congregations in Jerusalem being one church, the elders of that church are mentioned as meeting together for acts of government;[51] which proves that those several congregations were under one presbyterial government.

And whether these congregations were fixed or not fixed, in regard of officers or members, it is all one as to the truth of the proposition.

Nor doth there appear any material difference betwixt the several congregations in Jerusalem, and the many congregations now in the

[49] Acts 8: 1. And Saul was consenting unto his death. And at that time there was a great persecution against *the church which was at Jerusalem*; and they were all scattered abroad throughout the regions of Judea and Samaria, except the apostles. Acts 2: 47. Praising God, and having favour with all the people. And the Lord added to *the church* daily such as should be saved. Compared with Acts 5: 11. And great fear came upon all the church, and upon as many as heard these things. Acts 12: 5. Peter therefore was kept in prison; but prayer was made without ceasing of *the church* unto God for him. Acts 15: 4. And when they were come to Jerusalem, they were received of *the church*, and of the apostles and elders, and they declared all things that God had done with them.

[50] Acts 11: 30. Which also they did, and sent it to *the elders* by the hands of Barnabas and Saul. Acts 15: 4. And when they were come to Jerusalem, they were received of the church, and of the apostles and *elders*, and they declared all things that God had done with them. Ver. 6. And the apostles and *elders* came together for to consider of this matter. Ver. 22. Then pleased it the apostles and *elders*, with the whole church, to send chosen men of their own company to Antioch with Paul and Barnabas; namely, Judas surnamed Barsabas, and Silas, chief men among the brethren. Acts 21: 17. And when we were come to Jerusalem, the brethren received us gladly. Ver. 18. And the day following Paul went in with us unto James; and *all the elders* were present.

[51] Acts 11: 30. Which also they did, and sent it to the elders by the hands of Barnabas and Saul. Acts 15: 4. And when they were come to Jerusalem, they were received of the church, and of the apostles and elders, and they declared all things that God had done with them. Ver. 6. And *the apostles and elders came together for to consider of this matter.* Ver. 22. Then pleased it *the apostles and elders*, with the whole church, to send chosen men of their own company to Antioch with Paul and Barnabas; namely, Judas surnamed Barsabas, and Silas, chief men among the brethren. Acts 21: 17. And when we were come to Jerusalem, the brethren received us gladly. Ver. 18. And the day following *Paul went in with us unto James; and all the elders were present.* [And so forward.]

ordinary condition of the church, as to the point of fixedness required of officers or members.

Thirdly, Therefore the scripture doth hold forth, that many congregations may be under one presbyterial government.

II. *Secondly,* By the instance of the church of Ephesus; for,

First, That there were more congregations than one in the church of Ephesus, appears by Acts 20: 31,[52] where is mention of Paul's continuance at Ephesus in preaching for the space of three years; and Acts 19: 18, 19, 20, where the special effect of the word is mentioned;[53] and ver. 10 and 17 of the same chapter, where is a distinction of Jews and Greeks;[54] and 1 Cor. 16: 8, 9, where is a reason of Paul's stay at Ephesus until Pentecost;[55] and ver. 19, where is mention of a particular church in the house of Aquila and Priscilla, then at Ephesus,[56] as appears, Acts 18: 19, 24, 26.[57] All which laid together, doth prove that the multitude of believers did make more congregations than one in the church of Ephesus.

Secondly, That there were many elders over these many congregations, as one flock, appeareth.[58]

---

[52] Acts 20: 31. Therefore watch, and remember, that by *the space of three years,* I ceased not to warn every one night and day with tears.

[53] Acts 19: 18. And *many that believed* came, and confessed, and shewed their deeds. Ver. 19. *Many* of them also which used curious arts brought their books together, and burned them before all men: and they counted the price of them, and found it fifty thousand pieces of silver. Ver. 20. *So mightily grew the word of God and prevailed.*

[54] Acts 19: 10. And this continued by the space of two years; so that all they which dwelt in Asia heard the word of the Lord Jesus, *both Jews and Greeks.* Ver. 17. And this was known to *all the Jews and Greeks* also dwelling at Ephesus; and fear fell on them all, and the name of the Lord Jesus was magnified.

[55] 1 Cor. 16: 8. But I will tarry at Ephesus until Pentecost. Ver. 9. For *a great door and effectual is opened unto me,* and there are many adversaries.

[56] 1 Cor. 16: 19. The churches of Asia salute you. Aquila and Priscilla salute you much in the Lord, with *the church that is in their house.*

[57] Acts 18: 19. And he came to *Ephesus,* and left them there: but he himself entered into the synagogue, and reasoned with the Jews. Ver. 24. And a certain Jew, named Apollos, born at Alexandria, an eloquent man, and mighty in the scriptures, came to *Ephesus.* Ver. 26. And he began to speak boldly in the synagogue: whom when Aquila and Priscilla had heard, they took him unto them, and expounded unto him the way of God more perfectly.

[58] Acts 20: 17. And from Miletus he sent to Ephesus, and called *the elders of the church.* Ver. 25. And now, behold, I know that ye all, among whom I have gone preaching the kingdom of God, shall see my face no more. Ver. 28. Take heed therefore unto yourselves, and to all the flock, over the which the Holy Ghost hath made you overseers, to feed the church of God, which he hath purchased with his own blood. Ver. 30. Also of your own selves shall men arise, speaking perverse things, to draw away disciples after them. Ver. 36. And when he had thus spoken, he kneeled down, and prayed with them all. Ver. 37. And they all wept sore, and fell on Paul's neck, and kissed him.

Thirdly, That these many congregations were one church, and that they were under one presbyterial government, appeareth.[59]

Of Synodical Assemblies

The scripture doth hold out another sort of assemblies for the government of the church, beside classical and congregational, all which we call *Synodical.*[60]

Pastors and teachers, and other church-governors, (as also other fit persons, when it shall be deemed expedient,) are members of those assemblies which we call *Synodical,* where they have a lawful calling thereunto.

Synodical assemblies may lawfully be of several sorts, as provincial, national, and oecumenical.

It is lawful, and agreeable to the word of God, that there be a subordination of congregational, classical, provincial, and national assemblies, for the government of the church.

Of Ordination of Ministers

Under the head of Ordination of Ministers is to be considered, either the doctrine of ordination, or the power of it.

Touching the Doctrine of Ordination

No man ought to take upon him the office of a minister of the word without a lawful calling.[61]

[59] Rev. 2: 1. Unto *the angel of the church of Ephesus* write: These things saith he that holdeth the seven stars in his right hand, who walketh in the midst of the seven golden candlesticks; Ver. 2. I know thy works, and thy labour, and thy patience, and how thou canst not bear them which are evil: and thou hast tried them which say they are apostles, and are not, and hast found them liars: Ver. 3. And hast borne, and hast patience, and for my name's sake hast laboured, and hast not fainted. Ver. 4. Nevertheless I have somewhat against thee, because thou hast left thy first love. Ver. 5. Remember therefore from whence thou art fallen, and repent, and do the first works; or else I will come unto thee quickly, and will remove thy candlestick out of his place, except thou repent. Ver. 6. But this thou hast, that thou hatest the deeds of the Nicolaitanes, which I also hate. Joined with Acts 20: 17, 28. [See in [58].]

[60] Acts 15: 2. When therefore Paul and Barnabas had no small dissension and disputation with them, they determined that Paul and Barnabas, and certain other of them, should go up to Jerusalem unto the apostles and elders about this question. Ver. 6. And *the apostles and elders came together* for to consider of this matter. Ver. 22. Then pleased it *the apostles and elders, with the whole church,* to send chosen men of their own company to Antioch, with Paul and Barnabas; namely, Judas surnamed Barsabas, and Silas, chief men among the brethren: Ver. 23. And they wrote letters by them after this manner; *The apostles, and elders, and brethren,* send greeting unto the brethren which are of the Gentiles in Antioch, and Syria, and Cilicia.

[61] John 3: 27. John answered and said, A man can receive nothing, *except it be given him from heaven.* Rom. 10: 14. How then *shall they call on him* in whom they have not

Ordination is always to be continued in the church.[62]

Ordination is the solemn setting apart of a person to some public church office.[63]

Every minister of the word is to be ordained by imposition of hands, and prayer, with fasting, by those preaching presbyters to whom it doth belong.[64]

It is agreeable to the word of God, and very expedient, that such as are to be ordained ministers, be designed to some particular church, or other ministerial charge.[65]

---

believed? and how shall they believe in him of whom they have not heard? and how shall they hear without a preacher? Ver. 15. And *how shall they preach except they be sent?* as it is written, How beautiful are the feet of them that preach the gospel of peace, and bring glad tidings of good things! Jer. 14: 14. Then the Lord said unto me, The prophets prophesy lies in my name: I sent them not, *neither.have I commanded them,* neither spake unto them: they prophesy unto you a false vision and divination, and a thing of nought, and the deceit of their heart. Heb. 5: 4. And no man taketh this honour unto himself, *but he that is called of God,* as was Aaron.

[62] Tit. 1: 5. For this cause left I thee in Crete, that thou shouldest set in order the things that are wanting, and *ordain* elders in every city, as I had appointed thee. 1 Tim. 5: 21. I charge thee before God, and the Lord Jesus Christ, and the elect angels, that thou observe these things, without preferring one before another, doing nothing by partiality. Ver. 22. *Lay hands suddenly on no man,* neither be partaker of other men's sins: keep thyself pure.

[63] Numb. 8: 10. And thou shalt bring the Levites before the Lord; and the children of Israel shall put their hands upon the Levites: Ver. 11. And Aaron shall offer the Levites before the Lord for an offering of the children of Israel, that they may execute the service of the Lord. Ver. 14. Thus *shalt thou separate the Levites* from among the children of Israel; and the Levites shall be mine. Ver. 19. And I have given the Levites as a gift to Aaron, and to his sons, from among the children of Israel, to do the service of the children of Israel in the tabernacle of the congregation, and to make an atonement for the children of Israel; that there be no plague among the children of Israel, when the children of Israel come nigh unto the sanctuary. Ver. 22. And after that went the Levites in to do their service in the tabernacle of the congregation before Aaron, and before his sons: as the Lord had commanded Moses concerning the Levites, so did they unto them. Acts 6: 3. Wherefore, brethren, look ye out among you seven men of honest report, full of the Holy Ghost and wisdom, whom *we may appoint over this business.* Ver. 5. And the saying pleased the whole multitude: and they chose Stephen, a man full of faith and of the Holy Ghost, and Philip, and Prochorus, and Nicanor, and Timon, and Parmenas, and Nicolas a proselyte of Antioch; Ver. 6. Whom they set before the apostles; and when they had prayed, *they laid their hands on them.*

[64] 1 Tim. 5: 22. *Lay hands* suddenly on no man, neither be partaker of other men's sins: keep thyself pure. Acts 14: 23. And when they had ordained them elders in every church, and had *prayed* with *fasting,* they commended them to the Lord, on whom they believed. Acts 13: 3. And when they had *fasted and prayed,* and *laid their hands on them,* they sent them away.

[65] Acts 14: 23. [See before.] Tit. 1: 5. *For this cause left I thee in Crete,* that thou shouldest set in order the things that are wanting, and ordain elders in every city, as I had appointed thee. Acts 20: 17. And from Miletus he sent to Ephesus, and called the elders of the church. Ver. 28. Take heed therefore unto yourselves, and to *all the flock, over the which the Holy Ghost hath made you overseers,* to feed the church of God, which he hath purchased with his own blood.

He that is to be ordained minister, must be duly qualified, both for life and ministerial abilities, according to the rules of the apostle.[66]

He is to be examined and approved by those by whom he is to be ordained.[67]

No man is to be ordained a minister for a particular congregation, if they of that congregation can shew just cause of exception against him.[68]

Touching the Power of Ordination

Ordination is the act of a presbytery.[69]

The power of ordering the whole work of ordination is in the whole presbytery, which, when it is over more congregations than one, whether these congregations be fixed or not fixed, in regard of officers or members, it is indifferent as to the point of ordination.[70]

It is very requisite, that no single congregation, that can conveniently associate, do assume to itself all and sole power in ordination:

1. Because there is no example in scripture that any single congregation, which might conveniently associate, did assume to itself all and sole power in ordination; neither is there any rule which may warrant such a practice.

2. Because there is in scripture example of an ordination in a presbytery over divers congregations; as in the church of Jerusalem, where were many

[66] I Tim. 3: 2. A bishop then must be *blameless, the husband of one wife, vigilant, sober, of good behaviour, given to hospitality, apt to teach*; Ver. 3. *Not given to wine, no striker, not greedy of filthy lucre*; but *patient*, not a brawler, not covetous; Ver. 4. *One that ruleth well his own house*, having his children in subjection with all gravity; Ver. 5. (For if a man know not how to rule his own house, how shall he take care of the church of God?) Ver. 6. *Not a novice*, lest, being lifted up with pride, he fall into the condemnation of the devil. Tit. 1: 5. For this cause left I thee in Crete, that thou shouldest set in order the things that are wanting, and ordain elders in every city, as I had appointed thee. Ver. 6. If any be *blameless, the husband of one wife, having faithful children, not accused of riot or unruly*. Ver. 7. For a bishop must be *blameless*, as the steward of God; *not self-willed, not soon angry, not given to wine, no striker, not given to filthy lucre*; Ver. 8. But *a lover of hospitality, a lover of good men, sober, just, holy, temperate*; Ver. 9. *Holding fast the faithful word* as he hath been taught, that he may be able by sound doctrine both to exhort and to convince the gainsayers.
[67] I Tim. 3: 7. Moreover, he must have a good report of them which are without; lest he fall into reproach and the snare of the devil. Ver. 10. *And let these also first be proved*; then let them use the office of a deacon, being found blameless. I Tim. 5: 22. *Lay hands suddenly on no man*, neither be partaker of other men's sins: keep thyself pure.
[68] I Tim. 3: 2. A bishop then must be *blameless*, the husband of one wife, vigilant, sober, of good behaviour, given to hospitality, apt to teach. Tit. 1: 7. For a bishop must be *blameless*, as the steward of God.
[69] I Tim. 4: 14. Neglect not the gift that is in thee, which was given thee by prophecy, with the laying on of the hands of the *presbytery*.
[70] I Tim. 4: 14. [See in [69].]

congregations: these many congregations were under one presbytery, and this presbytery did ordain.

The preaching presbyters orderly associated, either in cities or neighbouring villages, are those to whom the imposition of hands doth appertain, for those congregations within their bounds respectively.

Concerning the Doctrinal Part of Ordination of Ministers

1. No man ought to take upon him the office of a minister of the word without a lawful calling.[71]

2. Ordination is always to be continued in the church.[72]

3. Ordination is the solemn setting apart of a person to some public church office.[73]

4. Every minister of the word is to be ordained by imposition of hands, and prayer, with fasting, by these preaching presbyters to whom it doth belong.[74]

5. The power of ordering the whole work of ordination is in the whole presbytery, which, when it is over more congregations than one, whether those congregations be fixed or not fixed, in regard of officers or members, it is indifferent as to the point of ordination.[75]

6. It is agreeable to the word, and very expedient, that such as are to be ordained ministers be designed to some particular church, or other ministerial charge.[76]

7. He that is to be ordained minister, must be duly qualified, both for life and ministerial abilities, according to the rules of the apostle.[77]

8. He is to be examined and approved by those by whom he is to be ordained.[78]

9. No man is to be ordained a minister for a particular congregation, if they of that congregation can shew just cause of exception against him.[79]

10. Preaching presbyters orderly associated, either in cities or neighbouring villages, are those to whom the imposition of hands doth appertain, for those congregations within their bounds respectively.[80]

11. In extraordinary cases, something extraordinary may be done, until a settled order may be had, yet keeping as near as possibly may be to the rule.[81]

[71] See before in [61]. [72] See before in [62]. [73] See before in [63].
[74] See before in [64]. [75] See before in [70]. [76] See before in [65].
[77] See before in [66]. [78] See before in [67]. [79] See before in [68].
[80] 1 Tim. 4:14. Neglect not the gift that is in thee, which was given thee by prophecy, with the laying on of the hands of the *presbytery*.
[81] 2 Chron. 29:34. But the priests were too few, so that they could not flay all the burnt-offerings: wherefore *their brethren the Levites did help them*, till the work was

12. There is at this time (as we humbly conceive) an extraordinary occasion for a way of ordination for the present supply of ministers.

The Directory for the Ordination of Ministers

It being manifest by the word of God, that no man ought to take upon him the office of a minister of the gospel, until he be lawfully called and ordained thereunto; and that the work of ordination is to be performed with all due care, wisdom, gravity, and solemnity, we humbly tender these directions, as requisite to be observed.

1. He that is to be ordained, being either nominated by the people, or otherwise commended to the presbytery, for any place, must address himself to the presbytery, and bring with him a testimonial of his taking the Covenant of the three kingdoms; of his diligence and proficiency in his studies; what degrees he hath taken in the university, and what hath been the time of his abode there; and withal of his age, which is to be twenty-four years; but especially of his life and conversation.

2. Which being considered by the presbytery, they are to proceed to enquire touching the grace of God in him, and whether he be of such holiness of life as is requisite in a minister of the gospel; and to examine him touching his learning and sufficiency, and touching the evidences of his calling to the holy ministry; and, in particular, his fair and direct calling to that place.

The Rules for Examination are these:

"(1.) That the party examined be dealt withal in a brotherly way, with mildness of spirit, and with special respect to the gravity, modesty, and quality of every one.

"(2.) He shall be examined touching his skill in the original tongues,

---

ended, and until the other priests had sanctified themselves; for the Levites were more upright in heart to sanctify themselves than the priests. Ver. 35. And also the burnt-offerings were in abundance, with the fat of the peace-offerings, and the drink-offerings for every burnt-offering. So the service of the house of the Lord was set in order. Ver. 36. And Hezekiah rejoiced, and all the people, that God had prepared the people: for the thing was done suddenly. 2 Chron. 30: 2. For the king had taken counsel, and his princes, and all the congregation in Jerusalem, to keep the passover *in the second month.* Ver. 3. *For they could not keep it at that time, because the priests had not sanctified themselves sufficiently,* neither had the people gathered themselves together to Jerusalem. Ver. 4. And the thing pleased the king and all the congregation. Ver. 5. So they established a decree to make proclamation throughout all Israel, from Beer-sheba even to Dan, that they should come to keep the passover unto the Lord God of Israel at Jerusalem: for they had not done it for a long time in such sort as it was written.

and his trial to be made by reading the Hebrew and Greek Testaments, and rendering some portion of some into Latin; and if he be defective in them, enquiry shall be made more strictly after his other learning, and whether he hath skill in logic and philosophy.

"(3.) What authors in divinity he hath read, and is best acquainted with; and trial shall be made in his knowledge of the grounds of religion, and of his ability to defend the orthodox doctrine contained in them against all unsound and erroneous opinions, especially these of the present age; of his skill in the sense and meaning of such places of scripture as shall be proposed unto him, in cases of conscience, and in the chronology of the scripture, and the ecclesiastical history.

"(4.) If he hath not before preached in public with approbation of such as are able to judge, he shall, at a competent time assigned him, expound before the presbytery such a place of scripture as shall be given him.

"(5.) He shall also, within a competent time, frame a discourse in Latin upon such a common-place or controversy in divinity as shall be assigned to him, and exhibit to the presbytery such theses as express the sum thereof, and maintain a dispute upon them.

"(6.) He shall preach before the people, – the presbytery, or some of the ministers of the word appointed by them, being present.

"(7.) The proportion of his gifts in relation to the place unto which he is called shall be considered.

"(8.) Beside the trial of his gifts in preaching, he shall undergo an examination in the premises two several days, and more, if the presbytery shall judge it necessary.

"(9.) And as for him that hath formerly been ordained a minister, and is to be removed to another charge, he shall bring a testimonial of his ordination, and of his abilities and conversation, whereupon his fitness for that place shall be tried by his preaching there, and (if it shall be judged necessary) by a further examination of him."

3. In all which he being approved, he is to be sent to the church where he is to serve, there to preach three several days, and to converse with the people, that they may have trial of his gifts for their edification, and may have time and occasion to enquire into, and the better to know, his life and conversation.

4. In the last of these three days appointed for the trial of his gifts in preaching, there shall be sent from the presbytery to the congregation a public intimation in writing, which shall be publicly read before the people, and after affixed to the church-door, to signify that such a day a

competent number of the members of that congregation, nominated by themselves, shall appear before the presbytery, to give their consent and approbation to such a man to be their minister; or otherwise, to put in, with all Christian discretion and meekness, what exceptions they have against him. And if, upon the day appointed, there be no just exception against him, but the people give their consent, then the presbytery shall proceed to ordination.

5. Upon the day appointed for ordination, which is to be performed in that church where he that is to be ordained is to serve, a solemn fast shall be kept by the congregation, that they may the more earnestly join in prayer for a blessing upon the ordinances of Christ, and the labours of his servant for their good. The presbytery shall come to the place, or at least three or four ministers of the word shall be sent thither from the presbytery; of which one appointed by the presbytery shall preach to the people concerning the office and duty of ministers of Christ, and how the people ought to receive them for their work's sake.

6. After the sermon, the minister who hath preached shall, in the face of the congregation, demand of him who is now to be ordained, concerning his faith in Christ Jesus, and his persuasion of the truth of the reformed religion, according to the scriptures; his sincere intentions and ends in desiring to enter into this calling; his diligence in praying, reading, meditation, preaching, ministering the sacraments, discipline, and doing all ministerial duties towards his charge; his zeal and faithfulness in maintaining the truth of the gospel, and unity of the church, against error and schism; his care that himself and his family may be unblameable, and examples to the flock; his willingness and humility, in meekness of spirit, to submit unto the admonitions of his brethren, and discipline of the church; and his resolution to continue in his duty against all trouble and persecution.

7. In all which having declared himself, professed his willingness, and promised his endeavours, by the help of God; the minister likewise shall demand of the people concerning their willingness to receive and acknowledge him as the minister of Christ; and to obey and submit unto him, as having rule over them in the Lord; and to maintain, encourage, and assist him in all the parts of his office.

8. Which being mutually promised by the people, the presbytery, or the ministers sent from them for ordination, shall solemnly set him apart to the office and work of the ministry, by laying their hands on him, which is to be accompanied with a short prayer or blessing, to this effect:

"Thankfully acknowledging the great mercy of God in sending Jesus Christ for the redemption of his people; and for his ascension to the right hand of God the Father, and thence pouring out his Spirit, and giving gifts to men, apostles, evangelists, prophets, pastors, and teachers; for the gathering and building up of his church; and for fitting and inclining this man to this great work:[82] to entreat him to fit him with his Holy Spirit, to give him (who in his name we thus set apart to this holy service) to fulfil the work of his ministry in all things, that he may both save himself, and his people committed to his charge."

9. This or the like form of prayer and blessing being ended, let the minister who preached briefly exhort him to consider of the greatness of his office and work, the danger of negligence both to himself and his people, the blessing which will accompany his faithfulness in this life, and that to come; and withal exhort the people to carry themselves to him, as to their minister in the Lord, according to their solemn promise made before. And so by prayer commending both him and his flock to the grace of God, after singing of a psalm, let the assembly be dismissed with a blessing.

10. If a minister be designed to a congregation, who hath been formerly ordained presbyter according to the form of ordination which hath been in the church of England, which we hold for substance to be valid, and not to be disclaimed by any who have received it; then, there being a cautious proceeding in matters of examination, let him be admitted without any new ordination.

11. And in case any person already ordained minister in Scotland, or in any other reformed church, be designed to another congregation in England, he is to bring from that church to the presbytery here, within which that congregation is, a sufficient testimonial of his ordination, of his life and conversation while he lived with them, and of the causes of his removal; and to undergo such a trial of his fitness and sufficiency, and to have the same course held with him in other particulars, as is set down in the rule immediately going before, touching examination and admission.

12. That records be carefully kept in the several presbyteries, of the names of the persons ordained, with their testimonials, the time and place of their ordination, of the presbyters who did impose hands upon them, and of the charge to which they are appointed.

13. That no money or gift, of what kind soever, shall be received from the person to be ordained, or from any on his behalf, for ordination, or ought else belonging to it, by any of the presbytery, or any appertaining to any of them, upon what pretence soever.

[82] Here let them impose hands on his head.

[229]

Thus far of ordinary Rules, and of course of Ordination, in the ordinary way; that which concerns the extraordinary way, requisite to be now practised, followeth.

1. In these present exigencies, while we cannot have any presbyteries formed up to their whole power and work, and that many ministers are to be ordained for the service of the armies and navy, and to many congregations where there is no minister at all; and where (by reason of the public troubles) the people cannot either themselves enquire and find out one who may be a faithful minister for them, or have any with safety sent unto them, for such a solemn trial as was before mentioned in the ordinary rules; especially, when there can be no presbytery near unto them, to whom they may address themselves, or which may come or send to them a fit man to be ordained in that congregation, and for that people; and yet notwithstanding, it is requisite that ministers be ordained for them by some, who, being set apart themselves for the work of the ministry, have power to join in the setting apart others, who are found fit and worthy. In those cases, until, by God's blessing, the aforesaid difficulties may be in some good measure removed, let some godly ministers, in or about the city of London, be designed by public authority, who, being associated, may ordain ministers for the city and the vicinity, keeping as near to the ordinary rules fore-mentioned as possibly they may; and let this association be for no other intent or purpose, but only for the work of ordination.

2. Let the like association be made by the same authority in great towns, and the neighbouring parishes in the several counties, which are at the present quiet and undisturbed, to do the like for the parts adjacent.

3. Let such as are chosen, or appointed for the service of the armies or navy, be ordained, as aforesaid, by the associated ministers of London, or some others in the country.

4. Let them do the like, when any man shall duly and lawfully be recommended to them for the ministry of any congregation, who cannot enjoy liberty to have a trial of his parts and abilities, and desire the help of such ministers so associated, for the better furnishing of them with such a person as by them shall be judged fit for the service of that church and people.

The Cambridge Platform 1648

APART FROM THE FAMOUS PILGRIM FATHERS, WHO WERE FROM A SEPARA-
tist background, practically all the early emigrants to New England were from the
mainstream of English Puritanism. Having been unable to conform in England to
the liturgy and order of the Established Church, they now dispensed with them
and sought to follow a more scriptural pattern. But for two decades they had no
confession of faith and no platform of church order. In 1646 the General Court of
Massachusetts Colony, which was the governing body, called a synod at Cambridge
to resolve several ecclesiastical issues. Three ministers were deputed by the Synod:
each was to draw up a model of church government. The consideration of these was
postponed until 1648 because of a prevailing infection at Cambridge.

When the Synod re-assembled, the model drawn up by Richard Mather of Dor-
chester (1596–1669), father of Increase Mather and grandfather of Cotton Mather,
was accepted in a modified form. The Preface to the Cambridge Platform was
written by John Cotton (1585–1657) of Boston, probably the ablest and most
influential of the early New England divines; its object was to vindicate the orthodoxy of the New England churches, which had been challenged by critics in England
and Scotland. The Preface expresses the churches' hearty assent to the newly published Westminster Confession of Faith, except for some sections on church discipline, and seeks to answer the objection that they gathered churches out of churches,
though they could hardly have done this in New England where there were no
'parish churches' at first.

The Cambridge Platform was adopted by the Massachusetts General Court in
1651, and remained the legally recognized standard there until 1780. It was much
more influential in practice than the English Savoy Declaration.

Bibliography
For historical background: *Magnalia Christi Americana*, Cotton Mather,
Hartford, Conn., 1853–1855 (reprint); *The Creeds and Platforms of Congregationalism*, Williston Walker, 1893 and 1960 (this contains a large bibliography); *The Congregationalism of the Last Three Hundred Years as seen in
its Literature*, H. M. Dexter, 1879; *Orthodoxy in Massachusetts*, Perry Miller.

The Cambridge Platform 1648

THE PREFACE

The setting forth of the public confession of the faith of churches hath a double end, and both tending to public edification. First the maintenance of the faith entire within itself: secondly the holding forth of unity and harmony, both amongst, and with other churches. Our churches here, as (by the grace of Christ) we believe and profess the same doctrine of the truth of the Gospel, which generally is received in all the reformed churches of Christ in Europe: so especially, we desire not to vary from the doctrine of faith and truth held forth by the churches of our native country. For though it be not one native country, that can breed us all of one mind; nor ought we for to have the glorious faith of our Lord Jesus with respect of persons: yet as Paul who was himself a Jew, professed to hold forth the doctrine of justification by faith, and of the resurrection of the dead, according as he knew his godly countrymen did, who were Jews by nature (Gal. 2: 15; Acts 26: 6, 7), so we, who are by nature Englishmen, do desire to hold forth the same doctrine of religion (especially in fundamentals) which we see and know to be held by the churches of England, according to the truth of the Gospel.

The more we discern (that which we do, and have cause to do with incessant mourning and trembling) the unkind, and unbrotherly, and unchristian contentions of our godly brethren and countrymen, in matters of church government: the more earnestly do we desire to see them joined together in one common faith, and ourselves with them. For this end, having perused the public confession of faith, agreed upon by the reverend assembly of divines at Westminster, and finding the sum and substance thereof (in matters of doctrine) to express not their own judgments only, but ours also: and being likewise called upon by our godly magistrates, to draw up a public confession of that faith, which is constantly taught, and generally professed amongst us, we thought good to present unto them, and with them to our churches, and with them to all the churches of Christ abroad, our professed and hearty assent and attestation to the whole confession of faith (for substance of doctrine) which the reverend assembly presented to the religious and honourable Parliament of England: Excepting only some sections in the 25, 30 and 31st Chapters of their confession, which concern points of controversy in church-discipline; Touching which we refer ourselves to the draft of church-discipline in the ensuing treatise.

The truth of what we here declare, may appear by the unanimous vote of the Synod of the Elders and messengers of our churches assembled at Cambridge, the last of the sixth month, 1648: which jointly passed in these words: This Synod having perused, and considered (with much gladness of heart, and thankfulness to God) the confession of faith published of late by the reverend Assembly in England, do judge it to be very holy, orthodox, and judicious in all matters of faith: and do therefore freely and fully consent thereunto, for the substance thereof. Only in those things which have respect to church government and discipline, we refer ourselves to the platform of church-discipline, agreed upon by this present assembly: and do therefore think it meet, that this confession of faith, should be commended to the churches of Christ amongst us, and to the Honoured Court, as worthy of their due consideration and acceptance. *Howbeit, we may not conceal that the doctrine of vocation expressed in* Chap. 10. S 1. *and summarily repeated* Chap. 13 and 1. *passed not without some debate. Yet considering, that the term of vocation, and others by which it is described, are capable of a large, or more strict sense, and use, and that it is not intended to bind apprehensions precisely in point of order or method, there hath been a general condescendency thereunto.*

Now by this our professed consent and free concurrence with them in all the doctrinals of religion, we hope it may appear to the world, that as we are a remnant of the people of the same nation with them: so we are professors of the same common faith, and fellow heirs of the same common salvation. Yea moreover, as this our profession of the same faith with them will exempt us (even in their judgments) from suspicion of heresy: so (we trust) it may exempt us in the like sort from suspicion of schism: that though we are forced to dissent from them in matters of church discipline: yet our dissent is not taken up out of arrogance of spirit in ourselves (whom they see willingly condescend to learn of them): neither is it carried with uncharitable censoriousness towards them (both which are the proper and essential characters of schism), but in meekness of wisdom, as we walk along with them, and follow them, as they follow Christ: so where we conceive a different apprehension of the mind of Christ (as it falleth out in some few points touching church order) we still reserve due reverence to them (whom we judge to be, through Christ, the glorious lights of both nations): and only crave leave (as in spirit we are bound) to follow the Lamb whithersoever he goeth, and (after the Apostle's example) as we believe, so we speak.

And if the example of such poor outcasts as ourselves, might prevail if not with all (for that were too great a blessing to hope for) yet with some or other of our brethren in England, so far as they are come to mind and speak the same thing with such as dissent from them, we hope in Christ, it would not only moderate the harsh judging and condemning of one another in such differences of judgment, as may be found in the choicest saints: but also prevent (by the mercy of Christ) the peril of the distraction and destruction of all the churches in both kingdoms. Otherwise, if brethren shall go on to bite and devour one another, the Apostle feared (as we also, with sadness of heart do) it will tend to the consuming of them, and us all: which the Lord prevent.

We are not ignorant, that (besides these aspersions of heresy and schism) other exceptions also are taken at our way of church-government: but (as we conceive) upon as little ground.

As 1 That by admitting none into the fellowship of our Church, but saints by calling, we rob many parish-churches of their best members, to make up one of our congregations: which is not only, to gather churches out of churches (a thing unheard of in Scripture): but also to weaken the hearts and hands of the best ministers in the parishes, by despoiling them of their best hearers.

2 That we provide no course for the gaining, and calling in, of ignorant, and erroneous, and scandalous persons, whom we refuse to receive into our churches, and so exclude from the wholesome remedy of church-discipline.

3 That in our way, we sow seeds of division and hindrance of edification in every family: whilst admitting into our churches only voluntaries, the husband will be of one church, the wife of another: the parents of one church, the children of another: the master of one church, the servants of another. And so the parents and masters being of different churches from their children and servants, they cannot take a just account of their profiting by what they hear, yea by this means the husbands, parents, and masters, shall be chargeable to the maintenance of many other churches, and church-officers, besides their own: which will prove a charge and burden unsupportable.

But for answer, as to the first. For gathering churches out of churches, we cannot say, that is a thing unheard of in Scripture. The first Christian church was gathered out of the Jewish church, and out of many synagogues in that church, and consisted partly of the inhabitants of Jerusalem, partly of the Galileans: who though they kept some communion in some parts of public worship with the temple: yet neither did they frequent the sacrifices, nor repair to the Sanhedrim for the determining of their church-causes: but kept entire and constant communion with the Apostles' church in all the ordinances of the gospel. And for the first Christian church of the Gentiles at Antioch, it appears to have been gathered and constituted partly of the dispersed brethren of the church at Jerusalem (whereof some were men of Cyprus, and Cyrene) and partly of the believing Gentiles. Acts 11: 20, 21.

If it be said the first Christian church at Jerusalem, and that at Antioch were gathered not out of any Christian church, but out of the Jewish temple and synagogues, which were shortly after to be abolished: and their gathering to Antioch, was upon occasion of dispersion in time of persecution.

We desire, it may be considered, 1 That the members of the Jewish church were more strongly and straitly tied by express holy covenant, to keep fellowship with the Jewish church, till it was abolished, than any members of Christian parish-churches are wont to be tied to keep fellowship with their parish-churches. The episcopal canons, which bind them to attend on their parish church, it is likely they are now abolished with the Episcopacy. The common law of the land is satisfied (as we conceive) if they attend upon the worship of God in any other church though not within their own parish. But no such like covenant of God, nor any other religious tie lieth upon them to attend the worship of God in their own parish church, as did lie upon the Jews to attend upon the worship of God in their temple and synagogues.

2 Though the Jewish temple Church at Jerusalem was to be abolished, yet that doth not make the desertion of it by the members, to be lawful, till it was abolished. Future abolition is no warrant for present desertion: unless it be lawful in some case whilst the church is yet in present standing to desert it; to wit, either for avoiding of present pollutions, or for hope of greater edification, and so for better satisfaction to conscience in either. Future events (or foresight of them) do not dissolve present relations. Else wives, children, servants, might desert their husbands, parents, masters, when they be mortally sick.

3 What the members of the Jewish church did, in joining to the church at Antioch in time of persecution, it may well be conceived the members of any Christian church may do the like, for satisfaction of conscience. Peace of conscience is more desirable than the peace of the outward man: and freedom from scruples of conscience is more comfortable to a sincere heart than freedom from persecution.

If it be said, these members of the Christian Church at Jerusalem, that joined to the church at Antioch, removed their habitations together with their relations: which if the brethren of the congregational way would do, it would much abate the grievance of their departure from their presbyterial churches.

We verily could wish them so to do, as well approving the like removal of habitations, in case of changing church-relations (provided, that it may be done without too much detriment to their outward estates) and we for our parts, have done the same. But to put a necessity of removal of habitation in such a case, it is to foment and cherish a corrupt principle of making civil cohabitation, if not a formal cause, yet at least a proper adjunct of church-relation; which the truth of the

Gospel doth not acknowledge. Now to foment an error to the prejudice of the truth of the Gospel, is not to walk with a right foot according to the truth of the Gospel, as Paul judgeth. Gal. 2: 14.

4 *We do not think it meet, or safe, for a member of a presbyterial church, forthwith to desert his relation to his church, betake himself to the fellowship of a congregational church, though he may discern some defect in the estate, or government of his own.*

For 1 Faithfulness of brotherly love in church-relation requireth, that the members of the church should first convince their brethren of their sinful defects, and duly wait for their reformation, before they depart from them. For if we must take such a course for the healing of a private brother, in a way of brotherly love, with much meekness, and patience: how much more ought we so to walk with like tenderness towards a whole church.

Again 2 By the hasty departure of sound members from a defective church, reformation is not promoted, but many times retarded, and corruption increased. Whereas on the contrary, while sincere members breathing after purity of reformation abide together, they may (by the blessing of God upon their faithful endeavours) prevail much with their elders and neighbours towards a reformation; it may be, so much, as that their elders in their own church shall receive none to the seals but visible saints: and in the classis shall put forth no authoritative act (but consultative only) touching the members of other churches: nor touching their own, but with the consent (silent consent at least) of their own church: which two things, if they can obtain with any humble, meek, holy, faithful endeavours, we conceive they might (by the grace of Christ) find liberty of conscience to continue their relation with their own presbyterial church without scruple.

5 *But to add a word farther, touching the gathering of churches out of churches, what if there were no express example of such a thing extant in the Scriptures? that which we are wont to answer the Anti-paedobaptists, may suffice here: it is enough, if any evidence thereof may be gathered from just consequence of Scripture light. Dr Ames' judgment concerning this case, passeth (for aught we know) without exception, which he gave in his 4th book of conscience[1] in answer to question 3.*

If any (he says) wronged with unjust vexation, or providing for his own edification or in testimony against sin depart from a church where some evils are tolerated, and join himself to another more pure, yet without condemning of the church he leaveth, he is not therefore to be held as a schismatic, or as guilty of any other sin. *Where the Tripartite disjunction, which the judicious Doctor putteth, declareth the lawfulness of the departure of*

---

[1] Dr William Ames, *De Conscientia*, Amsterdam, 1635.

[238]

a church-member from his church, when either through weariness of unjust vexation, or in way of provision for his own edification, or in testimony against sin, he joineth himself to another congregation more reformed. Any one of these, he judgeth a just and lawful cause of departure, though all of them do not concur together. Neither will such a practice despoil the best ministers of the parishes of their best hearers.

For 1 Sometimes the ministers themselves are willing to join with their better sort of hearers, in this way of reformation: and then they and their hearers continue still their church relation together, yea and confirm it more straitly and strongly, by an express renewed covenant, though the ministers may still continue their wonted preaching to the whole parish.

2 If the ministers do dislike the way of those, whom they otherwise count their best members, and so refuse to join with them therein; yet if those members can procure some other ministers to join with them in their own way, and still continue their dwelling together in the same town, they may easily order the times of the public assembly, as to attend constantly upon the ministry of their former Church: and either after or before the public assembly of the parish take an opportunity to gather together for the administration of sacraments, and censures, and other church ordinances amongst themselves. The first apostolic church assembled to hear the word with the Jewish church in the open courts of the temple: but afterwards gathered together for breaking of bread, and other acts of church-order, from house to house.

3 Suppose presbyterial churches should communicate some of their best gifted members towards the erecting and gathering of another church: it would not forthwith be their detriment, but may be their enlargement. It is the most noble and perfect work of a living creature (both in nature and grace) to propagate, and multiply his kind: and it is the honour of the faithful spouse of Christ, to set forward the work of Christ as well abroad as at home. The church in Cant. 8: 8–9, to help forward her little sister-church, was willing to part with her choice-materials, even beams of cedar, and such precious living stones, as were fit to build a silver palace. In the same book, the church is compared sometime to a garden, sometime to an orchard, Cant. 4: 12, 13. No man planteth a garden, or orchard, but seeketh to get the choicest herbs and plants of his neighbours, and they freely impart them: nor do they account it a spoil to their gardens, and orchards, but rather a glory. Nevertheless, we go not so far: we neither seek nor ask the choice-members of the parishes but accept them being offered.

If it be said, they are not offered by the ministers, nor by the parish churches (who have most right in them) but only by themselves.

It may justly be demanded, what right, or what power have either the ministers, or parish church over them? Not by solemn church covenant: for that, though it be the firmest engagement, is not owned, but rejected. If it be, by their joining with the parish, in the calling and election of a minister to such a congregation at his first coming, there is indeed just weight in such an engagement: nor do we judge it safe for such to remove from such a minister, unless it be upon such grounds as may justly give him due satisfaction. But if the union of such members to a parish church, and to the ministry thereof, be only by cohabitation within the precincts of the parish, that union, as it was founded upon human law: so by human law it may easily be released. Or otherwise, if a man remove his habitation, he removeth also the bond of his relation, and the ground of offence.

4 It need not to be feared, that all best hearers of the best ministers, no, nor the most of them, will depart from them upon point of church government. Those who have found the presence and power of the spirit of Christ breathing in their ministers, either to their conversion, or edification, will be slow to change such a ministry of faith, and holiness, for the liberty of church order. Upon which ground, and sundry other such like, there be doubtless sundry godly and judicious hearers in many parishes in England that do and will prefer their relation to their ministers (though in a presbyterial way) above the congregational confederation.

5 But if all, or the most part of the best hearers of the best ministers of parishes, should depart from them, as preferring in their judgments, the congregational way: yet, in case the congregational way should prove to be of Christ, it will never grieve the holy hearts of godly ministers, that their hearers should follow after Christ: yea many of themselves (upon due deliberation) will be ready to go along with them. It never grieved nor troubled John Baptist, that his best disciples departed from him to follow after Christ, John 3. But in case the congregational way should prove to be, not the institution of Christ (as we take it) but the invention of men: then doubtless, the presbyterial form (if it be of God) will swallow up the other, as Moses' rod devoured the rods of the Egyptians. Nor will this put a necessity upon both the opposite parties, to shift for themselves, and to seek to supplant one another: but only, it will call upon them ἀληθεύειν ἐν ἀγάπῃ to seek and to follow the truth in love, to attend in faithfulness each unto his own flock, and to administer to them all the holy things of God, and their portion of food in due season: and as for others, quietly to forbear them, and yet to instruct them with meekness that are

contrary minded: leaving it to Christ (in the use of all good means) to reveal his own truth in his own time: and meanwhile endeavouring to keep the unity of the Spirit in the bond of peace. Phil. 3: 15, 16; Eph. 4: 3.

To the 2nd Exception, That we take no course for the gaining and healing and calling in of ignorant, and erroneous, and scandalous persons, whom we refuse to receive into our churches and so exclude them from the remedy of church-discipline.

We conceive the receiving of them into our churches would rather lose and corrupt our Churches, than gain and heal them. A little leaven laid in a lump of dough, will sooner leaven the whole lump, than the whole-lump will sweeten it. We therefore find it safer, to square rough and unhewn stones, before they be laid into the building, rather than to hammer and hew them, when they lie unevenly in the building.

And accordingly, two means we use to gain and call in such as are ignorant or scandalous. 1 The public ministry of the Word, upon which they are invited by counsel, and required by wholesome laws to attend. And the Word it is, which is the power of God to salvation, to the calling and winning of souls. 2 Private conference, and conviction by the elders, and other able brethren of the church: whom they do the more respectively hearken unto, when they see no hope of enjoying church-fellowship, or participation in the sacraments for themselves, or their children, till they approve their judgments to be sound and orthodox, and their lives subdued to some hope of a godly conversation. What can classical discipline, or excommunication itself do more in this case?

The 3rd Exception wraps up in it a threefold domestical inconvenience: and each of them meet to be eschewed. 1 Disunion in families between each relation: 2 Disappointment of edification, for want of opportunity in the governors of families to take account of things heard by their children and servants. 3 Disbursements of chargeable maintenance to the several churches, whereto the several persons of their families are joined.

All which inconveniences either do not fall out in congregational-churches; or are easily redressed. For none are orderly admitted into congregational-churches, but such as are well approved by good testimony, to be duly observant of family-relations. Or if any otherwise disposed should creep in, they are either orderly healed, or duly removed in a way of Christ. Nor are they admitted, unless they can give some good account of their profiting by ordinances, before the elders and brethren of the church: and much more to their parents, and masters. Godly tutors in the university can take an account of their pupils: and godly householders in the city can take account of their children and servants, how they profit by the Word they have heard in several churches: and that to the greater edification of the whole family, by the variety of such administrations. Bees may bring more honey and wax into the hive, when they are not limited to one garden of flowers, but may fly abroad to many.

Nor is any charge expected from wives, children, or servants to the maintenance of congregational churches, further than they be furnished with personal estates, or earnings, which may enable them to contribute of such things as they have, and not of such as they have not. *God accepteth not robbery for a sacrifice.* And though a godly householder may justly take himself bound in conscience, to contribute to any such church, whereto his wife, or children, or servants do stand in relation: yet that will not aggravate the burden of his charge, no more than if they were received members of the same church whereto himself is related.

But why do we stand thus long to plead exemptions from exceptions? The Lord help all his faithful servants (whether presbyterial, or congregational) to judge and shame ourselves before the Lord for all our former compliances to greater enormities in church government, than are to be found either in the congregational or presbyterial way. And then surely, either the Lord will clear up his own will to us, and so frame and subdue us all to one mind, and one way (Ezek. 43: 10, 11), or else we shall learn to bear one another's burdens in a spirit of meekness. It will then doubtless be far from us, so to attest the discipline of Christ, as to detest the disciples of Christ, so to contend for the seamless coat of Christ, as to crucify the living members of Christ, so to divide ourselves about church communion, as through breaches to open a wide gap for a deluge of Antichristian and profane malignity to swallow up both church and civil state.

What shall we say more? Is difference about church order become the inlet of all the disorders in the kingdom? Has the Lord indeed left us to such hardness of heart, that Church government shall become a snare to Zion (as sometimes Moses was to Egypt, Ex. 10: 7) that we cannot leave contesting and contending about it, till the kingdom be destroyed? Did not the Lord Jesus, when he dedicated his sufferings for his church, and his also unto his father, make it his earnest and only prayer for us in this world, that we all might be one in him? John 17: 20, 21, 22, 23. And is it possible, that he (whom the Father heard always, John 11: 42) should not have this last most solemn prayer heard, and granted? or, shall it be granted for all the saints elsewhere, and not for the saints in England; so that amongst them disunion shall grow even about church-union, and communion? If it is possible, for a little faith (so much as a grain of mustard seed) to remove a mountain: is it not possible, for so much strength of faith, as is to be found in all the godly in the kingdom, to remove those images of jealousy, and to cast those stumbling-blocks out of the way, which may hinder the free passage of brotherly love amongst brethren? It is true indeed, the National covenant doth justly engage both parties, faithfully to endeavour the utter extirpation of the Antichristian hierarchy, and much more of all blasphemies, heresies, and damnable errors.

Certainly, if congregational discipline be independent from the inventions of men, is it not much more independent from the delusions of Satan? What fellowship hath Christ with Belial? light with darkness? truth with error? The faithful Jews needed not the help of the Samaritans, to re-edify the temple of God: yea they rejected their help when it was offered, Ezra 4. 1–3. And if the congregational way be a way of truth (as we believe) and if the brethren that walk in it be zealous of the truth, and hate every false way (as by the rule of their holy discipline they are instructed, 2 John 10: 11) then verily, there is no branch in the national covenant that engageth the covenanters to abhor either congregational Churches, or their way: which being duly administered, do no less effectively extirpate the Antichristian hierarchy, and all blasphemies, heresies, and pernicious errors, than the other way of discipline doth, which is more generally and publicly received and ratified.

But the Lord Jesus commune with all our hearts in secret: and he who is the King of his Church, let him be pleased to exercise his kingly power in our spirits, that so his kingdom may come into our churches in purity and peace. Amen. Amen.

CHAPTER I

Of the form of Church Government; and that it is one, immutable, and prescribed in the Word of God

1 Ecclesiastical polity or church government, or discipline is nothing else, but that form and order that is to be observed in the church of Christ upon earth, both for the constitution of it, and all the administrations that therein are to be performed.[1]

2 Church government is considered in a double respect either in regard of the parts of government themselves, or necessary circumstances thereof. The parts of government are prescribed in the Word, because the Lord Jesus Christ, the King and Law-giver of his Church, is no less faithful in the house of God than was Moses, who from the Lord delivered a form and pattern of government to the children of Israel in the Old Testament: And the holy Scriptures are now also so perfect, as they are able to make the man of God perfect and thoroughly furnished unto every good work; and therefore doubtless to the well ordering of the house of God.[2]

3 The parts of church government are all of them exactly described in the Word of God being parts or means of instituted worship according

[1] Ezek. 43: 11; Col. 2: 5; 1 Tim. 3: 15.
[2] Heb. 3: 5, 6; Ex. 25: 40; 2 Tim. 3: 16.

to the second Commandment: and therefore to continue one and the same, unto the appearing of our Lord Jesus Christ as a kingdom that cannot be shaken, until he shall deliver it up unto God, even the Father.[3] So that it is not left in the power of men, officers, churches, or any state in the world to add, or diminish, or alter anything in the least measure therein.[4]

4 The necessary circumstances, as time and place, etc. belonging unto order and decency, are not so left unto men as that under pretence of them, they may thrust their own inventions upon the churches:[5] Being circumscribed in the Word with many general limitations; where they are determined in respect of the matter to be neither worship itself, nor circumstances separable from worship:[6] in respect of their end, they must be done unto edification: in respect of the manner, decently, and in order, according to the nature of the things themselves, and civil, and church custom, doth not even nature itself teach you? yea they are in some sort determined particularly, namely that they be done in such a manner, as all circumstances considered, is most expedient for edification: so, as if there be no error of man concerning their determination, the determining of them is to be accounted as if it were divine.[7]

CHAPTER II

Of the Nature of the Catholic Church in general, and in special, of a Particular Visible Church

The Catholic Church is the whole company of those that are elected, redeemed, and in time effectually called from the state of sin and death unto a state of grace, and salvation in Jesus Christ.[8]

2 This church is either triumphant, or militant. Triumphant, the number of them who are glorified in heaven: militant, the number of them who are conflicting with their enemies upon earth.[9]

3 This militant church is to be considered as invisible, and visible. Invisible, in respect of their relation wherein they stand to Christ, as a body

---

[3] I Tim. 3: 15; I Chron. 15: 13; Ex. 20: 4; I Tim. 6: 13, 16; Heb. 12: 27, 28; I Cor. 15: 22.
[4] Deut. 12: 32; Eze. 43: 8; I Kings 12: 31–33.
[5] I Kings 12: 28, 29; Is. 29: 13; Col. 2: 22, 23; Acts 15: 28.
[6] Matt. 15: 9; I Cor. 11: 23; 8: 34.
[7] I Cor. 14: 26, 40; 11: 14, 16; 14: 12, 19; Acts 15: 28.
[8] Eph. 1: 22, 23; 5: 25, 26, 30; Heb. 12: 23.
[9] Rom. 8: 17; 2 Tim. 2: 12; 4: 8; Eph. 6: 12, 13.

unto the head, being united unto him, by the Spirit of God, and faith in their hearts: Visible, in respect of the profession of their faith, in their persons, and in particular churches: and so there may be acknowledged a universal visible church.[10]

4 The members of the militant visible church considered either as not yet in church order, or as walking according to the church order of the gospel. In order, and so besides the spiritual union, and communion, common to all believers, they enjoy moreover an union and communion ecclesiastical-political: so we deny an universal visible church.[11]

5 The state the members of the militant visible church walking in order, was either before the law, economical, that is in families; or under the law, national: or, since the coming of Christ, only congregational. (The term independent, we approve not). Therefore neither national, provincial, nor classical.[12]

6 A congregational church, is by the institution of Christ a part of the militant visible church, consisting of a company of saints by calling, united into one body, by a holy covenant, for the public worship of God, and the mutual edification one of another, in the fellowship of the Lord Jesus.[13]

CHAPTER III

Of the Matter of the Visible Church both in respect of Quality and Quantity

The matter of a visible church are saints by calling. By saints, we understand,

1 Such, as have not only attained the knowledge of the principles of religion, and are free from gross and open scandals, but also do together with the profession of their faith and repentance, walk in blameless obedience to the Word,[14] so as that in charitable discretion they may be accounted saints by calling[15] (though perhaps some or more of them be unsound, and hypocrites inwardly): because the members of such particular churches are commonly by the Holy Ghost called saints and faithful brethren in Christ, and sundry churches have been reproved for receiving,

[10] 2 Tim. 2: 19; Rev. 2: 17; 1 Cor. 6: 17; Eph. 3: 17; Rom. 1: 8; 1 Thess. 1: 8; Is. 2: 2; 1 Tim. 6: 12.

[11] Acts 19: 1; Col. 2: 5; Matt. 18: 17; 1 Cor. 5: 12.

[12] Gen. 18: 19; Ex. 19: 6.

[13] 1 Cor. 14: 23, 36; 1: 2; 12: 27; Ex. 19: 5, 6; Deut. 29: 1, 9–15; Acts 2: 42; 1 Cor. 14: 26.

[14] 1 Cor. 1: 2; Eph. 1: 1; Heb. 6: 1; 1 Cor. 1: 5; Rom. 15: 14; Ps. 50: 16–17; Acts 8: 37; Matt. 3: 6; Rom. 6: 17.

[15] 1 Cor. 1: 2; Phil. 1: 1; Col. 1: 2.

and suffering such persons to continue in fellowship amongst them, as have been offensive and scandalous: the name of God also by this means is blasphemed: and the holy things of God defiled and profaned, the hearts of the godly grieved: and the wicked themselves hardened: and helped forward to damnation; the example of such doth endanger the sanctity of others. A little leaven leaveneth the whole lump.[16]

2 The children of such, who are also holy.[17]

3 The members of churches though orderly constituted, may in time degenerate, and grow corrupt and scandalous, which though they ought not to be tolerated in the church, yet their continuance therein, through the defect of the execution of discipline and just censures, doth not immediately dissolve the being of the church, as appears in the church of Israel, and the churches of Galatia and Corinth, Pergamus, and Thyatira.[18]

4 The matter of the church in respect of its quantity ought not to be of greater number than may ordinarily meet together conveniently in one place:[19] nor ordinarily fewer than may conveniently carry on church-work.[20] Hence when the Holy Scripture maketh mention of the saints combined into a church-estate, in a town or city, where was but one congregation, it usually calleth those saints the church in the singular number, as the church of the Thessalonians, the church of Smyrna, Philadelphia, and the like:[21] But when it speaketh of the saints in a nation, or province, wherein there were sundry congregations, it frequently and usually calleth them by the name of churches, in the plural number, as the churches of Asia, Galatia, Macedonia, and the like:[22] which is further confirmed by what is written of sundry of those churches in particular, how they were assembled and met together the whole church in one place, as the church at Jerusalem, the church at Antioch, the church at Corinth, and Cenchrea, though it were more near to Corinth, it being the port thereof, and answerable to a village, yet being a distinct congregation from Corinth, it had a church of its own as well as Corinth had.[23]

5 Nor can it with reason be thought but that every church appointed and ordained by Christ, had a ministry ordained and appointed for the same: and yet plain it is, that there were no ordinary officers appointed by

[16] Eph. 1: 1; 1 Cor. 5: 2, 13; Rev. 1: 14, 15, 20; Eze. 44: 7, 9; 23: 38, 39; Num. 29: 20; Hag. 2: 13, 14; 1 Cor. 11: 27, 29; Ps. 37: 21; 1 Cor. 5; 6.
[17] 1 Cor. 7: 14.
[18] Jer. 2: 21; 1 Cor. 5: 12; Jer. 14; Gal. 5: 4; 2 Cor. 12: 21; Rev. 2: 14, 15; 21: 21.
[19] 1 Cor. 14: 21.
[20] Matt. 18: 17.
[21] Rom. 16: 1; 1 Thess. 1: 1; Rev. 2: 8; 3: 7.
[22] 1 Cor. 16: 1, 19; Gal. 1: 2; 2 Cor. 8: 1; 1 Thess. 2: 14.
[23] Acts 2: 46; 5: 12; 6: 2; 14: 27; 15: 38; 1 Cor. 5: 4; 14: 23; Rom. 16: 1.

Christ for any other than congregational churches: elders being appointed to feed, not all flocks, but the particular flock of God over which the Holy Ghost had made them the overseers,[24] and that flock they must attend, even the whole flock: and one congregation being as much as any ordinary elders can attend, therefore there is no greater church than a congregation, which may ordinarily meet in one place.

CHAPTER IV

Of the Form of a Visible Church and of Church Covenant

Saints by calling, must have a visible political union amongst themselves, or else they are not yet a particular church: as those similitudes hold forth, which Scripture makes use of, to show the nature of particular Churches: as a body, a building, or house, hands, eyes, feet, and other members must be united, or else, remaining separate are not a body.[25] Stones, timber, though squared, hewn and polished, are not an house, until they are compacted and united: so saints or believers in judgment of charity, are not a church, unless orderly knit together.

2 Particular churches cannot be distinguished one from another but by their forms. Ephesus is not Smyrna, and Pergamus Thyatira, but each one a distinct society of itself, having officers of their own, which had not the charge of others:[26] virtues of their own, for which others are not praised: corruptions of their own for which others are not blamed.

3 This form is the visible covenant, agreement, or consent whereby they give up themselves unto the Lord, to the observing of the ordinances of Christ together in the same society, which is usually called the Church-Covenant;[27] for we see not otherwise how members can have church-power one over another mutually.

The comparing of each particular church unto a city, and unto a spouse,[28] seemeth to conclude not only a form, but that that form, is by way of a covenant.

The covenant, as it was that which made the family of Abraham and children of Israel to be a church and people unto God, so it is that which now makes the several societies of Gentile believers to be churches in these days.[29]

4 This voluntary agreement, consent or covenant (for all these are here

[24] Acts 20: 28.   [25] I Cor. 12: 27; I Tim. 3: 15; Eph. 2: 22; I Cor. 12: 15–17.
[26] Rev. I.   [27] Ex. 19: 5, 8; Deut. 29: 12, 13; Zech. 11: 14; 9: 11.
[28] Eph. 2: 19; 2 Cor. 11: 2.   [29] Gen. 17: 7; Deut. 29: 12, 13; Eph. 2: 12, 19.

taken for the same): although the more express and plain it is, the more fully it puts us in mind of our mutual duty, and stirreth us up to it, and leaveth less room for the questioning of the truth of the church-estate of a company of professors, and the truth of membership of particular persons: yet we conceive the substance of it is kept, where there is a real agreement and consent of a company of faithful persons to meet constantly together in one congregation, for the public worship of God and their mutual edification: which real agreement and consent they do express by their constant practice in coming together for the public worship of God, and by their religious subjection unto the ordinances of God there: the rather, if we do consider how Scripture covenants have been entered into, not only expressly by word of mouth, but by sacrifice; by hand writing, and seal; and also sometimes by silent consent, without any writing, or expression of words at all.[30]

5 This form then being by mutual covenant, it followeth, it is not faith in the heart, nor the profession of that faith, nor cohabitation, nor baptism; 1 Not faith in the heart; because that is invisible: 2 not a bare profession; because that declareth them no more to be members of one church than of another: 3 not cohabitation; atheists or infidels may dwell together with believers: 4 not baptism; because it presupposeth a church estate, as circumcision in the Old Testament, which gave no being unto the church, the church being before it, and in the wilderness without it. Seals presuppose a covenant already in being, one person is a complete subject of baptism: but one person is incapable of being a church.

6 All believers ought, as God giveth them opportunity thereunto, to endeavour to join themselves unto a particular church and that in respect of the honour of Jesus Christ, in his example and institution, by the professed acknowledgment of, and subjection unto the order and ordinances of the Gospel: as also in respect of their good of communion, founded upon their visible union, and contained in the promises of Christ's special presence in the church: whence they have fellowship with him, and in him one with another:[31] also, for the keeping of them in the way of God's commandments, and recovering of them in case of wandering (which all Christ's sheep are subject to in this life), being unable to return of themselves; together with the benefit of their mutual edification, and of their posterity,[32] that they may not be cut off from the privileges of the covenant.

[30] Ex. 19: 5–8; 24: 3, 17; Josh. 24: 18–24; Ps. 50: 5; Neh. 9: 38; 10: 1; Gen. 17; Deut. 29.
[31] Acts 2: 47; 9: 26; Matt. 3: 13–15; 28: 19–20; Ps. 133: 2, 3; 87: 7; Matt. 18: 20; 1 John 1: 3.
[32] Ps. 119: 176; 1 Pet. 2: 25; Eph. 4: 16; John 22: 24, 25; Matt. 18: 15–17.

Otherwise, if a believer offends, he remains destitute of the remedy provided in that behalf, and should all believers neglect this duty of joining to all particular congregations: it might follow thereupon, that Christ should have no visible political churches upon earth.

CHAPTER V

Of the First Subject of Church Power or, to whom Church Power doth first belong

The first subject of church power, is either supreme, or subordinate and ministerial. The supreme (by way of gift from the Father) is the Lord Jesus Christ. The ministerial, is either extraordinary; as the Apostles, prophets, and evangelists, or ordinary; as every particular congregational church.[33]

2 Ordinary church power, is either the power of office, that is such as is proper to the eldership: or, power of privilege, such as belongs unto the brotherhood. The latter is in the brethren formally, and immediately from Christ, that is, so as it may according to order be acted or exercised immediately by themselves: the former, is not in them formally or immediately, and therefore cannot be acted or exercised immediately by them, but is said to be in them, in that they design the persons unto office, who only are to act, or to exercise this power.[34]

CHAPTER VI

Of the Officers of the Church, and especially of Pastors and Teachers

A church being a company of people combined together by covenant for the worship of God, it appeareth thereby, that there may be the essence and being of a church without any officers, seeing there is both the form and matter of a church, which is implied when it is said, the Apostles ordained elders in every church.[35]

2 Nevertheless, though officers be not absolutely necessary to the simple being of churches, when they be called: yet ordinarily to their calling they are, and to their well being: and therefore the Lord Jesus out of his tender compassion hath appointed and ordained officers which he would not

[33] Matt. 28: 18; Rev. 3: 7; Is. 9: 6; John 20: 21, 23; 1 Cor. 14: 32; Tit. 1: 5; 1 Cor. 5: 12.
[34] Rom. 12: 4, 8; Acts 12: 3; 6: 3, 4; 14: 23; 1 Cor. 12: 29, 30.
[35] Acts 14: 23.

have done, if they had not been useful and needful for the church; yea, being ascended into heaven, he received gifts for men, and gave gifts to men, whereof officers for the church are justly accounted no small parts; they being to continue to the end of the world, and for the perfecting of all the saints.[36]

3 The officers were either extraordinary, or ordinary: extraordinary, as apostles, prophets, evangelists; ordinary, as elders and deacons.[37]

The apostles, prophets, and evangelists, as they were called extra-ordinarily, by Christ,[38] so their office ended with themselves whence it is that Paul directing Timothy how to carry along church administrations, giveth no direction about the choice or course of apostles, prophets, or evangelists, but only of elders and deacons, and when Paul was to take his last leave of the church of Ephesus, he committed the care of feeding the church to no other, but unto the elders of that church. The like charge doth Peter commit to the elders.[39]

4 Of elders (who are also in Scripture called bishops) some attend chiefly to the ministry of the Word, as the pastors and teachers; others attend especially unto rule, who are therefore called ruling elders.[40]

5 The office of pastor and teacher appears to be distinct. The pastor's special work is, to attend to exhortation: and therein to administer a word of wisdom: the teacher is to attend to doctrine, and therein to administer a word of knowledge[41] and either of them to administer the seals of that covenant, unto the dispensation whereof they are alike called; as also to execute the censures, being but a kind of application of the Word, the preaching of which, together with the application thereof, they are alike charged withal.[42]

6 And forasmuch as both pastors and teachers are given by Christ for the perfecting of the saints, and edifying of his body, which saints, and body of Christ is his church.[43] Therefore we account pastors and teachers to be both of them church officers; and not the pastor for the church, and the teacher only for the schools, though this we gladly acknowledge, that schools are both lawful, profitable, and necessary for the training up of such in good literature, or learning, as may afterwards be called forth unto office of pastor or teacher in the church.[44]

[36] Rom. 10: 17; Jer. 3: 15; 1 Cor. 12: 28; Ps. 68: 18; Eph. 4: 8, 11–13.
[37] 1 Cor. 12: 28; Eph. 4: 11; Gal. 1; Acts 8: 6, 26, 19; 11: 28; Rom. 11: 7, 8.
[38] 1 Cor. 4: 9.   [39] 1 Tim. 3: 1, 2, 8–13; Tit. 1: 5; Acts 20: 17, 28; 1 Pet. 5: 1–3.
[40] 1 Tim. 3: 2; Phil. 1: 1; Acts 20. 17, 28; 1 Tim. 5: 17.
[41] Eph. 4: 11; Rom. 12: 7, 8; 1 Cor. 12: 8.
[42] 2 Tim. 4: 1, 2; Tit. 1: 9.   [43] Eph. 4: 11, 12; 1: 22, 23.
[44] 1 Sam. 10: 12, 19, 20; 2 Kings 2: 3, 15.

CHAPTER VII

Of Ruling Elders and Deacons

The ruling elder's office is distinct from the office of pastor and teacher. The ruling elders are not so called to exclude the pastors and teachers from ruling, but because ruling and governing is common to these with the other; whereas attending to teach and preach the Word is peculiar unto the former.[45]

2 The ruling elder's work is to join with the pastor and teacher in those acts of spiritual rule which are distinct from the ministry of the Word and sacraments committed to them.[46] Of which sort, these be, as followeth: 1 To open and shut the doors of God's house, by the admission of members approved by the church: by ordination of officers chosen by the church: and by excommunication of notorious and obstinate offenders renounced by the church: and by restoring of penitents, forgiven by the church.[47] 2 To call the church together when there is occasion, and seasonably to dismiss them again. 3 To prepare matters in private, that in public they may be carried to an end with less trouble, and more speedy dispatch.[48] 4 To moderate the carriage of all matters in the church assembled, as, to propound matters to the church, to order the season of speech and silence: and to pronounce sentence according to the mind of Christ, with the consent of the church. 5 To be guides and leaders to the church, in all matters whatsoever, pertaining to church administrations and actions. 6 To see that none in the church live inordinately out of rank and place; without a calling, or idly in their calling.[49] 7 To prevent and heal such offences in life, or in doctrine; as might corrupt the church. 8 To feed the flock of God with a word of admonition. 9 And as they shall be sent for, to visit, and to pray over their sick brethren. 10 And at other times as opportunity shall serve thereunto.[50]

3 The office of a deacon is instituted in the church by the Lord Jesus; sometimes they are called helps.

The Scripture telleth us, how they should be qualified: grave, not double tongued, not given too much to wine, not given to filthy lucre. They must first be proved and then use the office of a deacon, being found blameless.[51]

---

[45] Rom. 12: 7–9; 1 Tim. 5: 17; 1 Cor. 12: 28; Heb. 13: 17.   [46] 1 Tim. 5: 17.
[47] 2 Chron. 23: 19; Rev. 21: 12; 1 Tim. 4: 14; Matt. 18: 17; 2 Cor. 2: 7, 8; Acts 2: 6.
[48] Acts 21: 18, 22, 23.
[49] Acts 6: 2, 3; 13: 15; 2 Cor. 8: 10; Heb. 13: 7, 17; 2 Thess. 2: 10–12.
[50] Acts 20: 28, 32; 1 Thess. 5: 12; Jas. 5: 14; Acts 20: 20.
[51] Acts 6: 3, 6; Phil. 1: 1; 1 Tim. 3: 8, 9; 1 Cor. 12: 28.

The office and work of the deacons is to receive the offerings of the church, gifts given to the church, and to keep the treasury of the church: and therewith to serve the tables which the church is to provide for: as the Lord's table, the table of the ministers, and of such as are in necessity, to whom they are to distribute in simplicity.[52]

4 The office therefore being limited unto the care of the temporal good things of the church, it extends not unto the attendance upon, and administration of the spiritual things thereof, as the Word, and sacraments, or the like.[53]

5 The ordinance of the apostle, and practice of the church, commends the Lord's day as a fit time for the contributions of the saints.[54]

6 The instituting of all these officers in the church, is the work of God himself; of the Lord Jesus Christ; of the Holy Ghost,[55] and therefore such officers as he hath not appointed, are altogether unlawful either to be placed in the church, or to be retained therein, and are to be looked at as human creatures, mere inventions and appointments of man, to the great dishonour of Christ Jesus, the Lord of his house, the king of his church, whether popes, patriarchs, cardinals, archbishops, lordbishops, archdeacons, officials, commissaries, and the like. These and the rest of that hierarchy and retinue, not being plants of the Lord's planting, shall all certainly be rooted out, and cast forth.[56]

7 The Lord hath appointed ancient widows (where they may be had) to minister in the church, in giving attendance to the sick, and to give succour unto them, and others in the like necessities.[57]

CHAPTER VIII

Of the Election of Church Officers

No man may take the honour of a church-officer unto himself, but he that was called of God, as was Aaron.[58]

2 Calling unto office is either immediate, by Christ himself: such was the call of the apostles, and prophets: this manner of calling ended with them, as hath been said: or mediate, by the church.[59]

3 It is meet, that before any be ordained or chosen officers, they should first be tried and proved; because hands are not suddenly to be laid upon any, and both elders and deacons must be of honest and good report.[60]

[52] Acts 4: 35; 6: 2, 3; Rom. 12: 8.   [53] 1 Cor. 7: 17.
[54] 1 Cor. 16: 1–3.   [55] 1 Cor. 12: 28; Eph. 4: 8, 11; Acts 20: 28.
[56] Matt. 15: 13.   [57] 1 Tim. 5: 9, 10.   [58] Heb. 5: 4.
[59] Gal. 1: 1; Acts 14: 23; 6: 3.   [60] 1 Tim. 5: 22; 3: 10; Acts 16: 2; 6: 3.

4 The things in respect of which they are to be tried, are those gifts and virtues which the Scripture requireth in men, that are to be elected into such places, viz. that elders must be blameless, sober, apt to teach, and endued with such other qualifications as are laid down, 1 Tim. 3: 2; Tit. 1: 6–9. Deacons to be fitted, as is directed, Acts 6: 3; 1 Tim. 3: 8–11.

5 Officers are to be called by such churches, whereunto they are to minister; of such moment is the preservation of this power, that the churches exercised it in the presence of the apostles.[61]

6 A church being free cannot become subject to any, but by a free election; yet when such a people do choose any to be over them in the Lord, then do they become subject, and most willingly submit to their ministry in the Lord, whom they have so chosen.[62]

7 And if the church have power to choose their officers and ministers, then in case of manifest unworthiness and delinquency they have power also to depose them. For to open, and shut: to choose and refuse; to constitute in office, and remove from office: are acts belonging unto the same power.[63]

8 We judge it much conducing to the well-being, and communion of churches, that where it may conveniently be done, neighbour churches be advised withal, and their help made use of in the trial of church officers, in order to their choice.[64]

9 The choice of such church officers belongeth not to the civil magistrates, as such, or diocesan bishops, or patrons: for of these or any such like, the Scripture is wholly silent, as having any power therein.

CHAPTER IX

Of Ordination, and Imposition of hands

Church officers are not only to be chosen by the church, but also to be ordained by imposition of hands, and prayer, with which at ordination of elders, fasting also is to be joined.[65]

2 This ordination we account nothing else, but the solemn putting of a man into his place and office in the church whereunto he had right before by election, being like the installing of a magistrate in the commonwealth.[66]

Ordination therefore is not to go before, but to follow election.[67] The essence and substance of the outward calling of an ordinary officer in the

[61] Acts 14: 23; 1: 23; 6: 3–5. [62] Gal. 5: 13; Heb. 13: 17. [63] Rom. 16: 17.
[64] Cant. 8: 8, 9. [65] Acts 13: 3; 14: 23; 1 Tim. 5: 22.
[66] Num. 8: 10; Acts 6: 5, 6; 13: 2, 3. [67] Acts 6: 5, 6; 14: 23.

church, doth not consist in his ordination, but in his voluntary and free election by the church, and in his accepting of that election, whereupon is founded the relation between pastor and flock, between such a minister and such a people.

Ordination doth not constitute an officer, nor give him the essentials of his office. The apostles were elders, without imposition of hands by men: Paul and Barnabas were officers, before that imposition of hands, Acts 13: 3. The posterity of Levi were priests, and Levites, before hands were laid on them by the children of Israel.

3 In such churches where there are elders, imposition of hands in ordination is to be performed by those elders.[68]

4 In such churches where there are no elders, imposition of hands may be performed by some of the brethren orderly chosen by the church thereunto. For if the people may elect officers, which is the greater, and wherein the substance of the office consists, they may much more (occasion and need so requiring) impose hands in ordination, which is the less, and but the accomplishment of the other.[69]

5 Nevertheless in such churches where there are no leaders, and the church so desire, we see not why imposition of hands may not be performed by the elders of other churches. Ordinary officers laid hands upon the officers of many churches: the presbytery of Ephesus laid hands upon Timothy an evangelist. The presbytery at Antioch laid hands upon Paul and Barnabas.[70]

6 Church officers are officers to one church, even that particular, over which the Holy Ghost hath made them overseers. Insomuch as elders are commanded to feed, not all flocks, but that flock which is committed to their faith and trust, and dependeth upon them. Nor can constant residence at one congregation, be necessary for a minister, no, nor yet lawful, if he be not a minister to one congregation only, but to the church universal: because he may not attend one part only of the church, whereto he is a minister, but he is called to attend unto all the flock.[71]

7 He that is clearly loosed from his office-relation unto that church whereof he was a minister, cannot be looked at as an officer, nor perform any act of office in any other church, unless he be again orderly called unto office: which when it shall be, we know nothing to hinder, but imposition of hands also in his ordination ought to be used towards him again. For so Paul the apostle received imposition of hands twice at least, from Ananias, Acts 9: 17 and Acts 13: 3.

[68] 1 Tim. 4: 14; Acts 13: 3; 1 Tim. 5: 22.   [69] Num. 8: 10.
[70] 1 Tim. 4: 14; Acts 13: 3.   [71] 1 Pet. 5: 2; Acts 20: 28.

CHAPTER X

Of the Power of the Church, and its Presbytery

Supreme and lordly power over all the churches upon earth, doth only belong unto Jesus Christ, who is King of the church, and the Head thereof. He hath the government upon his shoulders, and hath all power given to him, both in heaven and earth.[72]

2 A company of professed believers ecclesiastically confederate, as they are a church before they have officers, and without them; so even in that estate, subordinate church power under Christ delegated to them by him, doth belong to them, in such a manner as is before expressed,[73] and as flowing from the very nature and essence of a church: it being natural to all bodies, and so unto a church body, to be furnished with sufficient power, for its own preservation and subsistence.[74]

3 This government of the church, is a mixed government (and so hath been acknowledged long before the term of independency was heard of:) in respect of Christ, the head and king of the church, and the sovereign power residing in him, and exercised by him, it is a monarchy. In respect of the body, or brotherhood of the church, and power from Christ granted unto them, it resembles a democracy, in respect of the presbytery and power committed to them, it is an aristocracy.[75]

4 The sovereign power which is peculiar unto Christ, is exercised, 1 In calling the church out of the world unto holy fellowship with himself 2 In instituting the ordinances of his worship, and appointing his ministers and officers for the dispensing of them. 3 In giving laws for the ordering of all our ways, and the ways of his house:[76] 4 In giving power and life to all his institutions, and to his people by them. 5 In protecting and delivering his church against and from all the enemies of their peace.[77]

5 The power granted by Christ unto the body of the church and brotherhood, is a prerogative or privilege which the church doth exercise: 1 In choosing their own officers, whether elders, or deacons.[78] 2 In admission of their own members and therefore, there is great reason they should have power to remove any from their fellowship again. Hence in case of offence any one brother hath power to convince and admonish an offending

[72] Ps. 2: 6; Eph. 1: 21, 22; Is. 9: 6; Matt. 28: 18.
[73] Chap. v. Section 2.
[74] Acts 1: 23; 14: 23; 6: 3, 4; Matt. 18: 17; 1 Cor. 5: 4, 5.
[75] Rev. 3: 7; 1 Cor. 5: 12. 1 Tim. 5: 17.
[76] Gal. 1: 4; Rev. 5: 8, 9; Matt. 28: 20; Eph. 4: 8, 12; Jas. 4: 12; Is. 33: 22.
[77] 1 Tim. 3: 15; 2 Cor. 10: 4, 5; Is. 32: 2; Luke. 1: 51.
[78] Acts 6: 3, 5; 14: 23; 9: 26.

brother: and in case of not hearing him, to take one or two more to set on the admonition, and in case of not hearing them, to proceed to tell the church: and as his offence may require the whole church hath power to proceed to the public censure of him, whether by admonition, or excommunication: and upon his repentance to restore him again unto his former communion.[79]

6 In case an elder offend incorrigibly, the matter so requiring, as the church had power to call him to office, so they have power according to order, the counsel of other churches where it may be had, directing thereto, to remove him from his office:[80] and being now but a member, in case he add contumacy to his sin, the church that had power to receive him into their fellowship, hath also the same power to cast him out, that they have concerning any other member.[81]

7 Church government, or rule, is placed by Christ in the officers of the church, who are therefore called rulers, while they rule with God:[82] yet in case of maladministration, they are subject to the power of the church, according as hath been said before. The Holy Ghost frequently, yea always, where it mentioneth church rule, and church government, ascribeth it to elders: whereas the work and duty of the people is expressed in the phrase of obeying their elders; and submitting themselves unto them in the Lord: so as it is manifest, that an organic or complete church is a body politic, consisting of some that are governors, and some that are governed, in the Lord.[83]

8 The power which Christ has committed to the elders, is to feed and rule the church of God, and accordingly to call the church together upon any weighty occasion,[84] when the members so called, without just cause, may not refuse to come: nor when they are come, depart before they are dismissed: nor speak in the church, before they have leave from the elders: nor continue so doing, when they require silence, nor may they oppose nor contradict the judgment or sentence of the elders, without sufficient and weighty cause, because such practices are manifestly contrary unto order, and government, and inlets of disturbance, and tend to confusion.[85]

9 It belongs also unto the elders to examine any officers, or members, before they be received of the church: to receive the accusations brought to the church, and to prepare them for the church's hearing. In handling of offences and other matters before the church they have power to declare

[79] Matt. 18: 15–17; Tit. 3: 10; Col. 4: 17; 2 Cor. 2: 7, 8.
[80] Col. 4: 17; Rom. 16: 17.   [81] Matt. 18: 17;
[82] 1 Tim. 5: 17; Heb. 13: 17; 1 Thess. 5: 12.
[83] Rom. 12: 8; 1 Tim. 5: 17; 1 Cor. 12: 28, 29; Heb. 13: 7, 17.
[84] Acts 20: 28; 6: 2; Num. 16: 12; Ezek. 46: 10; Acts 13: 15.   [85] Hos. 4: 4.

and publish the counsel and will of God touching the same, and to pronounce sentence with the consent of the church.[86] Lastly they have power, when they dismiss the people, to bless them in the name of the Lord.[87]

10 This power of government in the elders, doth not any wise prejudice the power of privilege in the brotherhood; as neither the power of privilege in the brethren, doth prejudice the power of government in the elders; but they may sweetly agree together, as we may see in the example of the apostles furnished with the greatest church power, who took in the concurrence and consent of the brethren in church administrations.[88] Also that Scripture, 2 Cor. 2: 9 and chap. 10: 6 do declare, that what the churches were to act and do in these matters, they were to do in a way of obedience, and that not only to the direction of the apostles, but also of their ordinary elders.[89]

11 From the premisses, namely, that the ordinary power of government belonging only to the elders, power of privilege remaineth with the brotherhood (as power of judgment in matters of censure, and power of liberty, in matters of liberty): it followeth, that in an organic church, and right administration, all church acts proceed after the manner of a mixed administration, so as no church act can be consummated, or perfected without the consent of both.

CHAPTER XI

Of the Maintenance of Church Officers

The apostle concludes, that necessary and sufficient maintenance is due unto the ministers of the Word: from the law of nature and nations, from the law of Moses, the equity thereof, as also the rule of common reason.[90] Moreover the Scripture doth not only call elders labourers, and workmen but also speaking of them doth say, that the labourer is worthy of his hire: and requires that he which is taught in the Word, should communicate to him, in all good things; and mentions it as an ordinance of the Lord, that they which preach the gospel, should live of the Gospel; and forbiddeth the muzzling of the mouth of the ox, that treadeth out the corn.[91]

2 The Scriptures alleged requiring this maintenance as a bounden duty, and due debt, and not as a matter of alms, and free gift, therefore people

[86] Rev. 2: 2; 1 Tim. 5: 19; Acts 21: 18, 22, 23; 1 Cor. 5: 4, 5.
[87] Num. 6: 23-26.
[88] Acts 14; 23; 15: 23; 6: 2; 1 Cor. 5: 4; 2 Cor. 2: 6, 7.   [89] Heb. 13: 17.
[90] 1 Cor. 9: 9, 15; Matt. 9: 38; 10: 10; 1 Tim. 5: 18.
[91] Gal. 6: 6; 1 Cor. 9: 9, 14; 1 Tim. 5: 18.

are not at liberty to do or not to do, what and when they please in this matter, no more than in any other commanded duty, and ordinance of the Lord: but ought of duty, to minister of their carnal things to them that labour amongst them in the Word and doctrine, as well as they ought to pay any other workmen their wages, or to discharge and satisfy their other debts, or to submit themselves to observe any other ordinance of the Lord.[92]

3 The apostle, Gal. 6: 6, enjoining that he which is taught communicate to him that teacheth in all good things: doth not leave it arbitrary, what or how much a man shall give, or in what proportion, but even the latter, as well as the former, is prescribed and appointed by the Lord.[93]

4 Not only members of churches, but all that are taught in the Word, are to contribute unto him that teacheth, in all good things.[94] In case that congregations are defective in their contributions, the deacons are to call upon them to do their duty:[95] if their call sufficeth not, the church by her power is to require it of their members, and where church power through the corruption of men, doth not, or cannot attain the end, the magistrate is to see ministry be duly provided for, as appears from the commended example of Nehemiah.[96] The magistrates are nursing fathers, and nursing mothers, and stand charged with the custody of both tables;[97] because it is better to prevent a scandal, that it may not come and easier also, than to remove it when it is given. It is most suitable to rule, that by the church's care, each man should know his proportion according to rule, what he should do, before he do it, that so his judgment and heart may be satisfied in what he doth, and just offence prevented in what is done.[98]

CHAPTER XII

Of Admission of Members into the Church

The doors of the churches of Christ upon earth, do not by God's appointment stand so wide open that all sorts of people good or bad, may freely enter therein at their pleasure; but such as are admitted thereto, as members ought to be examined and tried first; whether they be fit and meet to be received into church society, or not.[99] The eunuch of Ethiopia, before his admission was examined by Philip, whether he did believe on Jesus Christ with all his heart.[100] The angel of the church at Ephesus is commended, for

---

[92] Rom. 15: 27; 1 Cor. 9: 14. [93] 1 Cor. 16: 2. [94] Gal. 6: 6.
[95] Acts 6: 3, 4. [96] Neh. 13: 11. [97] Is. 49: 23.
[98] 2 Cor. 8: 13, 14. [99] 2 Chron. 23: 19; Matt. 13: 25; 22: 12. [100] Acts 8: 37.

trying such as said they were apostles and were not. There is like reason for trying of them that profess themselves to be believers.[101]

The officers are charged with the keeping of the doors of the church, and therefore are in a special manner to make trial of the fitness of such who enter. Twelve angels are set at the gates of the temple, lest such as were ceremonially unclean should enter thereinto.[102]

2 The things which are requisite to be found in all church members, are, repentance from sin, and faith in Jesus Christ.[103] And therefore these are the things whereof men are to be examined, at their admission into the church and which then they must profess and hold forth in such sort, as may satisfy rational charity that the things are there indeed. John the Baptist admitted men to baptism, confessing and bewailing their sins: and of others it is said, that they came, and confessed, and showed their deeds.[104]

3 The weakest measure of faith is to be accepted in those that desire to be admitted into the church:[105] because weak Christians if sincere, have the substance of that faith, repentance and holiness which is required in church members: and such have most need of the ordinances for their confirmation and growth in grace. The Lord Jesus would not quench the smoking flax, nor break the bruised reed, but gather the tender lambs in his arms, and carry them gently in his bosom.[106] Such charity and tenderness is to be used, as the weakest Christian if sincere, may not be excluded, nor discouraged. Severity of examination is to be avoided.

4 In case any through excessive fear, or other infirmity, be unable to make their personal relation of their spiritual estate in public, it is sufficient that the elders having received private satisfaction, make relation thereof in public before the church, they testifying their assents thereunto; this being the way that tendeth most to edification. But whereas persons are of better abilities, there it is most expedient, that they make their relations, and confessions personally with their own mouth, as David professeth of himself.[107]

5 A personal and public confession, and declaring of God's manner of working upon the soul, is both lawful, expedient, and useful, in sundry respects, and upon sundry grounds. Those three thousand (Acts 2: 37, 41) before they were admitted by the apostles, did manifest that they were pricked in their hearts at Peter's sermon, together with earnest desire to be delivered from their sins, which now wounded their consciences, and their ready receiving of the word of promise and exhortation. We are to

[101] Rev. 2: 2; Acts 9: 26.
[102] Rev. 21: 12; 2 Chron. 23: 19.
[103] Acts 2: 38–42; 8: 37.
[104] Matt. 3: 6; Acts 19: 18.
[105] Rom. 14: 1.
[106] Matt. 12: 20; Is. 40: 11.
[107] Ps. 66: 16.

be ready to render a reason of the hope that is in us, to every one that asketh us:[108] therefore we must be able and ready upon any occasion to declare and show our repentance for sin, faith unfeigned; and effectual calling, because these are the reason of a well-grounded hope.[109] I have not hidden thy righteousness from the great congregation, Ps. 40: 10.

6 This profession of faith and repentance, as it must be made by such at their admission, that were never in church-society before: so nothing hindereth but the same may also be performed by such as have formerly been members of some other church, and the church to which they now join themselves as members, may lawfully require the same. Those three thousand (Acts 2) which made their confession, were members of the church of the Jews before, so were they that were baptized by John. Churches may err in their admission: and persons regularly admitted, may fall into offence.[110] Otherwise, if churches might obtrude their members, or if church members might obtrude themselves upon other churches, without due trial, the matter so requiring, both the liberty of churches would hereby be infringed, in that they might not examine those concerning whose fitness for communion they were unsatisfied:[111] and besides the infringing of their liberty, the churches themselves would unavoidably be corrupted, and the ordinances defiled, whilst they might not refuse, but must receive the unworthy: which is contrary unto the Scripture teaching that all churches are sisters, and therefore equal.

7 The like trial is to be required from such members of the church, as were born in the same, or received their membership, and were baptized in their infancy, or minority, by virtue of the covenant of their parents, when being grown up unto years of discretion, they shall desire to be made partakers of the Lord's Supper: unto which, because holy things must not be given unto the unworthy, therefore it is requisite, that these as well as others, should come to their trial and examination, and manifest their faith and repentance by an open profession thereof, before they are received to the Lord's Supper, and otherwise not to be admitted thereunto.[112]

Yet these church-members that were so born, or received in their childhood, before they are capable of being made partakers of full communion, have many privileges which others (not church members) have not: they are in covenant with God; have the seal thereof upon them, viz. Baptism; and so if not regenerated, yet are in a more hopeful way of attaining regenerating grace, and all the spiritual blessings both of the

---

[108] 1 Pet. 3: 15.
[110] Matt. 3: 5, 6; Gal. 2: 4; 1 Tim. 5: 24.
[111] Cant. 8: 8.

[109] Heb. 11: 1; Eph. 1: 18.

[112] Matt. 7: 6; 1 Cor. 11: 27.

covenant and seal; they are also under church watch, and consequently subject to the reprehensions, admonitions, and censures thereof, for their healing and amendment, as need shall require.

CHAPTER XIII

Of Church-members, their Removal from one Church to another, and of Letters of Recommendation and Dismission

Church-members may not remove or depart from the church, and so one from another as they please, nor without just and weighty cause but ought to live and dwell together: forasmuch as they are commanded, not to forsake the assembling of themselves together.[113] Such departure tends to the dissolution and ruin of the body: as the pulling of stones, and pieces of timber from the building, and of members from the natural body, tend to the destruction of the whole.

2 It is therefore the duty of church members, in such times and places when counsel may be had, to consult with the church whereof they are members, about their removal, that accordingly they have their approbation, may be encouraged, or otherwise desist. They who are joined with consent, should not depart without consent, except forced thereunto.[114]

3 If a member's departure be manifestly unsafe, and sinful, the church may not consent thereunto: for in so doing, they should not act in faith: and should partake with him in his sin. If the case be doubtful and the person not to be persuaded, it seemeth best to leave the matter unto God, and not forcibly to detain him.[115]

4 Just reasons for a member's removal of himself from the church are, 1 If a man cannot continue without partaking in sin.[116] 2 In case of personal persecution, so Paul departed from the disciples at Damascus. Also, in case of general persecution, when all are scattered.[117] 3 In case of real, and not only pretended, want of competent subsistence, a door being opened for a better supply in another place, together with the means of spiritual edification.[118] In these, or like cases, a member may lawfully remove, and the church cannot lawfully detain him.

5 To separate from a church, either out of contempt of their holy fellowship, or out of covetousness, or for greater enlargements with just grief to the church; or out of schism, or want of love; and out of a spirit

[113] Heb. 10: 25.
[114] Pro. 11: 16.
[115] Rom. 14: 23; 1 Tim. 5: 22; Acts 21: 14.
[116] Eph. 5: 11;
[117] Acts: 9. 25, 29, 30; 8: 1.
[118] Neh. 13: 20.

of contention in respect of some unkindness, or some evil only conceived, or indeed, in the church, which might and should be tolerated and healed with a spirit of meekness, and of which evil the church is not yet convinced (though perhaps himself be) nor admonished:[119] for these or the like reasons to withdraw from public communion, in Word, or seals, or censures, is unlawful and sinful.

6 Such members as have orderly removed their habitation ought to join themselves unto the church in order, where they do inhabit if it may be: otherwise, they can neither perform the duties, nor receive the privileges of members;[120] such an example tolerated in some, is apt to corrupt others; which if many should follow, would threaten the dissolution and confusion of churches, contrary to the Scripture.[121]

7 Order requires, that a member thus removing, have letters testimonial; and of dismission from the church whereof he yet is, unto the church whereunto he desireth to be joined, lest the church should be deluded; that the church may receive him in faith; and not be corrupted by receiving deceivers, and false brethren.[122] Until the person dismissed be received into another church, he ceaseth not by his letters of dismission to be a member of the church whereof he was. The church cannot make a member no member but by excommunication.

8 If a member be called to remove only for a time, where a church is, letters of recommendation are requisite, and sufficient for communion with that church, in the ordinances, and in their watch: as Phœbe, a servant of the church at Cenchrea, had letters written for her to the church of Rome, that she might be received, as becometh saints.[123]

9 Such letters of recommendation and dismission were written for Apollos: for Marcus to the Colossians; for Phœbe to the Romans; for sundry others to other churches;[124] and the apostle telleth us, that some persons, not sufficiently known otherwise, have special need of such letters, though he for his part had no need thereof.[125] The use of them is to be a benefit, and help to the party for whom they are written; and for the furthering of his receiving amongst the saints in the place whereto he goeth; and the due satisfaction of them in their receiving of him.

---

[119] 2 Tim. 4: 10; Rom. 16: 17; Jude 19; Eph. 4: 2, 3; Col. 3: 13; Gal. 6: 1, 2.
[120] Is. 56: 8; Acts 9: 26.
[121] 1 Cor. 14: 33.
[122] Acts 18: 27.
[123] Rom. 16: 1, 2; 2 Cor. 3: 1.
[124] Acts 18: 27; Col. 4: 10; Rom. 16: 1.
[125] 2 Cor. 3: 1.

Chapter XIV

Of Excommunication and Other Censures

The censures of the church, are appointed by Christ, for the preventing, removing, and healing of offences in the church: for the reclaiming and gaining of offending brethren: for the deterring others from the like offences: for purging out the leaven which may infect the whole lump: for vindicating the honour of Christ, and of his Church, and the holy profession of the gospel: and for preventing the wrath of God, that may justly fall upon the church, if they should suffer his covenant, and the seals thereof, to be profaned by notorious and obstinate offenders.[126]

2 If an offence be private (one brother offending another) the offender is to go, and acknowledge his repentance for it unto his offended brother, who is then to forgive him,[127] but if the offender neglect or refuse to do it, the brother offended is to go, and convince and admonish him of it, between themselves privately: if thereupon the offender be brought to repent of his offence, the admonisher hath won his brother, but if the offender hear not his brother, the brother offended is to take with him one or two more, that in the mouth of two or three witnesses, every word may be established (whether the word of admonition, if the offender receive it, or the word of complaint, if he refuse it): for if he refuse it, the offended brother is by the mouth of the elders to tell the church, and if he hear the church, and declare the same by penitent confession, he is recovered and gained; and if the church discern him to be willing to hear, yet not fully convinced of his offence, as in case of heresy; they are to dispense to him a public admonition; which declaring the offender to lie under the public offence of the church, doth thereby withhold or suspend him from the holy fellowship of the Lord's Supper, till his offence be removed by penitent confession. If he still continue obstinate, they are to cast him out by excommunication.[128]

3 But if the offence be more public at first, and of a more heinous and criminal nature, to wit, such as are condemned by the light of nature; then the church without such gradual proceeding, is to cast out the offender, from their holy communion, for the further mortifying of his sin and the healing of his soul, in the day of the Lord Jesus.[129]

[126] 1 Tim. 5: 20; Deut. 17: 12, 13; Jude 23; Deut. 13: 11; 1 Cor. 5: 6; Rom. 2: 24; Rev. 2: 14, 15, 16, 20.
[127] Matt. 5: 23, 24; Luke 17: 3, 4.
[128] Matt. 18: 15–17; Tit. 3: 10.
[129] 1 Cor. 5: 4, 5, 7.

4 In dealing with an offender, great care is to be taken, that we be neither overstrict or rigorous, nor too indulgent or remiss; our proceeding herein ought to be with a spirit of meekness, considering ourselves, lest we also be tempted;[130] and that the best of us have need of much forgiveness from the Lord. Yet the winning and healing of the offender's soul, being the end of these endeavours, we must not daub with untempered mortar, nor heal the wounds of our brethren slightly. On some have compassion, others save with fear.[131]

5 While the offender remains excommunicate, the church is to refrain from all member-like communion with him in spiritual things, and also from all familiar communion with him in civil things, farther than the necessity of natural, or domestical, or civil relations do require: and are therefore to forbear to eat and drink with him, that he may be ashamed.[132]

6 Excommunication being a spiritual punishment, it doth not prejudice the excommunicate in, nor deprive him of his civil rights, and therefore toucheth not princes, or other magistrates, in point of their civil dignity or authority. And, the excommunicate being but as a publican and a heathen, heathens being lawfully permitted to come to hear the Word in church assemblies,[133] we acknowledge therefore the like liberty of hearing the Word, may be permitted to persons excommunicate, that is permitted unto heathen. And because we are not without hope of his recovery, we are not to account him as an enemy but to admonish him as a brother.[134]

7 If the Lord sanctify the censure to the offender, so as by the grace of Christ he doth testify his repentance, with humble confession of his sin, and judging of himself, giving glory unto God; the church is then to forgive him, and to comfort him, and to restore him to the wonted brotherly communion, which formerly he enjoyed with them.[135]

8 The suffering of profane or scandalous livers to continue in fellowship, and partake in the sacraments, is doubtless a great sin in those that have power in their hands to redress it; and do it not.[136] Nevertheless, inasmuch as Christ and his apostles in their times, and the prophets and other godly in theirs, did lawfully partake of the Lord's commanded ordinances in the Jewish church, and neither taught nor practised separation from the same, though unworthy ones were permitted therein;[137] and inasmuch as the faithful in the church of Corinth, wherein were many unworthy persons, and practices, are never commanded to absent themselves from the

---

[130] Gal. 6: 1. [131] Matt. 18: 34, 35; 6: 14, 15; Eze. 13: 10; Jer. 6: 14.
[132] Matt. 18: 17; 1 Cor. 5: 11; 2 Thess. 3: 6, 14. [133] 1 Cor. 14: 24, 25.
[134] 2 Thess. 3: 14, 15. [135] 2 Cor. 2: 7, 8.
[136] Rev. 2: 14, 15, 20. [137] Matt. 23: 3; Acts 3: 1.

sacraments, because of the same: therefore the godly in like cases, are not presently to separate.

9 As separation from such a church wherein profane and scandalous livers are tolerated, is not presently necessary: so for the members thereof, otherwise worthy, hereupon to abstain from communicating with such a church, in the participation of the sacraments, is unlawful. For as it were unreasonable for an innocent person to be punished for the faults of others, wherein he hath no hand, and whereunto he gave no consent: so is it more unreasonable, that a godly man should neglect duty, and punish himself in not coming for his portion in the blessing of the seals, as he ought, because others are suffered to come, that ought not,[138] especially considering that himself doth neither consent to their sin, nor to their approaching to the ordinance in their sin, nor to the neglect of others who should put them away, and do not: but on the contrary doth heartily mourn for these things, modestly and seasonably stir up others to do their duty.[139] If the church cannot be reformed, they may use their liberty, as is specified.[140] But this all the godly are bound unto, even every one to do his endeavour, according to his power and place, that the unworthy may be duly proceeded against, by the church to whom this matter doth appertain.

CHAPTER XV

Of the Communion of Churches one with another

Although churches be distinct, and therefore may not be confounded one with another: and equal, and therefore have not dominion one over another: yet all the churches ought to preserve church communion one with another, because they are all united unto Christ, not only as a mystical, but as a political head; whence is derived a communion suitable thereunto.[141]

2 The communion of churches is exercised sundry ways.

1 By way of mutual care in taking thought for one another's welfare.[142]

2 By way of consultation one with another, when we have occasion to require the judgment and counsel of other churches, touching any person, or cause wherewith they may be better acquainted than ourselves. As the church of Antioch consulted with the apostles, and elders of the church at Jerusalem, about the question of circumcision of the Gentiles, and about the false teachers that broached that doctrine.[143] In which case,

---

[138] 2 Chron. 30: 18; Gen. 18: 25.   [139] Eze. 9: 4.   [140] Chapter XIII, section 4
[141] Rev. 1: 4; Cant. 8: 8; Rom. 16: 16; 1 Cor. 16: 19; Acts 15: 23; Rev. 2: 1.
[142] Cant. 8: 8.   [143] Acts 15: 2.

when any church wanteth light or peace amongst themselves, it is a way of communion of churches (according to the Word) to meet together by their elders and other messengers in a synod, to consider and argue the points in doubt, or difference; and having found out the way of truth and peace, to commend the same by their letters and messengers to the churches, whom the same may concern.[144] But if a church be rent with divisions amongst themselves, or lie under any open scandal, and yet refuse to consult with other churches, for healing or removing of the same; it is matter of just offence both to the Lord Jesus, and to other churches, as betraying too much want of mercy and faithfulness, not to seek to bind up the breaches and wounds of the church and brethren;[145] and therefore the state of such a church calleth aloud upon other churches, to exercise a fuller act of brotherly communion, to wit, by way of admonition.

3 A third way then of communion of churches is by way of admonition, to wit, in case any public offence be found in a church, which they either discern not, or are slow in proceeding to use the means for the removing and healing of. Paul had no authority over Peter, yet when he saw Peter not walking with a right foot, he publicly rebuked him before the church.[146] Though churches have no more authority one over another, than one apostle had over another; yet as one apostle might admonish another, so may one church admonish another, and yet without usurpation. In which case, if the church that lieth under offence, do not hearken to the church which doth admonish her, the church is to acquaint other neighbour churches with that offence, which the offending church still lieth under, together with their neglect of the brotherly admonition given unto them;[147] whereupon those other churches are to join in seconding the admonition formerly given: and if still the offending church continue in obstinacy and impenitency, they may forbear communion with them; and are to proceed to make use of the help of a synod, or council of neighbour churches walking orderly (if a greater cannot conveniently be had) for their conviction. If they hear not the synod, the synod having declared them to be obstinate, particular churches, approving and accepting of the judgment of the synod, are to declare the sentence of non-communion respectively concerning them: and thereupon out of a religious care to keep their own communion pure, they may justly withdraw themselves from participation with them at the Lord's table, and from such other acts of holy communion, as the communion of churches doth otherwise allow, and require. Nevertheless, if any members of such a church as lieth under

[144] Acts 15: 6, 22, 23. [145] Eze. 34: 4.
[146] Gal. 2: 11–14. [147] Matt. 18: 15–17 by proportion.

public offence; do not consent to the offence of the church, but do in due sort bear witness against it, they are still to be received to wonted communion: for it is not equal, that the innocent should suffer with the offensive.[148] Yea furthermore; if such innocent members after due waiting in the use of all good means for the healing of the offence of their own church, shall at last (with the allowance of the council of neighbour-churches) withdraw from the fellowship of their own church and offer themselves to the fellowship of another; we judge it lawful for the other church to receive them (being otherwise fit) as if they had been orderly dismissed to them from their own church.

4 A fourth way of communion of churches, is by way of participation: the members of one church occasionally coming unto another, we willingly admit them to partake with us at the Lord's table, it being the seal of our communion not only with Christ, nor only with the members of our own church, but also with all the churches of the saints:[149] in which regard, we refuse not to baptize their children presented to us, if either their own minister be absent, or such a fruit of holy fellowship be desired with us. In like case such churches as are furnished with more ministers than one, do willingly afford one of their own ministers to supply the place of an absent or sick minister of another church for a needful season.

5 A fifth way of church communion is, by way of recommendation when a member of one church hath occasion to reside in another church;[150] if but for a season, we commend him to their watchful fellowship by letters of recommendation: but if he be called to settle his abode there, we commit him according to his desire, to the fellowship of their covenant, by letters of dismission.[151]

6 A sixth way of church communion, is in case of need, to minister relief and succour one unto another: either of able members to furnish them with officers; or of outward support to the necessities of poorer churches; as did the churches of the Gentiles contribute liberally to the poor saints at Jerusalem.[152]

3 When a company of believers purpose to gather into church fellowship, it is requisite for their safer proceeding, and the maintaining of the communion of churches, that they signify their intent unto the neighbour-churches, walking according unto the order of the Gospel, and desire their presence, and help, and right hand of fellowship which they ought readily to give unto them, when there is no just cause of excepting against their proceedings.[153]

[148] Gen. 18: 25.   [149] 1 Cor. 12: 13.   [150] Rom. 16: 1.   [151] Acts 18: 27.
[152] Acts 11: 22, 29; Rom. 13: 26, 27.   [153] Gal. 2: 1, 2, 9 by proportion.

4 Besides these several ways of communion, there is also a way of propagation of churches; when a church shall grow too numerous, it is a way, and fit season, to propagate one church out of another, by sending forth such of their members as are willing to remove, and to procure some officers to them, as may enter with them into church-estate amongst themselves: as bees, when the hive is too full, issue forth by swarms, and are gathered into other hives, so the churches of Christ may do the same upon like necessity; and therein hold forth to the right hand of fellowship, both in their gathering into a church; and in the ordination of their officers.[154]

Chapter XVI

Of Synods

Synods orderly assembled, and rightly proceeding according to the pattern, Acts 15, we acknowledge as the ordinance of Christ:[155] and though not absolutely necessary to the being, yet many times, through the iniquity of men, and perverseness of times, necessary to the well-being of churches, for the establishment of truth, and peace therein.

2 Synods being spiritual and ecclesiastical assemblies, are therefore made up of spiritual and ecclesiastical causes. The next efficient cause of them under Christ, is the power of the churches, sending forth their elders, and other messengers; who being met together in the name of Christ, are the matter of a synod: and they in arguing, debating and determining matters of religion according to the Word, and publishing the same to the churches whom it concerneth, do put forth the proper and formal acts of a synod; to the conviction of errors, and heresies, and the establishment of truth and peace in the churches, which is the end of a synod.[156]

3 Magistrates have power to call a synod, by calling to the churches to send forth their elders and other messengers, to counsel and assist them in matters of religion:[157] but yet the constituting of a synod is a church act, and may be transacted by the churches, even when civil magistrates may be enemies to churches and to church assemblies.[158]

4 It belongeth unto synods and councils, to debate and determine controversies of faith, and cases of conscience; to clear from the Word holy directions for the holy worship of God, and good government of the church;[159] to bear witness against maladministration and corruption in

[154] Is. 40: 20; Cant. 8: 8, 9.
[156] Acts 15: 2, 3, 6, 7–23, 31; 16: 4, 15.
[158] Acts 15.
[155] Acts 15: 2–15.
[157] 2 Chron. 29: 4, 5–11.
[159] Acts 15: 1, 2, 6, 7; 1 Chron. 15: 13.

doctrine or manners in any particular church, and to give directions for the reformation thereof: not to exercise church-censures in way of discipline, nor any other act of church-authority or jurisdiction: which that presidential synod did forbear.[160]

5 The synod's directions and determinations, so far as consonant to the Word of God, are to be received with reverence and submission; not only for their agreement therewith (which is the principal ground thereof, and without which they bind not at all): but also secondarily, for the power whereby they are made, as being an ordinance of God appointed thereunto in his Word.[161]

6 Because it is difficult, if not impossible, for many churches to come altogether in one place, in all their members universally: therefore they may assemble by their delegates or messengers, as the church of Antioch went not all to Jerusalem, but some select men for that purpose.[162] Because none are or should be more fit to know the state of the churches, nor to advise of ways for the good thereof than elders; therefore it is fit that in the choice of the messengers for such assemblies, they have special respect into such. Yet inasmuch as not only Paul and Barnabas, but certain others also were sent to Jerusalem from Antioch, Acts 15, and when they were come to Jerusalem, not only the apostles and elders, but other brethren also do assemble, and meet about the matter,[163] therefore synods are to consist both of elders, and other church members, endued with gifts, and sent by the churches, not excluding the presence of any brethren in the churches.

CHAPTER XVII

Of the Civil Magistrate's Power in Matters Ecclesiastical

It is lawful, profitable, and necessary for Christians to gather themselves into church estate, and therein to exercise all the ordinances of Christ according unto the Word, although the consent of magistrate could not be had thereunto, because the apostles and Christians in their time did frequently thus practise, when the magistrates being all of them Jewish or pagan, and mostly persecuting enemies, would give no countenance or consent to such matters.[164]

2 Church government stands in no opposition to civil government of commonwealths, nor any way entrencheth upon the authority of civil magistrates in their jurisdictions; nor any whit weakeneth their hands in

[160] 2 Chron. 29: 6, 7; Acts 15: 24, 28, 29. [161] Acts 15.
[162] Acts 15: 2.   [163] Acts 15: 2, 22, 23.   [164] Acts 2: 41, 47; 4: 1, 2, 3.

governing; but rather strengtheneth them, and furthereth the people in yielding more hearty and conscionable obedience unto them,[165] whatsoever some ill-affected persons to the ways of Christ have suggested, to alienate the affections of kings and princes from the ordinances of Christ; as if the kingdom of Christ in his church could not rise and stand, without the falling and weakening of their government, which is also of Christ: whereas the contrary is most true, that they may both stand together and flourish the one being helpful unto the other, in their distinct and due administrations.[166]

3 The power and authority of magistrates is not for the restraining of churches, or any other good works, but for helping in and furthering thereof;[167] and therefore the consent and countenance of magistrates when it may be had, is not to be slighted, or lightly esteemed; but on the contrary; it is part of that honour due to Christian magistrates to desire and crave their consent and approbation therein: which being obtained, the churches may then proceed in their way with much more encouragement, and comfort.

4 It is not in the power of magistrates to compel their subjects to become church members, and to partake at the Lord's table: for the priests are reproved, that brought unworthy ones into the sanctuary:[168] then, as it was unlawful for the priests, so it is as unlawful to be done by civil magistrates. Those whom the church is to cast out if they were in, the magistrate ought not to thrust into the church, nor to hold them therein.[169]

5 As it is unlawful for church officers to meddle with the sword of the magistrate, so it is unlawful for the magistrate to meddle with the work proper to church officers. The acts of Moses and David, who were not only princes, but prophets, were extraordinary; therefore not imitable. Against such usurpation the Lord witnessed, by smiting Uzziah with leprosy, for presuming to offer incense.[170]

6 It is the duty of the magistrate, to take care of matters of religion, and to improve his civil authority for the observing of the duties commanded in the first, as well as for observing of the duties commanded in the second table. They are called gods.[171] The end of the magistrate's office, is not only the quiet and peaceable life of the subject, in matters of righteousness and honesty, but also in matters of godliness, yea of all godliness.[172] Moses, Joshua, David, Solomon, Asa, Jehoshaphat, Hezekiah, Josiah, are much

[165] John 18: 36; Acts 25: 8.
[166] Is. 49: 23.
[167] Rom. 13: 4; 1 Tim. 2: 2.
[168] Eze. 44: 7, 9.
[169] 1 Cor. 5: 11.
[170] Matt. 20: 25, 26; 2 Chron. 26: 16, 17.
[171] Ps. 82: 1.
[172] 1 Tim. 2: 1, 2.

commended by the Holy Ghost, for the putting forth their authority in matters of religion: on the contrary, such kings as have been failing this way, are frequently taxed and reproved by the Lord, and not only the kings of Judah, but also Job, Nehemiah, the king of Nineveh, Darius, Artaxerxes, Nebuchadnezzar, whom none looked at as types of Christ (though were it so, there were no place for any just objection), are commended in the book of God, for exercising their authority this way.[173]

7 The object of the power of the magistrate are not things merely inward, and so not subject to his cognizance and view, as unbelief, hardness of heart, erroneous opinions not vented; but only such things as are acted by the outward man; neither is their power to be exercised, in commanding such acts of the outward man, and punishing the neglect thereof, as are but mere inventions, and devices of men;[174] but about such acts, as are commanded and forbidden in the Word; yea such as the Word doth clearly determine, though not always clearly to the judgment of the magistrate or others, yet clearly in itself. In these he of right ought to put forth his authority, though oft-times actually he doth it not.

8 Idolatry, blasphemy, heresy, venting corrupt and pernicious opinions, that destroy the foundation, open contempt of the Word preached, profanation of the Lord's day, disturbing the peaceable administration and exercise of the worship and holy things of God, and the like, are to be restrained, and punished by civil authority.[175]

9 If any church one or more shall grow schismatical, rending itself from the communion of other churches, or shall walk incorrigibly or obstinately in any corrupt way of their own, contrary to the rule of the Word; in such case, the magistrate is to put forth his coercive power, as the matter shall require. The tribes on this side Jordan intended to make war against the other tribes, for building the altar of witness, whom they suspected to have turned away therein from following of the Lord.[176]

[173] I Kings 15: 14; 22: 43; 2 Kings 12: 3; 14: 4; 15: 35; I Kings 20: 42; Job 29: 25; 31: 26, 28; Neh. 13; Jon. 3: 7; Ezra 7; Dan. 3: 29.
[174] I Kings 20: 28, 42.
[175] Deut. 13; I Kings 20: 28, 42; Dan. 3: 29; Zech. 13: 3; Neh. 13: 21; I Tim. 2: 2; Rom. 13: 4.
[176] Josh. 22.

The Savoy Platform 1658

THE SAVOY DECLARATION OF FAITH AND ORDER WAS THE PRODUCT OF *the phase of Independent ascendancy during the Commonwealth period just as the Westminster standards were the product of the phase of Presbyterian ascendancy. In the 1650's various extreme and heretical sects flourished especially in the Army, and the orthodox Independents were anxious to distinguish themselves from these. In 1658 with the compliance of Cromwell's government, ministers throughout the land of Independent (or Congregational) persuasion were summoned to a synod at the Savoy Palace in London. This was not an official synod, however, in the same sense as the Westminster Assembly, i.e. it was not commissioned by the civil authorities to lay down the pattern for an all-embracing national Church.*

The Assembly met on September 29th and a committee of distinguished divines – Thomas Goodwin, John Owen, Philip Nye, William Bridge, Joseph Caryl, and William Greenhill – was appointed to draw up a confession. All except Owen had been present at the Westminster Assembly, and the confession of faith they drew up is largely identical with the Westminster Confession. The Savoy Assembly was over by October 12, 1658, and even then had had time for prayer and fasting. The really original part of the Savoy Declaration was the Platform of Church Polity where the distinctive views of the English Congregationalists are set forth:

1. Full spiritual power and authority resides in a particular local congregation (IV–VI).

2. The essence of the call of a minister is his election by the congregation. Formal ordination is a ratification of this, and is normally to be performed by the eldership of the local congregation (XI, XII, XV).

3. Synods are expedient for the discussion and resolution of difficulties, but they have no power over churches and individuals. The system of standing synods subordinate to one another is rejected (XXVI–XXVII).

Besides the bibliography given in the previous section the following books may be mentioned:

Visible Saints: The Congregational Way (1640–1660), G. F. Nuttall, 1957.
Congregational History, 1567–1700, J. Waddington, 1874.
The Five Dissenting Brethren, B. Gustaffsson, Lund, 1955.

The Savoy Platform 1658

OF THE INSTITUTION OF CHURCHES,
AND THE ORDER APPOINTED IN THEM BY JESUS CHRIST

B Y the appointment of the Father all power for the calling, institution, order, or government of the church, is invested in a supreme and sovereign manner in the Lord Jesus Christ, as King and Head thereof.

II. In the execution of this power wherewith he is so entrusted, the Lord Jesus calleth out of the world unto communion with himself, those that are given unto him by his Father, that they may walk before him in all the ways of obedience, which he prescribeth to them in his Word.

III. Those thus called (through the ministry of the Word by his Spirit) he commandeth to walk together in particular societies or churches, for their mutual edification, and the due performance of that public worship, which he requireth of them in this world.

IV. To each of these churches thus gathered, according unto his mind declared in his Word, he hath given all that power and authority, which is any way needful for their carrying on that order in worship and discipline, which he hath instituted for them to observe with commands and rules, for the due and right exerting and executing of that power.

V. These particular churches thus appointed by the authority of Christ, and entrusted with power from him for the ends before expressed, are each of them as unto those ends, the seat of that power which he is pleased to communicate to his saints or subjects in this world, so that as such they receive it immediately from himself.

VI. Besides these particular churches, there is not instituted by Christ any church more extensive or catholic entrusted with power for the administration of his ordinances, or the execution of any authority in his name.

VII. A particular church gathered and completed according to the mind of Christ, consists of officers and members: The Lord Christ having given to his called ones (united according to his appointment in church-order) liberty and power to choose persons fitted by the Holy Ghost for that purpose, to be over them, and to minister to them in the Lord.

VIII. The members of these churches are saints by calling, visibly manifesting and evidencing (in and by their profession and walking) their

[276]

obedience unto that call of Christ, who being further known to each other by their confession of the faith wrought in them by the power of God, declared by themselves or otherwise manifested, do willingly consent to walk together according to the appointment of Christ, giving up themselves to the Lord, and to one another by the will of God in professed subjection to the ordinances of the Gospel.

IX. The officers appointed by Christ to be chosen and set apart by the church so called, and gathered for the peculiar administration of ordinances, and execution of power or duty which he entrusts them with, or calls them to, to be continued to the end of the world, are pastors, teachers, elders, and deacons.

X. Churches thus gathered and assembling for the worship of God, are thereby visible and public, and their assemblies (in what place soever they are, according as they have liberty or opportunity) are therefore church or public assemblies.

XI. The way appointed by Christ for the calling of any person, fitted and gifted by the Holy Ghost, unto the office of pastor, teacher or elder in a church, is, that he be chosen thereunto by the common suffrage of the church itself, and solemnly set apart by fasting and prayer, with imposition of hands of the eldership of that church, if there be any before constituted therein: And of a deacon, that he be chosen by the like suffrage, and set apart by prayer, and the like imposition of hands.

XII. The essence of this call of a pastor, teacher or elder unto office, consists in the election of the church, together with his acceptation of it, and separation *by fasting and prayer*: And those who are so chosen, though not set apart by imposition of hands, are rightly constituted ministers of Jesus Christ, in whose name and authority they exercise the ministry to them so committed. The calling of deacons consisteth in the like election and acceptation, with separation *by prayer*.

XIII. Although it be incumbent on the pastors and teachers of the churches to be instant in preaching the Word, by way of office; yet the work of preaching the Word is not so peculiarly confined to them, but that others also gifted and fitted by the Holy Ghost for it, and approved (being by lawful ways and means in the providence of God called thereunto) may publicly, ordinarily and constantly perform it; so that they give themselves up thereunto.

XIV. However, they who are engaged in the work of public preaching, and enjoy the public maintenance upon that account, are not thereby obliged to dispense the seals to any other than such as (being saints by calling, and gathered according to the order of the Gospel) they stand related to, as pastors or teachers; yet ought they not to neglect others living within their parochial bounds, but besides their constant public preaching to them, they ought to enquire after their profiting by the Word, instructing them in, and pressing upon them (whether young or old) the great doctrines of the Gospel, even personally and particularly, so far as their strength and time will admit.

XV. Ordination alone without election or precedent consent of the church, by those who formerly have been ordained by virtue of that power they have received by their ordination, doth not constitute any person a church officer, or communicate office power unto him.

XVI. A church furnished with officers (according to the mind of Christ) hath full power to administer all his ordinances; and where there is want of any one or more officers required, that officer, or those which are in the church, may administer all the ordinances proper to their particular duty and offices; but where there are no teaching officers, none may administer the seals, nor can the church authorize any so to do.

XVII. In the carrying on of church administrations, no person ought to be added to the church, but by the consent of the church itself; that so love (without dissimulation) may be preserved between all the members thereof.

XVIII. Whereas the Lord Jesus Christ hath appointed and instituted as a means of edification, that those who walk not according to the rules and laws appointed by him (in respect of faith and life, so that just offence doth arise to the church thereby) be censured in his name and authority: Every church hath power in itself to exercise and execute all those censures appointed by him in the way and order prescribed in the Gospel.

XIX. The censures so appointed by Christ, are admonition and excommunication: and whereas some offences are or may be known only to some, it is appointed by Christ, that those to whom they are so known, do first admonish the offender in private: in public offences where any sin, before all; or in case of non-amendment upon private admonition, the offence being related to the church, and the offender not manifesting his repentance, he is to be duly admonished in the name of Christ by the whole church, by the ministry of the elders of the church; and if this censure prevail not for his repentance, then he is to be cast out by excommunication with the consent of the church.

XX. As all believers are bound to join themselves to particular churches, when and where they have opportunity so to do, so none are to be admitted unto the privileges of the churches, who do not submit themselves to the rule of Christ in the censures for the government of them.

XXI. This being the way prescribed by Christ in case of offence, no church members upon any offences taken by them, having performed their duty required of them in this matter, ought to disturb any church order, or absent themselves from the public assemblies, or the administration of any ordinances upon that pretence, but to wait upon Christ in the further proceeding of the church.

XXII. The power of censures being seated by Christ in a particular church, is to be exercised only towards particular members of each church respectively as such; and there is no power given by him unto any synods or ecclesiastical assemblies to excommunicate, or by their public edicts to threaten excommunication, or other church censures against churches, magistrates, or their people upon any account, no man being obnoxious to that censure, but upon his personal miscarriage, as a member of a particular church.

XXIII. Although the church is a society of men, assembling for the celebration of the ordinances according to the appointment of Christ, yet every society assembling for that end or purpose, upon the account of cohabitation within any civil precincts and bounds, is not thereby constituted a church, seeing there may be wanting among them, what is essentially required thereunto; and therefore a believer living with others in such a precinct, may join himself with any church for his edification.

XXIV. For the avoiding of differences that may otherwise arise, for the greater solemnity in the celebration of the ordinances of Christ, and the opening a way for the larger usefulness of the gifts and graces of the Holy Ghost; saints living in one city or town, or within such distances as that they may conveniently assemble for divine worship, ought rather to join in one church for their mutual strengthening and edification, than to set up many distinct societies.

XXV. As all churches and all the members of them are bound to pray continually for the good or prosperity of all the churches of Christ in all places, and upon all occasions to further it (every one within the bounds of their places and callings, in the exercise of their gifts and graces), so the churches themselves (when planted by the providence of God, so as they may have opportunity and advantage for it) ought to hold communion amongst themselves for their peace, increase of love, and mutual edification.

XXVI. In cases of difficulties or differences, either in point of doctrine or in administrations, wherein either the churches in general are concerned, or any one church in their peace, union, and edification, or any member or members of any church are injured in, or by any proceeding in censures, not agreeable to truth and order: it is according to the mind of Christ, that many churches holding communion together, do by their messengers meet in a synod or council, to consider and give their advice in, or about that matter in difference, to be reported to all the churches concerned; howbeit these synods so assembled are not entrusted with any church power, properly so called, or with any jurisdiction over the churches themselves, to exercise any censures, either over any churches or persons, or to impose their determinations on the churches or officers.

XXVII. Besides these occasional synods or councils, there are not instituted by Christ any stated synods in a fixed combination of churches, or their officers in lesser or greater assemblies; nor are there any synods appointed by Christ in a way of subordination to one another.

XXVIII. Persons that are joined in church fellowship, ought not lightly or without just cause to withdraw themselves from the communion of the church whereunto they are so joined: nevertheless, where any person cannot continue in any church without his sin, either for want of the administration of any ordinances instituted by Christ, or by his being deprived of his due privileges, or compelled to any thing in practice not warranted by the Word, or in case of persecution, or upon the account of conveniency of habitation; he consulting with the church, or the officer or officers thereof, may peaceably depart from the communion of the church, wherewith he hath so walked, to join himself with some other church, where he may enjoy the ordinances in the purity of the same, for his edification and consolation.

XXIX. Such reforming churches as consist of persons sound in the faith and of conversation becoming the Gospel, ought not to refuse the communion of each other, so far as may consist with their own principles respectively, though they walk not in all things according to the same rules of church order.

XXX. Churches gathered and walking according to the mind of Christ, judging other churches (though less pure) to be true churches, may receive unto occasional communion with them, such members of those churches as are credibly testified to be godly, and to live without offence.

The Difference between Independency and Presbytery

Jeremiah Burroughs
[1599-1646]

ALTHOUGH BETWEEN THOSE WHO SOUGHT FURTHER REFORMATION OF
*the Church of England and those who defended the Elizabethan Settlement there
was a gulf in thought and practice, minor internal differences existed within the
Puritan movement itself. The most important of these proved to be over the question
of church government – between the two systems known as Independency and
Presbytery. In the sixteenth century the term 'presbyterian' was used as a synonym for 'Puritan', since the Puritans stood for a reformation of the discipline of the
Church of England along the lines set out in the Admonition to Parliament and
the Book of Discipline whereby the rule of presbyteries of ministers and lay elders
was to replace that of diocesan bishops. The Separatists, who rejected the whole
parochial structure of the Established Church and sought to gather churches of true
believers (for which, incidentally, they were mercilessly persecuted), were distinct
from the Puritans who often criticized them strongly, and were criticized by them
for remaining within a corrupt ecclesiastical system.*

*In the seventeenth century, however, there grew up within the Puritan movement
a powerful body of opinion espousing and advocating the principles of Congregationalism or Independency (though often they disowned the latter name). During
the ascendancy of Laud, several of this persuasion were forced to leave the country;
some found refuge in Holland and ministered to English congregations there, while
others crossed the Atlantic and founded the New England community. In Massachusetts
and Connecticut the Churches were organized in a closely knit pattern, yet on Congregational principles. The ecclesiastical practice of New England was defined in
the Cambridge Platform of 1648 (see pp. 233 ff.), and expounded and defended by
John Cotton in* The Keys of the Kingdom of Heaven, 1644, *and* The Way of
the Churches of Christ in New England, 1645. *A reply to the first of Cotton's
treatises was written by the famous Samuel Rutherford entitled:* Due Right of Presbyteries, 1644, *claiming that a form of Presbyterial government like that practised
in Scotland was scriptural.*

*When the Westminster Assembly met in 1643 and the whole form of the Church
of England was again in the melting-pot, the difference between Independency and
Presbytery became a practical hindrance to an agreed policy. Only a handful of the
members of the Assembly held Congregational principles. but they included some of
the ablest and most respected; moreover they represented a considerable body of
opinion outside the Assembly, especially in the Parliamentary army. The nucleus
was a group of five, all of whom had been exiles in Holland: Thomas Goodwin,
Philip Nye, Sidrach Simpson, Jeremiah Burroughs, and William Bridge, and who,
in January 1644 published* An Apologetical Narration, *which was in effect an
appeal to Parliament in defence of their position. When in October of the same
year the Assembly completed its proposed rule of church-government (see pp.
207 ff.), the Independents tabled objections to three. of its features: 1. Particular
congregations were placed under one presbyterial government. 2. A system of standing assemblies was to be set up, congregational, classical, provincial, and national,
and appeals might be made from the inferior to the superior. 3. No single congre-*

*gation was allowed the right of ordination. The subsequent controversy only em-
phasised the fact that there were real differences of interpreting the scriptural
teaching on church government.*

One of several writers who replied to the Apologetical Narration *was Charles
Herle, who on the death of William Twisse in 1646 became Prolocutor or Chairman
of the Westminster Assembly. Herle claimed that 'the difference between us and
our brethren who are for Independency is nothing so great as you seem to conceive
it; – at most it does ruffle a little the fringe, not any way rend the garment of
Christ'. This view was endorsed by spiritual men on both sides, among them Jeremiah Burroughs (see p. 353), one of the authors of the* Apologetical Narration,
*who dealt with the difference between Independency and Presbytery in the course
of a series of sermons on the Beatitudes – an illustration of the Puritans' view that
contemporary problems must be dealt with in the exposition of Scripture. Burroughs
claims that the controversy lies in whether 'the ruling power of any minister extends
further than his pastoral power for word and sacraments'. This is a stimulating
challenge, though it is doubtful whether the Presbyterians would have accepted this
definition of the issue. What is especially valuable in the following brief extract is
Burroughs' spirit and approach to the problem of resolving or at least of living with
the difference.*

The Difference between Independency and Presbytery

————

'Blessed are the peacemakers: for they shall be called the children of God.' – Matt. v. 9.

YOU know I have not as yet meddled with any matters of controversy among you, but give me leave in a few words plainly to speak a little to that great controversy that they call independency and presbytery. I will but show you, first, where lies the principal difference there; for a great many there are whose spirits are mighty hot and violent one against another. But come to demand of these men, Do you know the controversy? do you know what it is? They are not able to give you an account where doth the main thing lie. Some will tell you that Independents would have no kind of government at all, and a general toleration for all things; this, they think, is the difference. And upon this they are misled to those things that, were they rightly informed, they could not be misled unto; for I make no question, but many whose spirits are very hot this way, yet are very godly, holy, gracious men, and go according to their conscience, and think they do God good service in a very strong opposition of them, and were it not for that they would not do as they do. Therefore, but a word, to give you the main thing that is called independency, and that that is called presbytery, that hinders so much the peace among us.

The great thing is this, those that they call Independents, they are persuaded, first, that there can be no kind of power and authority in the Church, but that that is set in it by Christ, no officers at all but them that are set in it by Christ – some of the other judgments go thus far; but here it may be it may weigh a little further, that as every office in the Church and officer must be appointed by Christ, so the extent of that office, how far it should go, must be appointed by Christ. For as it is in the commonwealth – though this prove not, yet it may illustrate – as there can be no court and judicature in a commonwealth but by the authority of the supreme judicature, so no jurisdiction in the Church but by the authority of the supreme, Jesus Christ; and as it appoints the office, so it appoints the extent of the office, how far it should go. But this to make way.

Now for the controversy. Say those they call Independents, For our part we think this, that the ruling power of ministers, that Christ hath appointed to feed people by word and sacraments, extends no further than where Christ hath appointed them, for to feed, by word and sacraments, in their pastoral power. Look, how far Christ hath given them power and authority to feed a people by word and sacraments, to take charge of the souls of a people; so far Christ hath given them power to rule over them in his name, and no further.

Now those that they call presbyters, they think they may go further, that though such and such ministers have only a pastoral charge but in one congregation, he cannot challenge in any pastoral relation to come and preach and administer sacraments but in this congregation; yet they think that by joining with others, his ruling power shall have an extent to a hundred or a thousand congregations that his face never saw, when the pastoral charge of his word and sacraments doth extend in an ordinary way but to one. Now for my part, whoever thinks there is a greater controversy in these two, but this I am speaking of, he sees further than I can do in it. Here the controversy mainly lies, whether the ruling power of any minister extends further than his pastoral power for word and sacraments – whether he hath the charge of others to rule them together with others, and not the charge of them in an equal way to feed them in word and sacraments. Now I do not come to plead this way or that way for either side, but only so far as may be for peace.

If the controversy lies here, I appeal to your consciences, Are you so certain, so sure of one side, that you can join in a violent opposition of the other? Is one so clear and evident to you, as you can take upon you, you would answer it before Christ, to use all the power of civil magistracy for to force one or the other side? For so I speak of either; for I would account it a very great evil for those that profess independency to force such as profess presbytery to be of their minds or practice. And so I think it will not be acceptable to Jesus Christ for the one by a civil way to force the other, and it will never prove to be the way of peace.

But now if you will say, We will force them to do so; it is true you may by an iron chain tie men close together that they shall not be able to go at such a distance; but will that make peace here in the Church of Christ in respect of men's hearts?

There is one thing more that I have observed hath been a cause of the breaking of peace exceedingly, and that is, the mistake of the point of schism; for that because we have that word in the covenant, men think in conscience that what is indeed truly schism they are bound to oppose with all their might, let become of peace what will; for that the Scripture accounts schism, certainly we are bound by all lawful means, according to the covenant, to oppose.

[286]

But I beseech you consider this first whether if any man that is a member of a church – for this is cried out of – that whosoever shall depart from the church that is acknowledged by himself a true church, and especially shall join with others, this man is a schismatic.

For to understand this aright, that there may not be the breaking of more peace than need, suppose that there be some men truly godly and conscientious that are in a church, but there is something done in the church that they cannot believe to be the mind of Christ; nay, after all examination, after prayer, after seeking to God, yet they cannot see it to be the mind of Christ, but they should sin if they should join with them. They can testify to God, their own consciences witnessing for them, that they would gladly join with such a church in all the ways of God's worship, but in such and such ways they cannot without sin to their own consciences. They labour to inform themselves, they go to the elders, go to others in all humility to show their doubts in this thing; and after the receiving of reasons from them, they depart, and they do in conscience to God examine them between God and their souls, and pray over them, that God would reveal these things unto them if they be his mind. Now after all this is done, yet if they cannot see, what would you have these men do? Suppose there be a hundred of them; they cannot communicate, yet they are not presently to rend from the congregation, but to wait a while to see whether God will convince them. Now after all means used, and they cannot be convinced, shall these men live without the ordinances of the sacrament all the days of their lives? Hath Christ so tied a member of a congregation, that if he cannot without sin to him join with the church, that he must never join with any other? Truly there had need be clear warrant for this if any one shall affirm it. But now suppose these should in all humility desire that they might have liberty together to join in the ordinances of Christ. They hold all the foundations of this church, yea, they account them brethren, they look upon them as godly, and in those ordinances wherein they can, they will join with them; but they cannot in such and such, and they must either join in some other fellowship, or they must be without those ordinances all their days. Now if these men shall in their lives appear godly, and walk peaceably towards others, so far as they can see the mind of God, do you think in your consciences that this is the schism that is spoken against in Scripture, that we are to oppose, and that that men so oppose now, which they call schism? I would put the case thus: In the bishops' time there were a company, you know, that were accounted non-conformists, which were very godly men; they could not conform to kneeling, suppose, or in any other ceremony, either in baptism or the supper of the Lord, and so they could not join with the congregations in the supper of the Lord. Upon this the bishops called them schismatics; and it was upon no other ground, they said. Now there are many of our brethren at this day, yea, I believe most of the godly ministers in England within a few years, did account those men that could not join at sacraments, because of kneeling and the cross, to be in an error; I say, the most godly men in the kingdom did believe it, and I believe many do so still.

But you will say, Though withdrawing from a congregation indeed which they could not join withal without sin, that was not schism; yet if they had gathered into another congregation, that had been schism. Then this satisfies.

First, In the point of negative schism; but for positive schism, to that I put this consideration to you, only that we might a little mollify men's spirits: Suppose these men might have had leave from the state – as suppose this law had been made that all men whose consciences cannot be brought to submit to kneeling at sacrament, and the cross in baptism, and cannot acknowledge the authority of prelates, that they shall have in such places in the city such meetings and such congregations where they shall enjoy the sacrament without those ceremonies, and without the acknowledgment of the authority of bishops – I say, suppose the state had allowed this, had these men been schismatics? As suppose all our brethren of Scotland that were in England in former times, why, abundance of them that lived in parishes they could not kneel at sacrament; now if this liberty had been given them, that all of the kingdom of Scotland that lived in the city of London, that they should have some particular place in the city, and should enjoy what they would there.

Ay, you will say, if the state had allowed them, then they were not.

But now consider of this, Schism is a church sin; and if anything be schism before the state allow it, it is after the state allows it. When it comes to break any order in the state, then it is a sin of another nature; but when we speak of schism properly so called, it is only a sin of the church. Now, if it be a schism before the state allows it, it will be a sin when the state allows it, that is certain; the allowance or not allowance of the state doth not change the nature of the thing. And I am confident that there is scarce any of you that are godly but would have thought it in former times a great mercy if those that were Non-conformists had had so much favour from the state as to have liberty to have joined together in such and such places appointed for them; that so long as they are orthodox in their opinions, so long as they lived godly and peaceable, they should have had liberty. If this had been, I believe not one of you would have accounted them schismatics. Now, if there be other godly men in the kingdom whose consciences cannot be satisfied in some other things, and yet you know their lives are godly – you know they are orthodox in all fundamentals of religion, they join with you, they desire to communicate with you in hearing the word and prayer, and all ways wherein they can; now if they should have a desire to enjoy the ordinances of Christ in that way wherein they may do it with peace of conscience, why, they are cried out of as schismatics; it is against the covenant, and must not be suffered. Here lies a mistake; and were there a right understanding of things, there might be ways for brethren to live together in unity, and enjoy their consciences in the fear of God, and walking peaceably one with another. But this shall suffice for this thing, Blessed are they that are peacemakers in such times as these. For my part, so far, through God's mercy, God hath made me sensible of the evil of breaches of peace, that should my life go for the procuring of it, I should account it as great a mercy, next to the revealing Christ to me, as ever I had in my life. If, I say, my life might go for the making peace between these two sorts of men, and so it should be all your resolutions not to go violently on in any way, but to study what ways there may be for peace between brethren and brethren. Now I shall say no more about this, and it is like you may never hear me further to speak about such things as these are, except there should be very great occasion for it.

A Presbyterian View of the Difference with Independency

ALTHOUGH THE FOLLOWING EXTRACT HAS REFERENCE TO INDEPEND-
ency, the document from which it is taken was directed against Erastianism. The
Independents were not alone in obstructing the efforts of the majority party in the
Westminster Assembly to establish a Church of England on lines similar to the
presbyterian Church of Scotland. A few members of the Assembly, while not arguing for the retention of episcopacy, wished to preserve the arrangement established
at the Reformation whereby the government of the Church was ultimately subject to
the State. The Erastians, as they were called, though weak in the Assembly,
were strong in the House of Commons. The House objected in particular to the claim
that presbyteries should exercise independent jurisdiction in connection with excommunication and the suspension of scandalous offenders from the Lord's Supper.
They propounded a series of questions to the Assembly concerning the divine right
or jus divinum of church government. In reply the Assembly stated a single proposition: 'The Lord Jesus, as King and Head of His Church, hath therein appointed
a government, in the hand of Church officers, distinct from the Civil magistrate.'
Parliament's questions were also answered in detail by a special committee, but these
answers were never printed. In December 1646 a volume entitled Jus Divinum
Regiminis Ecclesiastici (The Divine Right of Church Government) was published by several London ministers; it is believed that this is based on the answers
of the Westminster Assembly to the Commons' questions.

Part of the Commons' first question asked which, if any, form of Church polity
was divinely ordained: 'Whether any particular church government be jure divino?
And what that government is?' Like the Scottish leaders, Henderson and Rutherford, many of the members of the Assembly held that not only was church government, in general, of Divine right, but that the particular form was also set out in
Scripture and therefore of Divine institution. In their Jus Divinum, the London
ministers emphasized particularly that it was presbytery and not independency
which was of Divine right, as may be seen from this brief extract.

This comparison of the two forms of polity is clearly an attempt to win support
for the one rather than the other, and not a serious attempt to resolve the differences
between them. It claims that, comparatively, 'The Independent government is no
government at all'. That independency was tantamount to anarchy was a favourite
charge, which the Independents countered by charging Presbyterianism with tyrannical tendencies. The London ministers' point-by-point comparison of the two
systems is not wholly satisfactory in its statement of the Independents' view (it
accuses them of not believing in the unity of the visible church, in ordination, or
in the rule of eldership of the local congregation with authority derived directly
from Christ), but it is illuminating as an indication of what the Presbyterians considered the defects of Independency.

A Presbyterian View of the Difference with Independency

B UT the Independent government seems to be a far more excellent way, and it is embraced by many godly and precious people and ministers.

Answer 1. What true excellency is there at all in the whole Independent government, save only in those particulars wherein it agrees with the presbyterial government; and only so far as it is presbyterial? therefore the presbyterial government is equally, yea primarily and principally excellent. Wherein is the excellency of the Independent way of government? Have they only those officers which Christ himself hath appointed pastors and teachers, ruling elders and deacons? So the Presbyterians. Have they those spiritual censures, of admonishing, excommunicating, and receiving again into communion, which Christ ordained in his church, for guarding his ordinances, and well-guiding of the flock? So the Presbyterians. Have they Congregational presbyteries duly elected and constituted, for the exercise of all acts of government proper and necessary for their respective congregations? So the Presbyterians. Have they liberty of electing their own officers, pastors, elders and deacons? So the Presbyterians. Have they power to keep the whole lump of the church from being leavened, and purely to preserve the ordinances of Christ from pollution and profanation, etc? So the Presbyterians, etc. So that wherein soever the Independent government is truly excellent, the Presbyterial government stands in a full equipage and equality of excellency.

2. What one true excellency is there in the whole Independent government in any one point, wherein it really differs from the Presbyterial government? Take for instance a few points of difference.

In the Independent government.

In the Presbyterial government.

No other visible Church of Christ is acknowledged but only a single congregation meeting in one place to partake of all ordinances.

One general visible Church of Christ on earth is acknowledged, and all particular churches, and single congregations are but as similar parts of that whole.

[294]

The matter of their visible Church must be (to their utmost judgment of discerning) such as have true grace, real saints.

Their Churches are gathered out of other true visible Churches of Christ, without any leave or consent of pastor or flock, yea, against their wills, receiving such as tender themselves, yea, too often by themselves or others, directly or indirectly seducing disciples after them.

Preaching elders are only elected, not ordained.

Ruling elders also preach.

The subject of church-government is the *cœtus fidelium* or community of the faithful.

The church-officers act immediately as the servants of the Church, and deputed thereby.

All censures and acts of government are dispensed in single congregations ultimately, independently, without all liberty of appeal from them to any superior church-assembly; so the parties grieved are left without remedy.

There are acknowledged no authoritative classes or synods, in common, great, difficult cases, and in matters of appeals, but only suasive and consultative, and in case advice be not followed, they proceed only to a non-communion.

The matter of the Church invisible are only true believers, but of the Church visible persons professing true faith in Christ, and obedience to him, according to the rules of the Gospel.

Parochial churches are received as true visible Churches of Christ, and most convenient for mutual edification: gathering churches out of churches, hath no footsteps in Scripture, is contrary to apostolical practice; is the scattering of churches; the daughter of schism, the mother of confusion, but the stepmother to edification.

Preaching elders are both elected and ordained.

Ruling elders only rule, preach not, 1 Tim. 5: 17.

The subject of church-government is only Christ's own church-officers.

The church-governors act immediately as the servants of Christ, and as appointed by him.

All censures and acts of government are dispensed in congregational presbyteries subordinately, dependently, with liberty of appeal in all cases to presbyterial or synodal assemblies; where parties grieved have sufficient remedy.

There are acknowledged, and with happy success used not only suasive and consultative, but also authoritative classes and synods in cases of great importance, difficulty, common concernment or appeals; which have power to dispense all church-censures, as need shall require.

Let these and such like particulars in the Independent way, differing from the Presbyterial be duly pondered, and then let the impartial and indifferent reader judge, whether they be not the deformities, at least the infirmities of that way.

3. How many true excellencies are there in the way of the Presbyterial government, wherein it utterly surpasses the Independent government? Read but the particulars of the former parallel in the Presbyterial government, and then consider how far this transcends, yea, how the Independent government is indeed no government at all, to the Presbyterial government; wherein is to be found such ample provision, and that according to the Word of God, for comely order against confusion; for peace and unity of the Church against schism and division; for truth of the faith against all error and heresy; for piety and unblameableness against all impiety and scandal of conversation; for equity and right against all maladministrations, whether ignorant, arbitrary or tyrannical; for the honour and purity of all Christ's ordinances against all contempt, pollution and profanation; for comfort, quickening and encouragement of the saints in all the ways of Christ; and consequently for the honour of God and our Lord Jesus Christ in all the mysterious services of his spiritual sanctuary: All which rich advantages how impossible is it they should ever be found in the Independent government so long as it continues Independent? And what though some pious ministers and people embrace the Independent way? This dazzles not the eyes of the intelligent but of the infirm; we are to be regulated by Scripture-warrant, not by human examples. The best of saints have failed in ecclesiastical affairs; what a sharp contention was there betwixt Paul and Barnabas, Acts 15: 39 etc.? what a dangerous dissimulation was there in Peter, the Jews, and Barnabas. Gal. 2: 11, 12, 13, etc.? and therefore it is not safe, prudent, or conscientious to imitate all the examples of the best, and yet how few are those that have engaged themselves in the Independent way, in comparison to the multitudes of precious ministers and people inferior to them neither in parts, learning, piety, nor any other spiritual gift, who are for the Presbyterial way of church-government. Notwithstanding let all the true Israel of God constantly follow not the doubtful practices of unglorified saints, but the written pleasure of the most glorious King of saints; and as many as walk according to this rule, peace shall be on them and upon the Israel of God.

The Heads of Agreement 1691

THE DIVISION IN NAME AND PRACTICE BETWEEN THE PRESBYTERIANS
and Independents (or Congregationalists), which had hindered the Puritan cause
in the Commonwealth period, continued throughout the era of persecution. There
was fellowship and co-operation on a local level – several County Associations
continued to operate – but there was no nation-wide unity despite endeavours on both
sides for a closer association and agreement. After the Revolution and the accession
of William III and Mary, the Presbyterians' hopes of comprehension in a reformed national Church were revived. Bills were introduced into Parliament to
this end, but were dropped and instead an Act of Toleration was passed in 1689.

The movement for association between Independents and Presbyterians in London
was now intensified. In 1690 a joint fund was set up to support weak congregations
and to assist the training of ministerial candidates. Efforts were made to draw up
a statement of church principles and practice which would be acceptable to both
groups. An Essay of Accommodation was considered, but in April 1691 the union
was declared on the basis of the Heads of Agreement which differed in several respects from the Essay. The principal agents in securing this agreement were Matthew
Mead, a Congregational pastor at Stepney and a former exile in Holland; John
Howe, formerly chaplain to Cromwell, pastor of Silver Street Presbyterian Church,
London, and perhaps the most eminent living Puritan of the day; and Increase
Mather, pastor of the First Church, Boston, New England, and son of Richard
Mather, the drafter of the Cambridge Platform, who was in England on a mission
from the New England churches at that time. This was essentially an agreement
of London ministers, but it was supported and endorsed by Nonconformists in
several counties. For example, John Flavel was instrumental in securing its acceptance in Cornwall and Devon.

The Heads of Agreement have been stigmatized as a compromise; this is true
inasmuch as neither party to the agreement explicitly disavowed its principles on
any of the hitherto divisive issues. For example, as to whether the ordination of
ministers should be by the elders of one congregation or by a presbytery of ministers,
the Agreement seems to incline to the latter, but certainly represents concessions by
both sides in comparison with the positions taken at the Westminster Assembly.
But the local congregation is seen as the working unit, though this may owe less to
a change of heart among the Presbyterians than to the enforced circumstances of
the Great Persecution.

A particularly forceful condemnation of the Heads of Agreement by the nine-
teenth-century English Presbyterian scholar, Peter Lorimer, illustrates the view
held by some seventeenth-century divines, that the differences between presbytery
and independency were fundamental and irreducible. 'What a contrast', writes
Lorimer, 'between the Presbyterian divines at Westminster, in 1644, and the Presbyterian divines of London, in 1691, with truly great men like John Howe and
Richard Baxter among the number, who, of their own accord, and without the least
pressure from without, virtually undid all the Church work which their Westminster predecessors had done only fifty years before.' He claims that they 'tacitly

[299]

gave up all the distinctive constitutional principles of presbyterianism'. Lorimer goes on to describe the Heads of Agreement as 'a union-arrangement under which, incredible as it may appear, all the material concessions were made upon one side, while nothing of any consequence whatever was conceded on the other! The practical effect of the whole transaction was, that the Presbyterians, while still retaining the old name, became in all other respects Congregationalists . . .' (from an article entitled: 'Early English Presbyterian History' in The Catholic Presbyterian, *XVII, May 1880).*

The London Agreement of which the Heads were the expression was short-lived. The understanding and co-operation seems to have been largely broken within a few years, due to doctrinal division. In the subsequent history of English Dissent the Congregational-Presbyterian differences were to become almost irrelevant as the fundamental doctrines of the Reformation, upon which the original Puritans had agreed almost to a man, were thrown into the melting pot, and 'moderate Calvinism' gave way to Deism and Socinianism.

The Heads of Agreement are significant, however, as a concrete expression of the general and deeply-rooted Puritan conviction that in terms of the great amount of common ground among the true heirs of the Reformation the differences were of comparatively small account.

Bibliography

For historical background: *Magnalia Christi Americana*, Cotton Mather, Hartford 1853 (reprint) *The Church of the Revolution*, John Stoughton, 1874, *The Creeds and Platforms of Congregationalism*, Williston Walker (with bibliography), 1893, reprinted, Boston, 1960.

The Heads of Agreement 1691

The Heads of Agreement
Preface

Endeavours for an agreement among Christians, will be grievous to none who desire the flourishing state of Christianity itself. The success of these attempts among us, must be ascribed to a presence of God so signal, as not to be concealed; and seems a hopeful pledge of further blessings.

The favour of our rulers in the present established liberty, we most thankfully acknowledge; and to them we are studious to approve ourselves in the whole of this affair. Therefore we declare against intermeddling with the national Church form; imposing these terms of agreement on others is disclaimed: all pretence to coercive power, is as unsuitable to our principles, as to our circumstances: excommunication itself, in our respective churches, being no other than a declaring such scandalous members as are irreclaimable, to be incapable of Communion with us in things peculiar to visible believers: and in all, we expressly determine our purpose, to the maintaining of harmony and love among ourselves, and preventing the inconveniences which human weakness may expose to in our use of this liberty.

The general concurrence of ministers and people in this city, and the great disposition thereto in other places, persuade us, this happy work is undertaken in a season designed for such divine influence, as will overcome all impediments to peace, and convince to that agreement which has been always among us in a good degree, though neither to ourselves nor others so evident, as hereby it is now acknowledged.

Need there any arguments to recommend this union? Is not this what we all have prayed for, and Providence by the directest indications has been long calling and disposing us to? can either zeal for God, or prudent regards to ourselves remissly suggest it, seeing the blessings thereof are so important, and when it has become in so many respects even absolutely necessary; especially as it may conduce to the preservation of the Protestant religion, and the Kingdom's weal; a subserviency whereto, shall always govern our united abilities, with the same disposition to a concurrence with all others who are duly concerned for those national blessings.

As these considerations render this agreement desirable, so they equally urge a watchful care against all attempts of Satan to dissolve it, or frustrate the good effects thereof so manifestly destructive to his kingdom. Therefore it is incumbent on us, to forbear condemning and disputing those different sentiments and practices we have expressly allowed for: To reduce all distinguishing names, to that of United Brethren: To admit no uncharitable jealousies, or censorious speeches;

much less any debates as to which party seems most favoured by this agreement. Such carnal regards are of small moment with us, who herein have used words less accurate, that neither side might in their various conceptions about lesser matters be contradicted, when in all substantials we are fully of one mind; and from this time hope more perfectly to rejoice in the honour, gifts, and success of each other, as our common good.

That we as united, may contribute our utmost to the great concernments of our Redeemer, it is mutually resolved, we will assist each other with our labours, and meet and consult, without the least shadow of separate or distinct parties: Whence we joyfully expect great improvements in light and love, through the more abundant supplies of the Spirit; being well assured we herein serve that Prince of Peace, of the increase of whose Government and Peace, there shall be no end.

THE following Heads of Agreement have been resolved upon, by the united ministers in and about London, formerly called Presbyterian and Congregational; not as a measure for any national constitution, but for the preservation of order in our congregations that cannot come up to the common rule by law established.

I. OF CHURCHES AND CHURCH-MEMBERS

1. We acknowledge our Lord Jesus Christ to have one Catholic Church, or Kingdom, comprehending all that are united to him, whether in heaven or earth. And do conceive the whole multitude of visible believers, and their infant seed (commonly called the Catholic visible Church) to belong to Christ's spiritual kingdom in this world: but for the notion of a Catholic visible Church here, as it signifies its having been collected into any formed society, under any visible human head on earth, whether one person singly, or many collectively, we, with the rest of Protestants, unanimously disclaim it.

2. We agree, that particular societies of visible saints, who under Christ their Head are statedly joined together, for ordinary communion with one another in all the ordinances of Christ, are particular churches, and are to be owned by each other as instituted Churches of Christ, though differing in apprehensions and practice in some lesser things.

3. That none shall be admitted as members, in order to communion in all the special ordinances of the Gospel, but such persons as are knowing and sound in the fundamental doctrines of the Christian religion, without scandal in their lives; and, to a judgment regulated by the Word of God, are persons of visible godliness and honesty; credibly professing cordial subjection to Jesus Christ.

4. A competent number of such visible saints (as before described) do become the capable subjects of stated communion in all the special ordinances of Christ, upon their mutual declared consent and agreement to walk together therein according to Gospel rule. In which declaration, different degrees of explicitness, shall no way hinder such churches from owning each other, as instituted churches.

5. Though parochial bounds be not of divine right, yet for common edification the members of a particular church ought (as much as conveniently may be) to live near one another.

6. That each particular church hath right to choose their own officers; and, being furnished with such as are duly qualified and ordained according to the Gospel rule, hath authority from Christ for exercising government, and of enjoying all the ordinances of worship within itself.

7. In the administration of church power, it belongs to the pastors and other elders of every particular church (if such there be) to rule and govern: and to the brotherhood to consent, according to the rule of the Gospel.

8. That all professors as before described, are bound in duty, as they have opportunity, to join themselves as fixed members of some particular church; their thus joining being part of their professed subjection to the Gospel of Christ, and an instituted means of their establishment and edification; whereby they are under the pastoral care, and, in case of scandalous or offensive walking, may be authoritatively admonished or censured for their recovery, and for vindication of the truth, and the church professing it.

9. That a visible professor thus joined to a particular church, ought to continue stedfastly with the said church; and not forsake the ministry and ordinances there dispensed, without an orderly seeking a recommendation unto another church, which ought to be given, when the case of the person apparently requires it.

II. OF THE MINISTRY

1. We agree, that the ministerial office is instituted by Jesus Christ, for the gathering, guiding, edifying, and governing of his Church; and to continue to the end of the world.

2. They who are called to this office ought to be endued with competent learning, and ministerial gifts, as also with the grace of God, sound in judgment, not novices in the faith, and knowledge of the Gospel; without scandal, of holy conversation, and such as devote themselves to the work and service thereof.

3. That ordinarily none shall be ordained to the work of this ministry, but such as are called and chosen thereunto by a particular church.

4. That in so great and weighty a matter as the calling and choosing a pastor, we judge it ordinarily requisite, that every such church consult and advise with the pastors of neighbouring congregations.

5. That after such advice, the person consulted about, being chosen by the brotherhood of that particular church over which he is to be set, and he accepting, be duly ordained and set apart to his office over them; wherein it is ordinarily requisite, that the pastors of neighouring congregations concur with the preaching elders, if such there be.

6. That, whereas such ordination is only intended for such as never before had been ordained to the ministerial office; if any judge, that in the case also of the removal of one formerly ordained, to a new station or pastoral charge, there ought to be a like solemn recommending him and his labours to the grace and blessing of God; no different sentiments or practice herein, shall be any occasion of contention or breach of communion among us.

7. It is expedient, that they who enter on the work of preaching the Gospel, be not only qualified for communion of saints; but also that, except in cases extraordinary, they give proof of their gifts and fitness for the said work, unto the pastors of churches of known abilities to discern and judge of their qualifications; that they may be sent forth with solemn approbation and prayer; which we judge needful, that no doubt may remain concerning their being called to the work; and for preventing (as much as in us lieth) ignorant and rash intruders.

III. Of Censures

1. As it cannot be avoided, but that in the purest churches on earth, there will sometimes offences and scandals arise, by reason of hypocrisy and prevailing corruption; so Christ hath made it the duty of every church, to reform itself by spiritual remedies, appointed by him to be applied in all such cases; viz., admonition, and excommunication.

2. Admonition, being the rebuking of an offending member in order to conviction, is in case of private offences to be performed according to the rule in Mat. 18: v. 15, 16, 17, and in case of public offences, openly before the church, as the honour of the Gospel, and nature of the scandal shall require: and if either of the admonitions take place for the recovery of the fallen person, all further proceedings in a way of censure, are thereon to cease, and satisfaction to be declared accordingly.

3. When all due means are used, according to the order of the gospel, for the restoring an offending and scandalous brother; and he notwithstanding remains impenitent, the censure of excommunication is to be proceeded unto; wherein the pastor and other elders (if there be such) are to lead, and go before the church; and the brotherhood to give their consent, in a way of obedience unto Christ, and unto the elders, as over them in the Lord.

4. It may sometimes come to pass, that a church-member, not otherwise scandalous, may sinfully withdraw, and divide himself from the communion of the church to which he belongeth: in which case, when all due means for the reducing him, prove ineffectual, he having hereby cut himself off from that church's communion; the church may justly esteem, and declare itself discharged of any further inspection over him.

IV. Of Communion of Churches

1. We agree, that particular churches ought not to walk so distinct and separate from each other, as not to have care and tenderness towards one another. But their pastors ought to have frequent meetings together, that by mutual advice, support, encouragement, and brotherly intercourse, they may strengthen the hearts and hands of each other in the ways of the Lord.

2. That none of our particular churches shall be subordinate to one another; each being endued with equality of power from Jesus Christ. And that none of the said particular churches, their officer, or officers, shall exercise any power, or have any superiority over any other church, or their officers.

3. That known members of particular churches, constituted as aforesaid, may have occasional communion with one another in the ordinances of the Gospel, viz., the Word, prayer, sacraments, singing psalms, dispensed according to the mind of Christ: Unless that church with which they desire communion, hath any just exception against them.

4. That we ought not to admit any one to be a member of our respective congregations, that hath joined himself to another, without endeavours of mutual satisfaction of the congregations concerned.

5. That one church ought not to blame the proceedings of another, until it hath heard what that church charged, its elders, or messengers, can say in vindication of themselves from any charge of irregular or injurious proceedings.

6. That we are most willing and ready to give an account of our church

proceedings to each other, when desired; for preventing or removing any offences that may arise among us. Likewise we shall be ready to give the right hand of fellowship, and walk together according to the Gospel rules of communion of churches.

V. OF DEACONS AND RULING ELDERS

We agree, The office of a deacon is of divine appointment, and that it belongs to their office to receive, lay out, and distribute the church's stock to its proper uses, by the direction of the pastor, and the brethren if need be. And whereas divers are of opinion, that there is also the office of ruling elders, who labour not in Word and doctrine; and others think otherwise; we agree, that this difference make no breach among us.

VI. OF OCCASIONAL MEETINGS OF MINISTERS, &C.

1. We agree, that in order to concord, and in any other weighty and difficult cases, it is needful, and according to the mind of Christ, that the ministers of several churches be consulted and advised with, about such matters.

2. That such meetings may consist of smaller or greater numbers, as the matter shall require.

3. That particular churches, their respective elders, and members, ought to have a reverential regard to their judgment so given, and not dissent therefrom, without apparent grounds from the Word of God.

VII. OF OUR DEMEANOUR TOWARDS THE CIVIL MAGISTRATE

1. We do reckon ourselves obliged continually to pray for God's protection, guidance, and blessing upon the rulers set over us.

2. That we ought to yield unto them, not only subjection in the Lord, but support, according to our station and abilities.

3. That if at any time it shall be their pleasure to call together any number of us, or require any account of our affairs, and the state of our congregations, we shall most readily express all dutiful regard to them herein.

VIII. OF A CONFESSION OF FAITH

As to what appertains to soundness of judgment in matters of faith, we esteem it sufficient, that a church acknowledge the Scriptures to be the

Word of God, the perfect and only rule of faith and practice; and own either the doctrinal part of those commonly called the Articles of the Church of England, or the Confession, or Catechisms, Shorter or Larger, compiled by the Assembly at Westminster, or the Confession agreed on at the Savoy, to be agreeable to the said rule.

IX. OF OUR DUTY AND DEPORTMENT TOWARDS THEM THAT ARE NOT IN COMMUNION WITH US

1. We judge it our duty to bear a Christian respect to all Christians, according to their several ranks and stations, that are not of our persuasion or communion.

2. As for such as may be ignorant of the principles of the Christian religion, or of vicious conversation, we shall in our respective places, as they give us opportunity, endeavour to explain to them the doctrine of life and salvation, and to our uttermost persuade them to be reconciled to God.

3. That such who appear to have the essential requisites to church-communion, we shall willingly receive them in the Lord, not troubling them with disputes about lesser matters.

As we assent to the forementioned Heads of Agreement; so we unanimously resolve, as the Lord shall enable us, to practise according to them.

SECTION V

The Unity of the Church

The Way to Peace

Walter Cradock

[1606–1659]

NONCONFORMITY IN WALES IS GENERALLY DATED FROM THE OUTBREAK
of the Laudian persecutions in 1633. Among several ministers suspended that year
was young Walter Cradock, curate at St Mary's, Cardiff. Born at Trefela, Mont-
mouthshire, and educated at Oxford, Cradock had come under the powerful influence of William Wroth (1570–1642), the apostolic rector of Llanvaches, whose
ministry attracted hungry souls from all over South Wales. After his suspension
Cradock took to itinerant preaching and apart from a year as curate at Wrexham,
where his ministry caused such a reformation that he was compelled to leave, he
resided at Llanvair Waterdine, Salop.

Wroth was not deprived of his living until 1638, and the following year he formed
an Independent congregation at Llanvaches. This church being 'cast into the
mould of Church order, according to the New England way' is claimed as the
first of this 'pattern' in Britain. Wroth himself is regarded as 'the father and founder
of Nonconformity in Wales'. Cradock became his assistant at Llanvaches and together they helped to form an Independent church on similar lines at Bristol. On
Wroth's death in 1642 Cradock became his successor not only in the pastorate
but as the recognized leader of the Independent Churches in Wales.

At the outbreak of the Civil War the Llanvaches Church together with Cradock
fled to Bristol, a Parliamentarian city of refuge, and the following year both churches
'emigrated' to London. There they joined together, worshipping at All Hallows
the Great where Cradock accepted a lectureship. In 1646, after the Bristol and Llanvaches churches had gone home again, Cradock returned to Wales where he renewed his evangelistic labours with such evident results that he could tell the House
of Commons in 1648: 'The Gospel is run over the mountains between Brecknock-
shire and Monmouthshire, as the fire in the thatch.' Those converted under his
ministry included Vavasor Powell and Morgan Llwyd.

Among Cradock's best-known works was his Gospel liberty in the extensions
and limitations of it, wherein is laid down an exact way to end the present
dissensions, and to preserve future peace among the saints, published in 1648
and reprinted in his Works, 1800. It consisted of nine sermons on I Corinthians
10: 23: 'All things are lawful for me, but all things are not expedient: all things
are lawful for me, but all things edify not.' The seventh sermon, which is reproduced on the following pages, bears directly on the Independent-Presbyterian
controversy.

Bibliography
Works, Walter Cradock, published by Thomas Charles of Bala and P.
Oliver of Chester, 1800.
History of Protestant Nonconformity in Wales, Thomas Rees, 1861.
The Welsh Saints, 1640–1660 (Walter Cradock, Vavasor Powell, Morgan
Llwyd), G. F. Nuttall, 1957.

The Way to Peace

All things are lawful for me, but all things are not expedient:
all things are lawful for me, but all things edify not

WE are come to the third doctrine, which, for brevity's sake, I brought in as the use and application of the two former, that seeing many things are lawful to the saints under the New Testament that were not to the saints under the Old; and seeing that of those many things that are now lawful there are but a few that are expedient, therefore the saints would be exhorted, in their walking, not only to eye that which is lawful, but also that which is expedient.

The last day I propounded one motive, which I have not yet finished; it was this, That this is the readiest way to end the controversies and to settle peace among the saints. I shall not repeat what was then delivered, but proceed in this use (because it is the chief of all) to answer an objection or two.

The first is this, you will say, Sir, you pretend to seek peace by this; is this the way to peace? methinks you seem to cross all people in your discourse, you speak against Anabaptists, and Independents, and Presbyterians; and is this the way to peace?

Beloved, to that, briefly, I answer in general, It is the way to peace, the right way. How? Thus, in all fallings out between man and man in civil things, what is the way to peace and reconciliation? The ordinary way is to divide stakes, to abate every one a little, every one to come to condescend to each other; that is the way to peace. We should do with our brethren just as God doth with us, or we with him, when we are fallen out: You know that sin is enmity against God, how comes there to be peace and reconciliation? You know the way is, God comes and meets us, and we are to meet him; as it is in Amos, Prepare to meet thy God, O Israel. We meet the Lord and he meets us (as we see in the parable of the prodigal and his father) and so there is peace. So there will never be peace among the saints as long as every one stands upon his points, and will not abate an ace; but he will go his way, and do what he list. The apostle's rule, Romans 12, is, Brethren, saith he, condescend to men of low estate:

There is the way: Be of the same mind one toward another (verse 16.) that is, away with jars and dissensions, I beseech you be of the same mind in the Lord. If we were of the same mind we should soon be at peace: Every one loves those that are of his mind; but which is the way? The way, is, Mind not high things; go not so high as to mind high things, and care not whether your brethren be edified, or whether they stumble; but condescend to them that are low; come down a little, every one abate a little; this is the way to peace. And so, in Acts 15, when there was dissension about circumcision, it is notably worth your observation; when they were come to the saints at Jerusalem, and the apostles were about the controversy, they answer not punctually, they do not blame the Gentiles or the Jews, but they divide stakes, and desire that the Jews would not enforce circumcision upon the Gentiles, and they desire that the Gentiles would not stand upon things strangled and blood, those things of all others did give most offence to the Jews; for it was notoriously infamous for them to do so; therefore they should condescend to them so far, and the other should condescend to them again; and so there was like to be peace, and the churches had joy; the honest, humble-hearted were glad. So, till people are willing to come down and condescend to their brethren, there will never be peace.

And do not conceive that it is not possible in things spiritual as well as civil; it is not impossible; there is a way in spiritual things also. The Lord hath promised one heart and one way; it is not impossible for us to be as one man to go in one way. Thus in general to answer the objection.

But, in particular, you say, you cross Independents and Presbyterians; and is this the way to make peace?

Hear me with patience: Concerning Independents, as you call them (though they will not own the name, but you fasten it on them) I must speak this, that, concerning their practice and what they do ordinarily, I cannot condemn them; neither do I know any godly, judicious Presbyterian that will be against most of their tenets: But know, concerning those you call Independents, that they have divers principles that are destructive; among the rest I warn you of one principle that will be wholly destructive to your own peace and the peace of others (though you see it not) the fancying and conceiting of a curious piece of discipline in the New Testament, in every tittle as it was in the Old; it will necessarily and infallibly follow, that any man that holds that must come to this, that we must have signs, and miracles, and apostles again. Experience shows that when men stand upon that, and cannot make it out, they conclude that there must be apostles and miracles, as of old; because they conceive that there must be a more curious piece in the New than in the Old Testament, and they are not able to find it; as one that puzzled himself and doted on such a thing; he cast his Bible aside, and said, We must of necessity have miracles and apostles as they had before. Therefore though, for the generality, your practice be good, yet labour to get out of that principle, or else remember it will be your ruin, and the ruin of all your churches.[1]

But then you say, you herein cross Presbyterians too.

In a word, let me tell you, that those that are now called Presbyterians, that are pious, and godly, and precious men (as many of them I knew) under the episcopacy were of this mind, they either held that there was no external way of government at all, or else they held that there is a latitude that we are not so absolutely and punctually tied in every thing: And if half a score years ago there was such a latitude, it were a strange thing if these Presbyterians should go now to frame such a curious piece in every point. So, I say, if those that are called Presbyterians agree with themselves, and their own principles, and what they were ten years since, they agree with this doctrine, and therefore there is no cause of offence to them.

But I have not yet done, because I am willing that there should be peace; let me come a little home to particulars, and I will show you this, that there is not true reason in the world (but that the devil bewitcheth men) why there should be any contention and strife between Presbyterians (I mean godly, religious people) and those that you call Independents. There is no true reason at all why there should be this contention, and I will demonstrate it four ways.

The first is this, because they are on both sides godly, precious men: I do not say that all are on either side, but the generality of them. And you know Abraham and Lot, when there was like to be a falling out about a greater thing, a matter of land, saith Abraham, Let there be no strife between thee and me, for we are brethren; if thou wilt take the one hand I will take the other. So these are godly men, as I acknowledge both sides to be; why should people be ready to nourish strife and contention between them?

---

[1] Cradock frequently attributes internal difficulties amongst the godly to the tendency which some had to claim a divine warrant for parts of their church order which, in fact, Scripture does not determine (e.g. the mode of baptism). He complains, 'the godly go one against another, and all *Jure Divino*; every one will have an absolute rule for all the Saints'. In contrast to this he says, 'where God hath left a latitude . . . let us take notice of it'.

There can be no question that the regulative principle of Scripture can be misused (as it was, to name an extreme case, by those seventeenth-century groups who asserted there was no scriptural warrant for congregational singing). It is against this abuse and not the principle as such that Cradock appears to be arguing.—EDITOR.

[316]

But the second reason that there should be no strife and contention between them is, because the business, the things that they differ in are very small, it is a very small, inconsiderable thing. I speak not of those (as Paul saith of oppositions of science, falsely so called; so I speak not of Presbytery, falsely so called; I know of no rule they go by) but of godly men, that out of judgment and conscience hold Presbytery. As a reverend, godly man, writing of Presbytery, The case between us and our brethren, saith he, it is not the rending of the garment, it is but the ruffling of the fringe. It is so far from being a fundamental difference that it is scarce a material difference; nay, it is not in the form; we agree both in the same form of government. We (saith he) agree in this, that there shall be such a government, and what this government shall be; only here is the difference, whose it shall be, to whom it shall belong; nor so much in that, as where it shall be; whether in a church or in a congregation of ministers belonging to divers churches. And so being but the ruffling of the fringe, what madmen are we to set the kingdom on fire, and make our lives burthensome, and draw new and heavier miseries on ourselves now than ever we felt by our very enemies. Therefore, being between brethren, and for a thing so small, why should there be strife among us?

Well, thirdly (which to me is the main, the chief) that this difference, which is between brethren, and about that which never was, and it is a hundred to one that it is a thing that never will be; we strive about a thing that is a great way off, it is a hundred to one if any of us ever come to the practice of that we strive for. We all agree there shall be a company of saints and a company of visible believers, and that there shall be power in the church to order and govern things; that the church shall determine, as it did in Jerusalem. Let us go so far, let us have churches reformed, and set the power in them, and let them rule, and then, if there be occasion for people to appeal, God will either open men's eyes, or else in expediency (as I shall show by and by) they shall be directed: But we strive (as I told you) as if you and I should strive who should enter into the gates of Venice first, and we know not whether either of us shall come there at all. We strive about tomorrow; we have present miseries enough, we need not strive about things that are to come ten years hence, and, it may be, will never come. We are fools; are we sure that the kingdom will stand? or that we shall have our lives? and yet we go and strive about a nick; that is, the farthest of all things: Whereas, as for outward things, sufficient for the day is the grief thereof. Go on in love, and when it comes to that we shall see more light. This is the greatest indiscretion in England, to strive about a thing that is never likely to come to pass.

Fourthly, and lastly, there should be no strife, because, as the Presbyterial, godly men, they cannot, nor will prove such a thing to be an absolute rule for all the churches and for all saints. Say there were such a rule in Acts 15; doth it follow that it is a rule for all churches and all saints? Why do we not also sell our lands, and give to our brethren? Let them but show me a ground why that example should be made an absolute rule. Therefore as a man cannot show, nor ever will, an absolute rule to bind all the saints throughout the world to do so; so, on the other side, the Independents cannot prove but it may be expedient in divers cases; therefore the one seems to act necessarily, the other probably, to be expedient by right reason and the law of nature, if a church cannot agree among themselves; and what cause of strife is there in this?

Suppose one should say to me, come out of that house, or else you will be destroyed, the house will fall upon you: I believe not that there is a necessity, but I think it is expedient, because the house is old; he thinks it is of necessity, and I think it expedient; is there any cause of strife in this? So put these together, and see how we are deluded by the devil and our own hearts to make strife about a thing that may never be; therefore there is no reason for it.

But, that I may satisfy you a little more, you will say, What, is there no more difference between Presbyterians and Independents? I have heard that there is more difference between them than between the cavaliers and the other party, that they are ready to cut one another's throats. If there be no more between them, how comes this contention among them?

I think, of all the contentions that ever were among the saints, from Christ's time till now, there was never such a mystery in any contention as there is in this: And (but that I would not take up so much time) I could go near to open this mystery, how the devil and our own hearts have got the strangest mystery to set the saints together by the ears, that ever was: But I cannot stay upon that.

But if you ask me, How comes it to pass? You know a little spark will bring a great flame; a little contention is as the letting out of waters. It is no wonder; it is the nature of contention to multiply, as it is the nature of fire to grow bigger; it comes from the devil and our own hearts.

If you ask me, How comes it from men?

I say, it comes from five sorts of people, and, it may be, you and I, and the most of us, have a hand in blowing this fire. The Lord show it to us all, that we may labour to be peace-makers, and so be blessed.

The first sort of people are weak, carnal Christians; there may be those that are called Independents that are carnal: I mean not carnal, as though they had no grace, but in the apostle's sense, 1 Cor. 3, Are ye not carnal? that is, those that have but a little grace, and have a great deal of rashness, and peevishness, and giddiness, and pettishness, and censoriousness: They are people that have a great deal of zeal, many of them, but it is without knowledge, without wisdom to manage it: They see part of the will of God, and of the truth of God, but not all (as the sun shines on one part of the earth, and the other is dark) and in that part they see the substance, but eye not the circumstance; they care not if all the world be against them, or whom they edify, or whom they destroy, if they have the command of Christ they will do it. And these people, though they be godly, as a godly man saith of them, there is a new light coming into their souls; but they have not grace to manage it, and so they go headlong. It is a good light, but they have not grace to manage it; and that light, by reason of their corruptions and temptations, kindles contention in the churches.

Therefore if we would have peace (which is our great desire) we must admonish and rebuke them sharply; they are full of censoriousness, and pettishness, and have many harsh and unseemly words: These must be reproved, and there must be a course taken to bind up their spirits, or else it will be hard to have peace.

Then, secondly, there is another generation of people, that exceedingly blow up the fire, that are contrary to those, that is, a generation of carnal men that have nothing of God in them; that usurp to themselves commonly the name of Presbytery; they would be called (though falsely) Presbyterians. Though Presbytery be an honourable word, and it is an honourable thing, and they be honourable men that hold it, and godly men: but many that would be called Presbyterians (taking a good name, and misapplying it to themselves) they are wolves in sheep's clothing; they talk of reforming the church, and yet they would set the saints, as so many tigers, together by the ears: I mean not by these any godly men; but you may know them, if you take notice of their persons; usually they are the prelatical men, such as were surrogates to bishops before, double-beneficed men, rich parsons, prebends, and canons; these men, that know not the power of godliness, whose hearts were at Oxford, and they would have been there too, but that they see more hope of preferment here; there are none that talk so much of Presbytery as they; and in these hoods and veils they study to devour the people of God: Beware of them.

But you will say, Why may not a double-beneficed man and a surrogate be a godly man?

He may be, and be truly converted; I condemn not all, but it is very rare: Therefore go farther, and you shall see the same principles in them

[319]

that were in the persecuting bishops, pride, and cruelty, and rage against the saints, and fire and faggot, etc. worse than was in the bishops; they have the same principles, and breathe out threatenings against the saints, fire and banishment, and yet they croak of reformation; they are wolves in sheep's clothing.

So, if you look on their ends, they are the same, they were rich men then, and so they are now, they are covetous, and greedy, and sensual, and proud, griping for livings, and means, and wealth; they chop and change livings, and use devices to get more means still; they are the same men still: And yet these own the name of Presbytery, and every one that is against them is against Presbytery (there is the mystery of iniquity) and shortly, if these get their wills, every godly man in England shall be accounted either to be an an Independent, or an Anabaptist, or an Antinomian, or some other scandalous note, that does not approve of their courses: And, as they say, every man shall be a Round-head that is rich, that hath something to lose among the Cavaliers. So these men having a mind to faction, meaning to rule the world, and to enjoy the sweets and the fat of it, they put foul names upon the saints: And so many godly men that preach against Antinomians and Anabaptists, they must be accounted Antinomians or Anabaptists: And this is ordinary amongst these men, therefore wonder not at this, for be sure of it that always there will be some to persecute the people of God, and put foul names upon them to cover the business. And observe from the beginning of the preaching of the Gospel, carnal men have taken good names to themselves, and thrown ill names upon godly people. So you shall see in Popery: What were they? Catholics; a good word: And what were true Christians? Lollards, Heretics, and Schismatics. And so in King James's time, what were the good fellows? Orthodox men: And what were the saints? Puritans: So now, what are the sides in the armies? The one are Cavaliers, a word of honour and knighthood: And what are the other? Round-heads. So episcopacy, it is a good word, and a thing that God in Scripture commends; but, by degrees, carnal men stole the name episcopacy and bishops and under that they persecuted the saints. So the saints have the worst end of the staff still, the worst names. As for these men, there is nothing to be done but to discover them, and to pray for them that the Lord would open their eyes; I mean not any godly man, Independent or Presbyterian, and therefore if thou be offended at this, thou showest thyself to be a man that feareth not God.

The third sort are Malignants, a lower sort of people, that are ill-affected to the commonwealth; and so out of a design that they see the commonwealth party, the godly Presbyterians or Independents, they have borne the brunt, as they know; and if we could take away the godly party of them (say they) we should do well enough; the rest would turn, and do I know not what: And what course take these? They come to the Independents, and present Presbytery to them, and say it is worse than episcopacy, and it is of Rome, and use abominable, bitter words, and so fill poor souls, especially the weak, with such conceits, as if Rome itself, and the pope himself, were coming to rule all.

Then for the other side (though they care neither for Presbytery nor Independency, but are downright Atheists) they go to the Presbyterians, and they say that the Independents are destructive to the commonwealth, that they have strange principles, that they will not fight in the wars because they may not have their liberty, they leave all to us, and they will be at no loss, and if that party were rooted out, we should be stronger, say they; and so they make them as hideous as they can; though it be untrue, for it is well known that they ran not away, but fought as courageously as any; but they represent them so; and when they have brought them both together by the ears, then they laugh in their sleeves.

You will say, There are some you know that are great Independents, and they are wondrously vexed because they have not their design.

But let me tell you, they grieve and mourn bitterly, not because they could not set up Independency; but this is their greatest grief, that the devil drives such a design, and giddy people do not take notice of the consequences of the divisions among us.

Brethren, beware of these; say to them as he did, Exodus 2, You will come and kill me, as you did the Egyptian yesterday: Take them up sharply and send them a going; you are firebrands of hell to set us together by the ears.

Fourthly, There are another sort of people, that is, the godly party (that you call the moderate party on both sides) those that are godly men; and there is flesh and spirit in these also, and they have a hand in it. As for the Independents, those that are moderate they hearken too much to the heady people I spake of before, and are provoked: So, on the other side, the godly men of the Presbytery adhere too much to those wolves in sheep's apparel, and the cruelty they threaten against the saints, they connive at it too much: Hence the wonder is how so many that were moderate in the bishops' time should now be ready to become persecutors of others. Wonder not, the reason is this, not because they are not godly and gracious men, but because there is some corruption in them; and they are drawn by carnal company that have not the fear of God, and have not

[321]

grace and strength enough to resist. Therefore, if we will have peace on both sides, we must reprove those people, and not talk as others talk, and do as others do. Those that you call Independents must not hearken to people that talk without reason in respect of their brethren. And those that are godly of the Presbytery must reprove those men that are full of fire and faggot, and nothing else; rather reprove them than connive at them.

Fifthly, and lastly (and so to end for this time) the last sort of people are the common, superstitious multitude. They exceedingly blow up the fire: How? They cry out of divisions, there are so many religions amongst us; there is this religion and that; and they are all for conformity; and, O, that the synod would settle some government, they care not what, if it be Rome itself; and it is dishonourable that we should have divisions and stirs among us: Thus the blind multitude cry, Whereas it is better to have division than an evil uniformity. It is true; the time will come that all shall be of one heart and one way, but it hath never yet been. There were abundance of differences in the apostles' times, in the first churches, between the Jews and Gentiles; and they were always wrangling about blood, and about the law and genealogies, yet they were churches of God, and dear to the Lord. So, I say, every little difference and dissent makes not a new religion: Opinions are profitable (in a sort) in the churches, that some should dissent from others sometimes.

Therefore (to conclude this use) labour to appease the multitude; the multitude are ignorant, labour to instruct and teach them. Presbytery and Independency are not two religions, but one religion to a godly, honest heart; it is only a little ruffling of the fringe; therefore make not the breach wider, and blow not the fire more. The Lord give you and me, every one of us, wherein by any of these sorts of people we find ourselves guilty, to endeavour to reform, and to follow the things that concern our peace, that however our enemies will not receive terms of peace, yet we may be at peace among ourselves, which the Lord grant.

What We Are to
Bear with in Others

Jeremiah Burroughs
[1599-1646]

THE ECCLESIASTICAL COURSE RUN BY JEREMIAH BURROUGHS WAS RE-
*markably similar to that of the four other 'Dissenting Brethren' at the Westminster
Assembly (see p. 283). They had all suffered persecution under Laud, had gone to
Holland, where they ministered to English congregations, and had returned to
positions of influence in England at the outbreak of the Civil War. Burroughs, at
first colleague to Edmund Calamy at Bury St Edmunds, and then rector of Tivet-
shall, Norfolk, until suspended in 1636, became teacher of the English Church in
Rotterdam over which William Bridge was pastor. His renown as a preacher
secured for him on his return to London the lectureships at Stepney and Cripplegate,
two of the largest congregations in England.*

*While playing a part in the activities of the Independents in the Westminster
Assembly, Burroughs was singularly free from party spirit. Being of a peaceable
disposition, he was deeply affected by the divisions of the times. His plea for unity
among brethren runs to three hundred pages in* Irenicum, to the Lovers of Truth
amd Peace, *more widely known by the sub-title,* Heart-Divisions Opened, *an
extract from which is reprinted here. This, indeed, was his last work, as he died
prematurely of consumption in 1646. In such a healing spirit as his lay the hope of a
united church, and we are reminded of Richard Baxter's observation that 'if all the
Episcopalians had been like Archbishop Ussher, all the Presbyterians like Stephen
Marshall, and all the Independents like Jeremiah Burroughs, the breaches of the
Church would soon have been healed'.*

What We Are to Bear with in Others

RULES TO KNOW IN WHAT THINGS WE ARE TO
BEAR WITH OUR BRETHREN

I. In the first place, though men be known to err in judgment in things not fundamental nor destructive, yet if after such knowledge of them, they would keep their judgments to themselves, so as not to hurt others, or disturb the peace, most men of moderate spirits, if not all, hold that such men are not to be punished either by Church or State. But though this be yielded to, yet the practices of many are against it, they have ways to draw forth men's judgments, though they would conceal them, and when they have drawn them forth they make them suffer for their judgments these three ways:

1. By requiring men to subscribe to things which they suspect are against their judgments. They invent Articles, which if put to them they know will pinch them, and draw forth their judgments, which when they come to know, they make them as Articles of accusation against them. Surely such dealings as these are very harsh.

But you will say, Blessed be God, we hope we have done with forcing men to subscribe.

God grant that we may never meddle with anything answerable to that tyranny; heretofore we groaned under the drawing out of men's judgments, and then the punishing them for them.

2. If such things be put into oaths – which though a man should not hold in every clause, yet he may be godly, and a good subject – and urge such oaths with violence under penalty, what is this but to punish a man for his judgment, though he would keep it to himself?

3. By propounding questions to men when they come to the choice of, or admission to, any place or preferment, to draw forth their judgments, such questions as concern not at all the qualification of men to such places, and then deny them those places, either because they are unwilling to answer, or if you will needs have them answer, they discover their judgments different from yours. Is not this to make men suffer for their judgments, though they would live peaceably, keeping them to themselves? Here is not that suffering of brethren that Christ would have.

[326]

II. Secondly, in things controversial and doubtful amongst godly and peaceable men, though there should be a declaration of difference of judgment, and some different practice, yet there is to be a forbearance of compulsory violence. We must not be to one another in such things as these are, as that giant we read of, who laid upon a bed all he took, and those who were too long, he cut them to size of his bed, and such as were too short he stretched them out to the length of it. Verily this is cruelty. God has not made men all of a length nor height; men's parts, gifts, graces differ; men's tempers, apprehensions, educations are various. And if there be no suffering of one another in things not clear, all the world must needs be quarrelling. There will be strengthening interests, sidings and opposings of one another continually, except not only men's bodies and estates, but their very souls also be brought under sordid slavery.

Our brethren in Scotland writing against the tyranny of Prelates, when they were under it, in that book, entitled, *English and Popish Ceremonies*, have this passage: 'If the error of conscience be about things unnecessary, then it is *tutior pars*, the surest and safest way, not to urge men to do that which in their consciences they condemn.' And the ministers of the Protestant Churches in France, giving their judgments on *De pace inter Evangelicos procuranda*, how peace amongst the Protestants in Germany may be had, set forth by Duraeus, say this: 'Let all matters controversial be brought into such a certain model, as may give satisfaction to both parties; and that if it be possible framed out of the very words of Scripture: and let no man require any thing else of his brother.' Zanchius in *Precep.* 4 has this notable speech: 'That which I say, is diligently to be observed, that those who would stir up Princes to have all people, Kingdoms, Commonwealths, which, not overthrowing the fundamentals of religion, differ from them in any thing, condemned of heresy, excluded from friendship, driven out of their territories—these are no friends, either to their princes, or to the Church of Christ.'

Many think they do great service to Christ, the Church and State, if they can stir up magistrates to suppress whatsoever they conceive are errors. It may be their hearts are upright in the main, they aim at peace, but certainly they cause much disturbance in Church and State.

Bishop Davenant in a little book entitled *Exhortation to Brotherly Love amongst Churches*, in the ninth chapter, has this title, 'Brotherly communion between Churches Evangelical is not to be cut asunder because of divers opinions about questions controversial.' And in the beginning of the tenth chapter, 'This is to be premised, The bonds of the brotherly communion of Christian Churches ought not to be dissolved upon every

THE REFORMATION OF THE CHURCH

difference of opinion, but only for the denying or opposing fundamentals.'
Here see the moderation of a Prelate.

Thus Cyprian of old delivered his opinion, and practised accordingly,
differing from many of his brethren, but withal professes, 'That he meant
not to prescribe or give Laws to any; that he would not contend with
any of his colleagues, so as to break divine concord, and the peace of our
Lord; that he was far from judging or censuring any of his brethren, or
cutting off from his communion any that were of a different mind; and
that in such case none ought to constrain his colleague by tyrannical
violence (therein glancing at the violent proceeding of Stephen to whom
he wrote), to a necessity of believing or following what he thinks meet'.
This modesty and charity of Cyprian is very often and very deservedly
commended by St Augustine, says Dr. Potter, an Episcopal man.

That this may go down the better, or at least that men's spirits may be
in some measure moderated, take these following considerations.

1. First, this contending about every difference of opinion, and urging
our brethren with what we conceive right in matters of controversy,
crosses the end of Christ in His administration of differing gifts to His
Church, and human society and His revealing truths in a different way,
some more darkly, some more clearly. Christ could easily have given
such gifts to all, or revealed all truths so clearly that every man should
have been able to have seen every truth. Surely Christ did not disperse
gifts, and reveal truths so differently, to the end, that there might be
continual matter of strife and contention in His Church, and in human
societies; not that there should be provocation to the exercise of cruelty
one upon another, but rather that there might be the exercise of love,
charity, forbearance, meekness, long-suffering of one towards another.
Christ bids us, charges us to be at peace amongst ourselves. If we should
say, O Lord Jesus, wouldst Thou have us be at peace one with another?
There are many things in Thy Word, that we and our brethren have
different apprehensions of ; for though (blessed by Thy Name) the great
necessary things of salvation be clearly revealed, yet many other things
are so dark to us, that through our weakness we cannot all of us see the
same thing. Now is it Thy mind, O blessed Saviour, that one man, who
conceives himself to understand the truth (and that it may be rightly),
compel another to his judgment? And dost Thou also require that we
must not bring our judgments to our brethren's till Thy light brings them?
How then is it possible we should be at peace one with another?

Do not all divines say that there are some things in Scripture wherein
the elephant may swim, some things wherein the lamb may wade? Matters

of discipline are acknowledged by all not to be revealed with such clearness, but that truly conscientious, upright, diligent men may not be able in many things to see the mind of Christ in them. And to what end hath Christ done this, think you?

2. Secondly, compulsion in such things as we are speaking of, is to strain justice so high, as to make it *summa justitia*, which is the degeneration of it, as physicians say of the uttermost degree of health, it is a beginning of sickness. If justice be wound up a peg too high, it breaks. Though justice were to be managed by the most holy, wise, self-denying, and meek men upon the earth, yet there would be much danger in winding it up to the highest, for it is administered by men full of infirmities, to men full of infirmities; therefore God will not have it strained too high, he will rather have charity to be above justice, than justice to be above charity. This I have out of Luther, who although he was a man of fiery spirit, and could tell how to contend where there was cause, yet in an Epistle that he writes to the divines of Nuremberg, upon occasion of dissensions risen among them, he says that judgment must serve, not rule over charity; otherwise it is one of those four things that Solomon says troubles the earth; namely, a servant ruling, or the maid heir to her mistress. If therefore you would have peace, says he, charity must rule over justice, you must not suffer justice to rule over charity.

3. Thirdly, if men go upon this principle, they will be in danger of opposing truth as well as falsehood, and compelling to falsehood as well as to truth; for in matters doubtful and controversial amongst good and peaceable men, it is not easy to have any such grounded confidence as to be out of all danger of mistake. There is more confidence needful in a thing that we impose upon others, than in what we practise ourselves. If a thing be to us rather true than otherwise, we may lawfully do it, but this is not enough to be a ground for the imposing it upon others, who cannot see it to be a truth; in such a case we need be very sure. The weak drizzlings of our probabilities, guesses, and opinions, are not enough to cause the streams of another man's conscience to stop, yea to turn its course another way; especially considering that in such things we have oftentimes misgiving thoughts ourselves; yea, and not long since we were confident, that what we now condemn was true, and what we now are ready to enjoin upon others, we then did as confidently condemn. There must be great care taken, that when we seek to pluck up the tares, we pluck not up the wheat also; this may be understood of things, of truths and falsehoods, as well as of persons; we may be mistaken in the one, as well as in the other. Pluck not up the tares. Christ does not forbid

casting out any wicked men from the Church, but as Jerome has it, in those countries tares were very like the wheat; therefore take heed, says Christ, what you do in plucking up; when you have to deal with men whose condition is any way doubtful, be sure they be hypocrites, or else meddle not with them, do not pluck them up upon every surmise, because you think they are not right, for then you may pluck up a wheat as well as a tare, he may prove to be a godly man; therefore you had better let tares grow. If you do but think that such men are not right, you were better let them continue in the Church, than be venturing upon them, to be in danger to pluck up the wheat.

Thus in respect of things good or evil, there are some things apparently evil, they are rather thistles and briers, than tares; we may freely pluck them up; but other things, though perhaps they may prove evil, yet they have some likeness to good, so as you can hardly discern whether they be good or evil; Now, saith Christ, take heed what you do then, do not out of eagerness to oppose all evil, to get out every tare, pluck out some wheat too; what if that you oppose with violence as evil, prove to be good? You had better let forty tares stand, than pluck up one wheat.

4. Fourthly, if men take this power upon them, to compel men to do whatsoever they conceive good, and to deny or forbear whatsoever they conceive evil, they take more power upon them than ever the Apostles took. The government of the saints under the Apostles, was a great deal more mild, sweet, gentle than this. The rule the Apostles went by was, 'Let us therefore, as many as be perfect be thus minded: and if in any thing ye be otherwise minded, God shall reveal even this unto you. Nevertheless whereto we have already attained, let us walk by the same rule, let us mind the same thing' (Phil. 3: 15, 16). If any should be otherwise minded than I or the other Apostles we will not force him, God will reveal it in due time; only let us walk up to what we have attained. This rule, Zanchius says, Augustine would repeat a thousand times; and Chrysostom has a good remark upon this place. He notes that the Apostle does not say, God will bring them to it, if they be otherwise minded, but God will reveal it, showing the love and goodness of God to those who are otherwise minded, excusing them that it was not through wickedness, but for want of knowledge that they did otherwise. In Acts 15, where the Apostles and elders were met together, the furthest they would take upon themselves, was to lay no other burden but 'these necessary things'. The false teachers put a yoke upon them, which was such a burden that neither they nor their fathers could bear (ver. 10), yet it was no juridical authority that these had over them; surely the yoke they put upon them in the

judgments of all was but doctrinal. But for us, say the Apostles, we finding what the mind of the Holy Ghost is, dare not yoke you as they did; all that we burden you with is these necessary things – no Church officers, no Synod can go further than this. Certainly every matter in controversy amongst godly and peaceable men cannot be conceived to be necessary.

Romans 14 is a very useful place for this, 'Him that is weak in the faith receive ye, but not to doubtful disputations'. Receive him, though he understands not all you do; do not trouble him, neither with nor for doubtful things. 'One believeth he may eat all things, another who is weak eateth herbs; let not him that eateth, despise him that eateth not; neither let him that eateth not, judge him that eateth. . . .' Upon this he gives general rules to do all to the glory of God. All these people were not in the right, for a man not to eat flesh out of conscience, when the thing was not forbidden, certainly was a sin; or to make conscience of a holy day, which God required not, was a sin. Now the Apostle did not come with his authority, and say, I will make you leave off keeping such days, or you shall eat, or to abstain thus as you do is evil, and it must not be suffered in you. No, the Apostle lays no Apostolical authority upon them, but tells them, that every man must be fully persuaded in his own mind, in what he does; and who art thou that judgest another man's servant? – the Lord hath received him. And yet the governors of the Churches in the primitive times might upon much stronger grounds have stood upon such a principle than any governors of the Church now can. There was less reason why they should suffer any difference in opinion or practice amongst them, than why we should suffer differences amongst us; for they had men amongst them immediately inspired, who could dictate the mind of Christ infallibly; they could tell them the certain meaning of any Scripture. The burden of being under the determinations of such men in points of differences, had not been so great as subjection to any governors now in such cases would be. Our differences are usually about the meaning of such or such Scriptures, in which both sides think they have the right; and profess one to another, as in the presence of God, the searcher of all hearts, that if they could but see the meaning of such a Scripture to be so as their brethren believe it is, they would soon agree: and yet though there were in these primitive times such means of reconciling differences more than we have, yet there was much mutual toleration amongst them; they used no compulsive violence to force those who through weakness differed from them, to come up to their judgments or practice. It is also more tolerable in Papists not to tolerate any difference

[331]

in opinion or practice, because firstly, they believe that they have an infallible Judge to decide all controversies. Secondly, they hold implicit faith in the judgment of their clergy, to be sufficient warrant to justify the belief or practice of the people, or of any particular man, and yet they suffer differences in opinions and practices amongst them. They have their several orders of their monks, priests, friars, Jesuits; they differ very much one from the other, and yet agreeing in the root, they are suffered, supposing those two helps to union; they have an infallible Judge, and implicit faith. We have cause either to admire their moderation in their mutual bearing one with another, or at the disquietness, the rigidness of spirits amongst us, who cannot bear with far lesser things in our brethren differing from us; for we profess we know no such external infallible Judge, upon whom we may depend; neither dare we warrant an implicit faith. We teach men that every man must be persuaded in his own heart; must see the rule of his own actions; must give an account of his own way to God: now what can men that have the most gracious and peaceable spirits imaginable, do in such a case? Before they believe or do what their brethren believe or do, they must have the authority of the Word on which to ground their faith or actions; and for the present, though sincerely willing to know God's mind, and diligently laborious to search it out, yet they cannot see it: and yet according to this sour, rigid principle, they must be forced to it by violence. What is this but to command the full tale of brick to be brought in, where no straw can be had? Straw might be had in Egypt by seeking for it; but here, after the most careful and painful seeking for it, yet it cannot be had.

5. Fifthly, by this principle, the finding out of much truth will be hindered; it will stifle men's gifts and abilities in arguing and discoursing about truths. We know fire is beaten out by striking the flint. Although differences be very sad, yet the truth that comes to light by them, may recompense the sadness. You cannot beat out a place for a window to let in light, but you must endure some trouble. Children will think the house is being pulled down when the window is being knocked out; but the father knows that benefit will come by it. He complains not that the dust and rubbish lies up and down in the house for a while, the light let in by it will recompense all. The trouble in the discussions of things by brethren of different judgments may seem to be great, but either you or your posterity hereafter may see cause to bless God for that light hath been or may be let into the Churches by this means; men of moderate spirits do bless God already. But if according to this principle, the governors of the Churches must suppress whatsoever they conceive not to be right,

to what purpose should there be arguing and discussing of several judgments and several ways?

You will say, those who are the governors, they, or those whom they call to consult with, may argue and discuss, but not others.

Is not this to deny the Church the benefit of the gifts and graces of thousands of others? The Church may soon receive as much prejudice by this, as the trouble caused by some differences comes to.

6. Sixthly, this lays a great temptation to idleness and pride before the guides of the Church. Men are naturally subject to sloth, and may not this principle suggest such a temptation as this: what need we take care or pains to search into truths, to be able to convince gainsayers, to carry things with strength of Scripture and reason, seeing we have power to compel men to yield to us? And men who can do least by reason and Scripture, are many times strongest in their violence this way; this strength must come in to make up their other weakness. But it may be conscience will not let them compel men presently; it will tell them they must seek first to convince men: but because the seeking to satisfy other men's consciences in things differing from us, is a troublesome work, the temptation that this principle presents may at least prevail thus far, that seeing besides means of conviction by arguing they have another help at hand to keep down error, namely, compulsory violence, making men who differ from them, to suffer for those things, therefore not to trouble themselves very much in the way of seeking to convince, but for their own case to rid their hands of such a burdensome work, to cast the trouble, and lay heavy burdens upon their brethren, this is easy for them to do, though hard for their brethren to suffer; But the tables may turn one day, wherein the sufferers shall have the greatest case, and the inflicters the sorest burden. But God forbid that their brethren should lay it upon them, though it were put into their power to do it.

The temptation to pride is not less, neither are men's hearts less prone to this. If it prevails, what domineering is there likely to be of one over another, yea of some few over many! If they judge in things never so doubtful, all must yield, at least for their profession and practice. This is a great power to be given to men over men in matters of faith and godliness. This is lording it over God's inheritance. It is observable, when the Church was in the lowest condition, this power was highest – the power of making canons in doubtful things to bind under penalties. And when this power was lowest, as in the primitive times, then the Church was highest.

7. Seventhly, this will be a means to bring gross ignorance upon the

face of the Churches and of the world. For, first, if men shall not be suffered to profess or practise otherwise than governors in Church or State shall determine they will not take pains to find out the truth themselves, but rather take things implicitly, which is the easiest way; they will think it to little purpose to take pains in examining things, when after all is done they must be bound up at least in their profession and practice, to what either is or shall be determined by those who have power of rule in their hands.

Our late prelates' design was to bring in ignorance that they might with more freedom rule over us as they pleased; and in nothing did they drive on this design more, than in the practice of this power, which they took themselves to command things doubtful and controversial, and by violence to urge their commands upon people: by which, had their power continued, gross ignorance would soon have been spread over the face of the land. From whence has come the gross ignorance of Popery, but from the prevailing of this principle? By which the people have been brought into such subjection under their guides, that they have lost their understandings in the matters of religion.

If it be said, But we will take care that those men who shall be consulted withal, and those who shall have power in their hands to determine, shall be wise, understanding, godly men, then the danger will not be so great.

Suppose those men who for the present have such power, have attained to the highest measure of knowledge and godliness that can be imagined to be in any men upon the earth, yet the people are under this temptation, to neglect the getting of knowledge themselves; and it may be the rather, because those who are appointed to determine things, are so understanding and so conscientious. Now these people growing ignorant, when these knowing and godly men who are now in place, shall be gone, who shall choose others in their places? I suppose it to be the opinion of most of you, and of the godly in the kingdom, and in all Reformed Churches, that either the body of the Church, the people, must choose their officers; or at least, that none must be put upon them without their consent. Well then, if the people through the prevailing of the former temptations grow ignorant; is it not like they will choose such guides and leaders as themselves are? Or if they shall not choose yet their negative voice will have such an influence into the choice, as it is very probable that in a generation or two, blind guides will be brought in, and so the blind leading the blind. And when by this, ignorance hath prevailed and gotten a hold in the Church, there is almost an impossibility ever to get it out again; this

[334]

brings men into the dark, and locks and bolts the doors upon them.

Hence men by pleading for this principle, may bring themselves and their posterity into greater bondage than they are aware; for although now while they have the power in their own hands, it may be well with them, yet hereafter others may have the power, and then it may prove ill enough. They may then complain of what now they plead for; though now the guides of the Church may be good and holy, yet they may live to see such a change, or at least their posterity that such a principle, acted by such men as they may be under, may wring them. Yea, it is the more strange that men should plead so much for this now, when as the sores of their necks, caused by the bondage under it a while since, are scarce yet healed.

8. Eighthly, there is yet a further danger in this, not only that men will neglect truth, but there will be a strong temptation to resist and reject truth; if God begins to dart in any light into a man's spirit that appears to cross what hath been determined of for opinion or practice under a penalty, the corruption of a man's heart will entice him to turn his mind from that light, not to let it into conscience or heart, lest it prevailing, should put him upon such ways, wherein he is like to suffer. This hath been common in former times; many have hid their eyes from those truths that would have kept them from conformity, because they foresaw what sad consequences would follow, if their consciences should not suffer them to conform.

But you will say, this supposes that some things will be urged that are contrary to truth, which is uncharitable to suppose.

Although in matters fundamental, there is no fear that godly men will err, yet let charity be stretched to the full latitude of it, and reverence of men in place raised to the uttermost height, if they will meddle with such things as are doubtful and controversial amongst godly and peaceable men, and force them upon others, that confidence of theirs that shall put them out of fear or erring, shall be to me a ground of great fear, that they will err.

But some will acknowledge that some liberty should be granted in things thus doubtful and controversial to men who are indeed conscientious, godly and peaceable men; but if this be yielded to, then men who are not conscientious, but of turbulent and corrupt spirits, will abuse it.

We have given rules to find out those who only pretend conscience, and if by those, or the like, it does not appear, but that men are indeed conscientious in their way, we should judge charitably of them. You think much if those be not admitted to communion with Christ and His

[335]

saints, when they profess godliness in word and life, and nothing appears to the contrary; why then should you think much to tolerate those as conscientious, who profess it in words and life, and nothing appears to the contrary?

Bishop Davenant in that exhortation to peace before quoted, as one means for peace, gives his opinion thus, 'Because it belongs only to God to teach the hearts of men, it is our duty always to make the best interpretation of things, and to presume of every one where the contrary appears not by manifest signs, that he is kept from assenting by his conscience rather than by obstinacy.'

As for the peaceableness of men's dispositions, let it be judged from their carriages in other things of as great moment, wherein the temptation for the attaining their own ends is as great, yea far greater than here: Do they not carry themselves in as peaceable, gentle, self-denying, a way as any? Mr Parker upon the Cross in chap. 5 sect. 14 pleads for himself and others who could not yield in some things enjoined upon them, when they were accused of pride, contempt, unpeaceableness: 'What signs', says he, 'do men see in us of pride, contempt, unpeaceableness? What be our *cætera opera* that betray such a humour? Let it be named wherein we go not two mile, where we are commanded to go but one; yea, whether we go not as many miles as any shoe of the preparation of the Gospel of peace will carry us. What payment, what pain, what labour, what taxation made us ever to murmur? Survey our charges where we have laboured, if they be not found to be of the faithfullest subjects that be in the land. We deserve no favour; nay, there is wherein we stretch our consciences to the uttermost to conform and obey in divers matters: Are we refractory in other things? As Balaam's ass said to his master, Have I used to serve thee so at other times?'

And whereas it is said, that some will abuse such liberty as this, it is answered, Surely those who are peaceable and conscientious, must not be deprived of what sufferance Christ allows them, because others who are in the same way, are, or may prove turbulent, and do or may not appear truly conscientious. This is as far beneath the rule of justice, as no sufferance in any thing conceived erroneous, is above it.

III. Thirdly, whatsoever errors or miscarriages in religion the Church should bear withal in men, continuing them still in communion with them as brethren, these the magistrate should bear with in men, continuing them in the Kingdom or Commonwealth, in the enjoyment of the liberty of subjects. Grant what possible can be granted to the magistrate in the extent of his power about religion, to be *custos utriusque tabulae*;

yet certainly no man can imagine that this his charge reaches further than the charge of the Church – that he is to be more exact in his oversight of these things, than the Church is to be; for whatever the power of the magistrate be in these things, yet to the Church especially are the oracles, the ordinances, the truths of God committed. The charge of the spiritual estate of men especially belongs to the Church. Now the Church is to bear with men in their infirmities, though they be ignorant of many things, yea after means used for information. No Church must cast off any from communion with it, but for such things that all the Churches of Christ ought to cast them off for. This is generally held by our brethren, if a man be rightly cast out of communion with one Church, he is thereby cast out of all; if this be so, then surely many things must be suffered before we proceed to cast out a member, it must not be for every error or miscarriage. Thus Bishop Davenant in his rules for peace: 'Those may not be cut off from communion with particular Churches who remain joined to the Catholic Church.'

Yea, none is to be cast out of communion, but for that which if whole Churches were guilty of, we must refuse communion with; yea, with all the Churches in the world, if they could be supposed to be so far left of Christ, as to be guilty of the same thing. If this be so, when a Church is about casting out any out of communion, it need be wary, and not presently call upon him, because there is something evil in him; and if the Church should be so, the civil magistrate much more, whose care of a man's spiritual estate is not so immediate and full as the Church's is.

From what has been said these two consequences are clear; first, Articles or rules for doctrine or practice in matters of religion to be imposed upon men, should be as few as may be; there is very great danger in the unnecessary multiplying them. This in all ages has caused division and exceeding disturbances in the Churches of Christ.

I find an excellent passage in an Epistle of Isaac Causabon to Cardinal Perron, which he wrote in the name of King James by his command, 'The King (saith he) thinks that the things that are absolutely necessary to salvation are not many, therefore His Majesty is of that mind that there is no shorter way for peace, than first by severing necessary things from things that are not necessary, and then to labour a full agreement in those; but as for things not necessary, let them be left to Christian liberty.' And again, 'These necessary things are few, and the King thinks this distinction to be of so great moment to lessen the controversies which this day do so exceedingly trouble the Church, that all who study peace, should most diligently explicate, teach, and urge this.'

[337]

God hath so graciously ordered things for the body, that the things necessary for life are not many, nor costly. The greatest stir in the world is about things not necessary; so for the soul.

A second consequence from what hath been said, is, we see hence who is most for peace; one professes what he is convinced of to be a truth and a duty, if it be not necessary he is not to force it upon his brethren, though he had never so much power in the Church or State to back him. The other holds this principle, that whatsoever he thinks to be a duty, he must force upon his brethren, not only by the power of the Church, but he must call in the power of the magistrate to back him in it.

But do not men in a Congregational way urge upon others their own conceptions and practices, according to the power they have, as much as any? If men will not enter into covenant, if they hold another kind of government in the Church differing from them, they will not receive them, nor communicate with them.

I would that all our controversy lay here, surely we should soon agree. Whosoever does as you say, cannot be justified in so doing; some men it may be through an earnest desire of promoting what they conceive to be the mind of Christ, have been too rigid in their dealings with their brethren. What has been said, will show the evil of their practice as well as of others.

As for entering into covenant, it is true, there is such a practice in the congregational Churches; and a covenant either explicit or implicit, I think all acknowledge: that is, there must be some agreement to join those together in a body, who formally were not joined, to make them to be of such a society, to have power in it for others for the choice of officers in this congregation, and to be under the care and charge of those officers more than members of another congregation. What shall join them, if not at least some mutual agreement to join in one body for such spiritual ends as Christ has appointed this body for, the very nature of a society that is embodied, carries this with it; and any farther than this I know none requires as necessary.

Indeed the more explicit this agreement is, the more is the edification. Surely there is no Christian but will acknowledge that the more one Christian opens his heart to another, and binds himself to walk in the ways of Christ with another, the more comfortable it is, and helps to edification; and upon this ground do the Congregational Churches practise this.

Suppose any godly man shall come and desire to join with any of them, but withal tell them, that for his part he yet cannot be convinced by anything he can find in Scripture that this way of covenanting is required. If the Church cannot satisfy such a man (being godly) in their practice, yet desire to know of him whether he be willing to join with them in all the ordinances of Christ, so far as he knows, a mere affirmative to this is a covenant sufficient to join him with them. The more fully he expresses this to them, it would be the more acceptable. Now then why is it that there is such a noise everywhere in exclamations against Church covenant, when it is nothing but this, which how any gracious heart upon due consideration can be against, I cannot see. And this is not only our present opinion, but that which ever since we knew any thing in that way, upon all occasions, we have held forth.

But what do you say to the other, If a man who you believe is godly, yet not being convinced of your way of government, but rather thinks the Presbyterian government to be the way of Christ, would you receive such a man into communion with you?

If any godly man whose conscience is not satisfied in that way of government, yet is so cast by Providence as he cannot join with those Churches where there is that government he thinks to be Christ's; and because he is desirous to enjoy what ordinances of Christ he can, therefore tenders himself to one of these congregational Churches. Such a man should be received to those ordinances he sees to be Christ's, if there be nothing else against him, but merely because after all due means used, yet through weakness he cannot see Christ's mind in some other ordinance. Christ does not lay so much upon the ordinance of government, as to exclude his saints all their days from all other Church ordinances, if through weakness they cannot be convinced of that.

Now let one who is in a congregational way, and cannot see Christ's mind in the Presbyterian government, yet come to one of those Churches, and say, he would gladly in all his ways see the mind of Christ, and enjoy all his ordinances, but he cannot see that a minister who takes only the charge to feed by Word and Sacraments one congregation, yet should with others have the charge of ruling a hundred or more, and till he be convinced otherwise, he cannot in his practice acknowledge that government to be Christ's, would you yet receive such a one to communion with you in all other Church ordinances? If you would, I make no question then but if we well understood one another, and were of quiet spirits, we might live together in peace.

Let not miscarriages in particular men or Churches in things of this nature, hinder our peace; what we say ought to be suffered in us, we profess to be our duty to suffer that or anything of the like nature in others, and where there has not been that brotherly and Christian forbearance as ought to be there has been sin committed against Christ: but let not this hinder brotherly and Christian agreement amongst ourselves, or any other Churches of Christ.

IV. Fourthly, evils that are small or uncertain, or come by accident, must rather be suffered than any good that is great, certain, and *per se*, should be hindered. We must take heed that in our zeal to oppose evil, we hinder not a greater good: If opposition of evil lies so far out of your reach as you cannot come at it but by hindering much good, you must be content then to let it alone.

V. Lastly, if the evils be such as only can be removed by supernatural means, we must not use violence for the removing of them, though God hath such authority over us, as he may justly punish us for not doing that which we are unable to do, by the strength of nature: yet one man has no such authority over another.

The power that God has given a magistrate, is but for a natural help at the most, and therefore it can go no farther than to help us in a natural way, to do what we are able to do by a natural power; when it hath gone so far, there it must rest.

Union among Protestants

John Owen
[1616–1683]

JOHN OWEN, BY GENERAL CONSENT THE GREATEST OF PURITAN DIVINES, *was born in 1616 at Stadhampton, Oxfordshire, where his father, Henry Owen, was minister. The boy entered Oxford in 1628, remaining until 1637 when he chose to leave the University rather than to comply with Archbishop Laud's new statutes requiring conformity. He was at first Domestic Chaplain to Sir Robert Dormer, and then Lord Lovelace; at this time his inner spiritual convictions were more burdensome than joyous and it was not until 1642 that he received a settled peace in his heart under the ministry of an unknown country preacher who occupied the pulpit of St Mary's Aldermanbury in the unexpected absence of the famous Edmund Calamy.*

About 1643 Owen was appointed to the living of Fordham, Essex, and the same year he wrote his first book on Church issues, entitled The Duty of Pastors and People Distinguished. *In this short book Owen supported the Presbyterian view of Church polity against Episcopacy. He had not yet studied the controversy between Independency and Presbytery, but when he did so, not long after, he came to believe that certain scriptural principles were best defended by the Independent position and that he had not been accurate enough in his use of terms in his earlier book (cf. Owen's* Works, *Gold Edition, 13, 222–3). Nevertheless this change of persuasion did not mean a total revision of his previous position. In contrast to his attitude to the Episcopal Church-State system, he did not regard the differences between Presbytery and Independency as necessarily irreconcilable (cf.* Works *14, 258, 338) and expressed hopes that 'so good a work' as the reconciliation of the differences might one day be obtained without any compromise of scriptural truth.*

In 1646 he moved to Coggeshall, and in the same year preached before Parliament for the first time. During the Civil Wars he adhered to the Parliamentary cause and was first Chaplain to Fairfax, and then to Cromwell in Ireland and Scotland. To him was given the unenviable privilege of preaching before Parliament on the day after the execution of Charles I. In 1651 Owen was appointed Dean of Christ-church, Oxford, and in the following year Vice-Chancellor of the University, where Cromwell, as Chancellor, left much of the administration to him. During the Commonwealth period he also served on several committees, including the Commission for the trying and ejecting of unworthy ministers. Owen fell from Cromwell's favour through his opposition to the proposal to make the Protector King.

During the Commonwealth and after, Owen was recognized as leader of the Independents, and in 1658 he played a large part in the Savoy Conference (see page 275). He lost both his Oxford offices before 1662 and so was not in a position to be deprived by the Act of Uniformity, though he suffered from the other penal statutes against dissenters. Declining invitations to New England (including an offer of the Presidency of Harvard College), he was active through the long years of persecution which followed the restoration of Charles II relieving impoverished Nonconformists and urging spiritual unity amongst oppressed evangelical ministers and congregations. He used his influence with the King to intercede for the release of John Bunyan, whom he greatly admired. When, after 1670, the Dissenters were able to meet publicly with less risk, Owen was Pastor of a congregation at Leaden-hall Street, London. He died at Ealing in 1683.

John Owen is best known to posterity for his writings, which are considerable in number as well as in quality. In addition to polemical works of more contemporaneous interest, his doctrinal and practical treatises have been read and admired ever since, as well as his monumental commentary on Hebrews. The tract Some Considerations about Union Among Protestants and the Preservation of the Interest of the Protestant Religion in the Nation *was first published in 1680. It appeared at a time when great excitement and alarm prevailed as to the progress and possible future triumph of Roman Catholicism in England. The King was pledged to establish the Roman religion in England though this was as yet unknown. His brother, the Heir-Apparent (who in 1685 became James II), was a declared Roman Catholic and efforts were in fact under way to exclude him from the succession. The discovery of the Popish Plot of 1678 aggravated popular anti-Roman feeling though the Nonconformists were treated alternately as allies against Rome and as traitors to the Protestant cause.*

Owen had already been recognized as a champion of Protestantism – Charles II's first Chancellor, Clarendon, said that he had done more for its cause than any man in England – and he now published several tracts refuting Roman Catholic principles and seeking to prevent their re-establishment in England. Union Among Protestants *is, as the title suggests, a plea for Protestants to put aside internal differences in the interests of the Protestant cause in England. At the same time, however, he points out that, contrary to the claims of its advocates, as long as the Anglican Church was maintained, it was 'vain to expect peace and union among Protestants.' Rather the continuance of such a false church structure gave to Popery a 'prevalent engine' by which to restore itself in England, and without which it would have no means of returning to this country except by 'force, war, and oppression . . .'. Then follow these prophetic words: 'But if the interest of Popery can possess this Church-State, either by the inclinations of them, or the greater number of them, who have the management of it, or by their dependence, as unto their interest, on the supreme authority, the whole nation will quickly be insensibly influenced and betrayed into Popery, as it were they know not how.'*

Bibliography

The Works of John Owen, 24 vols., edited by W. H. Goold, 1850–5.
Volume 1 contains a good biography by A. Thomson.
The Golden Book of John Owen, James Moffatt, 1904.

Union among Protestants

1. THE Protestant religion, introduced into this nation by the apostolical way and means of the holiness and laborious preaching of its professors, confirmed with the martyrdom of multitudes of all sorts, being now thoroughly fixed in the minds of the body of the people, and confirmed unto them by laws and oaths, is become the principal interest of the nation, which cannot be shaken or overthrown without the ruin of the government and destruction of the people. Nothing, therefore, less being included in the attempts of the Papists, with all their interest in Europe, for the re-introducing of their religion amongst us, the nation hath been constantly filled for a hundred years with fears, jealousies, and apprehensions of dangers, to the great disturbance of the government and disquiet of the subjects; nor can it be otherwise whilst they know that there is a pregnant design for their total subversion, together with the ruin of the Protestant religion in other places, which would have ensued thereon. But –

2. This religion, so received and approved by the people as the only true way to salvation (accompanied with an abhorrence of the superstition, idolatry, and heresies of the Church of Rome, partly on the general account of their own nature, and partly on particular reasons and provocations, from the attempts of those that belong unto that Church for the ruin of them and their religion), and jointly professed in the same confession of faith, hath been preserved by the means of a faithful, laborious ministry, under the care, protection, and outward government of the supreme power, as the greatest bulwark of the Protestant religion in Europe.

3. The only weakness in it, as the interest of the nation (before it was infested with novel opinions), was the differences that have been amongst many of the professors of it, from the very first beginning of the Reformation, and which are continued unto this day.

4. These differences, though consisting now in many particulars of less moment, arose originally solely from the constitution of an authoritative national Church-state. For some would have it to be of one sort, namely, episcopal; some of another, namely, presbyterian; some would have it of a divine original, others of a human, which must be the judg-

ment of the king and Parliament, who know it to be what they have made it, and nothing else; and some judge it a mere usurpation on the power of the civil government and the liberties of the people.

5. It is therefore acknowledged that the body of Christian people in this nation professing the Protestant religion, with a detestation of Popery, having the Gospel preached unto them, and the sacraments duly administered, under the rule of the king, are the Church of England. But as unto an authoritative national Church, consisting solely in the power and interest of the clergy – wherein the people, either as Christians, Protestants, or subjects of the kingdom, are not concerned – such as is at present established, farther inquiry may be made about it.

6. There is a threefold form of such a Church at present contended for. The first Papal, the second Episcopal, and the third Presbyterian.

7. The first form of an authoritative national Church-state amongst us, as in other places, was papal; and the sole use of it here in England was, to embroil our kings in their government; to oppress the people in their souls, bodies, and estates; and to sell us all, as branded slaves, unto Rome. These things have been sufficiently manifested. But in other places, especially in Germany, whilst otherwise they were all of one religion, in doctrine and worship, all conform to the Church of Rome, yet, in bloody contests, merely about this authoritative Church-state, many emperors were ruined, and a hundred set battles fought in the field.

8. At the Reformation, this Church-state was accommodated (as was supposed) unto the interest of the nation, to obviate the evils suffered from it under the other form, and render it of use unto the religion established. Yet experience manifests that, partly from its constitution, partly from the inclinations of them by whom it is managed, other evils have accompanied or followed it; which, until they are removed, the weakness of the Protestant interest, through mutual divisions, will remain among us. And, among others, they are these:

(1) An encroachment on the civil rights and government of the nation, in the courts and jurisdictions pretended to belong or to be annexed unto this Church-state, over the persons, goods, and liberties of the subjects (yea, in some cases, their lives). It is the undoubted right and liberty of the people of this nation, that no actual jurisdiction should be exercised over their persons, estates, or liberties, in a way collateral unto, and independent of, the public administration of justice unto all, derived from the sovereign power, and executed by known officers, rules, and orders, according unto the laws of the realm. If this be taken from them, all other pretences of securing the liberty and property of the subjects

are of no advantage unto them: for whilst they have justice, in legal public courts, duly administered unto them, they may be oppressed and ruined (as many are so every day) by this pretended collateral irregular power and jurisdiction over their persons, goods, and liberties; from which it seems to be the duty of the Parliament to deliver them. And it is the right of the kings of this nation that no external power over the subjects be exercised but in their name, by virtue of their commission, to be granted and executed according unto the laws of the land. This right of kings, and this liberty of subjects also, are so sacred as that they ought not to be intrenched on by any pretence of Church or religion; for what is of God's own appointment will touch neither of them. But the administration of this jurisdiction, as it is exercised with a side-wind power, distinct, different from, and in some things contrary unto, the public justice of the nation (wherein all the subjects have an equal interest), and by the rules of a law foreign unto that of the kingdom, is a great cause of the continuation of divisions among Protestants, unto the weakening of the interest of religion itself.

(2) It is accompanied with the prosecution and troubling of peaceable subjects in their liberties and estates – not for any error in the Christian faith, not for any declension from the Protestant religion or compliance with Popery, not for any immoralities, but merely and solely for their non-compliance with and submission unto those things which are supposed necessary for the preservation of their Church-state, which is of itself altogether unnecessary; for the whole complex of the imposed conformity in canonical obedience, ceremonies, rites, and modes of worship, hath no other end but the sustentation and preservation thereof, being things otherwise that belong not to Christian religion. This began, this will perpetuate, our divisions; which will not be healed whilst it is continued. And whilst the two parties of Papists and Protestants are at this day contending, as it were, for life, soul, and being (the long-continued design of the former, under various pretences, and by great variety of attempts, being come unto its fatal trial, as unto its issue), it will not be thought meet by wise men, whose entire interest in religion and the liberties of the nation are concerned in this contest, to continue the body of Protestants in divisions, with mutual animosities and the distrust of multitudes, on such unnecessary occasions.

(3) Whereas, by virtue of this state and constitution, sundry persons are interested in honours, dignities, power, and wealth, in all which they have an immediate (and not merely legal) dependence on the king since their separation from the Pope, they have constantly made it their business

[347]

to promote absolute monarchical power, without respect unto the true constitution of the government of this nation; which in sundry instances hath been disadvantageous to kings themselves, as well as an encumbrance to the people in Parliament: for although their constitution doth really intrench upon the king's legal power in the administration of their jurisdiction, yet, to secure their own interests, and to make a seeming compensation for that encroachment, many of them have contended for that absolute power in the king which he never owned nor assumed unto himself.

9. The evils and inconveniences of this constitution of an authoritative national Church-state have been greatly increased and propagated in this nation, as unto the heightening of divisions among Protestants, by the endeavours that have been made to confirm and continue this state in an extraordinary way. Such were the oath called 'Et cetera',[1] and the late oath at Oxford,[2] whereon many sober, peaceable Protestant ministers have been troubled, and some utterly ruined; which hath much provoked the indignation of the people against those who occasioned that law, and for whose sake it was enacted, and increased the suspicion that those who manage these things would have men believe that their state and rule is as sacred as the crown or religion itself, unto the great disparagement of them both: which things are effectual engines to expel all peace and union among Protestants.

10. Those who are for the presbyterian form of an authoritative national Church-state do, indeed, cut off and cast away most of those things which are the matter of contest between the present dissenting parties, and so make a nearer approach towards a firm union among all Protestants than

[1] The convocation of the English church held under Laud in 1640, drew up seventeen articles, entitled 'Constitutions and Canons Ecclesiastical', etc. They contain extreme views of the royal prerogative, and authorize the infliction of ecclesiastical and civil penalties upon Dissenters. The sixth canon embodies an oath to be taken by the clergy of the church; and in this oath these words occurred, 'Nor will I ever give my consent to alter the government of the church by archbishops, bishops, deans, and archdeacons.' This 'etc.' was the subject of complaint, and gave rise to the nickname by which the oath is commonly known. – Goold.

[2] While the plague was ravaging London in 1665, the Parliament met at Oxford, and imposed an oath on all Nonconformists, binding them never to take up arms against the king, or 'endeavour any alteration of government, either in church or state'. All who refused to take the oath were forbidden to approach within five miles of any city that returned a member to parliament, and any place where they had been ministers, or where they had preached after the act of oblivion. Strange requital for the faithfulness which many nonconformist ministers were at this time evincing in abiding by their posts in London, and supplying consolation to its inhabitants, diseased and dying in multitudes around them! – Goold.

the other do; yet such an authoritative Church-state, in that form, is neither proper for nor possible unto this nation, nor consistent with that pre-eminence of the crown, that liberty of the subjects, and freedom of the consciences of Christians, which are their due. But this being not much among us pretended unto, it need not farther be spoken of.

11. It is evident, therefore, that whilst the evils enumerated are not separated from the present authoritative national Church constitution, but the powers of it are put in execution, and the ends of it pursued, it is altogether vain to expect peace and union among Protestants in England.

It neither hath been so, nor ever will be so; fire and faggot will not be able to effect it. Who shall reconcile the endless differences that are and have been about the power, courts, and jurisdictions of this Church-state, whether they be agreeable unto the laws of the land and liberty of the subjects? The fixed judgment of many, that they have no legal authority at present, nor any power given unto them by the law of the land, whereon they dare not submit unto them, is no less chargeable, dangerous, and pernicious unto them, than are their uncouth vexations and illegal proceedings unto them who are unwillingly forced to submit unto them. And, whatever may be expected, the people of this nation will never be contented that their persons, goods, or liberties shall be made subject unto any law but the public royal law of the kingdom, administered in legal courts of justice. Who shall undertake that all Christians or Protestants in this nation shall ever submit their consciences and practices to a multitude of impositions no way warranted in the Scriptures? or how any of the other evils that are the causes of all our divisions shall be removed, cannot easily be declared.

12. If it shall be said, that if this authoritative national Church-state should be removed, and no other of another form set up in the room of it, or be divested of the powers claimed at present by it, it will be impossible to preserve the Protestant religion amongst us, to keep uniformity in the profession of it, and agreement amongst its professors, it is answered – (1) Nothing ought to be removed but what is a real cause, or unnecessary occasion at least, of all the deformity and disorder that is amongst us, and is likely so to continue. (2) That whilst we have a Protestant king and a Protestant parliament, Protestant magistrates and Protestant ministers, with the due care of the nation that they may so continue, and a Protestant confession of faith duly adhered unto, I shall not, under the blessing of the holy Providence, fear the preservation of the Protestant religion and interest in England, without any recourse unto such a Church-power as fills all with divisions. This, I say, is that Church of England which is

the principal bulwark of the Protestant religion and interest in Europe – namely, a Protestant king, a Protestant parliament, Protestant magistrates, Protestant ministers, a Protestant confession of faith established by law with the cordial agreement of the body of the people in all these things esteeming the Protestant religion and its profession their chief interest, in this world. To suppose that a few men, having obtained honours, dignities, and revenues unto themselves, exercising a power and authority (highly questionable, whether legal or no) unto their own advantage, oppressive unto the people, and by all means perpetuating differences among Protestants, are that Church of England which is justly esteemed the bulwark of the Protestant religion, is a high and palpable mistake. The Church of England, as unto its national interest in the preservation of the Protestant religion, is not only separable from it, but weakened by it. Yea, if there be such a national constitution as, in its own nature, and by the secular advantages which it supplies men withal, inclines them to prefer their own interest above that of the Protestant religion in general, it will always endanger that religion in any nation; for hereon they will judge, when they are pressed on any occasion or circumstance of affairs, that it is better to preserve their own interest, by virtue of some dispensations securing unto them their power and secular advantages, than to venture all by a rigid contest for the Protestant religion.

Nor is it morally possible that ever Popery should return into this or any other nation, but under the conduct of such a Church constitution; without this it hath no prevalent engine but mere force, war, and oppression.

But if the interest of Popery can possess this Church-state, either by the inclinations of them, or the greater number of them, who have the management of it, or by their dependence, as unto their interest, on the supreme authority; if that happen in any age to give countenance thereunto, the whole nation will quickly be insensibly influenced and betrayed into Popery, as it were, they know not how. Hence have been such national conversions to and fro in England as have been in no other places or countries in the world; for the care of the public preservation of religion being, as it is supposed, intrusted in this Church-state and the managers of it, if by any means it be possessed by Popery, or influenced by a popish prince, the religion of the whole nation will be lost immediately.

For as unto all other ministers who have the immediate guidance of the people, they will suppose that they can do nothing of themselves in this matter, but are only obliged unto the conduct of the Church-state itself. And having their station therein alone, and depending thereon, they may easily be either seduced by their interest or excluded from their duty by the power of that Church-state whereunto they are subject. By this means the whole interest of the Protestant religion in this nation, as unto its preservation, depends on such a state as, being the concernment of a few, and those such as have an especial interest of their own, distinct from that of the Protestant religion in general, may be easily possessed by Popery, and probably would be so, if they should have a popish prince to influence them.

But whereas the people are now possessed and fully persuaded of the truth of Protestant religion, if there be no public machine or engines insensibly to turn about the whole body of them, but they must be dealt withal individually or parochially, it will, as was said, be morally impossible that ever Popery should become the religion of this nation any other way but by the destruction or killing of the present inhabitants.

Allow that the Church-state supposed may, in those who have the trust and power of it, be seduced, corrupted, or any way induced or disposed unto the interest of Popery, as it may be; it is possible some individual persons may be found that, for the sake of truth, will expose their lives to the stake or otherwise – so did many in the days of Queen Mary, though now esteemed, by not a few, foolish zealots for their pains – but the body of the people, through their various legal relations unto this Church-state, deserting the care of their own preservation, by their trust in the conduct thereof, whereunto they are unavoidably compelled, will quickly be inveigled so as not to be able to extricate themselves. But set them at liberty, so as that every Parliament, every magistrate, every minister, every good Christian, may judge that the preservation of their religion is their own duty in all their capacities, and Popery with all its arts will know neither how to begin nor how to proceed with them.

If, then, there were no such Church-state as, being in the management of a few, is seducible, and not difficult to be possessed by the interest of Popery, whereby the whole nation would be at one betrayed, the Protestant religion is now so firmly seated in the minds of the people, so countenanced by law, so esteemed by all to be the principal interest of the nation, that the wit of all the Jesuits of the world knows not how to attack it, much less endanger it; which, if there be need, shall be farther demonstrated.

13. Nor is it a matter of art or difficulty to declare a way for the security of the Protestant religion, with the rights of the government and liberties of the subjects, with the due freedom of conscience, without any such Church-state; but it is what the principles of religion, common prudence,

[351]

and the honest interest of the nation do direct unto: as, to instance in the things that are most material unto that end –

(1) Let a solemn renunciation of Popery, suited unto the general principles of the Protestant religion, be established by law, to be made publicly by every person that is to partake of the rights and privileges already confirmed unto that religion, or which afterward shall be so; to be renewed as occasion shall require.

(2) Let there be one solemn stated confession of the Christian Protestant faith, such as is the doctrine of the Articles of the Church of England, especially as explained in the public authorized writings of the Church in the days of Queen Elizabeth and King James, before the inroad of novel opinions among us, to be subscribed by all enjoying a public ministry.

(3) Let the magistrate assume unto himself the exercise of his just power, in the preservation of the public peace in all instances; in the encouragement and protection of the professors of the Protestant religion; in securing unto all men their legal rights, already granted unto them, in their several places and stations; in the punishment of all crimes cognizable by human judgment; in deposing of men from their enjoyments or privileges, which they hold on any condition – as, suppose, their orthodox profession of the Protestant religion – if they fail in, or fall from, the performance of it; leaving only things purely spiritual and evangelical to the care and power of the churches, and all litigious causes, of what sort soever, with the infliction of all outward penalties, unto the determination of the laws of the land; – and a great progress will be made towards order and peace amongst us.

(4) Yea, these few things, in general, are only needful thereunto: [1] Let the king and Parliament secure the Protestant religion, as it is the public interest of the nation, against all attempts of the Papacy for its destruction, with proper laws, and their due execution. [2] Let the wisdom and power of the nation, in the supreme and subordinate magistrates, be exerted in the rule of all persons and causes, civil and criminal, by one and the same law of the land – in a compliance wherewith the allegiance of the subject unto the king doth consist; without which, government will never be well fixed on its proper and immovable basis. [3] That provision be made for the sedulous preaching of the Gospel in all parts and places of the land, or all parochial churches; the care whereof is incumbent on the magistrates. [4] Let the Church be protected in the exercise of its spiritual power by spiritual means only – as preaching of the Word, administration of the sacraments, and the like. Whatever is farther pretended as necessary unto any of the ends of true religion or its preservation

[352]

in the nation, is but a cover for the negligence, idleness, and insufficiency of some of the clergy, who would have an outward appearance of effecting that by external force which themselves, by diligent prayer, sedulous preaching of the Word, and an exemplary conversation, ought to labour for in the hearts of men.

(5) It is evident that hereon all causes of jealousies, animosities, and strifes among the Protestants, would be taken away; all complaints of oppression by courts and jurisdictions not owned by the people be prevented; all encroachments on the consciences of men (which are and will be an endless and irreconcilable cause of difference among us) be obviated; all ability to control or disturb the power and privilege of kings in their persons or rule, and all temptations to exalt their power in absoluteness above the law, will be removed; so as that, by the blessing of God, peace and love may be preserved among all true Protestants.

And if there do ensue hereon some variety in outward rites and observations, as there was in all the primitive churches, who pleaded that the unity of faith was commended and not at all impeached by such varieties; yet, whilst the same doctrine of truth is preached in all places, the same sacraments only administered – wherein every Protestant subject of the nation will be at liberty to join in Protestant Christian worship, and to partake of all Church ordinances in the outward way, and according unto the outward rites, of his own choosing, without the authoritative examination or prohibition of any pretended Church power but what, in his own judgment, he doth embrace – no inconvenience will follow hereon, unless it be judged such, that the Protestant religion, the liberty of the subjects, and the due freedom of the consciences of men sober and peaceable, will be all preserved.

The Scandal of
Division among the Godly

James Durham
[1622–1658]

FOR THE INFLUENCE OF JAMES DURHAM'S BRIEF LIFE UPON THE SCOTTISH Church we owe much to David Dickson. It was when Durham was a young captain in the Scottish army during the Civil War that the Glasgow Divinity Professor heard him leading his men in prayer, and claimed him for the ministry. After studying under Dickson, he was licensed to preach in 1646 and the following year became minister of Blackfriars Church, Glasgow. On Dickson's transfer to the Divinity Chair in Edinburgh, Durham was called to succeed him as Professor at Glasgow but before the appointment could take effect the General Assembly intervened to make him chaplain to the King. He later became pastor of the Inner Kirk of Glasgow where he died in 1658 at the early age of 36.

Durham is known today mainly through his works, most of which were published posthumously. Here again it was Dickson who discerned his ability and pressed him into his scheme for the provision of a series of commentaries. Durham's special contribution was his now well-known Commentary on Revelation. Of equal note was his Commentary on the Song of Solomon; his expositions of The Ten Commandments and Isaiah 53 have also justly been held in esteem down the centuries. A work of a somewhat different nature is his Treatise concerning Scandal which has long been looked upon as the Scottish classic on its subject. The story behind this work, from which the following material is taken, is interesting.

The latter part of Durham's brief ministry coincided with the contention that arose in the Scottish Church during the Commonwealth period. The dispute arose from 'the Engagement' which certain Scottish noblemen made with Charles I in 1649. This agreement was not accepted either by the Church or the Scottish Parliament which passed an Act of Classes debarring those who supported 'the Engagement' from places of trust and power. After the king's death and the subsequent invasion by Cromwell, the Scottish Parliament took fright, determined to welcome these men back, and so rescinded the Act of Classes. The Church ratified this decision by passing Public Resolutions, but there was a minority who strongly protested against it. The result was two parties in the Church in Scotland – the 'Resolutioners' and the 'Protesters'.

At the time when the dispute was so bitter that one party would have no dealings with the other, James Durham was esteemed by both sides so much that he was elected Moderator by both the competing Presbyteries in Glasgow. He was a man of moderate and peaceable spirit and there was none better fitted to undertake a work on offences in the Church – which Durham puts under the general heading of 'Scandal'; a fourth part of this book deals with the Scandal of Divisions. After completing the third part he was persuaded to write something relative to the sad controversy that was injuring the Scottish Church. Because of increasing infirmity he had to dictate the work which proved to be, as the original title reads, 'The Dying Man's Testament to the Church of Scotland'. Without making direct reference to the contemporary dispute he deals with the scandal of divisions among the godly in a tender, balanced, scriptural manner.

Historical Background
Men of the Covenant, Alexander Smellie, 1903, reprinted 1960.

The Scandal of Division among the Godly

THE DYING MAN'S TESTAMENT
TO THE CHURCH OF SCOTLAND;
OR,
A TREATISE CONCERNING SCANDAL

Matt. 18: 7. *Woe unto the world because of offences: for it must needs be that offences come: but woe to that man by whom the offence cometh.*

I Cor. 10: 32. *Give none offence, neither to the Jews, nor to the Gentiles, nor to the Church of God.*

Ps. 119: 165. *Great peace have all they which love thy law: and nothing shall offend them.*

GENERAL GROUNDS LEADING TO UNITY

AT a time when a Church lies under rents and divisions it is more difficult to speak particularly of what indeed is duty. For though the general be granted yet often it is difficult to take up the particular care, and still more difficult singly to follow the same. It is also more easy to prescribe rules to others than to follow them ourselves, especially when spirits are in such a heat and fervour of contention that they are some way drunken with affection to their own side and prejudice against the others, and distracted as it were with a sort of madness in pursuing their adversaries, as that great and meek divine Melancthon expressed it. It is hard to get affections that are in such a temper captivated to the obedience of light. Though we will not take on us to be particular and satisfying in this matter – wishing and hoping that it may be more effectually done by some other – yet having come this length we shall in an abstracted manner consider some things in reference thereto, and endeavour to hold forth what we conceive to be duty, especially to the ministers of the Gospel that have interest in such a Church; as also what may be required of others that may think themselves less concerned therein. In doing so we shall keep this order:

1. We shall lay down some general grounds which we take as granted.
2. We shall premise some preparatory endeavours agreeable to the same.

[358]

3. We shall speak negatively to what ought not to be done, or ought to be forborn.

4. We shall speak positively to the healing means called for in reference to several sorts of division, with some questions incident thereto.

5. We shall consider the grounds that do press the serious and condescending application of these or other healing means in such a case.

The first general ground, which we take for granted is this. That by way of precept there is an absolute necessity of uniting laid upon the Church, so that it falleth not under debate as a principle, whether a Church should continue divided or united, more than it falleth under debate, whether there should be preaching, praying, keeping of the Sabbath, or any other commanded duty; seeing that union is both commanded as a duty, and commended, as eminently tending to the edification of the Church, and therefore is so frequently joined with edification. Nor is it to be asked by a Church, what is to be done for the Church's good, in a divided way, thereby supposing a dispensation, as it were, to be given to division, and a forbearing of the use of means for the attaining thereof; or rather supposing a stating or fixing of division, and yet notwithstanding thereof, thinking to carry on edification? It is true, where union cannot be attained amongst orthodox ministers that agree in all main things (for, of such only we speak), ministers are to make the best use of the opportunities they have, and during that to seek the edification of the Church. Yet, that men should by agreement state a division in the Church, or dispense therewith, and prefer the continuing of division, as fitter for edification than union, we suppose is altogether unwarrantable. 1. Because that is not the Lord's ordinance, and therefore cannot be gone about in faith, nor in it can the blessing be expected, which the Lord doth command to those that are in unity (Ps. 133). 2. Because Christ's Church is but one Body, and this were deliberately to alter the nature thereof: and although those who deny this truth, may admit of division; yea, they cannot have union, that is proper Church union, which is union in government, sacraments, and other ordinances, because union or communion in these, doth result from this principle; yet it is impossible for those that maintain that principle of the unity of the Catholic visible Church, to own a divided way of administrating government or other ordinances, but it will infer either that one party hath no interest in the Church, or that one Church may be many; and so, that the unity thereof in its visible state is to no purpose: this then we take for granted. And though possibly it be not in all cases attainable, because the fault may be upon one side, who possibly will not act unitedly with others, yet is this still to be endeavoured, and every opportunity to be taken hold of for promoting of the same.

The second ground which we suppose is this, That as union is ever a duty, so, we conceive, if men interested will do their duty, there can be no division amongst orthodox divines or ministers, but it is possible also to compose it, and union is a thing attainable. For, (1) we are not speaking of composing divisions that are stated upon the fundamental things; nor, (2) are we speaking of removing all differences, as if all men were to be one in judgment in every point of truth; there may be difference where there is no division, as hath been said. Nor, (3) when we speak of men doing their duty, do we mean a full up-coming of every thing in knowledge and practice, and that in a sanctified manner, though that ought to be endeavoured; but it looketh principally to the doing of duty in reference to this particular (if it may be called so) of attaining union, a great part whereof doth consist in outward obvious things, which do neither require simply sanctification in the person (though in itself most desirable) nor perfection in the degree, some whereof we may afterward mention; so that the meaning is, if we consider union in itself, without respect to men's corruptions (which will make the least thing impossible when they are in exercise) it is a thing possible, according to the acknowledged principles that sober, orthodox men usually walk by, as experience hath often proven, and reason doth demonstrate in the particulars afterward to be instanced. And this consideration ought the more pressingly to stir up the endeavour of this duty, although oftentimes through men's corruption it hath been frustrated.

Thirdly, we permit, That in endeavouring union and healing, men would not straiten it to a universal union in everything, in judgment and practice, but would resolve to have it with many things defective that need forbearance in persons that are united, which we may take up in these particulars. 1. There may be difference of judgment in many things, I mean in such things that are consistent with the foundation, and edification; and such a forbearance would be resolved upon, and to do otherwise were to think that either men had no reason at all or that their understandings were perfect, or at least of equal reach. 2. There may be dissatisfaction with many persons, whether officers or members; and to expect a Church free of unworthy officers, or members, and to defer Church union thereupon, is to expect the barn-floor shall be without chaff, and to frustrate the many commands whereby this duty is pressed; for, so this command should be obligatory to no Church, but that that is triumphant; yet certainly our Lord Jesus gave this command to His disciples when Judas was amongst them; and Paul gave it and practised it, when some preached out of envy (Phil. 1), and when almost all sought their own things, and not the things of Christ. And certainly, if people ought to carry even to corrupt ministers who yet destroy not the foundation, as ministers, in the duties that becomes them to ministers in communion with them, while they continue such, then certainly ministers ought to keep that communion with ministers that becometh their relations, seing they are still ministers in that respect, as well as in the other. And if this corruption will not warrant separation in other ordinances (as was said in the close of the second part) then neither will it warrant division in the ordinance of government. 3. It may also be consistent with many particular failings, and defects in the exercise of government, as possibly the sparing of some corrupt officers and members; yea, the censuring of some unjustly, or the admission of some that are unfit for the ministry, and such like. These indeed are faults, but they are not such as make a Church to be no Church; and though these have sometimes been pretended to be the causes of schisms and divisions in the Church in practice, yet were they never defended to be just grounds of schisms and divisions, but were ever condemned by all Councils and Fathers, and cannot be in reason sustained. For, 1. there should be then no union expected here, except we supposed that men that have corruption, could not fall in these faults. 2. It is not unlikely some of these were in the primitive Churches; somewhat is inferred from Revelation chapter 2 in those Church officers tolerating of Jezebel and the Nicolaitans to seduce the people, and to commit fornication; yet neither is separation or division called for, or allowed either amongst ministers or people. Sure there were such corrupt acts of all kings amongst the Jews' Church officers; yet is it clear that Nicodemus and Joseph of Arimathea did continue to govern jointly, notwithstanding thereof, who yet cannot be counted accessory to any of their deeds; Because (which is a third reason) men in such cases have, even when they are present, to discountenance such corrupt acts, by not consenting thereto, and testifying against the same (yea, they may by so doing, stand in the way of many wicked acts, which by dividing they cannot do) which is sufficient for their exoneration both before God and men: As we may see in the instances of Joseph and Nicodemus mentioned, who continue united in the government, keep the meetings even when sentences pass against those who will acknowledge Christ, and orders for persecuting Him and them; and yet they are declared free, because they dissented from, and testified against the same. Yea, their freedom and exoneration by virtue of their dissent being present, is more solemnly recorded to their honour in the Gospel, than if they had divided. And yet the unity of the Church now hath the same ground, and no fewer motives to press it than it had then. 4. It may stand with some defects in worship, manner of Government, and rules that are necessary for good government in a Church. It is likely that many things of that kind were defective in the Church of Corinth, where the Sacrament was so disorderly admin-istrated, confusion in many things of worship, and some things still to be set in order; yet doth the Apostle nowhere press union more than in these Epistles, as formerly hath been marked; neither can it be thought that perfection in all these is ever to be expected, or that union, until such time is to be delayed. And if there be defects of that kind, it is union and not division that is to be looked upon as the commended mean for redressing of the same.

If it be asked then, With what kind of defects or discontents may a union be made up? or, what rules may be walked by therein? For answer, we offer these considerations or rules.

Rule 1. What cannot warrant a breach where there is union, that cannot warrantably be the ground to keep up a division. Now there are many miscarriages or defects, which are really gross, and yet will not warrant a schism, as all that write thereon do clear, and is obvious to all. The reason of the consequence is, because making up of a breach is no less a duty, than preventing thereof. And further, if it began upon such a ground, then the continuing thereof upon the same ground is but the continuing in the same sin; and it cannot be thought that any party by dividing upon an unjust ground, can afterward be justified upon the same ground. It remaineth, therefore, that if the ground was not sufficient at first to warrant a separa-tion or division, it cannot be sufficient afterward to continue the same.

Rule 2. Such defects as do not make communion in a Church, and in its ordinances sinful, will not warrant a separation or division from the same; for this followeth on the former. It is acknowledged by all that there is no separation from a true Church in such ordinances as men may without sin communicate into, although others may be guilty therein; as, suppose men to have access to government without such bonds and engagements, and such like, as may mar their freedom in following the light of the Word, in deciding whatever shall come before them, even though others should step over the same.

Rule 3. Men may keep communion with a Church, when their calling leadeth them thereto upon the one side, and they have access to the discharge of the same upon the other; this also followeth upon the former: for, if some acts of a man's station lead him to a united way of acting (as the duties of a fixed minister do) then he is obliged to follow the duties

[362]

of his calling, whilst there is no physical or moral impediment barring him in the same, and others being defective in their duty, will not absolve him from his, which he oweth by virtue of his station.

Rule 4. While the general rules tending to edification in the main are acknowledged, union is to be kept, even though there be much failing in the application; because, so there are fit weapons to make use of, and who knoweth but single and zealous improving of them, may help the application thereof; and if there be a failing therein, it is the person's deed, that by his vote so misapplies, and doth not involve any other in that guilt, beside that by joint and united acting much of that misapplication may through God's blessing be prevented.

Rule 5. Then there may and ought to be uniting when the evils that follow division or schism, are greater and more hurtful to the Church than the evils that may be supposed to follow on union. I speak not of ills of sin (for the least of these are never to be chosen) but of evils and inconveniences that may indeed be hurtful to the Church in themselves, and sinful in respect of some persons, yet are not so to all: Now, in such evils the lesser is to be chosen, because uniting and acting jointly in a Church way, doth belong to the policy and government of the Church, wherein Christian prudence is to have a main hand, so that when things cannot be done as men would simply, they are to do as they may comparatively, that is, to choose and make use of what may be most edifying, and least hurtful to the Church's edification (which is the great end that ought to sway in government) amongst all these means that seem probable and possible; so that the conscience may have testimony in this, that the way that had fewest inconveniences, and most advantages to edification, was chosen; and though some inconveniences fall out afterward, yet the conscience may be quiet on this ground: because, sometimes the Lord in His providence will order so in the matters of government that there is no side can be chosen without inconveniences; as suppose, there is not full satisfaction in any way that occurreth in planting such a congregation, in removing of such an offence, healing such a rent, and the like; but whatever side be looked to, many hindrances to edification appear, yet something must be chosen, and may be with peace to the conscience; because we are to regulate our own act suitably to the providences, and cases we meet with, and to the tempers of those we have to do with; but we are neither to regulate nor answer for providences, and the distempers of others. Indeed in such a case, the mind may be disquieted because of fear; and the consolation of the duty may be diminished, because of such circumstances; and affections may be grieved and jumbled, because there is not full satisfaction; yet may the conscience have quietness and peace in its duty notwithstanding; and men are specially to discern and to put difference between peace of conscience and the former discomposures: otherwise there will be many cases wherein it is impossible for a zealous minister to have peace, whatever side he choose, yea, whether he do or forbear.

If it be asked then, What way men may discern the side that is to be followed in such a case, when inconveniences threaten on all hands? *Answer.* By these and such like ways. 1. It is to be looked, what side hath the most dangerous and destructive inconveniences. 2. What inconveniences are most certain and inevitable, and the greatest and most inevitable inconveniences are to be shunned, and men would not choose a certain hurt to eschew that which is uncertain. 3. It would be looked what side duty lieth upon, or to what the command doth press; and although inconveniences seem to follow that yet it is to be followed as most safe. Now, as to all these, union hath the advantage of division: because, (1) It is a commanded mean tending to edification, which division is not. (2) Division hath no less nor fewer inconveniences following it, not less destructive to the Church, than union in the case supposed; yea, schism is one of the greatest hurts that can come to an orthodox Church, it being next to heresy in doctrine; and therefore no particular evil can be laid in the balance with it. (3) The ills of division are most inevitable, for the ills that follow union, through God's blessing may be prevented, it is not impossible, but in the way of division it is, because itself is out of God's way.

Rule 6. When men may unite without personal guilt, or accession to the defects or guilt of others, there may and ought to be union, even though there be failings and defects of several kinds in a Church. The reasons before given will clear this, because men are to reckon not for other men's carriages, but their own, and no such Church state is to be expected as is free of defects. Besides can it warrant a man to abstain from his duty because others do not theirs, while there is no sinful impediment lying in the way of his access thereto? If it be asked, What may be accounted such impediments, as a tender conscience may be justly scared by from uniting? It may be answered in these and such like: 1. If a person be put to comdemn anything he thinketh lawful in his own former practice, or the practice of others, or in some point of doctrine though never so extrinsic, if it be to him a point of truth. 2. If he be put to approve the deed, and practice of some others which he accounteth sinful, or to affirm somewhat as truth which he doth account an error. 3. When some engagement is required for the future, which doth restrain from any duty called for, or that may afterward be called for. These and such like involve persons in the sin of what is past, and also maketh them accessory to the inconveniences which may come; because they are bound up with their own consent, from endeavouring the preventing thereof in the way of duty, at least it is so to them, and so defileth their conscience. Therefore such entanglements are by all means to be forborn; but where no such thing is in condemning or acknowledging any thing that is past, nor any such restraining bond inconsistent with duty for the time to come, there may be access to union, even where there are many public defects, which is the thing laid down to be cleared.

In the fourth place we premit, that for attaining of union there would be, and there ought to be, large mutual condescending, that is, that both sides ought to stretch themselves, not only to forbear what is sinful; nor only to condescend to what may be thought simply necessary, and may be extorted as duty in any case; nor yet ought condescending to be upon one side levelled according to the length that another goeth, but condescending would be levelled mutually according as expediency calleth for, with respect to the edification of the Church; for which end even many infirmities of others are to be forborn, and things otherwise unreasonable in respect of these men we have to do with, yet respect to the Church's peace, ought to make men cede in these; for, if there ought to be condescending for private peace, much more ought it to be for Church peace and public edification: and though we cannot, nor will not now be particular in this, yet concerning it, we may lay down these considerations:

1. In what may involve a man in sin, or in the approbation thereof in others, there is no condescending, but what length may warrantably be gone, even to the utmost border of duty, men ought to go for this end; so that nothing ought to be a stop or march in condescension, but this, I cannot do this and sin against God; otherwise, one ought to be all things to others. This consideration will be more clear, by comparing it with the former rules, and what afterward may be said.

2. This condescension would be mutual upon both sides, that is, one party would not expect full submission from the other, for that is not union, but dominion. Hence the Apostle in his pressing of union in such cases, doth ordinarily pray, and obtest both sides. And seeing affection is the main ground of union, it is fit, there should be condescension for mutual testifying of respect each to other. This is also confirmed by an Epistle of Calvin's to Knox (afterward cited) wherein he presseth that condescension be mutual for removing of a division that was in his congregation at Frankfort.

3. Even that party that seemeth to be rightest in the matter, or to have authority on its side, or to have countenance from others, ought yet to condescend, yea in some things to be most condescending, because such are in some sort parents and strong; they ought therefore the more tenderly to bear and cover the infirmities of the weak: and because they are more sober and at themselves, they therefore ought to carry the more seriously toward others, whom they suppose to be in a distemper, and not to be equally gross in handling the tender things of the Church, whereof union is a main one. And considering that authority is given for edification, it is not unsuitable for it to condescend for attaining its end; for which cause we find often Paul, laying by his authority in such cases, and intreating and wooing, as it were, even the meanest dissenters, in this matter of union, as we see him, beseeching Euodias and Syntyche (who were it is likely but very private persons) to be of one mind (Phil. 4).

From what is said, we may lay down these negative conclusions, concerning the upmaking of a breach amongst godly and orthodox men, where a Church hath harmony in the fundamental points, faith, worship and government, and where the thriving of the Gospel is mutually designed.

1. Division ought not to be endeavoured to be removed in such a case, in such a way as doth undo or destroy either side, because that is not the good of the whole; for every part and side in such a case, is a part of the body, although it may be not so very considerable, and it is no wisdom to cut off a member of the body, and that way to cure a distemper therein, when possibly the purging away to corrupt humours from the body, or more gentle applications might recover the same.

2. We say that way of uniting is not to be admitted, but shunned, which may incapacitate any minister or member of the body that is fit for edifying of the same, from having access thereunto; for so the Church is prejudged, and men are rendered unable for edifying thereof. And this is not only when sentences are passed, or restraints laid on; but it may be in such like cases. As, 1. When by the terms of union some person is grieved and weighted, by annexing of some unnecessary thing which may be forborn, because by this men go about duty with heaviness, which is unprofitable to the Church. 2. It may be, when something that reflecteth upon any side, or person, unnecessarily, is interwoven because such things still keep up suspicion, and make the union the more heartless, and doth both make such persons more faint, and also in the lesser capacity to have weight with others for their edification, and doth leave a ground of dissatisfaction with such an agreement, that is ready afterward to break forth; Therefore union

[366]

would be essayed with all due respect from each to other, and without any note of disrespect.

3. We may gather, that no simply authoritative mean is the fit and only way of healing a rent Church. That is indeed the way of governing a united Church, but not the way of uniting a rent Church, especially a Church rent in particulars of practice and government; because the remedy must be extensive to both sides, and in such cases, at least as to these particulars. Authority usually is declined; and though it be unjustly declined possibly, yet when it is declined, it is unable to effectuate this end; and the remedy is to be applied, not as to what agreeth to a Church that is whole, but what agreeth to a Church in such a distemper; even as a sick body is to be nourished not always with the strongest and wholesomest meats which agree with such as are in health, but it is to be nourished with things suitable to its distemper, and are fit to cure it; yea, sometimes, with such things as may please the taste, when more healthful things are not admitted. Also when both judgments are to be informed, and affections are to be gained, there must be prudential and affectionate ways used for gaining these ends. Hence we see that not only in Church history, but in the Scriptures especially, the duty of union is more pressed by persuasions, entreaties, reasons to move to it, ills that follow the want thereof, and such like, than by an authoritative way, such as is used in the condemning of heretics, and other scandalous persons. And indeed union hath such conjunction with the will and affections, that it must be persuaded and cannot be so commanded. And amongst such persons as are supposed to be in this difference, private and particular condescension is most becoming that respect which each ought to other.

Fifthly, we premit, that suppose sufficient condescension should fail upon one side, yet ought the other to condescend fully the length that is possible.

1. Because Church union amongst Churchmen is no civil bargain to use prigging therein, but what is possible is duty out of obedience to God, who commandeth peace in other things (and so, much more in this) as far as is possible, or as in men lies. And, 2. Because respect is to be had to the Church's good, whose advantage we should seek, even though others were defective; and often such condescending gaineth more for the advantage of the Church, and commendation of the party condescending, than if there had been more sticking, as we may see in that praiseworthy instance of Basil's carriage, who stuck on nothing, but absolutely did lay by what was contended for, without respect to his own right or injury, for the Church's good. And oftentimes it is one party waiting for the other's

condescension, or taking occasion from their tenaciousness to stick, that doth keep the distance at a height.

Sixthly, oftentimes in such debates as are amongst orthodox divines and ministers, it seemeth they might be removed if one party should condescend according to the qualifications and cautions formerly laid down; yea, it seemeth it were safer for the Church's good in such a case that either party should practically condescend to the way of the other, than that division should be kept up upon such grounds. For, 1. It is not supposed here that there is any matter of faith in question, amongst such, often there was full harmony in the Confessions of Faith, as in the instances cited. 2. There is no question for government simply, nor for Councils and canons, these also were acknowledged; none did disclaim the general Councils, nor their acts. 3. The question often is not amongst them, whether others should be brought to their opinion or not, I mean as to the stick of the division, but often it is either, (1) upon some mistaken expression of another, or error in some lesser point of truth; and, in such a case, it is that great Augustine's word, 'Disputable errors, or uncertain faults, are not in their pursuit to be preferred to certain peace.' Or, (2) it is for some particular act of government, or other miscarriages by misapplying of rules, or not walking according to them, or something of that kind, as was in contrary ordinations of orthodox men, and such like: In which cases, we say (and it will be found from history) that it had been ever better for the Church, that either side had practically condescended to suffer the other to rule and govern, and personally to have kept themselves free from accession to their guilt, whether of crookedness, negligence, or the like, than to have raised or entertained divisions upon such accounts. For, often orthodox, and otherwise blameless men, have been made, by such divisions, factious and carnal in their carriage, and much unuseful; who otherwise had they been free of that temptation, might have proved sober, and profitable; and, when the temptation was over, were found to be such.

Seventhly, we may observe, that though in the primitive times there were diverse schisms and divisions, concerning Synods and government, yet we will find that these contests and divisions did flow from the matter and particular acts and actings thereof, and that there was hardly ever division tabled upon the formality of the constitution of a Council or Synod; nor yet, that much difference was put betwixt declining of their authority, and of the acts or censures passed by them.

Eighthly, although such debates concerning government seem most easy to be removed, yet often and almost ever, they have been most difficultly healed, and have been followed with greatest bitterness and contention in the Church; for, different judgments simply, and also different cere-monies, and different practices in other things, may consist without direct opposition or counteracting, and may either be the more easily borne or removed: but when it comes to government, whose sentence shall stand, whose ordination shall be acknowledged, who shall have place to decide such and such things, and the like, it is far otherwise. Hence it came to pass that men could keep union and communion with others that differed from them in far greater points of truth; but to persons that did not acknowledge their authority, or did acknowledge those that did controvert with them about that, they could by no means so condescend: because, 1. In government, men's own particular interest is more concerned than in points of truth, and that inadvertently stealeth in upon men. 2. Because, in government the question is not only for what is past, but there is a fear of what may come: Hence men that have some testimony in themselves that they are not ambitious of government, yet having taken up a prejudice against others, they are suspicious that if such had power, they would miscarry, not only in reference to them, but in reference to public concern-ment; and therefore in removing such a division that is in point of govern-ment, the great difficulty is not so much to heal and remove what is past, as to prevent the fear of what may come, if such continue to govern. And this maketh, that the result of such division is, That either they themselves, or such as they have confidence in particularly, may have the weight of government upon them, which may indeed be aimed at with some sincerity; because being some way alienated with prejudice, they do not think it fit for the good of the work, at least during that time, that any others should have such trust; and this made the heat of debates in the time of division, to break out mainly in the ordination of Bishops, and planting of Churches; because by that means their interest in the government was kept up, whereby there was after-access to the management of every other thing according as this succeeded.

SOME PREPARATORY ENDEAVOURS FOR UNITING

Although we have been somewhat large in these generals, because of the falling in of several things, yet we conceive it may be useful to the point, and we may have the speedier progress afterward in loosing this great question, What an orthodox Church divided in itself in some circum-stantial truths (to speak so) or contrary practices and actings, when still agreeing in the fundamentals of doctrine, worship, discipline and govern-ment, and having mutual esteem of the integrity one of another, what,

I say, such are called to do for the healing of that breach? In reference to which, these things, or this method would be followed:

1. All, especially ministers, would walk under the impression of the dreadfulness and terribleness of such a plague. It is like, if God were looked to as angry at a Church, and at ministers in such a time, men would be in the greater fitness to speak concerning a healing. Some time therefore would be bestowed on this, to let that consideration sink down in the soul, that the Lord's hand may be taken up therein; the many sad consequences thereof would be represented to the mind, and the heart would be furiously affected and humbled therewith, as if sword, pestilence or fire were threatened; yea, as if the Lord were spitting in ministers' faces, rubbing shame upon them, and threatening the making of them despicable, the blasting of the ordinances in their hands, the loosing the girdle of their loins, and authority amongst the people, the plucking up of the hedges to let in boars and wolves to spoil the vines, and destroy the flock; and, in a word, to remove His candlestick, so that ministers or other persons in such a case, have not only men that are their opposites to look to as angry at them, but they have the Lord to look to as their party, whose anger hath thus divided them; and the not observing of this, maketh men the more confident under such a judgment. Whereas, seeing it is a plague, men, even such as suppose themselves innocent, as to the immediate rise thereof, ought to humble themselves under the mighty hand of God, with respect to this as to other plagues.

2. Men would also look upon it as a snare. O how many temptations have such divisions accompanying them, especially to ministers; and also how many afflictions, crosses and reproaches, upon the back of these! Might it not make a minister tremble to think upon the matter of divisions that now beside all his former difficulties and straits, there is a snare and trial in everything; in every sermon that he preacheth it is thus, lest his own affection steal in for the zeal of God, to make him hotter and more vehement against those that oppose him in such things that are controverted, than he useth to be in things more nearly concerning to the glory of God, and lest by discovering his carnalness, he make his ministry despicable before others, when he heareth he is in hazard to be irritated by a contradiction; and though there be no contradiction, he is in hazard to lay the less weight upon what might be for his edification, because it is spoken by one who in such and such things differeth from him. When he is in any judicatory, there is a temptation waiting on, by the least motion of such things, to discompose all, and make such meetings scandalous and burdensome; by this all conversing almost becometh heartless and comfortless, the most

intimate brother is either suspicious, or suspected; all construction of men's ingenuity and sincerity in anything are, for the most part, grounded upon men's interests, as if men after that had no conscience of sinning, there is a failing of sympathy amongst brethren, etc. And may not these and many such like, make ministers circumspect in such a case, that they may be slow to speak to what may foment division, and wary in hazarding upon snares. Alas, it is unlike this, when men use more confidence and liberty in constructing, speaking and acting, and with less tenderness in times of division than at other times; and were men once impressed with the fear of sinning upon the occasions of divisions, they would be much more disposed for speaking of union.

3. Ministers and others would soberly retire to take a view of their own spiritual condition, and see if they have kept their own vineyard: and particularly, before the Lord, put themselves to these. 1. How union with Him hath been prized, and if there hath been studying to be, and abide, in Christ, and to keep themselves in the love of God. 2. If there be any ground of quarrel in the present strain or bygone practice, that might have influence to provoke the Lord to smite them in the general. Or, 3. and especially, If by their negligence and unfaithfulness, imprudence, heat, passion, tenaciousness, addictedness to other men, and too much loathness to displease them, prejudice at, and uncharitableness unto others, or the like, they have been any way accessory to the bringing in of this evil; for which cause they would take a view both of the sins that procure it, and the evils which do dispose for it, and increase it (which were formerly mentioned) and would be impartial and thorough in this; for, it is preposterous for men to meddle in removing public differences, while they know not how it standeth with themselves.

4. When that is done, there would be repentance suitable to what is found, and extraordinary humiliation and secret prayer to God, not only for themselves and for their own particular condition, but for the public, and particularly for healing of that breach, and that thereby God would spare His people, and not suffer His inheritance to be a reproach. It is no little furtherance to union, to have men in a spiritual, abstracted and mortified frame; for, we are sure, if it remove not difference, it will in a great part moderate the division, and restrain the carnalness that usually accompanieth it, and dispose men to be more impartial to hear what may lead further.

5. Men would not persist in this, but as they have interest, and are led by their places, they would endeavour soberly, warily and seriously, by speaking, writing, obtesting and otherwise, to commend union to these

[371]

that differ; yea, even they that differ, would commend it to these that differ from them. We see the Apostles do this frequently in the New Testament, and that not only in the general to Churches, but some persons are particularly by name obtested, as Phil. 4: 2. And in the primitive times, bishops and Churches who were not engaged, did seriously write, and sometimes did send some of their number to Churches and eminent persons that were divided, and often their interposing did prove effectual. And when that difference between Augustine and Jerome did come to some height, he (Augustine) pressed himself so on the other, for the begetting of a better understanding, and the abating of that difference, that he did prevail with him, and by their mutual apologies, and better understanding one of another, they came notwithstanding of their difference to have much respect one of another. For this end Polycarp came from Asia to Rome, to stay the division about Easter, which prevailed so far, that it desisted for a time. Also men, especially of the same judgment, would deal with others with whom in that they agree, to be condescending, and seriously obtest them; and when they exceed, would objurgate them for the Church's good. This is often of great weight, and often also, men that appear most in a difference, will be hotter and carry things further than less engaged men of the same judgment will allow, and such ought not to be silent in such a case. Thus Irenaeus (though of Victor's judgment in the matter of Easter) yet did boldly expostulate with him for his vehemency in pressing of the same, to the hurt of the Church's peace, charging him to forbear and to follow union notwithstanding; which act of his, is still highly commended, and (as Eusebius observeth) counted answerable to his name.

6. Serious and single thoughts of union would be laid down, and that would be purposely driven as the great duty; so that endeavours would not principally tend to strengthen a side, or exonerate themselves, or get advantage to others, but to make one of both; and therefore when one mean or occasion faileth, another would be essayed; neither would men weary or faint herein, although it prove often a most fainting business.

7. Men would endeavour all this with tenderness and respect to men's persons, actions and qualifications; for, oftentimes the rise of a division, is in the alienation of affections between some persons; which afterward disposeth to construct hardly both of their opinions and actions: and indeed often the stick is here, that men's affections are not satisfied one with another, and that maketh them that they do not trust each other: hence we see that in the Scripture, the commending of love, and of honouring and preferring of others in honour of ourselves, is ordinarily subjoined to the exhortations to union, or reproofs of division, as Phil. 2, Eph. 4, Matt. 18,

etc. And we see in the primitive times, when no mean could cure schisms, one party showing respect to another, or to some eminent head of the opposite party (it may be even after their death), did allay the same, and engage these that formerly shunned communion, to join with them. It is particularly observed, that when at Constantinople some had continued separated from the Bishop's government, and the Church thereof, after Chrysostom's deposition, for the space of thirty-five years, and were called Johannites; yet Proclus, who after some interval succeeded in that See, by recording Chrysostom's name amongst eminent persons, and making honourable merttion of him, and bringing his body from the place where it was buried in his exile, and burying it honourably at Constantinople in the great Church of the holy Apostles, did so appease and engage those that had disclaimed all the intervening Bishops that instantly they did acknowledge him and join with the Church. The like also is mentioned to have been the end of that schism at Antioch because of Eustachius, removal from them, when Callaudion the Bishop did return his body honourably to be buried, and went out with his party to receive the same solemnly some miles from the town; those also, who out of respect to him (to wit Eustachius) had continued separated from the succeeding Bishops for above a hundred years, now seeing the adverse party put respect on him, they also did from that time forth join with them. Both these are recorded in the Fifth Century; and if respect to dead men be prevalent to engage affections, certainly mutual respect and evidences of confidence amongst men living, would be much more weighty. This giving of respect would be manifested in these and the like. 1. Respectful mentioning in word or writ of the persons, and what concerns those that differ, especially such as are most eminent and leading amongst them. 2. There would be good constructions put upon their end and intentions, and sincerity, even in such actions as are displeasing. 3. Men's opinions and actions would not be loaded with gross absurdities and high aggravations, especially in public; because that tendeth but to make them odious, and standeth in the way of a future good understanding, when one hath proposed another as so absurd and hateful a person. 4. All personal reflections would be abstained, as also slighting answers, disdainful-like words and salutations, and such like, would be shunned; But on the contrary, there would be love, familiarity, tenderness; and if there have been any reflection or bitterness to occasion mistake, yea, if it have been unjustly apprehended, there would be condescending to remove the same. I have heard of a worthy person, who being led away in an hour of temptation, was by many of his former friends afterwards discountenanced, whereby he was, as it were, engaged in a kind

[373]

of discontent to defend his deed, and resent the disrespect of such persons, which almost grew to a rent: but having occasion to encounter one who was most opposite to his present way, who yet notwithstanding of all, did lovingly and familiarly, as ever, embrace him, without mentioning any such thing; it is said, That his heart melted instantly with the conviction of his former opposition, and so any further procedure towards a rent was prevented, when he saw there was yet again access to the affections of the most eminent of those he did differ from. 5. There would be expressions of mutual confidence in one another, which would appear not only in personal respects, but with respect to the ministry of such as they differ from, endeavouring to strengthen and confirm that, which was the thing that endeared Basil to Eusebius, that even while he differed, he endeavoured to have his ministry weighty amongst the people. 6. Respect would be shown to men of that judgment and side (it being such a difference as is supposed) they would be helped and furthered, and counted, notwithstanding thereof (if otherwise qualified), fit for trust and charge; for, this is not only engaging of a particular person, but of all the party, and doth hold forth a confidence in them notwithstanding of that; whereas the contrary is disobliging and irritating of all, because it proposeth all of such an opinion or practice to be unworthy of charge or trust, which no man can well digest; and it some way necessitates them in a divided way to endeavour some other way of entering, and to increase their diffidence of them who so partially (in their esteem at least) manage matters, and prefer the strengthening of a side, to the edification of the Church; as any different party cannot but expound it, seeing they seem to themselves to have some persuasion of their own integrity in the main work. 7. There would even be mutual visits and fellowship, civil and Christian, as hath been; yea, rather it would be increased; for if men have some confidence that others love their persons, respect them as ministers, and esteem of them as Christians, they will be easily induced to trust the other as such also. 8. If reflections and bitterness be vented by some (as even good men are too ready to indulge to themselves a liberty in debate to exceed in this) yet there would be no such meeting given. Luther is censured for exceeding in this, even by such as loved him; and it is a most excellent advertisement that Calvin giveth to Bullinger and others, thus provoked by him, that either they would not answer such a paper at all, or, in answering it, to remember, that they had a most eminent servant of Christ to answer, and so not to be provoked by his vehemency, seeing he also had corruptions; and thus expresseth his own resolution, *Etiamsi me diabolum vocaret, me tamen hoc illi honoris habiturum, ut insignem Dei servum agnoscam, etc.* It is upon this ground, that Augustine and others, most zealously affected with the schism of the Donatists, yet because they kept in other things sound in the Faith, they mention such of them as were sober, very honourably, and carried to them very brotherly; and particularly he used to visit their Bishops, if he had been going elsewhere for ordination or other affairs; and some of them also used to visit him, whom he entertained most kindly, ever speaking to improve both for begetting a better understanding, as may be gathered from instances cited out of his Epistles in what is before and after this. Sometimes also when he wrote to some of them, he desired them to write so to him, as he might acquaint his people with both their writings, and with his own, if they returned no answer, that thereby he might constrain them to reasonableness, yet saith, it shall be passed *Discessum militum*, that it might appear he intended not to make them odious. He doth also observe that a main thing that made the Donatists averse from yielding to union, was a suspicion which they had, that the Catholics would still persecute them if they had occasion, speaking of a Conference, he saith, *Dictum erat* (meaning by the Donatists) *quod adhuc nostri eos persecuturi essent;* which he with many words rejecteth, showing from Eph. 4 that they had learned to keep union with forbearance: elsewhere also he excuseth the too great vehemency of the expressions of some that were on his own side in that difference. All which showeth the great necessity that there is to recover affections in the pressing of union, and how far men ought to condescend in reference thereto, both in order to what is past, and for the preventing of what may be feared.

8. Then ministers would not only in their own practice, but in their doctrine, and otherwise, stir up others to the practice and life of religion. We ever find the Apostle useth this way upon the back of his exhortations to union, to press the working out of their salvation with fear and trembling, etc. And in the Epistles to Timothy and Titus, when he dissuades ministers from foolish and jangling questions, strifes and contentions, this remedy is either premitted or subjoined, that they would press the believers to be zealous of good works, and careful to maintain these (Tit. 3. 8, 9). That they would follow after love, righteousness, faith, peace with them that call on the Lord out of a pure heart (2 Tim. 2. 22, 23), for, when either ministers or professors are exercised and taken up with these things, there is little access to other things: then also they discern the necessity of union the more, and are the more disposed for it themselves, and others are the more easily induced to unite with them. Besides, it is never in such things that godly and orthodox men do differ, but it is in diverting from these; and therefore often much heat in particular differences, carrieth with it,

a decay and lukewarmness in more practical things; As on the contrary, zeal in these material things, doth ordinarily allay and mitigate heat and fervour in the other.

9. It is fit that there were solemn addresses to God for directing and guiding in the way to this end; for, He is *the God of peace*, and ought to be acknowledged in removing this great evil of division: Hence the Apostle subjoineth prayers for peace, unto his exhortations thereto; and we are commanded to pray for Jerusalem's peace, even Church peace no less than civil peace. It may be that the neglect of this is the cause that sound, godly and peaceable men, who love the welfare of Zion, do yet continue divided, and cannot fall upon means of healing, that thereby the necessity of the Lord's interposing may be discerned, and that there may be purposed addresses for this same thing, and that men may not undervalue the thing, nor their adversaries in it, so as not to account it a rod, seeing it is God they have to do with, nor be content to lie under it without aiming and dealing to have it removed by Him, as we would deal for the removal of any temporal plague, or expect a blessing upon this Gospel.

APPENDICES

Appendix 1:
The Church Membership of Children

Thomas Shepard

[1605-1649]

.

IT IS AN INTERESTING FACT THAT IN ENGLAND IN RECENT YEARS THOSE *who have frequently been foremost in preserving the doctrines of Divine grace, human depravity and saving faith – doctrines which Puritanism was once pre-eminent in expounding – have not observed the Puritan practice of baptizing the infants of believers. The reasons for this deviation from the general Reformed view of baptism are, however, not new. There were groups of Christians in England who ceased to observe infant baptism from the time of the Reformation, although it was not until the Commonwealth period when an eminent evangelical minister John Tombes (1603–1676) published a refutation of the practice, and a Baptist Confession was drawn up in 1646, that the scattered congregations of Baptist con-victions (about 54 in number at this time) began to increase in influence. The names of a comparatively small group of godly ministers, men such as Henry Jessey and Vavasor Powell, became associated with these convictions, and in the persecution period, following 1662, the records of the Baptist Chapel at Broad-mead, Bristol, give us a fine example of the piety of the people of these churches in times of suffering (cf.* The Records of a Church of Christ Meeting in Broad-mead, Bristol, 1640–1687, *edited by E. B. Underhill, 1857;* Baptist Confessions of Faith, *W. L. Lumpkin, Judson Press, 1959.*)

The Puritan reply to the allegedly unscriptural nature of the practice of infant baptism centred around their teaching on the Covenant of Grace (cf. John Flavel, Works, *vol. 6, pp. 318–378, and John Owen,* Works, *vol. 16, pp. 258–268) and, as well as countering the claim that the practice was not consistent with the spirituality of the New Testament, they urged the pastoral and spiritual import-ance of the ordinance in its bearing on the bringing up of children within the Church (cf. Thomas Goodwin,* Works, *vol. 9, pp. 426–498, and* The Biblical Repertory and Princeton Review, *1861). After the Puritan period, the Baptist position was strengthened by such writers as Abraham Booth and John Gill (Body of Divinity, Bk. 3) and, in an indirect way, by the labours of such pioneer mission-aries as William Carey and Adoniram Judson.*

Alexander Carson's Baptism: Its Mode and Subjects *(1854, reprinted 1959) presents what is still probably the best available examination of infant baptism from the Baptist standpoint, while John Murray,* Christian Baptism *(1952) gives a clear modern treatment of the position that baptism is a seal of the Covenant of Grace and that as this Covenant makes promises with regard to believers' children it warrants the administration of the ordinance to them.*

It is to be regretted that discussion on this question has frequently been marred by bigotry, a bigotry which leaders on both sides sought to allay in the seventeenth century. The ministers appointed in 1653 by Cromwell as 'Triers' to approve candidates for the ministry had four Baptists amongst them and candidates of Baptist views were accepted if they were qualified in other respects. Where men were spiritually minded and united in the doctrines of grace harmonious co-operation was possible, as is well illustrated by John Owen's numerous friendships with Baptist ministers. While some lesser men aggravated the differences, Christians like John Bunyan on one side (in his work on Terms of Communion *and* Fellowship of Christians at the Table of the Lord) *and* Flavel *on the other laboured for peace and mutual understanding. The material extant upon the controversy certainly shows the need for caution and sympathy with the difficulties of others; as John Flavel says: 'There are difficulties in this controversy which may puzzle the minds of well-meaning Christians.'*

Thomas Shepard was one of the best known of the New England Puritans, being especially noted for the humbling and heart-searching character of his ministry. After leaving Cambridge in 1625 he endured many afflictions for his fruitful preaching of the Gospel in Essex, Yorkshire and Northumberland, before he was finally forced, at the age of 30, to cross the Atlantic in 1635. In 1632 he had married Margaret Stoutville, who thereafter shared in her husband's trials. After an unsuccessful attempt to sail from Harwich in 1634 – the ship being nearly wrecked by storm – their first son died from a resulting sickness. Shepard was at this time so closely hunted by the bishops' agents that he was unable to attend the funeral. Their second child was about three months old when they finally sailed, and after a hazardous voyage Margaret Shepard only lived long enough to see her husband settled at Newtown, Massachusetts, before she died. Her death was a few days after the baptism of their baby, and in his Autobiography *(printed in A. Young,* Chronicles of the First Planters of the Colony of Massachussetts Bay, *from 1623 to 1636, 1846) Shepard, for the sake of his child in later years, makes the following observations on these two events:*

'On the seventh of Feb., God gave thee the ordinance of baptism, whereby God is become thy God, and is beforehand with thee, that whenever thou shalt return to God, he will undoubtedly receive thee; this is a most high and happy privilege, and therefore bless God for it. And now, after this had been done, thy dear mother died in the Lord, departing out of this world to another, who did lose her life by being careful to preserve thine; for in the ship thou were so feeble and froward both in the day and nights, that hereby she lost her strength and at last her life. She hath made also many a prayer and shed many a tear for thee, and this hath been oft her request, that if the Lord did not intend to glorify himself by thee, that he would cut thee off by death rather than to live to dishonour him by sin. And therefore know it, that if thou shalt turn rebel against God, and forsake him, and care not for the knowledge of him, nor believe in his Son, the Lord will make all these mercies, woes, and all thy mother's prayers, tears, and death, to be a swift witness against thee at the great day.'

Shepard's published works were popular in his own day and in the next century men like Jonathan Edwards and George Whitefield bore witness to their value. A complete edition was published in 3 vols. at Boston, in 1853, with a good record of his life by John A. Albro.

The Church Membership of Children

CLEARED UP IN A LETTER IN ANSWER TO THE DOUBTS
OF A FRIEND

WHEN we say that children are members by their parents' covenant,
I would premise three things for explication.

1. That children of godly parents come to the fruition of their membership by their parents' covenant, but that which gives them their right and
interest in this membership is God's covenant, whereby He engageth
Himself equally to be a God to them and to their seed. This I suppose is
clear.

2. That according to the double seed – viz., (1) Elect seed; (2) Church
seed; so there is a double covenant, (i) External and outward; (ii) Internal
and inward. And because the covenant makes the Church, hence there is
an inward and outward membership and Church estate; there is an outward
Jew and an inward Jew (Rom. 2: 28, 29). All are not Israel (i.e. the elect
seed) that are of Israel (i.e. the Church seed, or in outward covenant), to
whom the apostle saith belongs the adoption, the covenant, and the
promises; that is, the external adoption, whereby God accounts them His
children, or the children of His house and family, the children of the
church; and accordingly have the promises belonging to them in respect
of outward dispensation, although they be not children by internal
adoption, to whom belong the promises by effectual and special communication of saving grace. It is clearer than the day that many who are inwardly,
or in respect of inward covenant, the children of the devil, are outwardly,
or in respect of outward covenant, the children of God. Is. 1: 2, 'I have
brought up children,' and yet 'rebellious'; and in the next verse they are
called 'my people' (i.e. by outward covenant) and yet worse than the ox
or ass. Deut. 32: 19, 20, they are called sons, and yet provoking God to
revengeful wrath; and children, and yet without faith. And look, as some
may be externally dogs, and yet internally believers (as the woman of
Canaan, whom, in respect of outward covenant, Christ calls a dog, and the
Jews who yet rejected Him children, Matt. 15: 26), so many may be
externally children, in respect of external covenant, and yet internally dogs
and evil men; and we see that the purest Churches of Christ are called

[383]

saints, and faithful, and children of God, and yet many among them hypocrites and unbelievers; because they that, in respect of Church estate, and outward covenant and profession, are outwardly or federally saints, are many times inwardly and really unsound. Hence, therefore, it is, that when we say that children are in covenant, and so Church members, the meaning is, not that they are always in inward covenant, and inward Church members, who enjoy the inward and saving benefits of the covenant, but that they are in external and outward covenant, and therefore outwardly Church members, to whom belong some outward privileges of the covenant for their inward and eternal good.

These things being clear, I then rather make mention of them to undermine divers usual objections against the membership and covenant interest of children; as, that they have no saving grace many times; and that they make no actual profession of any grace, and that many of them degenerate and prove corrupt and wicked, etc.; for suppose all these, yet God may take them into outward covenant (which is sufficient to make them the Church seed, or members of the Church) although He doth not receive them into inward covenant, in bestowing upon them saving grace, or power to profess it; nay, though they degenerate and grow very corrupt afterward.

3. Because you may question what this outward covenant is, to which the seals are annexed, and under which we shall prove children are comprehended; and because the knowledge of it is exceeding useful and very pleasant, I shall therefore give a short taste of it, as a light to our after discourse, especially as it is considered in the largest extent of it. This outward covenant, therefore, consists chiefly of these three branches, or special promises:

1. The Lord engageth Himself to them, that they shall be called by His name, or His name shall be called upon them, as it is (Is. 63: 19). They shall be called the sons of God (Hos. 1: 10), and the people of God (Deut. 29: 12, 13); thou becamest mine (Ezek. 16: 8). They may not be His sons, and people, really and savingly, but God will honour them outwardly (at least) with this name and privilege; they shall bear His name, to be called so, and consequently to be accounted so by others, and to be reckoned as of the number of His visible Church and people, just as one that adopts a young son; he tells the father, if he carry it well toward him, when he is grown up to years he shall possess the inheritance itself; but yet, in the meanwhile, he shall have this favour, to be called his son, and be of his family and household, and so be reckoned among the number of his sons. See Rom. 9: 4.

2. The Lord promises that they shall, above all others in the world, have the means of doing them good, and of conveying of the special benefits of the covenant. Nay, they shall be set apart above all people in the world, to enjoy these special benefits of remission of sins, power against sin, eternal life, etc., and shall certainly have these, by these means, unless they refuse them; this is evident from these and such like Scriptures and examples: What privilege hath the Jew? (saith the apostle, Rom. 3: 1, and what advantage by circumcision, if by nature under wrath and sin? for upon that ground the apostle makes the question): he answers, It is much every way, but chiefly because to them were committed the oracles of God, i.e. the Word, promises, covenant, which are the ordinary means of saving grace and eternal good. Others hear the Word, but these in outward covenant enjoy it by covenant and promise; and hence these, in the first place and principally, are sought after by these means; and therefore Christ forbids His disciples at first to go preach in the way of the Gentiles (persons out of covenant), but to the lost sheep of the house of Israel (Matt. 10: 6); and Himself tells the woman of Canaan that He came not but to the lost sheep of the house of Israel (Matt. 15: 24). And although He bids His disciples go preach to all nations, yet (Acts 3: 26) it is said, Unto you first hath He sent Christ, because you are children of the promise and covenant (ver. 25); repent therefore, and be converted (ver. 19). Do not resist or refuse Christ, for He hath first sent Christ to you, to bless you and turn you from your iniquities; and the promise is full and fair (Rom. 11: 23). If they abide not in unbelief (i.e. in refusing grace and Christ when offered), they shall be graffed in, for God is able to do it, and will do it; and the reason why the Lord gave His people up to their own counsels, was because 'my people would none of me', after all the means God used for their good (Ps. 81: 11-13, and Deut. 7: 6). The Lord hath chosen you, above all people on the earth, to be a special people to Himself, and thou art a holy people unto the Lord. How a holy people? By inward holiness? No, verily; for many of them were inwardly unholy, both parents and children, but thou art holy, i.e. thou art externally sanctified and set apart, by special means of holiness, to be a special people unto God. And therefore (Is. 5: 7) the men of Judah are called God's pleasant plant, i.e. planted into the root and fatness of the Church, and therefore had all means used for their further special good (ver. 4). 'What could be done to my vineyard that hath not been done?' And hence it is, that though the Word may come to heathens as well as Church members, yet it comes not to them by way of covenant, as it doth to Church members; nor have they any promise of mercy aforehand as Church members have; nor is it chiefly belonging to such, but unto the

children of the covenant and the promise, as hath been said. And hence also it follows that God never cuts off the seed of His servants from the special benefits of the covenant, until they have had the means thereunto, and they have positively rejected those means; and hence the Jews (who are made the pattern of what God will do toward all Gentile churches, Rom. 11) were never cast off till by positive unbelief they provoked the Lord to break them off by rejecting and refusing the means of their eternal peace.

3. The Lord promiseth that the seed of His people (indefinitely considered) shall have this heart (viz. which would refuse special grace and mercy) taken away, as well as means used for that end; this is evident from Deut. 30: 6, 'The Lord thy God will circumcise thy heart and the heart of thy seed to love the Lord'; He will cut off the uncircumcision, and sin, and resistance of the heart against God; He will take away the stony heart; not indeed from all in outward covenant particularly, but from these indefinitely; so that there is no promise to do this for any out of the visible Church (though God of His sovereignty and free mercy sometimes doth so), but the promise of this belongs indefinitely to those of His Church, among whom usually and ordinarily He works this great work, leaving Him to His own freeness of secret mercy, to work thus on whom He will, and when He will; in the meanwhile no man can exclude himself, or any others within this covenant, from hope of this mercy and grace, but may with comfort look and pray for it; for this is God's covenant, that the Redeemer shall come out of Sion, and turn away ungodliness from Jacob. (Rom. 11: 26, 27); for the covenant of God doth not only run thus, If thou believe and receive grace, thou shalt have it; but thus also, I will circumcise your heart, I will take away the stony heart, I will turn away ungodliness from you, I will enable to believe. And hence these three things follow from these things thus opened:

1. That as the covenant runs not only thus, viz., 'If thou believest thou shalt be saved', but also, 'I will enable to believe', so a man's entrance into covenant is not only by actual and personal profession of faith (as some say), because God's covenant runs a peg higher, viz. to make and enable some to believe, and so to make that profession.

2. That the very outward covenant is not merely conditional, but there is something absolute in it; and hence it follows that it is a great mistake of some who think that circumcision and baptism seal only conditionally, the outward covenant being, say they, merely conditional; for those three things mentioned in the outward covenant, you see, are in some respect absolute, and if the covenant was only conditional, then the Lord was no more in covenant with Church members than with pagans and infidels;

for it may be propounded conditionally to all such, that if they believe they shall be saved; but assuredly God's grace is a little more extensive to the one than to the other.

3. Hence you may see what circumcision once did, and baptism now seals unto; even to infants the seal is to confirm the covenant; the covenant is, that God (outwardly at least) owns them, and reckons them among His people and children within His visible Church and kingdom, and that hereupon He will prune, and cut, and dress, and water them, and improve the means of their eternal good upon them, which good they shall have, unless they refuse in resisting the means; nay, that He will take away this refusing heart from among them indefinitely, so that though every one cannot assure himself that He will do it particularly for this or that person, yet every one, through this promise, may hope and pray for the communication of this grace, and so feel it in time.

These things thus premised, to clear up the ensuing discourse, I shall now do two things. 1. Leave a few grounds and reasons to prove that children are in Church covenant, and so enjoy Church membership by their parents. 2. I shall then answer your scruples.

Argument 1. To the first. The truth of it is manifest by clearing up this proposition, viz. that one and the same covenant, which was made to Abraham in the Old Testament, is for substance the same with that in the New; and this under the New Testament the very same with that of Abraham's under the Old.

I say, for substance the same; for it is acknowledged that there was something proper and personal in Abraham's covenant, as to be a father of many nations; but this was not of the substance of the covenant, which belongs to all the covenanters, and unto which the seal of circumcision was set; for all Abraham's seed, neither in those nor these days, are the fathers of many nations, nor did circumcision seal it.

Again: it is confessed that the external administrations of this one and the same covenant are diverse; but still the covenant for substance is the same. For that old covenant was dispensed with other external signs, sacrifices, types, prophecies, than this under the new. There was something typical in Abraham's covenant concerning Canaan, a type of heaven; but yet the same covenant remains now with a more naked manner of dispensation, or promise of heaven. And hence it follows that, if it may appear that the covenant itself is one and the same now as then, then as now, then it will undeniably follow that, if the new covenant under the gospel be not a carnal covenant, no more was that; if the new covenant be not proper to Abraham's natural seed, no more was that which was made with Abraham;

if the substance of that covenant was, 'I will be a God to thee and thy seed', then this very covenant remains still under the Gospel, it being one and the same with that; if, by virtue of that covenant, the children were made members of the Church, and hence had a Church privilege, and seal administered, then, the same covenant remaining the same, and in the same force and benefit, our children also are taken into the like membership. It remains therefore to prove that which all our divines have long since made good against the Papists, that the covenant then and now is for substance one and the same; or that the covenant made with Abraham was a Gospel covenant, and this Gospel covenant the same that was made with Abraham.

1. The covenant made with Abraham is renewed in the gospel, as to the main thing in it, viz. I will be their God, and they shall be my people (Heb. 8: 10; Jer. 31: 33); and though the seed be not expressed, yet it is understood, as it is Gen. 17: 8, and if need be shall be proved hereafter.

2. Because Abraham's covenant is of gospel and eternal privileges; not proper therefore to him, and his fleshly posterity; for righteousness by faith was sealed up by circumcision (Rom. 4: 11), which is a Gospel privilege, and is the ground of all other privileges; and yet in Gen. 17: 7, there is no expression of this righteousness by faith, but it is understood therefore in this, I will be their God. So the promise of eternal life and resurrection thereunto is wrapped up in this, 'I am the God of Abraham, Isaac, and Jacob.'

3. Because there was never any covenant but it was either of grace or works; that of works on Mount Sinai, that of grace which was made with Abraham; and hence (Gal. 3: 17) the covenant which was confirmed afore by Christ, the law four hundred and thirty years after cannot disannul. And what was that covenant before? Surely it was the covenant of grace, because it was confirmed by Christ: and what was this covenant confirmed by Christ but the covenant made with Abraham? for of this the apostle speaks (ver. 14, 16) and he calls it expressly by the name of Gospel, or the Gospel covenant (ver. 8, 9).

4. Because, when God reneweth His promise and covenant made with Abraham with His people at the plains of Moab (Deut. 30: 6), it runs in these words, viz.: 'I will circumcise thy heart, and the heart of thy seed.' Now, this is a gospel privilege and a gospel covenant, as appears by comparing this text with Rom. 10: 8, wherein the righteousness of faith, or the gospel, is brought in speaking the words of this covenant, saying, 'The word is nigh thee, in thy heart and mouth' (Deut. 30: 11-14). Now, if that place (Gen. 17: 7) should be said to be obscure concerning the

promise (I will be a God to thy seed) yet here in this place God speaks plainly, which by comparing the Scriptures is a gospel promise, and of a gospel privilege, and therefore to be preached by ministers of the gospel, and to be believed by the professors of it.

5. Because this promise (I will be a God to thee and thy seed) doth not belong to Abraham and his seed as after the flesh, or as lineally descended of Abraham, but as believers; and this is most evident, Rom. 11, wherein it is said of the Jews, (1) That they were broken off (made no people, no church) by unbelief (ver. 20), (2) That by faith they shall be graffed in again (ver. 23). If, therefore, they were broken off the Church by unbelief, then they stood as members of the Church by faith; and if by faith they should be graffed in, then they stood by faith at first. Again: it is said, in this Rom. 11: 28, that they are loved for the fathers' sakes, surely not as natural fathers, but as spiritual by faith; and hence (Neh. 9: 8) it is expressly said, that God found Abraham faithful before Him, and made a covenant with him.

Again: if the posterity of Abraham were members upon this ground only or chiefly (viz. because they were lineally descended of Abraham, then Esau, Ishmael) the Jews (Rom. 11: 20) could never have been cast off from being members of the Church, because they were always the natural offspring and posterity of Abraham. Hence, therefore, it follows that, if they were ingraffed in the Church as believers (the fathers as actually believing, the children as set apart by promise of God to be made to believe and in their parents' faith accounted believers) then all believers at this day have the same privilege, and the covenant then, being made only in respect of faith, must needs be gospel covenant, the same with God's covenant at this day. And hence, also, it follows that if they were members as believers, then not as members of that nation. They were not, therefore, members of the Church, because they were descended of Abraham, and were in a national Church, and were by generation Jews. Circumcision was a seal of righteousness by faith (Rom. 4: 11); therefore they were sealed as believers.

Thus much for the first argument, wherein I have been the larger, because much light is let in by it, to answer divers mistakes. I shall name the rest with more brevity.

Argument 2. If it was the curse of Gentiles to be strangers to the covenant of promise (made with the Jews) before they became the churches of God, then by being churches this curse is removed; and hence (Eph. 2: 12, 13) the apostle saith they were strangers to the covenant and commonwealth of Israel, but are not so now. If you say that the Ephesians were in covenant,

[389]

but not their seed, and so they were not strangers, I answer, that the apostle doth not set out their cursed estate merely because they were without any covenant, but because they were strangers to that covenant of promise which the Israelites had: for if their children had it not, they were then as without covenant, so without God and without hope, as pagans are, which is notoriously cross to the current of all Scripture, as may afterward appear.

Argument 3. The apostle expressly saith, 'Your children are holy' (1 Cor. 7: 14); and if federally holy, then of the Church (for real holiness cannot be here meant), and in the covenant of it; even as it is said (Deut. 7: 6) thou art 'a holy people unto the Lord thy God', few of which number were really and savingly holy; but they were all so federally, or by covenant and so became God's special Church or people.

If you say that this holiness is meant of matrimonial holiness, viz. that your children are not bastards, but legitimate, the answer is easy; for upon this interpretation the apostle's answer should be false; for then, if one of the parents had not been a believer, and so by his believing sanctified his unbelieving wife, their children must have been bastards; whereas you know that their children had not been in that sense unclean or illegitimate, although neither of them were believers; for the apostle's dispute is plain, viz., that, if the believing husband did not sanctify his unbelieving wife, then were your children unclean, i.e. say you, bastards; but it is evident that children may be in this sense clean, and yet no faith in either parent to sanctify one another to their particular use, unless you will say that all children of heathens are bastards, because neither of the parents believes.

Argument 4. Rom. 11: 17, The Jews are cut off from the fatness of the olive tree, and the Gentiles put in, or ingraffed in their room. Now, this ingraffing is not into Christ by saving faith, for it is impossible that such should ever be broken off who are once in; it must therefore be meant of their ingraffing into the external state of the visible Church, and the fatness and privileges thereof, of which Church Christ is the external and political head, into whom (in this respect) they are ingraffed by external visible faith and covenant. Hence thus I reason: that if the Jews and their children were ingraffed members of the Church, then the Gentile Churches ingraffed into the same state, and coming in their room, are, together with their children, members of the Church; when the Jews hereafter shall be called, they shall be ingraffed in as they were before, them and their seed (ver. 23). In the meanwhile the apostle puts no difference between the present ingraffing of the Gentiles now and of theirs past, or to come, and therefore they and their seed are ingraffed members now.

Argument 5. Because there is the same inward cause moving God to take in the children of believing Church members into the Church and covenant now, to be of the number of His people, as there was for taking the Jews and their children; for the only cause why the Lord took in the Jews and their children thus, was His love and free grace and mercy. Deut. 4: 37, 'Because he loved thy fathers, therefore he chose their seed', which choosing is not by eternal election, or choosing to glory, for many of their seed never came to glory, but unto this privilege, to be his people above all others in outward covenant with him; which is exceeding great love, if you remember what hath been said of the branches of this outward covenant and visible church estate. And hence (Deut. 10: 15), 'because the Lord had a delight in thy fathers', hence He chose their seed above all people, as at that day, viz. to be his people; so that I do from hence fully believe that either God's love is in these days of His gospel less unto His people and servants than in the days of the Old Testament, or, if it be as great, that then the same love respects the seed of His people now as then it did. And therefore, if then because he loved them he chose their seed to be of his Church, so in these days, because he loveth us, he chooseth our seed to be of his Church also.

Argument 6. Because our Saviour speaks plainly of all children who are brought to him, that of such is the kingdom of heaven; and none are ordinarily heirs of the kingdom of glory but such as are of God's visible Church and kingdom here. The objections against this place I think not worth confuting, because I hope enough is said to clear up this first particular, to prove the children of confederate believers to be in covenant, and Church members.

I now proceed to the second thing, viz. to answer your objections.

Objection 1. If children (say you) be members, as it was in Abraham's covenant, then wives and servants, and all the household, are to be taken in; for so it was Gen. 17 and Gen. 35: 2, 3; and then what churches shall we have but such as you fear God will be weary of and angry with?

Answer. Churches at first (by your own confession) were in families, where therefore God's grace did the more abound by how much the less it did abound abroad. And hence Abraham's family and household was a Church of God: but yet consider withal that all were not of this family church, merely because they were of the family or household, but because they were godly, or the children of such as were godly in the family; for Abraham's servants and household were such as he could and did command to keep the way of the Lord, and so were obedient to God in him (Gen. 18: 19); and we see they did obey, and did receive that new, strange, and painful sign of circumcision, about the nature and use of which, no

[391]

doubt, he first instructed them; and in the place you mention (Gen. 35: 4), they 'gave to Jacob all their strange gods and earrings' to worship God more purely. And it is evident (Ex. 12: 45) that every one in the family had not to do with the seals of the Church, and therefore now not of the Church, though of the family; for a foreigner or hired servant was not to eat of the passover, nor was every one who was bought with money to eat of it until they were circumcised (ver. 44), nor were any such to be circumcised until they were willing and desirous to eat the passover, and that unto the Lord; then, indeed, they and theirs were first to be circumcised, (ver. 48); and although this be not expressly set down (Gen. 17) in Abraham's family, yet I doubt not but that as one Scripture gives light unto another, so this Scripture in Exodus shows the mind of God in the first beginning of the Church, as well as in these times: if, therefore, the servants who were godly in the family were only to be circumcised, and their children born in the house with them, then this example is no way leading to corrupt churches, as you fear it will, but rather the contrary, that if proselyte servants then were received into the Church together with their seed, much more are they received now; and if they did not defile the Church then, neither should we think that they will do so now.

And, I beseech you, consider of it, that God was then as careful of keeping his Church holy as in these days, especially in the first constitution of it, as in this of Abraham's (Gen. 17). And hence God was as much provoked by the unholiness then as by any unholiness now (1 Pet. 1: 16). Suppose, therefore (as you imagine), that all the household, whether profane or holy, were to be received into the covenant, and so to the seal of it, do you think that this course of admitting all profane persons then would not make the Lord soon weary of, and angry with, those family Churches, as well as of national or congregational, now, upon the like supposition? If, therefore, any servants born in the house, or hired, were admitted, surely they were not such unholy ones, whom the Lord could not but be as much angry with then as now; but they were godly and holy, at least in outward profession, upon which ground the Lord commanded them to be circumcised.

I know there are some, and very holy and learned also, who think that if any godly man undertakes to be as a father to an adopted pagan or Indian, that such a one, not grown up to years, is, from the example in Gen. 17, to be received into the covenant of the Church, and the seal of it; and I confess I yet see no convicting argument against it, if it could be proved that some servants bought with Abraham's money were such, and were under years; but I see as yet no convicting argument for this assertion from this example, and therefore I stick to the former answer, and see no reason from any rule of charity but to believe that all those in Abraham's family were either visibly godly or the children of such, to whom circumcision belongs, and consequently might as well partake of Church membership as Abraham himself; which sort of servants, in these days, may as well be admitted to Church membership without fear of defiling the Church as their masters themselves.

Objection 2. If children (say you) be members, then all children, good and bad, must be received, as Jacob and Esau, etc.

Answer. Why not? For if there be any strength in this argument, it holds as strongly against the admission of professing visible believers; where, though all are externally and federally holy, yet some, yea, many, yea, the greatest part of such, may be inwardly bad, and as profane in their hearts as Esau; and must we therefore refuse them to be Church members because many of them may be inwardly bad? Verily, there must then never be churches of God in this world. So it is among children: they are all outwardly holy, yet many of them may be inwardly unholy, like Esau: must we not, therefore accept them to membership? It is a miserable mistake to think that inward, real holiness is the only ground of admission into Church membership, as some Anabaptists dispute; but it is federal holiness, whether externally professed, as in grown persons, or graciously promised unto their seed.

Reply 1. But you here reply, If so, then they are of the church when they are grown up, and profane until they are cast out; and to take in profane is sinful. (Ezek. 44.)

Answer. It is very true; for it is herein just as it is in admitting professing believers; they may prove profane, and continue so in Church membership until they are cast out; but is this therefore any ground to keep out those who are personally holy by their own profession? No, verily; why, then should such as are parentally and federally holy be kept out from Church membership because they may prove profane, and being profane must remain Church members till they be cast out.

Reply 2. But then (you say) they must be Church members though their parents themselves and the whole Church be unwilling thereunto, even as (say you) a man that marrieth a woman, her children must be his, and he be a father to them, though he, and she, and they should say he shall not be a father-in-law to them.

Answer. This similitude of marriage doth neither prove nor illustrate the thing; for the relation between father and such children is absolute and natural, and hence continues though they say he shall not be their father, and though he profess he will not; but the relation founded upon Church covenant between member and member is not natural, nor only and always absolute, but also conditional, which condition not being kept, the relation may be and is usually broken; for look, as the Jews were not so absolutely God's people, but, if they did in time reject the gospel, they were to be cast off, and indeed are so at this day (Rom. 2: 25; Hos. 2: 2; Acts 13: 46, 51), so it is with all Gentile Churches, and the members thereof; and as for that which you last say, that they may refuse their parents' covenant at age as well as own it, and so may members go out at pleasure, which is disorder, I answer, that the like may be said of such members as come in by personal profession, for they may renounce their own covenant with God and the Church: one may do so, and so may twenty; yet, though this be wickedness and disorder, yet the Church may proceed against them, and so it may against their children, who are bound to own the covenant made with God, and of God with them in their parents, as well as any Church members are to own their own covenant by their own personal profession. What disorder, therefore, will come in as you conceive this way, will come in by your own way, and what course you should take to heal the one, by the same you may heal the other.

Objection 3. If children (say you) be members, then their seed successively, until they be either dissolved or excommunicated; and if so, then what churches shall we have?

Answer 1. What churches shall we have? Truly, not always Churches of angels and saints, but mixed with many chaffy hypocrites, and ofttimes profane persons. But still I say this objection holds as firm against gathering churches of visible professing believers; for God knows what churches we may have of them, even heaps of hypocrites and profane persons, for I know not what can give us hope of their not apostatizing, but only God's promise to be a God to them and to preserve them; and truly the same promise being made to the seed gives me as much ground of faith to hope well of churches rising out of the seed of the godly, as of the professing parents themselves. I know one may have more experimental charity concerning some few professing the fear of God; but my Church charity is equal about them, especially considering that those whom God receives into Church covenant, he doth not only take them to be a people to him, but to establish them to be such, viz., for time to come. And hence God is said to establish his covenant with Isaac, not Ishmael, who was to be rejected (Gen. 17: 19), and God is said to gather them into covenant, to establish them to be a people, both young and old, present posterity and that which was to come (Deut. 29: 11–15).

2. God was as holy and as exactly requiring holiness from the Jewish church as well as from Christian churches: now, do you think that the covenant which then wrapped up the Jews' children into Church membership was a highway of profaneness and unholiness in the members thereof, and of defiling and polluting God's Church? or was it a way and means of holiness, and to keep them from being profane? To affirm the first is something blasphemous and very false, for it is expressly said (Jer. 13: 11) that 'as the girdle cleaveth to the loins of a man, so he caused the whole house of Israel (not grown men only) to cleave to him, that they might be to him a people, (which was by covenant,) and for a name, for a praise and for a glory'. God's name, glory, praise, was the end, and the covenant was the means hereunto; and therefore it was no way or means of unholiness in the Church; but if you say it was a means of holiness, why then should we fear the polluting of Churches by the same covenant, which we have proved wraps in our seed also? Indeed, they did prove universally profane in the Jewish Church; so they may in ours; but shall man's wickedness in abusing God's grace, and forsaking his covenant, tie the hands or heart of God's free grace from taking such into covenant? What though some did not believe? saith the apostle (Rom. 3: 3, 4), 'Shall their unbelief make the faith of God without effect? God forbid.'

3. Suppose they do prove profane and corrupt churches; yet even then, when they are corrupt, they are such churches where ordinarily God gathers out his elect, and out of which (till purer are gathered, or these wholly rejected) there cannot be expected ordinarily any salvation; for so saith our Saviour, 'Salvation is of the Jews' (John 4: 22), even in that very corrupt and worst estate of the Church that ever it was in.

Objection 4. If children be members, then they must come to the Lord's Supper; for you know no difference between member and member in point of privilege, unless they be under some sin.

Answer 1. Yes, verily, there is a plain difference between member and member (though professing believers) in point of privilege, though they lie under no sin; for a man may speak and prophesy in the Church, not women. A company of men may make a church, and so receive in and cast out of the Church, but not women, though professing saints.

2. All grown men are not to be admitted (though professing believers) to the Lord's Supper: my reason is, a man may believe in Christ, and yet be very ignorant of the nature, use, and ends of the Lord's Supper: now, such may be baptized as soon as ever faith appears (Mark 16: 16), but they may not be admitted to the Lord's Supper, because they will be guilty of the body and blood of the Lord, if they through their ignorance cannot

discern the Lord's body. I know no reason but ignorant persons may be as well suspended from the use of this privilege, though they be true believers (for faith may consist with much ignorance), as well as distracted persons, who, notwithstanding, may be believers also.

3. If, therefore, children be able to examine themselves and discern the Lord's body, they may then eat; and herein there is no difference in this privilege between member and member.

4. Children not being usually able to examine themselves, nor discern the Lord's body, hence they are not to be admitted to the use of this privilege; and yet they may be such members as may enjoy the benefit of other privileges, even that of baptism; for baptism seals up our first entrance into the covenant. This first entrance is not always by personal profession of faith, but by God's promise of working, or of vouchsafing the means of working of it: now, children (as is proved) being under this covenant (as we see all the posterity also of Abraham was), hence, though children cannot profess faith, nor actually examine themselves, yet they may receive, and must receive, baptism, being already under God's covenant; but because the Lord's Supper doth not seal up this first entrance and first right to the covenant, but our growth and fruition of the covenant, hence this act on our part is required to participate in this, which the apostle calls self-examination, and the act of taking and eating Christ, and of discerning the Lord's body, and of doing this in remembrance of Christ which every baptized person and Church member is not always able to do. A child may receive a promise aforehand of a rich estate given him, and this promise sealed up to him, his father receiving it for him; but it is not fit that he should be put to the actual improvement and fruition of that estate until he is grown up, understands himself, and knows how to do it: so it is here; the sacrament of the Lord's Supper requires ability, (1) To take Christ as our own; (2) To eat Christ; that is, to take fruition of Him; the which acts of faith God doth not require of all those immediately who are wrapped up in covenant with Him.

Objection 1. But here you say that that examination (1 Cor. 11) is required of all that be members, and that at all times, as well as at their first coming to the Lord's Supper.

Answer. This examination is indeed required of all those members who should partake of the Lord's Supper, but it is not required (as you seem to say) of every one to make him a member, so that none can be a member but him that is able to examine himself; for God's covenant to work faith, and to give power to examine one's self afterward, may make some as truly members as those who are able to act and express their faith. Now, I have proved that God's covenant is aforehand given to children; and to give them the seal of the first entrance into it many years after is as vile a thing as for them that are able and fit to examine themselves to have this sacrament of the Lord's Supper denied or delayed till many years after.

Objection 2. But you say, It is left to every one's conscience to examine himself, not that others should examine them, and consequently, if children be members, then it must be left upon their conscience.

Answer. We know in our own consciences that children usually cannot examine themselves: now, if the leaders and the Church are bound to see Christ's rules observed by others, and if this examination be the rule that all must walk by who participate here, then they must not suffer such young ones, no, nor persons grown up and entered in by personal profession, to receive this seal as they know are unable thus to do. I think, if Churches should degenerate in these days, this course of discipline should be attended (especially by the elders) toward any of their members, which way soever they have entered, whether by their own or by their parents' covenant. And I have oft feared that there is some need already of it, even toward some who enter by their own covenant, and may have faith, but are miserably to seek in the nature, use and, ends of the Lord's Supper, and consequently unfit to discern of Christ's body, and so to come to that sacrament.

Objection 5. If children may be members, and yet not come to the Lord's Supper, then it may come to pass that a whole Church may be a Church, and yet not have the Lord's Supper, or ought not to have it.

Answer 1. So there may; for a Church may be a true Church, and yet want the benefit of some one or more of God's ordinances, sometimes pastors, sometimes elders, sometimes seals.

2. A Church of professing believers may degenerate, and turn profane, and sottish, and so have no just right to the seals; and their officers may leave them, and so have no use of the seals; yet I suppose it is a Church of Christ still, though degenerate, though unfit to enjoy seals: will you therefore think the way of their membership unlawful, viz., by professing their faith, because such a rare thing as this may happen? Why, then, should you think the way of children's membership unlawful, because of the like rarity in such a dark and gloomy state of them as you mention?

Objection 6. If children be members, then there will be many in the Church who are not saints by calling, nor faithful in Christ Jesus, which ought not to be if the Church could see it; but these may be too plainly seen.

Answer 1. I do think it is true that poor children may be and are looked upon with too many dejected thoughts of unbelief, despising of them as children of wrath by nature, and not with such high thoughts of faith as children and sons of God by promise, as I have shown. And I think herein is our great sin, as it was in Christ's own disciples, who were the first that we read of that would not have little children brought unto him, for which he rebuked them, showing their privilege; and for want of which faith in God's promise about our children, certainly God smites and forsakes many of our children.

2. If, therefore, you think that Church members must consist only of saints by calling, so that your meaning is, such saints as are so by outward and personal profession, from the call of the Gospel, are only to be Church members, this is an error; for, (1) You know that they who define a Church to be a number of visible saints, they usually put this phrase in, 'and their seed', who may not profess faith perhaps as their fathers do, and you shall find that the Israel of God, under the Old Testament, are all of them said to be adopted (Rom. 9: 4) chosen, and called, (Is. 41: 8, 9) and faithful (Is. 1: 21) and yet we know they were not all so by personal profession, but in respect of their joint federation and the outward covenant of God with them. (2) The outward covenant is not always first entered into by personal profession of faith, but by God's covenant of promise to work, or to use the means to work faith. Hence it undeniably follows that as many may be in Church covenant before they profess faith personally, so many may be members of the Church without this profession of faith; for this covenant of working faith (as hath been formerly explained) doth not only belong to the Jews, but to Gentile Churches also, and believers, as hath been proved, and might further be confirmed.

Objection. But say you, If we saw hypocrites, we were to cast them out as well as profane persons; and we see no grace in many children, and therefore they must not be received in.

Answer 1. If you see children of whom you cannot say that they are faithful personally, yet they may be faithful federally (as hath been showed) for they may lie under God's covenant of begetting faith by some means in them, and then you are not to cast them out, but accept them, as God doth.

2. The children of godly parents, though they do not manifest faith in the gospel, yet they are to be accounted of God's Church until they positively reject the Gospel, either in themselves or in their parents; and therefore God did never go about to cast off the Jews and their seed, until they put forth positive unbelief; the Lord promised to give them

the means of faith, and did so; and when Christ was come, and the gospel sent first unto them for their good, the Lord herein fulfilled His covenant mercy, as toward His beloved people; but when they rejected these means, and cast off Christ and His gospel, then (Rom. 11) they were broken off, and not before. Now, hypocrites are such as profess Christ in words, and yet deny Christ in deed (Titus 1: 16; 2 Tim. 3: 5). Hence they are such as positively refuse Christ; hence the case of children in whom no positive unbelief appears is not the same with this of hypocrites or profane persons; and when young children shall grow positively such, I know not but they may be dealt with as any other members for any such like offence.

Thus you see an answer to your six objections. In the end of your paper there are two questions, which I suppose may not a little trouble against their baptism and membership. To these briefly.

Question 1. What good (say you) is it either for a wicked or an elect child, till he be converted, to be in the church? or what good may any have by being in the church, till they can profit by what they enjoy?

Answer 1. The apostle puts the like case, and gives you an answer (Rom. 3: 1, 2), 'What advantage hath the Jew? and what profit is there of circumcision?' What use or profit could the infants then make of their church covenant, membership, or seal, who understood none of these things? Do you think the Lord exposed His holy ordinances then unto contempt, and is more careful that they may be profitably used now? Was there no good by circumcision? Yea, saith the apostle, much every way.

2. What profit is it to persons grown up to years, and yet secretly hypocrites, who enter into the church by profession of the faith? You will say there is good and profit in respect of the privileges themselves, but, they abusing them, they had, in this respect, better have been without them, because they bring hereby upon themselves greater condemnation. The same say I of children, whom God receives into his church by promise and covenant of doing them good, although at present they may not be so sensible of this good.

3. To speak plainly, the good they get by being thus enriched is wonderful. And here there is more need of a treatise than of a letter, to clear up the benefits from all scruples arising by being in outward covenant in church fellowship, even unto infants. I confess I find little said by writers upon this subject, and I believe the doubts against children's baptism, as they arise by blindness in this particular, so I think that God suffers that opinion to take place, that by such darkness he may bring out light in this particular. I will only hint unto you some few of my many thoughts,

which have long exercised me for many years in this thing. The good by children's membership, especially when sealed, is in four things.

1. In respect of God. God shows hereby the riches of His grace toward them, in taking them to be His people; in adopting them to be His children; in preventing them with many special promises aforehand of doing them good; by all which the Lord doth, as it were, prevent Satan, in wooing their hearts, as it were, so soon to draw them to Him before he can actually stir to draw their souls from Him. So that I beseech you, consider; suppose they cannot as yet understand, and so make profit by all this; yet is it not good for them, or for any of us, to partake of God's grace before we know how to make use of it? Is it not good for God to be good to them that are evil? Is it not good for God to glorify and make manifest His grace to man, though man knows not how to make use of His grace? Was it not rich grace for Christ to wash Peter's feet, and yet he not know at present what it meant, only (saith Christ) 'thou shalt know hereafter'? Is it not good for God to give life to us, and to let us be born in such and such a place of the gospel where it is preached, and to lay in mercy aforehand for us, before we know how to be thankful, or know how to use any of these outward mercies? And is it no mercy or favour to have so much spiritual mercy bestowed on children beforehand, before they can be thankful or make use thereof? (Deut. 7: 6, 7). The choosing of them to be His people above all other people (which you know was from the womb), it is called God's setting His love upon them, and the reason of this love (ver. 8) is said to be because God loved them; this love was not electing and peculiar love (for thousands of these perished and went to hell), but it was His external, adopting love, to choose them to be His people, and to improve all means for their good, and to give them the good of all those means unless they refuse, and to give indefinitely among them, and particularly to many of them, such hearts as that they shall not be able to refuse the good of those means (as hath been showed formerly), this is love; great love and mercy; not shown or promised to any who are not of the visible Church throughout the whole world. By which God is glorified, and let Him be so, though we cannot see how to profit by it when it first breaks out. Have not you profited much by considering God's preventing grace, long before you understood how to make use of it? Hath not God received much glory from you for it? Hath this grace then, think you, been unprofitably spent on God's part? No, verily. The case is the same here; David blesseth God for being his God from his mother's belly, and from the womb (Ps. 22: 9, 10), and God's grace is shown through this expression (Is. 46: 3).

2. There is much good hereby in respect of the parents; for suppose the children cannot profit by it, yet parents may; and it is in respect of them very much that God looks upon their children, thus to receive them into covenant (Deut. 4: 37). For (1) Parents may hereby see and wonder at the riches of God's grace, to become a God not only to themselves, but to take in their seed also, whose good they prize as their own, and as if done to themselves; hence Abraham fell down upon his face adoring God, when he heard of this covenant (Gen. 17). See also how Moses aggravates this love in the eyes of all that had eyes to see (Deut. 10: 14, 15). (2) Hereby God gives parents some comfortable hope of their children's salvation, because they be within the pale of the visible church; for as out of the visible church (where the ordinary means of salvation be) there is ordinarily no salvation (Acts 2: 47). So, if children were not of Christ's visible church and kingdom, we could not hope for their salvation, no more than of pagans or Turks; for if they be without God, they are without hope (Eph. 2: 12); and to be without hope of such, to whom God hath made such promises of salvation not given to pagans, nor proper to Abraham, is very hard, and horrid to imagine; for the promise runs universally, that 'the seed of the upright (whether Jews or Gentiles) shall be blessed' (Ps. 112: 1, 2; Prov. 20: 7). (3) Hereby parents are stirred up the more earnestly to pray for them, because God's covenant and promise is so large toward them, at which prayer looks, and by which it wrestles with God; and hence we find that Moses and others, they use this argument in their prayers: 'O God of Abraham, Isaac, and Jacob', etc. (4) Hereby they may not only hope and pray, but are encouraged to believe concerning their children and the rest of those who are in covenant among them, that God will do them good, as they conclude mercy to the remnant, forgiveness of their sins, with faith upon this ground, 'Thou wilt perform the truth to Jacob, and the mercy to Abraham sworn unto our fathers in days of old' (Micah 7: 18, 20). This, indeed, is the children's faith for themselves and their children; but so it may be a ground of parents' faith. And if we pray for our children, why should we doubt (leaving only secrets to God) if we see them die before they reject the gospel positively? I see no reason for any man to doubt of the salvation of his child if he dies, or that God will not do good to his child in time if he lives. (5) This stirs up their hearts to be the more sincerely holy, and keep in with God, because of their children; and to educate them with more care and watchfulness, because they are the Lord's children as well as theirs; they are not common, but holy vessels, and therefore let them see that they be not defiled; and hence we find that when God

exhorts to any duty of holiness in Scripture, he oft makes this the ground of it, 'I am your God'; and hence God aggravates their sin in offering their children to Molech (Ezek. 16), because they were his children, that should have been better used.

3. In respect of themselves the good is very great. (1) It is a special means to prevent sin (Deut. 29). I make this covenant, not only with him that is present, but with your seed also, who are not here (ver. 15), lest there should be among you man or woman, family or tribe, whose heart turns away from God, and lest there should be a root of gall and wormwood; and indeed it mightily works on the heart to think, Shall I, whom God hath chosen to be His, be my own, or be the devil's, or be my lusts'? etc. (2) It is a strong motive and engagement upon them to forsake sin, even the uncircumcision and sin of their hearts, as is evident, Deut. 10: 15, 16. The Lord had a delight to choose the seed of your fathers, even you, to be his people, as it is this day: what follows? 'Therefore circumcise the foreskin of your hearts, and be no more stiffnecked'. (3) It is a special help, as to avert their hearts from sin, so to convert and turn them to God, and to make them look toward God, that He would turn them, when perhaps they are without any hope (in other respects) of mercy, or of being able by any means they can use to turn themselves; this is evident, Acts 3: 19, with ver. 25. Repent and be converted, for you are the children of the covenant which God made with our fathers; this draws their hearts, when they see how God calls them to return (Jer. 3: 22). Come unto Me, ye backsliding children, etc.: we come unto Thee, for thou art the Lord our God. When backsliding Ephraim could not convert himself, he cries unto God, 'O, turn me, and I shall be turned, for thou art the Lord my God' (Jer. 31: 18), which places cannot be meant of being their God only by internal covenant, in giving to them the special benefits of the covenant, for then they should be in covenant with God, and have remission of all their sins, etc., before they were turned, or before faith; and therefore it is meant of being a God in outward and external Church covenant, which is no small motive and loadstone to believe. And although many do not believe, and will not be turned, yet this covenant is a high privilege and great favour, fit in itself to draw to God, though many believe not; and hence the apostle saith that the privilege of the Jews is great in having God's oracles (which contain God's covenant) committed to them, though some believe not, which unbelief makes not (he saith) the faith of God, i.e. God's promise or covenant, of none effect, or an ineffectual and fruitless covenant; for this Word of God's covenant shall take some effect among some such as are in it; which

therefore is a privilege, though many perish, as is evident (Rom. 9: 4, 6).
(4) It is a special means of binding them fast to God when they are turned.
Jer. 13: 11, 'As the girdle cleaveth unto a man, so have I caused the whole
house of Israel to cleave unto me, that they may be for a name and glory.'·
Deut. 30: 20, 'Thou shalt cleave unto him, because he is thy life, and the
length of thy days'; He was not their life spiritually and savingly (for
many thus exhorted were dead and in their sins), but federally, or in
outward covenant. (5) If they shall forsake and break loose from God,
and from the bond of His covenant, and have (as much as in them lies)
cast themselves out of covenant by their own perfidiousness and breach
of covenant, that one would think now there is no more hope, yet it is
a special means to encourage their hearts to return again, even when
they seem to be utterly cast off; and therefore it is said (Jer. 3: 1), 'Though
thou hast committed whoredom with many lovers (whereby the covenant
was broken), yet return unto me'; so (Deut. 4), if when you are scattered
among the nations, and shall serve wood and stone, and be in great tribu-
lation, if from thence thou seek the Lord thy God, thou shalt find him,
He will not forsake thee; and what is the reason of it? viz., His remembrance of the covenant with their fathers, for so it is Deut. 4: 27–31.
But I forbear to name more such things as these which come by outward
covenant to inchurched members.

4. In respect of others their good is very great; for, (1) Now they may
enjoy the special watch and care of the whole church, which otherwise
they must want. (2) They hereby have the more fervent prayers of others
for their good; and hence (Rom. 9: 1–3) we see how Paul upon this ground
had great zeal in his prayers for the Jews, not only because his countrymen, but especially because to them did belong the adoption and covenants, and they had gracious fathers, etc. So (Ps. 89: 49), 'Lord remember
thy former loving kindnesses, which are sworn to David in truth.' And
hence we see Moses oft pleads and prevails with God in prayer for the
sinning Israelites, viz. 'O, remember Abraham, Isaac, and Jacob.'

Now, I pray you, lay all these things together, and then see whether
you have any cause to say, What profit is there by covenant and Church
membership of persons not yet able to profess the faith of Jesus Christ?

Question 2. You say, when families were Churches, all of the family
were of the Church, and when a nation was a Church, all that were of
that nation were of that Church; but now, believers being matter of the
Church, what if none were admitted till they can hold forth visible faith?
would not many of these things be more clear?

Answer. In these words there is a threefold mistake.

1. That all of the family and nation in former times were of the Church: this is false; for God never took any to be His Church but as they were believers, at least externally, in that nation. I say believers; which either are professed believers, or promised believers, such as by outward covenant shall have the means to be made believers in that nation; and hence you have heard that the nation of the Jews stood by faith, and were broken off by unbelief; and if any rejected the covenant, as Ishmael and Esau, they were not of that Church, though they did and might dwell in that nation, as doubtless thousands did.

2. You think that visible personal faith only makes the Church, and members of it; which is an error, as may appear from many things already said; for children may be in God's account professors of the faith parentally as well as personally; i.e., in the profession of their parents as well as in their own. And hence you shall find that the covenant God entered into with the parents of church members personally, the children are said to have that covenant made with them many hundred years after. See, for this purpose, among hundreds, these few Scriptures (Hag. 2: 5). In Haggai's time God is said to make a covenant with them then when they came out of Egypt (which was not personally, but parentally); so (Hos. 12: 4, 5), when God entered into covenant with Jacob at Bethel, God is said to speak with us who lived many years after; and hence the children many years after challenge God's covenant with them, which was made with their fathers for them (Mic. 7: 19, 20). Hence, also, those children are said to come to Christ who were not able to come themselves but only were brought in the arms of others to Christ. It is a known thing among men, that a father may receive a gift or legacy given to him and his heirs, and he and his heirs are bound to perform the condition of the covenant and promise by which it is conveyed, and that the child doth this in his father.

3. You think that if men only grown up and able to profess faith should be of the church, then all things would be more clear about children. Truly, I believe the quite contrary, upon the grounds before laid down; for, (1) Hereby pollution of the church shall not be avoided, but rather introduced, to exclude children from a holy-making covenant, as we have proved. (2) Hereby that good and benefit of their covenant should be lost (not gained) by excluding them out of covenant. The wisdom of man furthers not the righteousness of God. And here let me conclude with the naked profession of my faith to you in this point, which is a bulwark of defence against all that is said by Anabaptists against baptizing of infants.

1. That the children of professing believers are in the same covenant God made with Abraham: Abraham was a father of many nations, and not of one nation only; and hence the same covenant made with him and the believing Israel in that nation, the same covenant is made with all his believing seed in all other nations. 2. That baptism is a seal of our first entrance and admission into covenant; and therefore is to be immediately applied to children of believing parents as soon as ever they be in covenant, and that is as soon as they become the visible seed of the faithful for so the covenant to Abraham runs ('I will be thy God, and the God of thy seed'), not only his elect seed, but church seed (as hath been showed), not only of his seed in that one nation, but in all nations.

These two things I cannot tell how to avoid the light of, they are so clear; and the ignorance of these makes so many Anabaptists (as they are called), and I never yet met with any thing written by them (and much I have read) that was of any considerable weight to overthrow these. But I forget myself, and trouble you: my prayer is, and shall be, that the Lord would give you understanding in all these things.

Appendix 2:
Episcopalian Writers on Church Government

THE FOLLOWING ARTICLE FIRST APPEARED IN DECEMBER, 1879, UNDER the title: 'Recent Episcopalian Writers on Church Government' in The Catholic Presbyterian, a monthly journal edited by Dr W. G. Blaikie. It was signed with the initials, J. K., but we have been unable to trace the exact identity of the writer.

Episcopalian Writers on Church Government

IN A recent number of *The Catholic Presbyterian*, reference was made to the approval, by Dean Stanley, of the views regarding the form of Church government in apostolic times, expressed by Dr Lighftoot, the Bishop of Durham – so well known for his scholarly commentaries on the Epistles to the Galatians, Philippians, and Colossians, and more recently for his thorough and conclusive refutation of the leading statements in 'Supernatural Religion.' We propose to make a few quotations from the bishop's commentary on the Philippians, in which the subject is very fully and fairly discussed, merely reminding our readers that the great point in dispute between Episcopalians and Presbyterians is, whether the office of a 'bishop' is distinct from, and superior to, that of a presbyter, or not, rather identical with it.

At p. 93, Dr Lightfoot states:

'It is a fact now generally recognized by theologians of all shades of opinion, that, in the language of the New Testament, the same officer in the Church is called indifferently "bishop" and "elder" or "presbyter".'

On pp. 94–8, we find these remarks:

'Of the identity of the "bishop" and "presbyter" in the language of the apostolic age, the following evidence seems conclusive:

'(1) In the opening of this epistle [to the Philippians], St Paul salutes the "bishops and deacons." Now, it is incredible that he should recognize only the first and third order, and pass over the second, though the second was absolutely essential to the existence of a Church, and formed the staple of its ministry. It seems, therefore, to follow of necessity that the "bishops" are identical with the "presbyters". . . .

'(2) In the Acts (20: 17), St Paul is represented as summoning to Miletus the "elders" or "presbyters" of the Church of Ephesus. Yet, in addressing them immediately after, he appeals to them as "bishops" or "overseers" of the Church (20: 28).

'(3) Similarly, St Peter, appealing to the "presbyters" of the Churches addressed by him, in the same breath urges them to "fulfil the office of bishops" with disinterested zeal (1 Pet. 5: 1, 2).

'(4) Again, in the First Epistle to Timothy, St Paul, after describing the qualifications for the office of a "bishop" (3: 1–7), goes on at once to say what is required of "deacons" (3: 8–13). He makes no mention of presbyters. The term "presbyter", however, is not unknown to him: for, having occasion, in a later passage, to speak of Christian ministers, he calls these officers no longer "bishops", but "presbyters" (5: 17–19).

'(5) The same identification appears still more plainly from the apostle's directions to Titus (1: 5–7): "That thou shouldest set in order the things that are wanting, and ordain *elders* in every city, as I appointed thee: if any one be *blameless*, the husband of one wife, having believing children, who are not charged with riotousness, or unruly: for a *bishop* must be *blameless*", etc.

'(6) Nor is it only in the apostolic writings that this identity is found. St Clement of Rome wrote, probably, in the last decade of the first century, and in his language the terms are still convertible. Speaking of the apostles, he says, that, "preaching in every country and city, they appointed their first-fruits, having tested them by the Spirit, to be *bishops* and *deacons* of them that should believe", §42. A little later, referring to the disorganized state of the Corinthian Church, he adds: "Our apostles knew, through our Lord Jesus Christ, that there would be strife concerning the authority of the *bishopric*. . . . We shall incur no slight guilt if we eject those who have presented the offerings of the *bishopric* unblameably and holily. Blessed are the *presbyters* who have gone before, whose departure was crowned with fruit and perfection."

'This is the last instance of identification. With the opening of the second century, a new phraseology begins. In the genuine epistles of Ignatius, the terms are used in their more modern sense.'

From Dr Lightfoot's paper on the 'Christian Ministry', appended to his commentary on the Epistle to the Philippians, we proceed to make some extracts. Speaking of apostolic times, he says (pp. 192–8):

'The duties of the presbyters were twofold. They were both rulers and instructors of the congregation. This double function appears in St Paul's expression "pastors and teachers" (Eph. 4: 11), where, as the form of the original seems to show, the two words describe the same office, yet the work of *teaching* must have fallen to the presbyters from the very first, and have assumed greater prominence as time went on. With the growth of the Church, the visits of the apostles and evangelists to any individual community must have become less and less frequent, so that the burden of instruction would be gradually transferred from these missionary preachers to the local officers of the congregation. Hence St Paul, in two passages

[411]

where he gives directions relating to bishops or presbyters, insists specially on the faculty of teaching as a qualification for the position (1 Tim. 3: 2; Titus 1: 9).

'It is clear, then, that at the close of the apostolic age, the two lower orders of the ministry [viz, the presbyterate and diaconate] were firmly and widely established; but traces of the third and highest order, the episcopate, properly so called, are few and indistinct.

'For, the opinion hazarded by Theodoret, and adopted by many later writers, that the same officers in the Church who were first called apostles came afterwards to be designated bishops, is baseless. If the two offices had been identical, the substitution of the one name for the other would have required some explanation. But, in fact, the functions of the apostle and the bishop differed widely. The apostle, like the prophet or the evangelist, held no *local* office. He was essentially, as his name denotes, a missionary, moving about from place to place, founding and confirming new brotherhoods. The only ground on which Theodoret builds his theory is a false interpretation of a passage in St Paul. At the opening of the epistle to Philippi, the presbyters (here called bishops) and deacons are saluted, while, in the body of the letter, one Epaphroditus is mentioned as an "apostle" of the Philippians. If "apostle" here had the meaning which is thus assigned to it, all the three orders of the ministry would be found at Philippi. But this interpretation will not stand. The true apostle, like St Peter or St John, bears this title as the messenger, the delegate, of Christ Himself; while Epaphroditus is only so styled as the messenger of the Philippian brotherhood, and, in the very next clause, the expression is explained by the statement that he carried their alms to St Paul. The use of the word here has a parallel in another passage (2 Cor. 8: 23), where messengers (or apostles) of the Churches are mentioned. It is not, therefore to the apostle that we must look for the prototype of the bishop.

'The history of the name [bishop] itself suggests a different account of the origin of the episcopate. If "bishop" was at first used as a synonym for "presbyter", and afterwards came to designate the higher office under whom the presbyters served, the episcopate, properly so called, would seem to have been developed from the subordinate office. In other words, the episcopate was formed, not out of the apostolic order, by localization but out of the presbyteral, by elevation; and the title, which originally was common to all, came at length to be appropriated to the chief among them.'

There is scarcely any need for further quotation. Enough has been adduced to show that Bishop Lightfoot acknowledges the early Christian Church to have been without episcopal organization. But he tries to prove that James, the Lord's brother, may be regarded as an example of a Christian bishop, in the later and more special sense of the term. While, however, it is urged that such an instance is found in the *Jewish* Christian Church, he grants that the New Testament presents no distinct traces of such organization among the Gentile Christians. Yet, when we reach the second century, mention is made of bishops, in the later meaning of the word: episcopal government is already begun, and ever become more and more firmly established. To what must its origin be traced?

Dr Lightfoot can find no firmer basis for the system than *expediency*; episcopacy, it is affirmed, arose out of the emergency in which the early Christian Churches were placed. For, when dissensions were caused by Jewish and Gentile converts, when false teachers, also, had begun to make their evil influence felt within the Christian Church, it seemed only proper that some one of the elders should be placed over the rest, having authority to deal with those who were producing schism and anarchy. Moreover, in these days of persecution, when Christ's flock was still small, scattered, and feeble, it was highly advisable to have one presbyter placed over the Church, as a common leader and counsellor. Thus, it is stated, episcopacy gradually and naturally grew out of the pressing needs of the Church.

This is a very different position from that occupied by the High Church party, which claims a 'Divine right' in a favour of episcopacy. There is scarcely even the shadow of a claim to Scripture proof.

But let us also consider the acknowledgments of another esteemed Episcopal writer – Dean Alford, whose Greek Testament is so well known and so highly appreciated. On Acts 20: 17, where it is stated that Paul sent to Ephesus, and called the *elders* of the Church, he observes that 'the elders are called, in verse 28, bishops or overseers. This circumstance began very early to contradict the growing views of the apostolic institution and necessity of prelatical episcopacy. Thus, Irenaeus, III. xiv. 2, p. 201, "the *bishops and presbyters*[1] were called together in Miletus, from Ephesus, and the other neighbouring cities". Here we see (1) the two, bishops and presbyters, distinguished, as if *both* were sent for, in order that the titles might not seem to belong to the same persons, and (2) other neighbouring Churches also brought in, in order that there might not seem to be ἐπίσκοποι in one Church only. That neither of these was the case, is clearly shown by the plain words of this verse: he sent *to Ephesus* and summoned the *elders of the Church*. So early did interested and disingenuous interpretations begin to cloud the light which Scripture might have thrown on ecclesiastical

---

[1] The italics all through are Alford's own.

questions. The English version has hardly dealt fairly in this case with the sacred text, in rendering ἐπισκοπους, verse 28, "*overseers*"; whereas, it ought there, as in all other places, to have been *bishops*, that the fact of *elders and bishops having been originally synonymous* might be apparent to the ordinary English reader, which now is not.'

This is something more than a candid admission on the part of the Dean; it is more than we might expect, and perhaps as much as we could wish. He seems like a Presbyterian contending for parity among ministers, rather than a veritable episcopal dignitary.

Again, when commenting on the expression 'bishops and deacons' in Phil. 1: 1, he refers to his remarks, just quoted, on Acts 20: 17; and cites the following from Theodoret: 'He [Paul] calls the elders [presbyters] "bishops" [or overseers], for they had *both* names at that period.'

Commenting on 1 Tim. 3: 1, 'If any man seeks the overseership (office of an overseer, or bishop)', he remarks, 'it is merely laying a trap for mis-understanding, to render the word, at that time of the Church's history, "the office of a bishop". The "bishops" of the New Testament have, officially, nothing in common with our bishops. In my note on Acts 20: 17, I have stated that the English version ought to have been consistent with itself, and to have rendered ἐπισκοπους everywhere *bishops*, not *bishops* and *overseers* as suited ecclesiastical prejudices. But it would be better to adopt the other alternative, and always to render ἐπισκοπους overseers. Thus we should avoid any chance of identifying it with a present and different office, and take refuge in the meaning of the word itself, which, at the same time, bears an important testimony to the duties of the post. The identity of the bishop [or overseer] and presbyter [or elder] in apostolic times is evident from Titus 1: 5–7.' And when he comes to the last-mentioned passage, where Paul first speaks of 'elders' (or presbyters), and then refers to these as 'overseers', he remarks that these are 'most plainly identi-fied with the presbyter spoken of before'.

Such acknowledgments as these, which all fair minds must make, are reassuring to a Presbyterian. Other testimonies of the like kind, from other Episcopalian writers, may be given in a future number.